I0868176

The Translatability of Revolution

Harvard East Asian Monographs 415

The Translatability of Revolution

Guo Moruo and Twentieth-Century Chinese Culture

Pu Wang

Published by the Harvard University Asia Center
Distributed by Harvard University Press
Cambridge (Massachusetts) and London 2018

© 2018 by The President and Fellows of Harvard College
Printed in the United States of America

The Harvard University Asia Center publishes a monograph series and, in coordination with the Fairbank Center for Chinese Studies, the Korea Institute, the Reischauer Institute of Japanese Studies, and other facilities and institutes, administers research projects designed to further scholarly understanding of China, Japan, Vietnam, Korea, and other Asian countries. The Center also sponsors projects addressing multidisciplinary and regional issues in Asia.

Names: Wang, Pu, 1980– author.
Title: The translatability of revolution : Guo Moruo and twentieth-century Chinese culture / Pu Wang.
Other titles: Harvard East Asian monographs ; 415.
Description: Cambridge, Massachusetts : Published by the Harvard University Asia Center, 2018. | Series: Harvard East Asian monographs ; 415 | Includes bibliographical references and index.
Identifiers: LCCN 2017060559 | ISBN 9780674987180 (hardcover : alk. paper)
Subjects: LCSH: Guo, Moruo, 1892–1978. | Marxian Historiography—China—History—20th century. | Translators—China—History—20th century. | Historiography—China—History—20th century. | China—Intellectual life—1949–1976. | China—Historiography—History—20th century.
Classification: LCC PL2778.O2 W36 2018 | DDC 895.18/5109—dc23 LC record available at https://lccn.loc.gov/2017060559

Index by Stephen Ullstrom

∞ Printed on acid-free paper

Last figure below indicates year of this printing
27 26 25 24 23 22 21 20 19 18

To my mother, Zhang Xiuping; my wife, Jing (Qinyun) Li;
and my daughter, Rosemary

Contents

Figures

Acknowledgments

This book took its initial shape in my dissertation project when I was a PhD candidate at New York University and was finished during my fourth year of work at Brandeis University. Over this course of time, I have accumulated a staggering amount of intellectual and emotional debts. First, I wish to express my gratitude to Xudong Zhang for his mentorship, which combined generosity and a lassez-faire policy with timely interventionism in my scholarly training. This book is a testimony to his influence on every aspect of my intellectual formation. I also thank Richard Sieburth, who initiated me into comparative poetics and translation studies and provided unflagging support. A polymath, translator, and essayist, he remains my role model. Peter Button's enthusiasm was very helpful at the early stage of this project. As the chair of NYU's Comparative Literature Department and a deconstructionist teacher, Jacques Lezra played a constructive role in my research. The encouragement and assistance of many other NYU faculty members were equally vital to my development. I particularly thank Kristin Ross, Emily Apter, Harry Harootunian, Shiqi Liao, Rebecca Karl, Daniel Javitch, Catherine Stimpson, and Malcolm Semple. Wendy Larson gave me valuable feedback as an outside reader of my dissertation and has supported my work ever since. Since I moved to Massachusetts, David Der-wei Wang's guidance has been indispensable to the final revisions of this book, and I owe him special thanks.

I am very grateful for the privilege to work with many other outstanding scholars since my college years. In a life-changing way, the teachings of Hong Zicheng, Zang Di, Dai Jinhua, Wen Rumin, Yang Zhu, Chen Xiaoming, Wu Xiaodong, He Guimei, Zhang Xianglong, Yan Buke, Deng Xiaonan, Zhang Lianrong, and Yang Lihua introduced me to the humanities. The lectures Wang Hui gave during his stay at NYU in 2007 had a direct impact on the framework my research took. Fredric Jameson kindly shared with me his ideas on related topics in 2012–13. Always inspiring and engaging, Luo Gang, Ni Wenjian, Cai Xiang, Jiang Tao, Leng Shuang, Jin Yongbin, He Jixian, and Jiang Hui offered me various opportunities to present or publish my work in progress in Chinese and gave me valuable feedback. Mark Elliott, Lawrence Wong, Uganda Kwan, Wei Jian, and Fujita Rina generously invited me to share the preliminary output of this project in a series of workshops and conferences. Lucas Klein reviewed my dissertation with illuminating comments. Chen Pingyuan, Richard Wagner, Charles Laughlin, Michael Gibbs Hill, Ban Wang, Drucilla Cornell, Gao Yuandong, Jiang Langlang, Hu Xudong, Wang Feng, Cheng Kai, Mingwei Song, Carlos Rojas, Kawai Kozo, Chen Yue, and Liao Mingjiu gave me many important suggestions. Some portions of an earlier draft of chapter 3 were included as an article in *Translation and Modernization in East Asia* (Chinese University of Hong Kong, 2017), and for their assistance I thank Lawrence Wong and the CUHK Research Center for Translation.

My colleagues at Brandeis University have provided me an intellectual home and a productive working environment. I thank Robin Feuer Miller, Stephen Dowden, David Powelstock, and Yu Feng for their generosity and understanding. Matthew Fraleigh became a go-to person whenever I was hit by anxiety or puzzlement about my career. Harleen Singh has equally represented the best friendship one could expect from a colleague. Aida Wong and Xing Hang gave very useful advice. Conversations and collaborations with Chandler Rosenberger have been an enjoyable part of my life on campus. Billy Flesch, Rami Targoff, Jeronimo Arellano, and Nagmeh Sohrabi have also been great sources of professional and moral support.

The strong friendship I have developed with a diverse group of peers played a no less significant role in the making of this book. Liu Ziling, Li Chun, and Li Bin shared their digital archives, which tremendously facilitated my project. Li Mengyun, Yu Yang, Liu Fei, and Wu Xiangting have always reminded me to rethink my perspectives on life. Many of my ideas germinated in my cohort experience with Xiang He, Zhuo Liu, Jenny Lee, Julian Suddaby, Wenjin Cui, Daniel Hoffman-Schwartz, Sage Anderson, Lori Cole, Sun Yi, Loraine Wong, Yue Zhuo, Sonia Werner, Phil Kaffen, Qin Wang, and Eric Hodges. My friendship with Zhu Kang and Zhu Yu was deepened when they visited NYU, and ever since I have benefited from exchanging ideas with them. Brad Tabas and I had a theoretical reading group for just the two of us when we were in Paris. On a series of conference trips, Michel Bot and I debated on so many things. Sandra Rozental and Jeane Miller were my interlocutors and counselors when we shared study space at NYU's Humanities Initiative. Bilal Hashmi had a sympathetic eye when reading my early draft. I had the chance to learn a lot from Satoru Hashimoto's critique of my manuscript, among other things. I also enjoyed my collaborations with Tie Xiao, Max Bohnenkamp, and Roy Chan. Fan Xue, Liu Ying, Yang Daguo, Heather Inwood, and Li Zhang have been my fellow travelers despite the distance that divides us now. Lea Schneider, Liu Kui, Jin Lang, Chen Hailong, Bian He, Xingyi Wang, Xiaolu Ma, Jingling Chen, Gu Xiaolu, and many others have helped me in ways they might have forgotten. To all my friends around this tiny globe I offer this book, which silently records their wonderful presence in my life.

A series of fellowships and grants made my research and writing possible. At NYU, I enjoyed generous support from the Graduate School and was lucky to receive a Mellon Dissertation Fellowship and a Fellowship of the Humanities Initiative, which accelerated the writing of my early draft. At Brandeis, I enjoyed support from Tomberg Research Funds, Norman Funds, a Mandel Faculty Grant, and a Provost Research Grant, without which the completion of this book would have been unthinkable. In 2015–16, I was awarded a Chiang Ching-kuo Junior Faculty Grant, which enabled me to extend my sabbatical at a crucial stage of my writing.

I have relied on the resources and assistance of some of the best research libraries, including NYU Bobst Library, New York Public Library, Columbia Libraries (especially the Starr East Asian Library), Harvard Libraries (especially the Harvard-Yenching Library), Peking University Libraries, and Brandeis University Library. I thank the Klassik Stiftung Weimar for providing Goethe's drawing. I am very grateful to Guo Pingying for authorizing my use of Guo Moruo's photos and to Li Bin and the Guo Moruo Memorial Museum for coordinating the transaction of the images.

I thank my editor, Robert Graham, for his continuous support and understanding. I appreciate Kristen Wanner's help in setting up a good format for multilingual passages. My gratitude goes to Laura Poole for her excellent editorial work. I am very grateful for the criticisms of all the anonymous reviewers, which helped me rethink and revise this monograph. I am solely responsible for all the remaining errors and shortcomings of this book.

I wish to express my deepest gratitude to my mother, Zhang Xiuping, and my father, Wang Xingsheng, for their unconditional love, tolerance, and patience. I thank my parents-in-law for their support over the past few years. In 2014, I was able to see my maternal grandmother for the last time via video talk. Her memory was with me when I did the final revisions for this book. My aunts, uncles, and cousins have also been a source of moral support. Jing (Qinyun) Li, my wife and soul "enemy," has been here in every capacity to endure me, spur me, and test me since we met in college. Our two young children, Rosemary Rouran and Winston Qidan, had their own methods of influencing the pace of my work and hesitantly decided to accommodate a writing father. Now, as when it was then conceived, I dedicate this book to my mother, my wife, and my daughter: *Das Ewig-Weibliche / Zieht uns hinan.*

Abbreviations

CCP	Chinese Communist Party
GMD	Guomindang (also known as the Nationalist Party or Kuomintang)
GQ J/K	*Guo Moruo quan ji, kaogu bian* 郭沫若全集・考古編
GQ J/L	*Guo Moruo quan ji, lishi bian* 郭沫若全集・歷史編
GQ J/W	*Guo Moruo quan ji, wenxue bian* 郭沫若全集・文學編
GHY	*Guo Moruo yanjiu wenxian huiyao* 郭沫若研究文獻匯要
GZL	*Guo Moruo yanjiu ziliao* 郭沫若研究資料
N	*Nüshen: juqu shige ji* 女神：劇曲詩歌集
SPG	*Selected Poems from* The Goddesses

For more details, see the bibliography.

Conventions

Throughout this book, when citing the original German text of Goethe's *Faust,* I use the Deutscher Klassiker edition. For the English translation of *Faust,* I use the Norton edition by Walter Arndt and put the English quotes in parentheses following the German originals. After the first reference, I refer to *Faust* only by line numbers in parentheses.

My English back-translations of all the quotes from Guo Moruo's Chinese translation of *Faust* are provided in brackets following the quotes.

Similarly, when citing the original texts of classical Chinese poems, I provide the well-established English translations in parentheses. I provide my own English translations of Guo's Chinese translations of other foreign texts (such as Shelley's poems) and his vernacular translations of classical Chinese poetry in brackets following the Chinese quotes.

Unless otherwise indicated, all the translations of Chinese materials are mine.

INTRODUCTION

SPIRIT: . . . Thus at Time's scurrying loom I weave and warp.
—Johann Wolfgang von Goethe, *Faust*

[The spirit of Guo's poetry] is totally the spirit of the age—the Zeitgeist of the twentieth century.
—Wen Yiduo, "Zeitgeist in *The Goddesses*" (1923)

We can draw a mathematic equation: revolutionary literature = Function (Zeitgeist).
—Guo Moruo, "Revolution and Literature" (1926)

In [my historical drama] I grasped relatively better this Zeitgeist of the Warring States era [475–221 BCE].
—Guo, "The Peaches Offered to Reality" (1943)

Goethe's *Faust* . . . is a developmental history of Zeitgeist.
—Guo, "A Concise Interpretation of *Faust*" (1947)

"Right now I am undertaking a complete translation of Goethe's *Faust I*."[1] Thus Guo Moruo 郭沫若 (1892–1978) stated in a letter dated July 26, 1920. Then a Chinese student in Japan, Guo had recently adopted "Moruo" as his pen name and started to rise as a lyric poet on the scene of Chinese New Literature (*xin wenxue* 新文學). In the summer of 1920, taking his own cramped room for Faust's "narrow, high-vaulted Gothic chamber," Guo busied himself translating *Faust I* from German into Chinese.[2] Unfortunately, he failed to secure a publisher and had to leave the translated manuscript in a drawer when the summer ended. Here comes one of the most intriguing anecdotes in modern Chinese history of translation: about a month later, when Guo decided to take another look at his translation, he found that more than a third of the manuscript had been gnawed and destroyed by rats. Moreover, "his state of mind was not improved by [his Japanese wife, Satō] Tomiko's comment

1. Guo, "Lun shi tongxin," 111.
2. Goethe, *Faust*, 12.

that this catastrophe was clearly an omen intended to show him that he ought not to devote himself to literature."[3]

It must be immediately added, however, that this "omen" proved untrue. Less than a decade later, in late 1927 and early 1928, right before he was forced into exile because of the Nationalist Party's (Guomindang, GMD) anticommunist terror, Guo retranslated *Faust I* and had it see the light of the day. Two more decades having gone by, in 1947, when the civil war between the GMD and the communists drew to a deadlock, he finished his translation of *Faust II*. On that occasion, he characterized Goethe's epic drama as a "developmental history of Zeitgeist [*shidai jingshen* 時代精神]," and announced its relevance to the ongoing revolution, as if this German tragedy—an "allegory of the nineteenth century"—had been written for twentieth-century China.[4] Such links between translation and revolution, between the literary-intellectual transformation and a reimagination of the "Zeitgeist," between cultural production and political intervention, are the main subject matter of this book.

At the beginning of that 1920 letter, Guo transcribed his rendition of a passage from the opening act of *Faust*, "Night" ("Nacht"):

> So schaff' ich am sausenden Webstuhl der Zeit,
> Und wirke der Gottheit lebendiges Kleid.[5]
>
> (Thus at Time's scurrying loom I weave and warp / And broider at the Godhead's living garb.)[6]
>
> 我駕起時辰機杼，
> 替 "造化" 製造有生命的衣裳。[7]

3. Roy, *Kuo Mo-jo*, 94. Roy's narrative is based on Guo's autobiographical account. See Guo, *Chuangzao shinian*, in *GQJ/W*, 12:76.

4. Guo, "Fushide jian lun," 3. For a characterization of *Faust* as an "allegory of the nineteenth century," see Schlaffer, *Faust zweiter Teil*; Moretti, *Modern Epic*, 11–98.

5. Goethe, *Faust: Texte*, 37, lines 508–9. In the following, I only refer to the line numbers in parentheses when citing the German original text of *Faust* from this edition.

6. Goethe, *Faust*, 16. Throughout this book I use the Norton edition for the English translation of *Faust*. Hereafter only the line numbers are provided.

7. Guo, "Lun shi tongxin," 111.

[I drive Time's loom, / Manufacturing for the Nature of creation a living garb.][8]

"This song," Guo told his correspondent, "is sung by *Erdgeist*," the Earth Spirit. He continued: "The Earth Spirit is nothing but the symbol of the 'creative spirit' [*chuangzao jingshen* 創造精神]—*geschäftiger Geist*."[9] One may pause here and ask: does *chuangzao jingshen* really equal *geschäftiger Geist*?

Geschäftiger Geist is a phrase that Faust uses to express his worship of the Earth Spirit (see line 511); the German word *geschäftiger* means busy, active, sedulous, laborious, or bustling. *Chuangzao jingshen* means literally "creative spirit." In my view, this is not necessarily a mistranslation but forms a fleeting moment of creative translation in that forgotten letter. A key word of Guo's works and modern Chinese culture in general, *chuangzao* in Chinese signifies creation, and like the Greek *poiein*, it includes all forms of material, imaginative, and even political making or production. As we shall explore in more detail, Guo's embrace of creative spirit and especially the forms of creative destruction (resembling Faust's identification with the Earth Spirit) led to a controversial career ranging across literary production, historical scholarship, revolutionary activism—and translation.[10] This book not only sees the practice of translation as central and intrinsic to Guo's cultural practice, it also aims to unravel a creative mode of translation as historical imagination at the core of the long Chinese Revolution, stretching from the May Fourth New Culture Movement (1915–25) all the way to the Maoist Cultural Revolution (1966–76).[11] The young Guo's translation of *geschäftiger Geist* into *chuangzao jingshen*, in this sense, contains a prolepsis of his journey that would epitomize,

8. Throughout this book I provide my own back-translations (into English) of the Chinese passages I quote from Guo's interlingual or intralingual translations. They are in brackets below such quotes.

9. Guo, "Lun shi tongxin," 111.

10. Zhou Yang 周揚 seems to be the only one who has brought up this correspondence between Guo's lyrical position and Faust's identification with the Earth Spirit. See Zhou Yang, "Guo Moruo he ta de Nüshen," in *GZL*, 675.

11. For a more detailed discussion as to how to periodize the Chinese Revolution, see below.

in a problematic way that this book shall demonstrate, the laborious spirit or the spiritual labor of the Chinese Revolution.

Let us advance forward to the epilogue of China's revolutionary journey and Guo's own: in the People's Republic (1949–present) founded by the Chinese Communist Party (CCP), the aged Guo became an icon of the progressive intelligentsia's espousal of socialism. At the Ninth National Congress of the CCP, held in 1969 to mark the height of the Cultural Revolution, Guo was elected to the Central Committee—while many Chinese intellectuals were sidelined in sociopolitical life. Hailing to Maoism in public, in private he resumed the practice of translation in the same year. On the margins of a pocket book of poetry, he wrote down his renditions of a series of nineteenth-century English poems.[12] In addition to this split-persona act, he submerged himself in the writing of his last major book, *Li Bai and Du Fu* (*Li Bai yu Du Fu* 李白與杜甫), a study of Tang poetry that became a contentious monument of scholarship of the Cultural Revolution. To offer a class analysis of Du Fu (712–70), Guo produced vernacular translations of this acclaimed Tang poet's works.

Still, Guo could not escape from the final spasms of Maoist politics, as he was involved in a poetic conversation with Mao Zedong 毛澤東 (1893–1976). In 1973 he received a poem from Mao. Written in a traditional form of *qilü* 七律, Mao's poem singled out Guo's 1940s interpretation of the thought of Confucius (551–479 BCE) as a revolutionary "Zeitgeist" in pre-Qin China.[13] Stressing the necessity of Qin Shi Huang 秦始皇 (the First Emperor of Qin, 259–210 BCE) remolding Chinese society, Mao anachronistically picked Confucius as his last enemy and denounced Guo's previous view of ancient history: "My friend, please stop criticizing Qin Shi Huang."[14] Guo's final political trial was uncannily defined by an eternal return of Confucius, Qin Shi Huang, and the classical poetic style.

Guo survived Mao and the Cultural Revolution. The word *jizhu* 機杼, which he had chosen to translate Goethe's word *Webstuhl* (loom), reappeared in one of the last political poems he composed. The poem,

12. The late Guo's translations of those poems were discovered after Guo's death in his Beijing residence. See Guo, trans., *Ying shi yi gao*, especially 146–47. Also see Feng Xigang, *Guo Moruo de wannian suiyue*, 213–14.

13. See chapter 5 and conclusion.

14. Mao Zedong, "Qilü, du *Fengjian lun* cheng Guo lao," 361.

titled "Welcome the Year of 1977," endorsed the purge of the ultra-leftist faction: "A new historical [epoch] is reorganizing the [Time's] loom [*jizhu*]."[15] On his deathbed, this translator of *Faust* was praised by Zhou Yang 周揚 (1908–89), the CCP's former tsar of literature, as an encyclopedic Goethe of China's own.[16] Yet this effusive comparison must have been ironic to the ailing Guo since only recently in *Li Bai and Du Fu* had he cited the line of Friedrich Engels (1820–95): "Each of [Hegel and Goethe] was an Olympian Zeus in his own sphere, yet neither of them ever quite freed himself from German philistinism."[17] Guo died in summer 1978. Deng Xiaoping 鄧小平 (1904–97) delivered the memorial address at his funeral, defining Guo as a "writer, poet, dramatist, Marxist historian and paleographer" as well as a "revolutionist" and "cultural fighter."[18] Months later, Deng launched the "reforms and opening-up," effectively starting a burial of the Maoist era. Guo did not have the chance to judge whether China's farewell to revolution meant a redemption or yet another wager with the "negative spirit."[19]

These glimpses into the translingual creativity of Guo's early days and the political vagaries of his final years offer a montage of the turbulent trajectory that was not only his long career but also the Chinese Revolution, spanning six decades from the May Fourth Movement to the Cultural Revolution. Sketchy though it is, this montage suffices to illustrate how deeply Guo's work was embroidered in the cultural-political fabric of that long revolution. One way of problematizing Guo's peculiar existence in modern Chinese culture could be to characterize China's revolutionary ethos manifested in his activity as a creative translation of the Faustian drama: ever striving and seldom satisfied, Guo devoted himself to revolution as the laborious spirit, necessary negativity, and

15. Guo, "Yingjie yi jiu qi qi nian," in *GQJ/W*, 5:148.

16. According to Zhou's recollection, "this Chinese translator of *Faust*, upon hearing my words, smiled." See Zhou Yang, "Beitong de huainian," 9.

17. Guo, *Li Bai yu Du Fu*, 12. The quote is from Engels, *Ludwig Feuerbach and the End of Classical German Philosophy*, 600.

18. Deng Xiaoping, "Zai Guo Moruo tongzhi zhuidao hui shang de daoci," i.

19. In Goethe's *Faust*, Mephistopheles is the personification of "der Geist der stets verneint" (line 1338, "the spirit that eternally negates" [English translation modified]). In the 1940s, Guo expounded the role of Mephistopheles as "the negative spirit" (*fouding de jingling* 否定的精灵) of capitalism—see chapter 3.

above all, the "Zeitgeist." He tried to distill a revolutionary "Zeitgeist" from both *Faust* and ancient Chinese history. His oeuvre thus lends itself powerfully to an exploration of the dialectic of translation, revolution, and historical imagination (a dialectic comparable to "Time's scurrying loom") in twentieth-century China.

With such a focus on translation, revolution, and historical imagination, this book examines the cultural dynamics of China's revolutionary century. At the center of this study is a critical engagement with the multifaceted works of Guo Moruo, a towering figure in twentieth-century Chinese culture. Pioneering a new lyrical voice, he eventually became the inaugural president of socialist China's Academy of Sciences. Applying Marxism to the study of Chinese antiquity, he contributed to the paleographical-philological interpretations of the oracle bone and bronze inscriptions—China's most archaic written system. Championing the genres of historical drama and autobiography in modern Chinese literature, he fatefully wound up being Mao Zedong's last poetic interlocutor. No less important, he devoted almost three decades to translating Goethe's *Faust* into Chinese. Guo's career has generated as much controversy as it has admiration. While the CCP once enshrined him as a flag-bearer of progressive culture, current discourses on Chinese modernity have often marginalized—if not stigmatized—his work as an infamous example of revolutionary romanticism. However, precisely because of its controversial nature, I believe that revisiting this thorny case will help us better understand the cultural complexity of the Chinese Revolution. This book therefore attempts the first comprehensive study of Guo's lifework as a whole in the English-speaking world.[20] Working through different genres and periods of this encyclopedic author's writings, and engaging the texts of many related writers and thinkers (such as Goethe, Shelley, Lu Xun, Feng Zhi, Wen Yiduo, Marx, Engels, Lukács, and Mao), my inquiry confronts two issues crucial to revolutionary cultural politics: translation and historical interpretation.

20. Two preexisting book-length studies in English (one being David Roy's 1971 biographical study and the other being Xiaoming Chen's 2007 intellectual-historical case study) are exclusively preoccupied with Guo's early years.

Recent scholarship has scarcely treated Guo's oeuvre as a whole and even less touched on his career as a translator. In fact, he should be counted as one of the most prolific translators of twentieth-century China. My examination emphasizes that Guo's works of translation are as wide-ranging as his creative texts. He turned his hand to rendering into Chinese, among many other texts, the poetic works of Percy Bysshe Shelley (1792–1822), *The Rubáiyát of Omar Khayyám*, *Zur Kritik der Politischen Ökonomie* by Karl Marx (1818–83), as well as some excerpts from the young Marx and Friedrich Engels's *German Ideology* and *Holy Family* (Guo's dream of translating *Das Kapital* never materialized, though), *Young Werther's Sorrows* and *Hermann and Dorothea* by Johann Wolfgang von Goethe (1749–1832), *Wallenstein* by Friedrich Schiller (1759–1805), *Virgin Soil* by Ivan Turgenev, *Social Organization and Social Revolution* by Japanese economist Kawakami Hajime 河上肇, *A Century of Archaeological Discoveries* by Adolf Michaelis, and *The Science of Life* (coauthored by H. G. Wells). What dominated this splendid variety of translingual productions was, of course, Guo's translation of Goethe's *Faust*. Furthermore, Guo engaged himself in the inventive practice of modern vernacular translation (*jinyi* 今譯) of such ancient texts as the poems from the *Book of Songs* (*Shi jing* 詩經, *Shi jing* hereafter) and the Chu-styled songs of Qu Yuan 屈原 (340?–278 BCE). Even his paleographical interpretation of oracle bone and bronze inscriptions can be seen in the light of intralingual translation. My study aims to reveal the various forms of translingual practice as a condition for cultural-political interventions; it also highlights the forgotten fact that intralingual translations formed a key operation in revolutionary uses and abuses of ancient legacies. Together, the acts of translating the foreign and rewriting the ancient demarcated a precarious zone of revolutionary imaginaries.

Consequently, this book pays particular attention to two overarching and intertwined aspects of Guo's lifework and twentieth-century Chinese culture. One is the translingual dimension of revolutionary cultural practice, especially Guo's decades-long engagement in translating *Faust*. The other is his continuous rewriting of Chinese antiquity in lyrical, dramatic, and historiographical-philological forms, including not only the interpretative enterprise of "reversing the verdict" (*fan'an* 翻案) but also his vernacular translation of classical poetry. Interrogating the links between translation and historical imagination, I find in revolutionary cultural practice a transcoding of different historical conjunctures into the "now-time" (to echo Walter Benjamin) filled with possibilities and "saturated with tensions."[21]

As I shall elaborate later, in this book, translation primarily means specific interlingual and intralingual acts of translating. Meanwhile, it also signifies various forms of literary "rewriting," intellectual "transcoding," and even ideological reversal.[22] Pursuing a broader perspective of translation as an active agency in transforming traditions and instantiating cultural-political changes, I extend my discussion to the issue of twentieth-century China's rewritings of national antiquity and trace the imaginaries of revolution in both translingual practice and historical interpretation. On one hand, his translation of *Faust* became an allegory of the inconclusive Zeitgeist, amounting to an act of self-periodization. On the other hand, his transcoding of antiquity spiraled into the final scandals of Maoism, forming a retrospective from which to view the Chinese Revolution as the constant translation and reversal of historical time.

By "historical time," I mean neither the linear and homogeneous time of progression nor the apocalyptic and messianic time of redemption. Instead, I aim to grasp the open-ended experience of historical possibilities and conditions.[23] A radical example of the intensity, heterogeneity, and mutability of such a temporal experience, the Chinese Revolution was recognizably a long, continuous "cultural revolution," which meant a "formation of revolutionary subjectivity" amid competing tendencies and trajectories.[24] A central task of my examination is to contend that the

21. Benjamin, "On the Concept of History," 395, 396.

22. For a discussion of translation as rewriting, see Lefevere, *Translation, Rewriting, and the Manipulation of Literary Fame*. I borrow the term "transcoding" from Fredric Jameson, according to whom "a process of transcoding" is "the invention of a set of terms, the strategic choice of a particular code or language, such that the same terminology can be used to analyze . . . two very different structural levels of reality." Jameson, *The Political Unconscious*, 40.

23. For a critique of "homogenous" historical time, see Benjamin, "On the Concept of History."

24. According to Jameson's definition, "cultural revolution" is a process "in which the formation of revolutionary subjectivity is transformed into the restructuration of collective subjectivities along the logic of a new mode of production." Jameson, "Cultural Revolution," 267. Also see below.

translatability/reversibility of historical time formed a subjective dynamic, a structural problem, and a symptomatic crisis intrinsic to twentieth-century Chinese culture.

Guo Moruo: Life and Work

In 1892, Guo was born into a wealthy merchant family in Leshan, Sichuan Province. He spent his childhood and teenage years during the final decline of the Qing empire (1644–1911), a period when China fell prey to the escalating competition of Western and Japanese powers in a capitalist-imperialist world system. In his hometown, he received a half-traditional, half-modern education and started to learn foreign languages such as Japanese and English. In 1910, he was enrolled in a high school in Chengdu, the capital city of Sichuan. There, he witnessed the 1911 revolution that overthrew the Qing rule.

For Guo, the irony of that revolution lay in the fact that right after the founding of Asia's first modern republic in 1912, he had to accept an arranged marriage. Like many Chinese students dreaming of individual liberation and national modernization, Guo decided to escape from the old-styled family and pursue higher education in Japan. Since the Meiji Restoration, Japan became a modernized oppressor hungering for colonial interests in China and played a mediating role in the transmission of Western knowledge into China. Guo's travel to Japan in 1914 led to a complicated case of transnational engagement in the history of the Sino-Japanese contact and conflict, exerting a decisive influence on his personal, intellectual, and political development.[25]

His education in Japan initiated Guo into a fascination with Western culture in general and German culture in particular. Having attended Tokyo First Higher School and Okayama Higher School, he made significant progress in his language capabilities of Japanese, German, English, and Latin.[26] His rekindled interest in Confucianism and Daoism was

25. See Dong Bingyue, *"Guomin zuojia" de lichang.* Also see Yan Lu, *Re-Understanding Japan.*

26. As a premedical student, Guo was required to learn German, and the teaching materials for this language were primarily German literary texts.

mediated by his encounter with the discourse of Spinozan pantheism.[27] He submerged himself in works of Heinrich Heine (1797–1856), Goethe, Schiller, Rabindranath Tagore (1861–1941), Shelley, Shakespeare, and other foreign authors.[28] In 1915 he made his first attempt at translation, rendering Heine's poems into Chinese. In 1916, he fell in love with Satō Tomiko 佐藤富子(1894–1995), the daughter of a Japanese Protestant minister, and soon started their cohabitation. Their common-law marriage never received blessings from their parents. In 1918 Guo went on to study medical science at Kyushu Imperial University (fig. 1), moving with Satō and their first son to Fukuoka, a main city of Kyushu.

While living on the other side of the East China Sea, Guo took attentive note of the Literary Revolution taking place back in his homeland, and he started to write both fictional and lyrical pieces. In 1919–20, Guo was drawn under a spell of the powerful free verse of Walt Whitman (1819–92), and this new poetic inspiration erupted into the writing of what later became the major works of Guo's first book of poetry and poetic drama, *Goddesses* (*Nüshen* 女神). As his vernacular poems stormed on the scene of New Poetry (*xin shi* 新詩), he also published translations of excerpts from Goethe's *Faust* and discussed poetic pantheism in his correspondences with Zong Baihua 宗白華 (1897–1986) and Tian Han 田漢 (1898–1968). In 1921, Guo cofounded, with a number of other Chinese students in Japan, the Creation Society (*chuangzao she* 創造社). Initially an antiestablishment "lonely army" heralding romanticism and *l'art pour l'art* aesthetics, this literary society transformed itself into a Marxist group conducting theoretical warfare toward the end of the 1920s.[29] Guo's 1922 rendering of *Sorrows of Young Werther* offered him

27. During his early days of study abroad, Guo practiced the "meditative sitting" advocated by neo-Confucian thinker Wang Yangming 王陽明 (1472–1529) and reread the work of ancient Daoist philosopher Zhuangzi 莊子 (370–287 BCE). In a 1925 essay titled "In Praise of Wang Yangming" ("Wang Yangming lizan" 王陽明禮讚), Guo wrote that his practice of Wang Yangming's philosophy in 1914–15 led him to a true understanding of Zhuangzi's ideas, which in turn led him to Indian philosophy and "the idealist philosophers of continental Europe, especially Spinoza"—"I thus discovered a metaphisical world that is crystalline and solemn." *GQJ/L*, 3:290. Also see Jianmei Liu, *Zhuangzi and Modern Chinese Literature*, 21–45.

28. Guo, "Wo de xuesheng shidai," in *GQJ/W*, 12:17.

29. Maike Ang (Guo Moruo), "Wenxue geming zhi huigu," 552. Also see Cheng Fangwu, "Xin wenxue de shiming."

FIGURE 1 Guo Moruo (second from right) as a medical student in Kyushu, Japan, 1923. Courtesy of Guo Pingying.

an opportunity to propose his pantheism (*fanshenlun* 泛神論) of vitality and sentimentality.[30] Also in 1922, Guo translated a set of Shelley's poems and finished his vernacular renditions of a group of love songs from

30. For a discussion of the "Werther fever" in China, see Lee, *The Romantic Generation of Modern Chinese Writers*, 283–86.

Shi jing. He attempted to reinvent the traditional spirit of Confucianism as a "pantheist ideal" of self-fulfilling personality, humanity, and even utopian communism.[31] Taken together, the early Guo's liberating verse, his appropriation of Western culture, and his rediscovery of ancient Chinese spirituality called into being a "macrocosm" of pantheistic mutability that served as a demarcation of the emerging space of the New Culture.[32]

In other words, Guo's creative energies exploded in a short span of time, roughly from 1919 through 1923, and immediately earned him a celebrity status in China. This may sound like a familiar story: a youngster receives Western influences and bursts onto a non-Western national literary scene. Scholars partly owe this narrative of Guo's sudden rise to his luminous autobiography, which crystalizes his self-fashioning of an expressive ego. Yet unlike other archetypical Chinese romantics such as Xu Zhimo 徐志摩 (1897–1931), very soon Guo moved from literature to intellectual and political arenas.

David Roy's 1971 biography described the range of Guo's activity: "Kuo Mo-jo is possibly the most versatile Chinese intellectual of our day. There is hardly an area of twentieth-century Chinese cultural life in which his influence has not been felt. . . . [He] has made substantial contributions in such diverse fields as poetry, drama, fiction, autobiography, translation, intellectual and cultural history, archeology, paleography, and cultural and political propaganda."[33] Roy's biographical narrative stops right at the point of Guo's conversion to Marxism. The young Guo felt frustrated with the particular exploitation of the Creation Society by Shanghai print capitalism and the general suppression of Chinese society by external imperialist powers and internal warlords. A sense of disillusionment led him to search for intellectual and political alternatives while he was dividing his time between Shanghai and Fukuoka. In a 1924 letter to Cheng Fangwu 成仿吾 (1897–1984), a fellow Creationist, Guo announced his communist vision, hoping to create a world where "every-

31. See, for example, Guo, "Zhongguo wenhua zhi chuantong jingshen," in *GQJ/L*, 3:255–63. Also see Xiaoming Chen, *From the May Fourth Movement to Communist Revolution*, chapter 3.

32. I borrow the word from the scene about the "sign of the Macrocosm" in *Faust*. Goethe, *Faust*, 14.

33. Roy, *Kuo Mo-jo*, 1.

one will be able to develop his or her talents."[34] After engaging himself in political debates with anarchists and statists, he moved to Guangzhou in 1926, heralding the transformation of May Fourth literary youths into political youths against the backdrop of the formation of the united front of the GMD and CCP.

Commissioned to be in charge of political propaganda, Guo participated in the Northern Expedition (1926–27) that aimed to end the rule of warlords. Vetted by the GMD and CCP, Guo decided to denounce his superior Jiang Jieshi 蔣介石 (Chiang Kai-shek, 1887–1975), who later became the de facto autocrat of the GMD regime, and joined the CCP's military uprising when the GMD right wing severed the coalition in 1927. He was lucky enough to survive GMD's persecution of the communists. In the wake of this revolutionary crisis, Guo and the Creation Society feverishly engaged in the debates about "revolutionary literature" (*geming wenxue* 革命文學).[35] Hiding himself in Shanghai, he resumed his translation of *Faust* and left for Japan in early 1928.

During his decade-long exile in Japan, Guo translated Marx's works and started his career as a leftist historian of ancient China. Though his Marxist historiography has been criticized for dogmatism, his incorporation of the Morgan-Engels perspective and his deciphering of Shang-Zhou oracle bone and bronze inscriptions were groundbreaking by consensus. Under the surveillance of Japanese police, Guo also initiated his autobiographical writing. When the War of Resistance Against Japanese Aggression (1937–45) broke out, Guo abandoned Satō and their five children, left behind his paleographical manuscripts, and secretly went back to China in mid-1937. Subsequently he took charge of political propaganda in the Anti-Japanese United Front of the GMD and CCP—their second coalition. In 1938, he married Yu Liqun 于立群 (1916–79), a communist actress who later became an artist of calligraphy.

When the relationship between the two political parties became strained in the early 1940s, Guo was once again politically marginalized by the GMD. In contrast, the CCP decided to promote Guo's status as the "leader of today's revolutionary culture," using him as a symbolic figure to

34. Guo, "Gu hong," in *GQJ/W*, 16:8.
35. See Lee, "Literary Trends: The Road to Revolution," especially 196–203.

reach solidarity with the intelligentsia.[36] Working in Chongqing—the wartime capital of the GMD-controlled region—under the leadership of Zhou Enlai 周恩來 (1898–1976), Guo composed five historical plays over 1942 to 1943. He resumed historical studies, launching a provocative and systematic reinterpretation of the pre-Qin antiquity in his twin projects of *The Bronze Age* (*Qingtong shidai* 青銅時代, 1945) and *Ten Critiques* (*Shi pipan shu* 十批判書, 1945). The dramatic poetics and intellectual rhetoric of his historical interpretations fused into a perspective of "people-centrism" (*renmin benwei zhuyi* 人民本位主義), which needs to be examined in a larger context of the struggles for "people's democracy" (*renmin minzhu* 人民民主).[37]

In mid-1945, on the eve of China's bitter victory over Japan, Guo traveled to the Soviet Union on the invitation of the Soviet Academy of Sciences. By then he had worked as a major activist in the movements protesting the GMD's monopoly of power and proposing a coalition government.[38] When the postwar GMD-CCP negotiations gave way to an all-out civil war, Guo refused to accept the membership of the Academia Sinica (established by the GMD) and moved to Hong Kong in 1947. It was yet another retreat from politics that propelled him to complete his rendering of *Faust II* in the same year.

After the founding of the People's Republic in 1949, Guo was elected the chairman of the Chinese Federation of Literary and Art Circles, president of the Academy of Sciences, and vice chairman of the People's Congress. A 1951 recipient of the Stalin Peace Prize, he worked as a cultural diplomat, a CCP ideologue, and a historian (fig. 2). In 1953, he translated Qu Yuan's poems into modern vernacular, concluding his interpretation of this ancient poet. During the Great Leap Forward (1958–60), he supported Mao's proposal of "revolutionary romanticism" (*geming langmanzhuyi* 革命浪漫主義). He composed two more historical plays, attempting to combine the agenda of "reversal of the verdict" with the allegorical praise of the Maoist line.

36. Zhou Enlai, "Wo yao shuo de hua," in *GZL*, 371.

37. See Guo, *Shi pipan shu*, 423.

38. See Guo's account of the democratic movements in the GMD-controlled region, "Minzu yundong zhong de er san shi," in *GQJ/W*, 20:182–93.

FIGURE 2 Guo Moruo, 1952. Courtesy of Guo Pingying.

Indeed, the polemical drive of subversion can be readily discerned in Guo's post-1949 works, such as his reevaluation of historical personalities including Cao Cao 曹操 (155–220, a statesman and poet who reunited northern China) and Wu Zetian 武则天 (624–705, the only female emperor in Chinese history); his questioning of the authorship of Wang Xizhi 王羲之 (303–61) on the calligraphic masterpiece "Preface of the Orchid Pavilion" ("Lan ting xu" 兰亭序); and finally his political criticism and self-criticism. Such "destructive energies of historical materialism," however, were at least partly unleashed to cater to the accelerating pace of Maoist politics.[39] One of the last and most scandalous targets of reappraisal was his own past. When faced with the frenzy of ultraleftism at the beginning of the Cultural Revolution, Guo negated his past achievements, only to find the life of one of his children cut short. It is equally worth noting, though, that as a protégé of Zhou Enlai, Guo used his remaining prowess to help restore scholarly and cultural activities in the early 1970s.[40]

Inseparable from his subversive tendencies was Guo's role as "a commemorative agent of the new regime."[41] He fulfilled this role by becoming a poetic automaton, churning out countless classical-style poems on various occasions. A veteran of vernacular New Poetry, he mobilized the high-cultural value of traditional poetic prosody at the service of revolution.[42] His poetic exchanges with Mao fueled the cult of personality and helped produce an anachronistic form of politically symbolic action. In short, the combination of Guo's obsession with polemic vigor and his loyalty to Maoism defined a peculiar, if not perilous, existence of the socialist scholar-official.

Guo's last days after the Cultural Revolution were torn apart between his call for China's "springtime of science" and his fidelity to Maoist politics.[43] After he passed away at the age of eighty-six, according to his will his ashes were scattered on the agricultural land of Dazhai, a people's commune Mao had promoted as a socialist model. This may be seen as his last endorsement of revolution, whereas the whole country showed the

39. Benjamin, "Paralipomena to 'On the Concept of History,'" 406.
40. See Feng Xigang, *Guo Moruo de wannian suiyue*, 261–358.
41. Larson, *Literary Authority and the Modern Chinese Writer*, 152.
42. See Haosheng Yang, *A Modernity Set to a Pre-Modern Tune*, chapter 4.
43. Guo, "Kexue de chuntian."

desire for a postrevolutionary path that would lead China into marketization and capitalization.[44]

A Controversial Legacy

The life and work of Guo immediately present a series of difficulties for my inquiry. First, one has to wrestle with the sheer quantity of his textual output. The current edition of *Complete Works of Guo Moruo* (*Guo Moruo quan ji* 郭沫若全集) is composed of up to thirty-eight volumes. But it is by no means complete, as it does not collect, among other things, his correspondences and diaries—not to mention the voluminous and various works of his translations. The second difficulty concerns the wide range of the work. Guo moved with ease into so many different domains of literary, cultural, and intellectual practice that it seems almost unfeasible to bring them together in a single study. The third problem derives from the numerous revisions he made on his works for reasons not limited to political ones throughout his lifetime. Therefore, no studies of Guo's oeuvre can pretend to be exhaustive. My own study, for example, will not do full justice to his miscellaneous essays and speeches. Nor will I have space to deal with his works of Chinese calligraphy.

The majority of preexisting commentaries have tended to single out certain genres, topics and periods in Guo's lifework. In particular, the issue concerning Guo's conversion from a romantic writer into a leftist intellectual has attracted most critical attention. In socialist China, a number of critics already attempted—with varying degrees of success—to frame Guo's "transition from pantheism to communism" in a triumphalist narrative about the Chinese intelligentsia's progression toward Marxism.[45] Scholars in the English-speaking world have gauged the

44. For more detailed narratives of Guo's life, see the following biographical studies: Gong Jimin and Fang Rennian, *Guo Moruo nianpu*; Gong Jimin and Fang Rennian, *Guo Moruo zhuan*; Qin Chuan, *Wenhua juren Guo Moruo*. For biographical studies of Guo's later life, see two books by Feng Xigang: *Guo Moruo de wannian suiyue* and *Wenge qian de Guo Moruo*.

45. See, for example, Ai Yang, "Shi lun Guo Moruo qianqi sixiang fazhan," in *GZL*, 489–509; and Song Yaozong, "Dui Guo Moruo qianqi sixiang fazhan de yixie lijie,"

continuities and discontinuities between Guo's romantic and communist phases. Roy's biographical study situates Guo's vicissitude between romanticism and communism in his personal life and social environment. Leo O. Lee's study of the "romantic generation" in modern Chinese literature sees Guo as the "most successful of romantics turned Communist."[46] Marián Gálik's examination traces the "development" of the early Guo "from aesthetico-impressionist to proletarian."[47] In her book on Chinese modernism, Shu-mei Shih also devotes one short chapter to discussing Guo's early fictional writings in the context of the rise of cosmopolitan psychoanalysis in China.[48] Xiaoming Chen's book uses the early Guo to explain why "China saw some of its best brains turn to the Communist cause."[49] He suggests that the "tension between Confucian moralism and Marxist historical materialism was at the core of an overall predicament in Guo's communist thinking," and schematizes his thinking into a "Confucian/Marxist/Leninist Communist synthesis."[50]

Clearly, a lot of ink has been spilled on the initial period of Guo's career, whereas studies of the equally significant and far more controversial manifestations of his post-1927 leftist career (to say nothing of his post-1949 works) remain sporadic.[51] Roy's and Chen's books alleviate my burden of providing an explanation of when, where, and how Guo's reorientation toward the left took place. Meanwhile, my approach differs from either Roy's biographical treatment or Chen's idea of intellectual continuity. Emphasizing that many of Guo's later developments were germinated in the force field of his early works, I nevertheless hope to historicize his early phase as the "origin" or "unfolding structure" of an open-ended process within the totality of modern Chinese cultural poli-

---

in *GZL*, 510–24. The Chinese critics' preoccupation with Guo's early intellectual outlook culminated in Chen Yongzhi's book-length study, *Guo Moruo sixiang zhengti guan.*

46. Lee, *Romantic Generation of Modern Chinese Writers*, 177–200.

47. Gálik, *Genesis of Modern Chinese Literary Criticism*, 28–103.

48. Shih, *The Lure of the Modern*, 96–109.

49. Xiaoming Chen, *From the May Fourth Movement to Communist Revolution*, 1.

50. Ibid., 9, 111.

51. Arif Dirlik's study of Guo's Marxist historiography needs to be mentioned; see my chapter 4 for details. In her study of autobiographical writing in modern China, Wendy Larson finds in Guo's turn to politics a discontentment with the ineffectual textual/mental labor. See Larson, *Literary Authority and the Modern Chinese Writer*, 113–52.

tics.[52] Combining the method of historicization with symptomatic reading, I try to understand the mechanism of self-transformation and self-reversal in Guo's "change of direction" (*fangxiang zhuanhua* 方向轉換) via the medium of its own language—especially its own translingual rhetoric.[53] Then I bring this perspective to Guo's later developments, so as to restore the high quantity, unstable quality, and radical reversibility of his works as a site of constant repositioning that calls for a critical reading within a larger logic of cultural revolution.

The daunting task of confronting Guo's oeuvre as a whole consequently comes inexorably down to a challenge about how to address the controversial nature of Guo's role in the Chinese Revolution. Though he was popular among some like-minded Chinese youths in the 1920s, there was no shortage of critics who even saw him as one of the "talented scholars-cum-hooligans."[54] In the 1940s and 1950s, the CCP praised Guo as a pioneer of "revolutionary romanticism" and accorded him the iconic status that was only second to that of Lu Xun 魯迅 (1881–1936), a founding father of modern Chinese literature.[55] But for his opponents, Guo represented the worst combination of a romantic man of letters and a revolutionary politician, especially given his notoriety for vicissitudes in aesthetic sensibility, political attitude, and even personal affairs.[56]

Controversy continues to haunt Guo's posthumous reputation. As Chen rightly states, "when the Maoist revolution died, Guo was a noticeable figure in and at its deathbed."[57] Since his death, Guo's image has gradually lost its officially endorsed luster. A disapproving or even denigrating reappraisal emerged in due course, offering a "reflection" on either

52. Here I use the word "origin" in the Benjaminian sense of *Ursprung*. See Steiner, "Introduction," 15–16.

53. The phrase "change of direction," presumably borrowed from the Japanese, was widely used to describe the turn to Marxism and communism in the 1920s in China. See Cheng Fangwu, "Quanmian de pipan zhi biyao."

54. This dismissive phrase comes from Lu Xun's stigmatization of the Creationists in general. See Lu Xun, "A Glance at Shanghai Literature," 129.

55. See Zhou Yang, "Guo Moruo he ta de Nüshen."

56. For example, during the Cold War, GMD-affiliated scholars in Taiwan condemned Guo for his lack of moral integrity. See Jin Dakai, *Guo Moruo zong lun*. Jin seems to be especially indignant at what he finds as Guo's inclination for erotic relationships with women.

57. Chen, *From the May Fourth Movement to Communist Revolution*, 111.

Guo's dogmatic embrace of violent radicalism or his approach to politics.[58] Jin Qiu notes that Guo's post-1949 involvements in revolutionary culture and party politics are considered particularly scandalous, since some "believe [that] Guo advanced his political career at the cost of his personal and academic integrity."[59] Many also hold that his tendency of "catching the fashionable trends of the time" is an unfortunate example of how the "inner space of freedom" of modern Chinese intellectuals "has been gradually invaded and devoured by the external political power."[60] Therefore, while Lu Xun's work has entered the canon of world literature, Guo's lifework is now sometimes considered to be little more than an embarrassing reminder of a questionable revolutionary romanticism and is consigned to the pages of chronicles or textbooks of modern Chinese literature. Although scholarly works on Guo have formed a verifiable subfield in Chinese, since the 1990s it has been exhausted by efforts to protect Guo's image against denigrations in public media and mostly isolated by the main currents of modern China studies.[61] This marginalization indicates the dwindling relevance of revolutionary legacies in the post–Cold War and postsocialist atmosphere. In the changed ideological landscape, the corpus of Guo's work stands more like a poisonous asset inherited from a bygone revolutionary culture.

In this book I undertake the challenge to reclaim this asset—not to redeem Guo's image but to rekindle a critical debate on the cultural legacies of the Chinese Revolution. Both the iconic halo previously surrounding Guo and the postsocialist pejorative depiction of him represent a tendency to reduce the social, intellectual, and cultural complexities of the Chinese Revolution to a level of teleological narratives and self-closed judgments. Fully aware of all the difficulties and controversies facing the

58. A critique of Guo's unconditional embrace of revolutionary destruction can be found in Kubin, "'Invincible for Aye!'" More disparaging criticisms of Guo are included in Ding Dong, ed., *Fansi Guo Moruo*. Some of them deviate from the historical facts, triggering corrective responses: see Cao Jian, ed., *Gongzong pingjia Guo Moruo*. In my opinion, a more sophisticated critique of Guo as an opportunist comes from a much earlier book published in Hong Kong during the Cold War: Shi Jian, *Guo Moruo pipan*.

59. Jin Qiu, "Between Power and Knowledge," 146.

60. Jianmei Liu, *Zhuangzi and Modern Chinese Literature*, 21.

61. For a comment on the marginalization of Guo Moruo studies, see Cai Zhen, "Guo Moruo yan jiu san yi," in *GHY*, 13:408–9.

present study, I maintain that without a reexamination of Guo's career, our understanding of twentieth-century Chinese culture would be incomplete. Offering a case study of Guo's self-revision and "self-correction," Jianmei Liu points out that "by self-consciously subjecting himself to politics, Guo Moruo became a political instrument as well as an ideological instrument."[62] Yet it is precisely this mechanism of "self-conscious instrumentalization" that deserves further interrogation. In other words, I am not interested in pursuing biographical reevaluations of Guo's personality, but I propose to see his lifework as a social text that interweaves a "synthetic ensemble of problems" about revolutionary cultural politics.[63] Crucial to my task is an effort to further contextualize, conceptualize, and problematize the entanglement of Guo's work with the Chinese Revolution.

A Long Revolution, a Short Century, and a Translatable Zeitgeist

In this book, the phrase "the Chinese Revolution" does not signify a single event but refers to a period of radical sociopolitical change and, by extension, a new experience of historical time in modern China. From a perspective of the *longue durée*, the whole history of China's rocky journey from tradition into modernity can be recognized as a "great Chinese revolution," encompassing "five wars of foreign aggression," "five revolutionary civil wars," and far more social upheavals from the late Qing years all the way to the post-Maoist era.[64] More pertinent to my study is the periodization of "China's revolutionary century," articulated by the contemporary Chinese intellectual Wang Hui: "China's whole 'revolutionary century' . . . [encompasses] the era stretching from the Republican Revolution in 1911 to around 1976 (the end of the Cultural Revolution)."[65]

62. Jianmei Liu, *Zhuangzi and Modern Chinese Literature*, 44.

63. This phrase is borrowed from Jean-Paul Sartre's formulation of the "progressive-regressive method"; see Sartre, *Critique de la raison dialectique*, 1:91.

64. Fairbank, *The Great Chinese Revolution*, x.

65. Wang Hui, "Depoliticized Politics," 29.

Such a characterization of the long Chinese Revolution as a short century echoes the historical reflection of the "short twentieth century" as an age of "extremes."[66] A forceful philosophical redemption of the twentieth century comes from French philosopher Alain Badiou's periodization of a global revolutionary century starting from Russia's October Revolution and ending with China's Cultural Revolution.[67] In Badiou's view, the Chinese Revolution is of world-historic significance, and the failure of the Cultural Revolution "signals the closure of an entire sequence" of radical praxis.[68]

A long revolution, a short century: this is the epoch to which Guo's cultural practice bears intimate testimony, as we have seen how his lifework not only overlapped squarely with but also lay fully embedded in this condensed revolutionary century. Therefore, the Chinese Revolution denotes a singular historical process composed of plural revolutions. Hosting a seemingly never-ending list of radical movements and unleashing the unprecedented energies of social change, China's twentieth century was driven by a profound sense of incomplete modernization, unfinished transformation, and stalled revitalization—a Faustian dissatisfaction that would repetitively invite the next installment of the revolutionary performance. It is no surprise that Lu Xun once observed: "Revolution, counterrevolution, non-revolution. . . . Revolution, re-revolution, re-re-revolution, re-re-re . . ."[69] The singular-plural Chinese Revolution erupted into a series of inventions, repetitions, revisions, and translations of the revolutionary temporality.

In ancient times, the Chinese word *geming* 革命 originally meant a reversal or transfer of the heavenly mandate. A returned loan word from Japan, *geming* became a modern equivalent of "revolution," and was used to denote a radical modern transformation of every aspect of social and cultural life.[70] The word even attained an absolute and cosmic value: "The

66. See Hobsbawm, *The Age of Extremes*. Hobsbawm's periodization of the short twentieth century has the outbreak of the World War I as its beginning and sees the collapse of the Soviet bloc as its ending.

67. Badiou, *Le Siècle*, 12.

68. Ibid., 61.

69. Lu Xun, "Xiao zagan," 556.

70. For more etymological information about *geming*, see Lydia Liu, *Translingual Practice*, 335.

spirit of revolution is the substance of the universe."[71] This newly intensified cultural politics of historical time was registered in the conception of Zeitgeist (*shidai jingshen*), another term that was invested with "cosmological force previously ascribed to the *Dao* or heaven."[72] As can be seen in the epigraphs, "Zeitgeist" is a key word around which Guo's discursive productions gravitate. The centrality of the term "Zeitgeist/*shidai jingshen*" in twentieth-century Chinese discourse seems at first to be little more than a prop of the once dominant essentialist outlooks. Highlighting the term, I am *not* interested in recuperating an idealistic philosophy of history. Yet it may be useful to unpack the "ways of seeing culture and society" this "significant, indicative" word "bound together."[73] Such an investigation will help us question the word's binding power and discover the "historicity" and "spirituality" it was once called on to signify.

The term "Zeitgeist" bears a strong imprint of the "temporalization of history" and "acceleration of time" in modernity.[74] It was not so much a well-defined concept as a linguistic figuration/legitimation of the post–French Revolution urgency of social change. Reinhart Koselleck points out: "The [French] Revolution was transformed for everyone into a historico-philosophical concept, based on a perspective which displayed a constant and steady direction."[75] In his early writings, G. W. F. Hegel (1770–1831) combined "spirit" and "time" in an idealist outlook of revolution: "Great revolutions which strike the eye at a glance must have been preceded by a still and secret revolution in the spirit of the age."[76] Taking a further step, the young Karl Marx not only suggested that philosophy be "the spiritual essence of its time," but also demanded the actualization of spirituality in historical time.[77] According to Karl Löwith's account of nineteenth-century European thought, in Goethe's *Faust* there existed only "Geist der Zeiten," designating past historical ages; later *Zeit* became singular and the newly coined "Zeitgeist" emerged as a discourse that prioritized the present and was primarily concerned with a secular

71. Guo, "Yuzhou geming de kuang ge," 29.
72. Denton, "General Introduction," 26.
73. Williams, *Keywords*, 15.
74. Koselleck, *Futures Past*, 5.
75. Ibid., 48.
76. Hegel, *Early Theological Writings*, 152.
77. "Die geistige Quintessenz ihrer Zeit." Marx, "Der leitende Artikel," 97.

teleology of unilinear progression.[78] As Koselleck observes, the epoch from 1770 to 1830 witnessed the explosion of the *Zeit*-related neologisms in the German context, and among them "Zeitgeist" was "certainly the most widespread compound and the most often invoked."[79]

A similar reorganization of the temporal direction shaped the literary domain of modernity. For example, a perception of "the spirit of the age" electrified what James Chandler calls "the case of Romantic historicism" in nineteenth-century British literature.[80] Shelley defended poetry's function as a manifestation of "the spirit of the age," a theme we encounter time and again in Guo's work.[81] Similarly, William Hazlitt (1778–1830) attempted to represent the spirit of the age in his "contemporary portraits," claiming, for instance, that "Mr Wordsworth's genius is a pure emanation of the Spirit of the Age."[82] Such uses of the phrase preconditioned a modern concern about how to "date" and represent the historical specificity in literature.[83]

To better interrogate the experience of self-periodization registered in China's short twentieth century, one can probably divide *shidai jingshen* into *shidai* 時代 and *jingshen* 精神. *Shidai*, literally meaning epoch, energized the collective historical outlook in twentieth-century China. Guo once allegorized the epoch/*shidai* as a "mademoiselle *Shidai*": "Mademoiselle *Shidai*, you seem to be too light-hearted and rushed, changing the fashion for too many times and making us unable to catch up."[84] According to Lung-Kee Sun's study on the explosive proliferation of the word *shidai* in republican China, "among its various usages, *shidai*'s most important connotation came to be 'the present time' . . . always with the implication that it is a time of breathlessly rapid changes and incessant innovation." In the post–May Fourth period, more radical invocations of this catchword indicated a "deepening revolutionization of the Chinese consciousness," marking the young intellectuals' feverish redefinition of ideological agenda, anxious reorientation of political

78. See Löwith, *From Hegel to Nietzsche*, 200–206.
79. Koselleck, *Futures Past*, 258.
80. See Chandler, *England in 1819*.
81. Shelley, *A Defence of Poetry*, in *Shelley's Poetry and Prose*, 535.
82. Hazlitt, *The Spirit of the Age*, 187.
83. See Chandler, *England in 1819*, 3–45.
84. Guo, *Chuangzao shinian xubian*, in *GQJ/W*, 12:228.

identity, and accelerating demand for rupture with even the recent past.[85] The Creationists' turn to leftism in the late 1920s is an example in point: Feng Naichao 馮乃超 (1901–83) explained their change of the course by arguing for the need of literature to "express the *Tempo* of the epoch (*shidai*)."[86] Xiaobing Tang suggests that Feng's notion of epoch "enabled a periodizing narrative of social development."[87] In China's search for modernity, Leo Lee identifies a "mode of consciousness of time and history as unilinear progress," containing "the valorized notion of the present as a new 'epoch.' "[88] It can be added as a side note that in Guo the mademoiselle *Shidai* eventually made way for the "epoch of Mao Zedong" (*Mao Zedong shidai*).[89]

Such practices of specifying, periodizing, and spiritualizing the historical present are a main object of my inquiry. I find that Guo's work embodies a new operative as well as impulsive language of periodization and self-periodization within China's revolutionary century. The discourse of "epocality" (*shidaixing*) was not simply an echo of the one-directional temporality as some commentaries seem to indicate. In fact, Guo's case affords a lens from which to see that the conception of Zeitgeist/*shidai jingshen* was more fluid—and translatable—than schematic.

This new politics/poetics of time can be traced to Guo's early definition of "revolutionary literature." With a mathematic formula of "literature = Function (Zeitgeist)," the young Guo elucidated the relationship between *shidai* and *jingshen* by referring to revolution: "Every age progresses revolutionarily, and every age has its own Zeitgeist. . . . The content of revolutionary literature changes as soon as the Zeitgeist changes."[90] Guo's emphasis falls more on the unitary drive of revolution than on the multiplicity of epochal changes. Every epoch, in other words, is pregnant with a revolutionary spirit and expresses it. This formulation

85. Sun, "Chinese Intellectuals' Notion of 'Epoch' (Shidai) in the Post–May Fourth Era," 45.

86. Feng Naichao, "Yishu yu shehui shenghuo," 12; emphasis in original.

87. Tang with Hockx, "The Creation Society," 128.

88. Lee, "In Search of Modernity," 122.

89. On the occasion of his resumption of the CCP membership in 1958, Guo declared: "We are living in the great epoch of Mao Zedong." Guo, "Xuexi Mao zhuxi," in *GQJ/W*, 17:281.

90. Guo, "Geming yu wenxue," in *GQJ/W*, 16:33.

of *shidai jingshen*, which seems to echo an evolutionary theory of literature, actually bears an inkling of the romantic-pantheistic or quasi-Spinozan expressionism.[91] While *shidai* can refer to a multiplicity of historical epochs, they are all "modifications" or stages of the same universal spirit that is revolution as such.[92] Such a relationship between *jingshen* (spirit) and *shidai* (epoch) is structurally similar to the dialectical interaction between a theme and its variations.

This theme-variation approach leads us to the second part of the Chinese compound word for Zeitgeist, that is, *jingshen*. As Wendy Larson has noted, like *geming*, *jingshen* is most likely a "returned loan word" from Japan. Originally derived from the Chinese classics, it was borrowed from the modern Japanese use around the turn of the twentieth century, and readopted into Chinese vocabulary to be an equivalent of spirit.[93] The ideological concept of spirit/*jingshen* became "a fundamental aspect of the theory of the mind in revolutionary China."[94] It was repeatedly invoked in a transformative collective subjectivity-in-making; the culmination of such valorization is quintessentially found in Mao's formula on historical practice: "Spirit can transform into matter."[95]

Commenting on Hegel's *Phenomenology of Spirit*—a philosophical origin of such idealist emphases on Spirit and its "labor of the negative"—Fredric Jameson proposes to "translate" the Hegelian *Geist* as "the social collectivity," noting that the amorphous concept of spirit, when used to name the collective in history, prevents the historical uncertainties from sliding into a rigid teleology.[96] Jameson goes on to argue that Hegel's dialectic of spirit can be understood via "the musical phenomenon of the

91. For a reading of this view of Guo's in terms of the evolutionist logic in modern Chinese literature and thought, see Zhiguang Yin, *Politics of Art*, 142–43. Yin links Guo's notion of Zeitgeist to "a historiography that later on became one of the major legitimizing factors for Chinese Communist revolutionary discourse."

92. For a definition of the relationship between substance and modes in the philosophy of Spinoza, see Deleuze, *Expressionism in Philosophy*, 13–22. For an evaluation of the "Spinozistic crescendo" in the romantic reception of the pantheist tradition, see McFarland, *Coleridge and the Pantheist Tradition*, 53–106.

93. Larson, *From Ah Q to Lei Feng*, 96.

94. Ibid., 95.

95. Mao Zedong, "Ren de zhengque sixiang shi cong nali lai de," 193. For a discussion of the utopian spirit in Maoism, see Meisner, *Marxism, Maoism, and Utopianism*.

96. Hegel, *Phenomenology of Spirit*, 10; Jameson, *The Hegel Variations*, 14.

theme and variations": the theme of spirit as social-historical collectivity is "fragile and precarious," and only through variations can it be represented.[97] In light of Jameson's reading, the discursive dynamic of *shidai* and *jingshen* can be further reconsidered. In Guo's work, *shidai jingshen* signifies what Sun calls a "suprapersonal historical agency."[98] Yet this spirit should not be reduced to a predetermined teleological authority. As Peter Osborne contends: "Modernity is a form of historical time which valorizes the new as the product of a constantly self-negating temporal dynamic. Yet its abstract temporal form remains open to a variety of completing articulations."[99] Seen from the citations I have used as the epigraphs, Guo not only invokes the Zeitgeist/*shidai jingshen* to refer to a present time, he also applies this term in his narratives about the past ages and frame it in a transnational/translingual context. *Jingshen*, when conditioned by *shidai*, can be seen as a code name for the unstable collective-subjective experience of revolution that is always open to new articulations or imaginations but can only be represented through the displacement of various historical schemes. Guo's work as a whole is actually organized by a dialectical tension between *shidai* (variations) and *jingshen* (theme), which enables the translation between a constellation of different historical moments and a configuration of the present.

Perhaps few other uses of the term "Zeitgeist" are more symptomatic than Guo's interpretation of *Faust* as a "developmental history of Zeitgeist." From a perspective of translingual practice, China's revolutionary century can be seen as a "translated modernity," imitating, compressing, and subverting the major themes of Western modernity (from enlightenment to romanticism to communism).[100] This timeframe of catching up is dialectically determined by an experience of sudden interruptions, frustrating delays, missed opportunities, and coexisting temporalities—in a word, by a profound sense of "nonsynchronism" that bears remote resemblance to the German case of "contemporaneity of the

97. Jameson, *The Hegel Variations*, 23, 24.

98. Sun, "Chinese Intellectuals' Notion of 'Epoch' (Shidai) in the Post–May Fourth Era," 45.

99. Osborne, *Politics of Time*, xii.

100. For the perspective of "translated modernity," see Lydia Liu, *Translingual Practice*.

non-contemporaneous."[101] Guo's conception of Zeitgeist is intertwined with a translation of the nineteenth-century epic *Faust*—a text of "nonsynchronism" in its own right—into an allegory of twentieth-century China's ongoing modernization.[102] This book emphasizes the translation between heterogeneous temporal frameworks as a chief experience of this translingual revolution.

The experience of nonsynchronism is further intensified by the no less crucial factor of revolutionary China's changing attitudes toward its own long ancient past, ranging from iconoclastic amnesia to creative misuse. Despite its antitraditional tendencies, the Chinese Revolution was caught between the legacy of a once-revered national history and the impulse toward the tabula rasa of creative destruction.[103] The temporal confusion, disorientation, or reorientation finds a powerful expression in Guo's oscillation between his studies of ancient history and his imagination of the revolutionary now. For instance, his "grasp" of Confucian humanism as the revolutionary Zeitgeist of the Warring States era, resonating with the struggle for "people's democracy," involved a moment of "anachronism" that was manifested in the untimely figuration of Confucius and Qin Shi Huang in the Maoist era.[104] Hence, translingual practice and anachronistic imagination: it is these two motives that animate a conception of Zeitgeist.

As Chandler indicates, it is a typical "Romantic-historicist" notion to see an author as a representative of the spirit of his or her age.[105] Indeed, Guo fashioned his own activity as the expressive instrument of his epoch (first as a "lyre" of a cosmic spirit, and then a "gramophone" of the

101. For a critical account of the experience of nonsynchronism and its representations in German culture and philosophy, see Comay, *Mourning Sickness*, especially 1–25. The phenomenon of "noncontemporaneity" is famously theorized by Ernst Bloch in his diagnosis of German culture and society. Bloch, *Heritage of Our Times*, 106.

102. See Moretti, *Modern Epic*, especially chapter 2.

103. See Levenson, *Confucian China and Its Modern Fate*, 1:140–45.

104. Interestingly, in the vocabulary of Guo and his revolutionary comrades, the Chinese term for anachronism was also a *shidai*-related compound neologism—*shidai cuowu*. See the conclusion to this book.

105. For a relevant discussion of the discourse of the poet as the "representative" in the romantic and historicist traditions, see Chandler, *England in 1819*, 174–86.

revolutionary consciousness, and finally a "trumpet of the Party").[106] Yet this book historicizes the "representativeness" of Guo's work and the translatability of an imagined "Zeitgeist" as a conjuncture of cultural-political symptoms, crises, and tensions—a conjuncture that demands a reinterpretation of the Chinese Revolution as a "cultural revolution." According to Jameson, "cultural revolution" means a "permanent struggle between the various coexisting modes of production," and is "beyond the opposition between synchrony and diachrony, and [corresponds] roughly to what Ernst Bloch has called the *Ungleichzeitigkeit* (or 'nonsynchronous development') of cultural and social life."[107] The concept-figure of Zeitgeist/*shidai jingshen* in Guo's oeuvre should not be equated to a formula of what Benjamin calls "homogeneous, empty time."[108] Behind the façade of its ideological rigidity, it bears traces of a heterogeneous or "nonsynchronous development" that cannot be exhausted by any teleological historicism and testifies to the productive interventions within the self-periodization of the Chinese Revolution.

As a result, Guo's transformation of *Faust* into an allegory of the Zeitgeist can be mapped onto an implicit act of periodizing the three decades of his translingual engagement as an open-ended process that Mao and the CCP called the New Democratic Revolution—an epoch lasting from the May Fourth Movement to the founding of the People's Republic.[109] Inscribed in these three decades was the bulk of Guo's achievements in poetry, translation, drama, autobiography, and historical scholarship. The following period, stretching from the founding of the People's Republic to the end of the Cultural Revolution—three more decades—can be described as a process of Maoist attempts to go beyond and overcome the legacy of the New Democratic Revolution. It presented a permanent crisis, rather than a fulfillment, of the revolution itself, which will be examined in my account about how Guo's later work revived, revisited, and reversed his early motives. Composed of these two consecutive periods, the six-decade sequence from the May Fourth era to the final years

106. According to Lin Lin's recollections, Guo expressed in 1936 that he "was willing to be a trumpet of the Party." See Lin Lin, "Zhe shi dang laba de jingshen," 433. For the other two audio-instrumental figures of "lyre" and "gramophone," see chapter 1.

107. Jameson, *The Political Unconscious*, 97.

108. Benjamin, "On the Concept of History," 395.

109. See Mao, "On New Democracy."

of the Cultural Revolution defines the historical frame of my inquiry. The imprint Guo's lifework has left on this revolutionary sequence contains the figuration of a translatable Zeitgeist, complicating the lingual, cultural, and temporal schemes.

Cultural Politics of Fan*: Translation and Historical Interpretation*

In other words, my account is concerned with how a "spiritual" transcoding of the historical momentum constituted a cultural-political logic of the revolutionary century. This perspective determines my focus on translation and historical interpretation. Since the hermeneutic turn in translation theory, scholars have seen the act of translation as a "motion" of understanding, interpretation, and rewriting.[110] For example, resisting the worship of originality and the hierarchy of influence, André Lefevere sees translation as "the most . . . recognizable type of rewriting," and emphasizes the "importance of rewriting as the motor force behind literary evolution."[111] Challenging the translator's invisibility, current translation studies attach more importance to the creative agency of the translating culture and valorizes translation as a "locus of difference."[112] In line with this theoretical emphasis on the "politics of translation," Lydia H. Liu has used the phrase "translingual practice" to ground her seminal study of "an earlier moment of historical transaction between China and the West in language practices."[113] For her, "translingual practice" includes not only actual translation but also adaptation, appropriation, and other interlingual activities. It points to the "condition" of interlingual "discursive practices" in early twentieth-century China.[114] Since the publication of Liu's book, the gap between the field of modern Chinese literature and

110. See, for example, Steiner, *After Babel*, especially chapter 5 ("The Hermeneutic Motion").

111. Lefevere, *Translation, Rewriting, and the Manipulation of Literary Fame*, 9, 2.

112. Venuti, *The Translator's Invisibility*, 42.

113. Lydia Liu, *Translingual Practice*, 25. For a postcolonial intervention on translation theory, see Spivak, "The Politics of Translation."

114. Lydia Liu, *Translingual Practice*, 26.

that of translation studies has surely been narrowed, and a series of splendid studies on translation in late Qing and early Republican eras have appeared. Some of them use "translation" as a powerful trope for different kinds of cultural translation, mediation, and appropriation.[115] Theodore Huters's emphasis on the "productive hybridity" in China's appropriation of Western ideas in the era from 1894 to 1919 also contains a perspective of cultural translation.[116] Underscoring the "interdisciplinary nature" of translation studies, Lawrence Wang-Chi Wong points out the "close relationship" of the changing linguistics of modern Chinese translation to "the social, cultural, political and literary domains."[117] Michael G. Hill's recent study of Chinese translator Lin Shu (1852–1924) resists the use of translation as a "trope" and instead treats it as "a specific historical activity."[118] His emphasis of translation as a nonnormative labor is also meant to "bring new depth" to the practices of cultural appropriation in late Qing and early Republican China.[119]

From Liu to Hill, one can discern a persistent deconstruction of the traditional hierarchy of source language and target language. Translation, either broadly defined or specified as a mental labor, is now examined as an active agency in China's literary, cultural, and institutional change of that period.[120] In particular, this rich scholarship suggests that the late Qing and early Republican translingual/transcultural productions translated Western texts and ideas into the moment of China's own crisis within a world-historical timeframe of modernity. Joan Judge's attention to a "new hermeneutic of historical change" in the late Qing literature of Western women exemplars, Andrew Jones's observation of China's appropriation of "developmental thinking," Hill's account of Lin Shu's reflections on modernity in his translations of Charles Dickens, and Wong's inquiry into the Europeanization of May Fourth language—these

115. See, for example, Hu Ying, *Tales of Translation.*
116. Huters, *Bringing the World Home*, 8.
117. Wong, *Fanyi yu wenxue zhijian*, 371, 228.
118. Hill, *Lin Shu, Inc.*, 13.
119. Ibid.
120. Ibid., 8–15.

case studies all point to the translingual making of a new historical experience.[121]

Inspired by this turn to translation in modern Chinese studies, I see in Guo's translingual practice a continued evolution of this historically conditioned agency of cultural appropriation, and try to show how his case dramatized the relationship between translation and revolution during a different period, that is, the period from the May Fourth era to the Maoist era. The centrality of translation in this book first derives from the rich variety of translingual productions in the works of Guo and his contemporaries. Following Hill's example, I start with particular attention paid to the historicity of translation practices and even "the technical aspects of translation" that Liu's approach does not address.[122] As Lawrence Venuti suggests, "a foreign text is the site of many different semantic possibilities that are fixed only provisionally in any one translation, on the basis of varying cultural assumptions and interpretive choices, in specific social situations, in different historical periods."[123] The possibilities available in a translation site are actually not limited to the semantic ones but include semiotic, rhetorical, and formal ones, all conditioned by linguistic, literary, and intellectual politics. Challenging the paradigm of foreignization versus domestication in translation theory, I take Guo's translations to be a barometer registering the making of a modern Chinese literary language and the exigencies of revolutionary politics. Thus, the specificity of translingual practice actually brings to the fore the deep interaction of the poetics/politics of translation with many other genres of textual production. As a result, I also embrace a broader definition of translation as a practice of rewriting traditions, appropriating cultures, and imagining historical changes.

In particular, this book emphasizes that Guo's labors of translation are bound indissolubly with a creative mode of historical imagination. Like translation, historical interpretation is a form of rewriting. The modern Chinese word for "translation" is *fanyi* 翻譯, composed of two characters *fan* and *yi*. Not dissimilar to the prefix "trans-" in English, *fan* 翻

121. See Judge, *The Precious Raft of History*, 12–16; Jones, *Developmental Fairy Tales*, 9; Hill, *Lin Shu, Inc.*, chapter 4; Wong, *Fanyi yu wenxue zhijian*, 212–28.

122. Lydia Liu, *Translingual Practice*, 26.

123. Venuti, *The Translator's Invisibility*, 18.

connotes cross-bordering and transgression; more important, it literally means overturning and reversal. Rich in implications, this character is in a way a miniature of the subversive energies of the Chinese Revolution, as illustrated in the famous phrase *fanshen* 翻身(turning over the body).[124] Interestingly enough, *fan*/reversal also appears in another key word of China's revolutionary culture and politics, *fan'an* 翻案, meaning "reversing the verdict." Expressing an epistemological break in the reevaluation of antiquity, the leitmotif of "reversal of the verdict" pervades Guo's historical interpretations. The cultural productivity—and creative destructiveness—of such reversals needs to be examined on a level of the political poetics of historical writing.

Intellectual historians have routinely noted a revolution of historical thinking in modern China, traceable at least to Liang Qichao 梁启超's call for "new historiography" (*xin shixue* 新史学).[125] In particular, a lot of attention has been paid to how "historical consciousness . . . has been overwhelmingly framed by the nation-state" and how such a nationalist knowledge production has transformed Chinese history into a "linear, evolutionary history."[126] What I am more interested in is the contentious and precarious role of the rewriting of ancient heritage in China's revolutionary culture. The leftist efforts to "reverse" (*diandao* 颠倒) traditional narratives and to "make the past serve the present" meant a constant transcoding of ancient history.[127] Dirlik's study of Marxist historiography has highlighted the contribution Guo made to the "revolutionization" of the historical consciousness in 1920s and 1930s China.[128] Moreover, Guo's case also demands a scrutiny that covers his

124. William Hinton's account of the Chinese Revolution in rural regions is famously titled with the phrase of *fanshen*: "The Chinese Revolution created a whole new vocabulary. A most important word in this vocabulary was *fanshen*. Literally, it means 'to turn the body', or 'to turn over.'" Hinton, *Fanshen*, vii.

125. See, for example, Levenson, *Confucian China and Its Modern Fate*; Tang, *Global Space and the Nationalist Discourse of Modernity*; and Q. E. Wang, *Inventing China through History*.

126. Duara, *Rescuing History from the Nation*, 1.

127. See Mao Zedong, "Kanle *Bishang Liangshan* hou xie gei Yang Shaoxuan Qi Yanming er tongzhi de xin." Mao's slogan "gu wei jin yong" (making the past serve the present) is announced in Mao Zedong, "Zhi Lu Dingyi," 598.

128. Dirlik, *Revolution and History*, 259.

paleographical-philological works, his historical drama, and his translations of ancient poetry.

The issue of historical interpretation can be approached in close relationship with the issue of translation as an interpretative act of rewriting. To begin with, from Guo's early anarchist or romantic uses of Confucian traditions to his discovery of early China as a transition from matriarchy to slavery, and to his theatrical interpretations of Chinese antiquity, the controversies of *fan'an* are inseparable from translingual/transcultural practice. For example, in the early 1930s, Guo's Marxist studies of antiquity were immediately described by reviewers as *fan'an* and generated debates on how to appropriate the "developmental" formula originated in European historical thought.[129] More important, Guo's practice of vernacular translation and paleographical transcoding amount to radical examples of what Roman Jakobson theorizes as "intralingual translation."[130] Here, translation is no longer just a trope for historical interpretation but becomes its actual condition. Finally, reaffirming the same dynamic of interpretative subjectivity in his practice of translation, Guo's historical rewritings transcode ancient legacies into contemporary interventions, into a past "filled full by the now-time."[131]

Consequently, I extend my discussion of the dialectics between translation and revolution to the issue of historical rewriting, attempting to reveal the reversal (*fan'an*) of historical knowledge from the 1920s to 1970s as an interpretative translation (*fanyi*) of antiquity into revolutionary imaginaries, which was more complex than an adaptation of the linear narrative mode.[132] In this sense, the Chinese character *fan* (trans- or reversal) can serve as a linchpin that links translation and historical rewriting. Preexisting scholarship has scarcely taken note of the correspondence between Guo's translingual practice and historical interpretation. But this book uses their convergence in cultural politics to contend that a con-

129. For a description of Guo's Marxist historiography as *fan'an*, see Wen Fu, "Ping Guo Moruo Zhongguo gudai shehui yanjiu," in *GHY*, 9:3; for a critique of Guo's use of Western conceptions of history, see Su Chi, "Ping Guo Moruo Zhongguo gudai shehui yanjiu," *GHY*, 9:11.

130. Jakobson, "On Linguistic Aspects of Translation," 127.

131. Benjamin, "On the Concept of History," 395.

132. In this regard, my inquiry also follows the example of Hayden White's literary analysis of historical knowledge. See White, *Metahistory*.

stant translation of historical time is intrinsic to the experience of revolution.

Chapter Layout

This book is organized into two parts. Each part is composed of three chapters. Part I explores Guo's translingual practice side by side with his poetic and political development at the epicenter of the making of China's revolutionary culture. Chapter 1 traces the origins of the cultural-political logic of translatability to Guo's "phase of pantheism" during the May Fourth period. Focusing on the romantic rhetoric of apostrophe that animates and weaves together his early poetic creations and his translations of such poets as Shelley, Whitman, and Goethe, I try to disclose the apostrophic or vocative politics of lyricism in China's New Culture. This lyrical politics then gave rise to a radical ideology of pantheistic translatability, according to which both lyric poetry and translation function as the occasions whereby the subjective expression becomes the objective "instrument" of spirit or history. I argue that, in dialogue with a "Romantic historicism" in Shelley's view of poetry as the "lyre" of "the spirit of the age," Guo's ideal of pantheistic translation preconditioned a revolutionary subjectivity.

Chapter 2 concentrates on the translingual dimension of the emergence of "revolutionary literature" in late 1927 and early 1928, a fleeting yet critical moment that Guo characterized as a "caesura of the revolution." Revolving around the activities of the Creation Society, this chapter locates a series of translingual moments in this historical conjuncture—the Chinese transliteration of the Hegelian-Marxian concept "Aufheben" as *aofuhebian* 奥伏赫變, Guo's naming of his book of poetry as *Reconvalescence*, and most important, the cross-reference of "Rhine wine" (*laiyin de putao* 萊茵的葡萄) between Guo's translation of *Faust* and his political lyric poetry. They offer us a "dialectical image" of history's caesura and standstill.

Chapter 3 concludes part I by examining Guo's translation of *Faust* as a whole. Rediscovering the forgotten fragments of Guo's initial manuscripts in 1919 and 1920, my analysis first focuses on the unstable nature of the poetic language of his translation over the three decades. Delineating a genealogy of the interpretations of *Faust* in revolutionary China, the chapter then compares Guo's 1947 reading of *Faust* as a "developmental history of Zeitgeist" with other thematic readings offered by Zong Baihua, Hu Qiuyuan 胡秋原 (1910–2004), Feng Zhi 馮至 (1905–93), and György Lukács (1885–1971). Guo was particularly attentive to the theme of Germany's nonsynchronous development in *Faust II*, and he transformed it into an allegory of China's unfulfilled modernization and ongoing revolution. A translation of *Faust* turned out to be a Faustian act of constant self-periodization, in which the Chinese Revolution would find its own thematic of historical time.

If part I underscores a translingual trajectory of the so-called New Democratic Revolution (1919–49), then part II interrogates the various genres of Guo's reinterpretations of Chinese antiquity across the 1949 divide. For one thing, the interactions between his translingual, historiographical, and autobiographical practices have never been fully explored. Chapter 4 adventures into the isomorphism between autobiography and historiography in Guo's works at the turn of the 1920s and 1930s. Just as he uses the autobiographical narrative to establish an immediate correspondence between individual experiences and modern China's "epoch" of "social revolution," his deciphering of ancient inscriptions relies on an epistemological translation of the visual existence of Chinese pictographs into the emblem of historical developmental stages according to the Marxist periodization. The interpenetration of autobiography and historiography serves to transcode the particularity of both prehistorical pictographs and personal details into a universal urgency of revolution.

Chapter 5 focuses on the political poetics of Guo's rewriting of Chinese antiquity in dramatic and scholarly forms. In the 1940s, Guo's historical plays and historical scholarship interpreted the "Zeitgeist" of the Warring States era as a tragic spirit of "people's revolution" and produced a political imagination of "the people" (*renmin*). This staging of "the people" in ancient costume negotiated with a long Marxist tradition of polemics on historical literature, humanism, tragedy, and the popular character. Rather than reducing it to a merely partisan perspective, I demonstrate how Guo's conception of the tragic in ancient history formed an ambivalent intervention of leftist humanism into the CCP's strategies of "people's democracy" (*renmin minzhu*). This chapter then ends with a diagnosis of Guo's post-1949 historical drama and scholarship, suggesting that the crisis of historical literature in socialist China was the crisis of people's democracy itself.

With a fresh look at Guo's "modernizing translation" of ancient Chinese poetry into modern vernacular, chapter 6 drives home my argument about the convergence of translation and historical interpretation. I trace the full genealogy of Guo's "modernizing translation of ancient texts" from his lyrical renditions of *Shi jing* to the incorporation of his later translations of *Shi jing* in Marxist historiography, to his full rendering of Qu Yuan's poetry in the 1950s, and finally to his translation of Du Fu's poetry as "class analysis" in the early 1970s. In this case, literary translation and historical imagination share the same cultural-revolutionary logic.

Revolving around the thematic axes of translation and historical interpretation, the six chapters represent my attempts to link different moments or aspects of Guo's work to a larger problem about the cultural productivity and heterogeneity of the Chinese Revolution. In a final twist, the conclusion turns to the late Guo's poetic conversation with Mao in ancient style, a conversation that marks an anachronistic ending of China's revolutionary century. After revisiting Guo's thesis—"Marx enters the temple of Confucius"—my critique of translatability and reversibility ends with the problem of "revolutionary romanticism." Complicating such issues as revolutionary subjectivity and romantic "occasionalism," the conclusion tries to theorize the broader relevance of Guo's lifework in our reflection on the imagination and translation of the now-time.

PART I

The Translingual Making of a Chinese Zeitgeist

CHAPTER I

Apostrophe, Translatability, and the Origins of Guo's Lyrical Politics

Perhaps nothing is more typical of the lyrical intensity of Guo's early work than the following lines:

> Universe, O universe!
> Why do you exist?
> Whence do you come?
> . . . .
> Are you a life-endowed flux,
> or are you a lifeless mechanism?[1]

Addressing the universe, this stanza is from Guo's famous piece "The Nirvana of the Feng and Huang" ("Feng huang niepan" 鳳凰涅槃), originally published in 1920 and included in *The Goddesses*. The apostrophic effect here is so commonly seen in lyric poetry that one may have ignored an interesting paradox involved here: if the universe is indeed a "lifeless mechanism," how can it be called on and addressed in the first place? It is in fact nothing but the apostrophizing gesture of the poet (here masked as the Chinese mythic *Feng* bird, a male phoenix) that "endows" life to the universe by invoking its name and questioning it. The power of Guo's poetic operation in this passage thus derives less from the poem's

1. Guo, "Feng Huang niepan," in *N*, 47–49; *SPG*, 11–12. For a critical edition of *Nüshen* that reflects Guo's later revisions and other variations, see *Nüshen huijiaoben*.

philosophical-cosmological content than from its apostrophic form. In other words, the figure of apostrophe presumes that lyric poetry is a shamanistic—so to speak—ritual of the language, in which the poet is enabled and empowered on a rhetorical level to name, invoke, and address any object as a "life-endowed" entity.

The significance of apostrophe in Guo's early poetry, translation, and criticism furnishes a critical perspective from which to revisit the making of the lyrical as a May Fourth ideology and institution. As is well known, Jaroslav Průšek was among the first scholars that raised the issue of the lyrical as a key characteristic of modern Chinese literature.[2] David Der-wei Wang's recent book sees "lyricism" as a "poetics of selfhood that informs the historical moment and helps define Chinese modernity in a different light," thereby reviving the interest in "the lyrical" (*shuqing* 抒情).[3] My focus on apostrophe and pantheistic translatability as a latent rhetorical condition for revolutionary politics is intended to contribute to and further complicate the discussion of modern Chinese lyricism.

In "The Nirvana of the Feng and Huang," the young poet's apostrophic move is not meant to seriously refer to the universe as an object of inquiry, but to call into being an ever-expanding spiritual atmosphere in which a new temporal-spatial experience becomes possible. The hyperbolic questions he poses demarcate the imaginary world picture of the May Fourth New Culture Movement: the modernizing drive of enlightenment and disenchantment on one hand, and the cult of impulse and "life" on the other; the value of "Mr. Science" on one hand, and the vitality of romanticism on the other. This pantheistic vision defined Guo's first—and best-known—book of poetry, *The Goddesses*. Published in 1921 and consisting of fifty-seven poetic pieces, *The Goddesses* was a key text of the May Fourth Literary Revolution. One finds in this book the hypostasis of the sublime ego: "I am the total sum of the universal *Energy* . . . / My 'I' is about to explode!"[4] And the erotic free love as the essential symbol of the May Fourth emancipatory politics: "I would compare your enchanting lips / to a wine-cup . . . I would compare your breasts / to two

2. See Průšek, *The Lyrical and the Epic*.
3. David Wang, *The Lyrical in Epic Time*, ix.
4. Guo, "Tian gou," in *N*, 81–82.

grave mounds."[5] And an aestheticized version of death drive: "I have a knife / . . . She smilingly says to me: / Moruo, you hurry up and kiss me / so that I can dispense you with all the ennui."[6] The will to power is also the early Guo's trademark: "The surging flood wells up before me: / Unending destruction, unending creation, unending effort! / Ah, power, power!"[7] It seems justifiable to either praise or implore Guo's lyricism as the womb of the cult of revolutionary renewal: "I will go forth and create a new sun / To contain your new light and new heat."[8]

Just as its making of a "young style"[9] partakes in the self-mythologization of the May Fourth culture, so *The Goddesses* has become a myth in the history of China's New Poetry. New Poetry was experimented as early as 1916 by Hu Shi 胡適 (1891–1962), yet it was in Guo's poetry that Wen Yiduo 聞一多 (1899–1946), a poet-critic, saw the expression of the Zeitgeist: "When it comes to 'New Poetry,' only Guo Moruo's poetry merits this word 'new'! Not only is his work artistically remote from old classical poetry, but more importantly, his spirit is totally the spirit of the age (*shidai de jingshen*)—the Zeitgeist of the twentieth century."[10]

This perspective of poetic modernity was reinforced in Qian Xingcun's 錢杏邨 (1900–1977) comment: "*The Goddesses* was not only the first book of poetry in modern Chinese poetry, but also remains the only one."[11] Subsequently in the 1940s, Zhou Yang homogenized this view into a grand narrative about the "May Fourth spirit":

> Guo Moruo . . . was the poetic representative of the great May Fourth Enlightenment Movement, a prophet of new China. . . . His poetry expresses the spirit of May Fourth . . . In terms of content, it expresses selfhood, glorifies individuality, and fulfills the so-called "self-consciousness of being a human;" and in terms of form, it gets rid of the chains of ancient

5. Guo, "Venus," in *N*, 181; *SPG*, 48.
6. Guo, "Si de youhuo," in *N*, 190.
7. Guo, "Li zai diqiu bianshang fanghao," in *N*, 101; *SPG*, 24.
8. Guo, "Nüshen zhi zaisheng," in *N*, 5; *SPG*, 3 (translation modified).
9. See Huang Houxing, *Guo Moruo: "Qingchun xing" de shiren*.
10. Wen Yiduo, "Nüshen zhi shidai jingshen," 3.
11. Qian Xingcun, "Guo Moruo jiqi chuangzuo," 28.

> metrics and moves toward free verse. All this was what that epoch required of New Poetry.[12]

Commenting on this critical discourse, Jiang Tao concludes that "from the poetic form to the selfhood and to the Zeitgeist, the legitimacy of New Poetry was reaffirmed, and the paradigm of *The Goddesses* reception was established."[13]

Dissecting the grammar of mythmaking in *The Goddesses*, Jiayan Mi "translates" or reduces Guo's whole book into a "long single sentence with a thematically coherent content (subject-predicate-object form)": the grand "I" destroys the "old," "liberates" the body, and "creates" "a free" self, a "new sun," "a new society," and a "new world."[14] What is missing in this narrative rewriting is precisely the element of apostrophe that is essentially nonnarrative and therefore cannot be renarrativized into any syntactical arrangement of "subject-predicate-object." In fact, apostrophe, as a rhetorical operation, pervades *The Goddesses*, his other works such as *The Starry Sky* (*Xing kong* 星空, 1923), and even his nonpoetical pieces. In this chapter I seek some key traces of the May Fourth spiritual productivity in the apostrophic mode of the young Guo's literary creation and translation. In my view, his early contribution to Chinese literary modernity is intertwined with the logic of apostrophe, without which his pantheistic verse and poetic translation would have been inconceivable.

The centrality of apostrophe in *The Goddesses* can be sensed first and foremost in Guo's heightened odic voice: "O earth, my mother, / My spirit is your spirit!"[15] The identification of the self ("I") with the sublime (the earth, the sun, or the universe as "you") leads to an act of self-glorification of lyric poetry: "Sun! You, please shine all my poems into a golden foam!"[16] The aesthetic of the sublime as vastness and intensity also evokes the darkness, marking a modern sensibility:

12. Zhou Yang, "Guo Moruo he ta de Nüshen," in *GZL*, 669.
13. Jiang Tao, *"Xinshi ji" yu zhongguo xinshi de fasheng*, 249.
14. Mi, *Self-Fashioning and Reflexive Modernity in Modern Chinese Poetry*, 27.
15. Guo, "Diqiu, wo de muqin," in *N*, 118; *SPG*, 32 (translation modified).
16. Guo, "Taiyang lizhan," in *N*, 144; *SPG*, 40 (translation modified).

The night! The dark night!
You're the true Democracy!
You embrace in your arms the whole humanity.[17]

This apostrophic praise then turns into a naming of the new experience of the industrial age, which further serves the hypostasis of the lyrical subjectivity:

O, O [哦哦], you, blazing headlights of motorcars!
You twentieth-century Apollo!
Have you not changed your mount for a motorcar?
I would like to be your driver—will you hire me?[18]

With the appearance of the "O, O" [哦哦] as a signal, Guo's apostrophe sometimes reaches such an accelerated lyrical drive that there seems almost no time to finish a properly apostrophic addressing, no time to establish the "I–you" relationship. Poetry is reduced into a name-calling of every image that figures instantaneously in its lyrical realm:

O, O [哦哦]! Nature, how bold your sweep!
The *Symphony* that is Nature!
Hero-poet!
Proletarian poet![19]

This linguistic excitement amounts essentially to a self-affirmation of the lyrical, in which the spasmodic addressing becomes an epiphany of the signifier itself rather than any specific signified (such as the eye-catching but actually empty referent of the "proletarian poet"). Even the canonization of this book of poetry is already inscribed intrinsically in the apostrophic climax of "Introductory Poem" ("Xu shi" 序诗): "O, *The Goddesses*! / You, go find those men and women who have the same wavelength as mine."[20]

17. Guo, "Ye," in *N*, 177.
18. Guo, "Ri chu," in *N*, 91; *SPG*, 20 (translation modified.)
19. Guo, "Xue zhao," in *N*, 121; *SPG*, 33 (translation modified).
20. Guo, "Xu shi," in *N*, 1.

The pervasive existence of apostrophe in Guo's early work, however, seems too familiar and common to merit any critical treatment. Most scholars simply take for granted the apostrophic mode as a given trait of Guo's poetry. From a postromantic vantage point, this apostrophic gesture may even be disdained as an old-fashioned aesthetic manner, of which the "O, O" is an embarrassing signal. For example, C. T. Hsia once stated that Guo's "overuse of exclamatory sentences betray[s] a lack of poetic sensitivity."[21] The lack of interest in the apostrophic verse recalls to mind Jonathan Culler's observation: "To the Romantics apostrophe was natural and insignificant; to us it is wholly artificial and insignificant. It can always be ignored."[22] Culler is a rare critic who addresses our neglect of apostrophe. His theorization of the embarrassing power of the "O" suggests that the issue of apostrophe is actually intrinsic to the "poetics of the lyric."[23]

With examples from the works of Shelley, Keats, Wordsworth, and Blake, Culler implies that apostrophe is key to understanding the role of romanticism in literary modernity. If the enlightenment outlook tends to draw a line between the subject and object, then the romantic verse uses the apostrophic act to fulfill a ritual of the mutual identification between the subject (self) and object (universe). As Culler points out, apostrophe presumes a "prophetic" or "vocative" gesture of pantheism: "the apostrophizing poet identifies his universe as a world of sentient forces."[24] To put it in Guo's language: the universe is "a life-endowed flux." This dimension of apostrophe seems to reaffirm the conventional image of the early Guo as a poet-prophet of May Fourth China. Yet my focus on apostrophe concerns a further questioning of Guo's early lyrical and political formation: by problematizing apostrophe, can we reach a new diagnosis of the dynamic of romanticism/pantheism?

Culler's criticism starts with (rather than stops at) this "condition of visionary poet who engages in dialogue with the universe."[25] For him, Shelley's "Ode to the West Wind" counts as "the clearest example of the way in which the apostrophic mode . . . poses the problem of the poetic

21. C. T. Hsia, *A History of Modern Chinese Fiction*, 96.
22. Culler, "Apostrophe," 137.
23. Ibid.
24. Ibid., 139.
25. Ibid., 143.

subject" (my later discussion particularly turns to Guo's translation of this masterpiece).[26] In Shelley's poem, the poet calls on the west wind to transform himself into "a wave, a leaf and a cloud," hopes to become the wind itself, and finally asks the wind to permeate the whole universe.[27] Apostrophe, Culler indicates, is not intended to concretize such a relationship between the I and the wind but functions as an "image of voice," constructing the speaker as a prophetic "poetical spirit."[28] What the apostrophic discourse truly evokes is a poetic presence, a "moment when poetic voice constitutes itself."[29] In other words, apostrophe is a "sign of action which knows its own fictive nature."[30] Even though the apostrophic act seems to address the external world, it actually forms a process of internationalization, a return to the lyrical language or subjectivity itself. This internalization "works against" the narrative temporality. Representing the vocative language and resisting the sequential time, apostrophe stands for the "*now* of discourse, of writing," a temporality "toward which the lyric strives." Instead of narrating an event, apostrophe "produces a fictive, discursive event."[31]

Culler's deconstruction of the narrative-teleological time and the lyrical authenticity can surely help illuminate the conditions of Guo's lyrical voice and demystify his pantheistic romanticism. But my reading of Guo's early works is not intended to simply repeat Culler's deconstructionist tour. Revisiting the early Guo's role in the May Fourth cultural production, I would rather attempt to restore the apostrophic temporality—the now-time of lyrical discourse itself—as part and parcel of the emerging historical time and as a new possibility of the historical experience. In other words, my textual-rhetorical analysis will not avoid the dimension of historicization, but will inquire into the way history was actually envisioned as a social-collective experience within a lyrical language-in-making. I am interested not only in the rhetorical configuration of a romantic lyrical voice, but also in the historical formation of this lyrical mode.

26. Ibid., 142.
27. See Shelley, *Shelley's Poetry and Prose*, 298–301.
28. Culler, "Apostrophe," 142.
29. Ibid., 143.
30. Ibid., 146.
31. Ibid., 153; emphasis in original.

More important, the perspective of apostrophe will allow me to examine Guo's poetic development as an unfolding structure of translingual practice that was key to the emergence of political lyricism in revolutionary China. To read his poetic works side by side with his poetic translations does not merely mean an expansion of the scope of discussion. Poetic writing and translation are two inseparable aspects of the early Guo's textual practice as a whole: calling on each other, they provide the rhetorical conditions for each other. What interconnects these two domains is precisely an apostrophic or vocative mode. Just as Guo translates the apostrophic impulse from modern Western literature into his own verse, his ideal of poetic translation constitutes a major occasion for his formulation of a lyrical ideology. With the issue of apostrophe as a main point of entry, the following analysis of some crucial translingual moments in Guo's contribution to May Fourth lyricism aims to reveal the interconnections between poetic creation and translation. By doing so, it traces a symptomatic configuration of "mutability" and translatability in Guo's pantheism, which points to the potential intersection between romanticism and revolutionary politics.

A Lyrical Locality

Before examining the apostrophic mode as a translingual core of Guo's poetic imagination, I find it necessary to locate the early Guo's lyrical position, that is, to disclose how a new lyrical voice in modern Chinese literature was positioned and how this positioning was overdetermined historically. Nowhere is the lyrical locality of the early Guo revealed more clearly than in "Panorama from Fudetate Yama" ("Bili shan tou zhanwang" 筆立山頭展望), which is worth a full quotation:

Pulse of a metropolis!
Surge of life!
Beating, panting, roaring,
Spurting, flying, leaping,
The whole sky covered with a pall of smoke:
My heart is ready to leap from my mouth.

Hills, roofs, surge on,
Wave after wave they well up before me.
Symphony of myriad sounds,
Marriage of man and Nature.
The curve of the bay might be Cupid's bow
Man's life his arrow, shot over the sea.
Dark and misty coastline, steamers at anchor,
Steamers in motion, steamers unnumbered,
Funnel upon funnel bearing its black peony!
Ah, emblem of the twentieth century!
The stern mother of modern civilization![32]

Dated June 1920, this poem offers a panoramic viewing that assumes a relationship between the individual and the vast landscape. This positioning of the subject in confrontation with the sublime gives the lyrical sovereignty a vantage point of both mastery and awe. According to Jiang Tao, "landscape poetry" constituted a major type of early New Poetry, reinventing landscape as a rhetorical device.[33] In Guo's poem, the panoramic mapping of the coastal landscape is also a lyrical movement in which the division between the subject and the world collapses into a heightened celebration of modernity. Although in the romantic tradition the sublime landscape refers usually to nature, Guo's sublime in this poem is the industrialization of nature. The young poet sees industrial mobility as an intensified stage of natural vitality. This vision reaches its climax when Guo takes a decisive metaphorical move of analogizing an image of the industrial sublime, the funnel, to an image of natural beauty, the peony. This analogy between industry and nature is meant to express an ecstatic identification with the modernized mode of production.

The poet ends this piece by apostrophizing the globalizing force of industrial modernity as a "stern mother." The sternness refers to the cold necessity of modernization as the trend of human history. Yet the gendered image of mother, in contrast to the masculine sternness of the industrial power, produces a suggestive poetic effect in line with the image of peony. However stern it is, capitalistic modernity is still imagined as a glorifiable

32. Guo, "Bili shan tou zhanwang," in *N*, 97–98; *SPG*, 23.
33. Jiang Tao, *Gongyu li de ta*, 74–76.

maternal body, a mother embodying both productive forces and reproductive energy. Here the cults of power and the "eternal feminine" as two of Guo's persistent themes come into a modernistic unity. One might even say that the marriage of industry and nature leads to figuring an androgynous body of the modern.

Such a lyrical sensibility is preconditioned by the sociohistorical whereabouts of Guo as a young member of China's May Fourth intellectual community, a "medical student as romantic artist" at Kyushu Imperial University in Fukuoka.[34] This locality, at the turn of the 1920s, exposed the young student-poet all at once to the natural landscape of the West Pacific, to Japan's modernization, and to East Asia's changing cultural-political climate. To begin with, the steamer had long been an emblem of technological productivity, sea power, and world trade in Chinese collective memory of an encounter with capitalism since the time of the Qing empire's humiliating defeat at the hands of British warships in the Opium War of 1840–42. It is not only with cheap commodities but also with gun-boat diplomacy that capitalism "batters down all Chinese walls."[35] Ever since, the Chinese had admired the "rapid improvement of all instruments of production" and "the immensely facilitated means of communication."[36] However, Meiji Japan's steamer warships routed China's navy in the First Sino-Japanese War (1894–95) and therefore dashed the Qing empire's last hope for a technology-centered modernization. Guo was among republican China's overseas students living in Japan on a government stipend, and he witnessed modern Japan's transition from the Meiji period (1868–1912) to the Taisho period (1912–26). Ito Toramaru's insightful study argues that Guo and other early members of the Creation Society were in fact "Taisho youths" in terms of their sentimentalist ethos.[37] The Taisho period was marked by Japan's economic boom and fateful turn to imperialism. As Harry Harootunian's study has reminded us, Japan's industrialization did not take off until the Taisho years, when European powers had their hands tied in the bloody World War I. Accompanying Japan's economic success was a cultural turn of

34. See Roy, *Kuo Mo-jo*, 72.
35. Marx, *The Communist Manifesto*, 59.
36. Ibid.
37. See Ito Toramaru, *Lu Xun, Chuangzao she yu riben wenxue*, 143–78.

consumerism: "The heroism of production was being replaced by heroic consumption."[38]

On one hand, Guo was a firsthand witness to Japan's economic takeoff. His later autobiography records his impressions of Japan's capitalist golden age and in particular his disgust at the lavish lifestyle of the nouveau riche.[39] On the other hand, stationed in Kyushu rather than cosmopolitan Tokyo, Guo was never surrounded by "café girls" or cinematic sensations characteristic of Tokyo's new urban life.[40] Kyushu was not the center of Taisho consumerism, but it was a crucial site of East Asian trade. Fudetate Yama is a mountain of Kyushu overseeing the major sea routes between the Japanese islands and Korea and China. Guo's locality exposed his lyrical eyes to a new industrial landscape and a natural scene combining the oceanic view with longer hours of sunlight:

> Seated alone by the north window I look all round.
> In the womb of nature spring is having its fetal stirring!
> . . . .
> The depths of the sky are a jade blue flecked with scudding clouds,
> White clouds whose chyle-tinted edges almost dazzle the eye.[41]

The landscape functioned as a romantic climate for the new cultural-political "fetal movement." What Guo truly looked at, either from his window or from atop a Japanese mountain, was the May Fourth New Culture back in China and the new dynamic of East Asian modernity. Like its Japanese counterpart, the Chinese bourgeoisie enjoyed a rare and steady economic development during World War I. This short-lived golden age of the Chinese bourgeoisie predetermined the flowering of the New

38. Harootunian, *Overcome by Modernity*, 19.

39. See, for example, Guo's retrospective account of his observation of Japan's burgeoning bourgeois lifestyle in *GQJ/W*, 12:42–45.

40. In this regard, Guo was in contrast to some of his friends who were students in Tokyo at the time, such as writer and dramatist Tian Han 田漢 (1898–1968). For Guo's narration about his visit to Tian in Tokyo, their fantasy of the "café atmosphere" in the upscale Ginza district, and their encounter with German Expressionist cinema in the equally famous Kanda district, see *GQJ/W*, 12:113–15. For Tian Han's cultural experience in Tokyo, see Luo, *The Avant-Garde and the Popular in Modern China*, chapter 1.

41. Guo, "Chun zhi taidong," in *N*, 212–13; *SPG*, 61 (translation modified).

Culture Movement in the late 1910s. With the end of the war, China unfortunately became once again the major target of imperialist expansion and competition. In the meantime, Lenin's Soviet Russia also looked to the Far East, viewing China as a potential volcano of world revolution. The outbreak of the May Fourth social movement in 1919 was not only an immediate response of Chinese students to the national humiliation by the Versailles Peace Conference, it also unleashed the widespread desire for new possibilities of sociohistorical change.[42]

Guo's spiritual "wavelength" was the same as that of the May Fourth emancipatory cultural politics, yet as a poet he was not at the center of that movement. Kyushu offered him a locality of perspectival significance in a doubled sense: inside but marginal to Japan's modernization, close enough to but distanced from a mobilized China. In some of his poems, this geographical distance turned into an advantage: he was enabled by this locality to transform "new China" into an imaginary domain, into an addressee for his new apostrophic power. Determined by the unevenness of East Asian modernity, his lyrical position was the ecstatic speculator's view of the ocean, history, and politics that were all stirred up. From this panoramic vantage point, the poet was to appreciate, address, and apostrophize the sublime of an open-ended history.

Apostrophizing Whitman: A Global Synchronization

Like "Panorama from Fudetate Yama," the majority of the above-cited poems from *The Goddesses* are dated 1919–20. Late 1919 and early 1920 witnessed the volcanic outburst of Guo's poetic energies. The poems written during this short span of time bear an unmistakable influence of Walt Whitman. Guo once offered a chronological order of poetic influences on his early career: "First is Tagore, second Heine, third Whitman, fourth Shelley, fifth Goethe."[43] Guo emphasized that his "encounter with Whit-

42. Regarding the rise of culture as a political domain in the May Fourth Movement, see Wang Hui, *Wenhua yu zhengzhi de bianzou.*

43. Guo, "Guo Moruo shizuo tan," in *GZL*, 213.

man's *Leaves of Grass* took place in the same year as the outbreak of the May Fourth Movement."[44] For him, "Whitman's verse style, which is stripped of all the old conventions, resonated so perfectly with the May Fourth spirit of *Sturm und Drang* that I was completely aroused by his sublime, splendid and open voice."[45] The liberating effect of Whitman's work on Guo was "like a storm": "His wild free verse incited my own creative desire whose floodgate had already been opened."[46] It caused what he called "an irrepressible impulse, a craze-like fervent sentiment": "Before translating *Faust*, I experienced a poetic outburst from 1919 to 1920, a period during which most poems of *The Goddesses* were written."[47] Repeatedly describing this outburst as a one-time experience of poetic craze, he remembered the attacks of inspiration as neural breakdowns: "During the three or four months at the turn of 1919 and 1920, I experienced the poetic ecstasy almost every day. Whenever an inspiration attacked me, I felt like having a fever . . . , quivering too much to be able to hold my pen."[48] He also said: "Under the inspiration's attacks, I was like a Shaman writing oracles, and sometimes my writing was not speedy enough to catch the instantaneous inspiration." This poetic spasm disappeared quite soon: "My poetic explosion was really a one-time thing during the May Fourth Movement."[49]

Guo's retroactive account of that Whitmanian period amounts to a pathological allegory of the May Fourth spiritual emancipation, a sublimated image of libidinal economy, and a celebration of world literature. The encounter with Whitman's poetry has since then become a commemorated moment in modern Chinese literary history. For instance, Achilles Fang once argued that "the true background of the new poetry of China [was] Whitmanism," and Guo was "the apostle of Chinese Whitmanism": "With him, as with Whitman, poetry was an outlet for relieving himself of irrepressible *egotism and eleutheromania*, two things most solicitously suppressed by all traditionalists. . . . The

44. Guo, "Xu wo de shi," in *GQJ/W*, 19:408.
45. Guo, "Wo de zuoshi de jingguo," in *GZL*, 228.
46. Guo, *Chuangzao shinian*, in *GQJ/W*, 12:67.
47. Guo, "Xie zai sange panni de nüxing houmian," in *GQJ/W*, 6:143–44.
48. Guo, *Chuangzao shinian*, in *GQJ/W*, 12:68.
49. Guo, "Wo de zuoshi de jingguo," in *GZL*, 229–31.

emergence of Kuo Mo-jo on the Chinese poetic scene was almost miraculous; it marked the end of tradition."[50]

What I want to focus on is an apostrophic moment in Guo's engagement with Whitman, which is in my view an origin of the new lyrical politics in twentieth-century Chinese culture. "Good Morning" ("Chen an" 晨安), a poem written under Whitman's influence, represents an extreme of the apostrophic mode. Its content and form are identical, because in this poem the only "happening" or "event" is a linguistic ritual of morning greeting. The poem can be translated thus: a morning, the poet greets the world. But even this summary is counterproductive, because the whole poem is a purely apostrophic operation and therefore excludes any narrative possibility:

> Good morning! Rolling ocean that knows no rest!
> Good morning! Shimmering glow of the rosy dawn!
> Good morning! White clouds welling up like poetry from its source!
> Good morning! Silken rain-threads [*si yu*] evenly drawn! You language of poetry [*shi yu*]!
> Good morning! Crests over the sea burning with the fire of passion!
> Good morning! Morning breeze combing the soul!
> You morning breeze, please bear away my voice to the four quarters![51]

With a series of apostrophes, the opening stanza situates the poetic voice in a vast world, where the poet (the greeting subject) and the natural forces (the addressees) join each other in a confirmation of vitality. Meanwhile, this ritual of greeting immediately refers back to itself and reinforces a self-image of lyric poetry as such. The analogy drawn between clouds and poetry is recognizable as a celebration of the mutability of poetic language, which is to be affirmed in the Chinese pun between "rain-threads" and "language of poetry." Finally, the lyrical voice finds its ultimate metaphor in the image of "morning breeze" that is supposed to pervade the whole world. This is a circle of poetic self-empowerment: the natural mobility is called into presence by the poet's apostrophic discourse

50. A. Fang, "From Imagism to Whitmanism in Recent Chinese Poetry," 188, 185, 186; emphasis in original.

51. Guo, "Chen an," in *N*, 93; *SPG*, 21 (translation modified).

and becomes a metaphoric correlative, with which poetry fulfills an imagination of its own mobility, its own transportation and communication ("please bear away my voice to the four quarters"). What this apostrophic act means to call into being is nothing but the apostrophic language itself. In so doing, this stanza lays out the condition of lyric poetry: the greeting addressed to the world prepares the coronation of a lyrical power.

Guo's apostrophic sequence then turns into a global tour of the poetic-political imagination. With almost every line starting with "good morning," the whole poem is an endless list of morning salutes. From the proximity of Guo's Kyushu location, the voice moves to his homeland, China, to Russia, to India, to Egypt and Europe, to the New Continent, and all the way across the Pacific back to East Asia. On the surface, the addressees seem to be randomly picked. Yet as a ritual of drawing a cosmopolitan panorama or a phenomenological world-picture, this global mapping actually demarcates an amorphous ideological domain of the May Fourth imagination.

Guo first pays salute to a new China: "Good morning! My youthful homeland! / Good morning! My newborn kinsfolk!"[52] The salute is extended to Lenin's young Russia, as the ongoing Bolshevik Revolution inspired awe and curiosity among the young Chinese: "Good morning! The Russia who inspires me with awe! / Good morning! The pioneer I hold in awe!"[53] The next addressee, however, is the Oriental spirit represented by "Tagore of Bengal." If the poet's respect for India and Egypt echoes the attention China had paid to the fate of other old civilizations since the late Qing period, then the sympathies Guo expressed toward Belgium and Ireland was a response to another discourse in modern China: the international solidarity with the "countries of the weak and oppressed."[54] Meanwhile, the poet's references to natural sublimes (such as "snow-capped Himalayas") soon gives way to his juxtaposition of the Suez Canal and pyramids—modern and ancient gigantic projects—which shows a proto-Faustian admiration for industrial productive power. On top of this cult of productive forces, Guo turns attention to the new

52. *N*, 93–94; *SPG*, 21.

53. *N*, 94; *SPG*, 21.

54. This internationalist theme can be traced to the late Qing period. For the May Fourth writers' interest in the literature of "oppressed nations," see, for example, Hockx, "Literary Association (*Wenxue yanjiu hui*)."

fashions of modern arts, saying "good morning" to "D'Annunzio flying on the bomb" and "Thinker of Rodin seated before the Pantheon."[55] He does not forget to extend greetings to "the band of friends, half working half studying."[56] What he refers to is obviously the overseas Chinese students participating in the work-study movement in France. At the time of writing, Guo surely could not predict that he would become a political protégé of Zhou Enlai, and his own funeral would have Deng Xiaoping delivering the official verdict: both Zhou and Deng were members of that "band" of students in France. This imagined friendship is an imprint of the temporality shared by the modern-minded Chinese youths.

In other words, all the images or signs poeticized in Guo's apostrophic movement derive from the new symbolic currency circulated in the New Culture community. Notably, they do not conform to a consistent ideological doctrine but form an open symbolic constellation. The power of this poem lies precisely in its Whitmanian "rhetoric of inclusivity," in its celebration of cultural-political possibilities that are yet to be substantialized in any domain of value production.[57]

Within this mobilization of Whitman's style of listing, Guo apostrophizes the name of Whitman:

> Good morning! Graves of Washington, of Lincoln, of Whitman!
> Ah! Ah! Whitman! Whitman! The Pacific that is Whitman!
> Ah! Ah! The Pacific!
> Good morning! The Pacific![58]

The admiration for the United States as a land of true modernity is another conventional theme in modern Chinese culture. More remarkably, when the name of Whitman is addressed, the sequential pattern of "good morning" is interrupted into a pure outcry of "Ah! Ah!" Whitman's name catapults the poem into an ecstatic outburst, where the apostrophic voice

55. *N*, 95. In this poem's later versions, the line about D'Annunzio's violent futurism is deleted.

56. *N*, 95; *SPG*, 22.

57. Moretti, *Modern Epic*, 64.

58. *N*, 96; *SPG*, 22.

finally unifies itself with a proper name as the metaphor of lyrical power. Whitman's name must be understood here as an image of the possibility of modern lyric poetry. The repeated calling of this name—first time in its English original and then in Chinese, as if it were a magic formula—is both a moment of this poem's externalization (intended to reach the limit of referential inclusivity) and a moment of its ultimate internalization (a self-referential identification with the lyrical). The analogy between Whitman and the Pacific—the largest ocean, the ocean dividing or linking Guo's East Asia and Whitman's America—is yet a further step of lyric poetry's maximization. What Guo apostrophizes is the invocative power of China's New Poetry. This lyrical possibility has a test drive in this poem's global tour, a tour that constantly returns to itself and reaffirms its rhetorical mechanism and condition: "Ah! Ah! Whitman!"

It is now clear that Guo's true affinity to Whitman lies in the tendency of name-calling and list-making. Poeticizing the New World, Whitman's "chaotic enumeration" and "magic of proper nouns" produce a "democracy of things" in the age of America's rise.[59] Franco Moretti sees Whitman's list-mania as a central formal principle in response to the emergence of the world market and the development of capitalism:

> In "Song of the Open Road," for example, the many places mentioned have the 'you' apostrophizing [the things] all gradually superimposed upon them, transforming the list from a purely descriptive sequence into an endless, tense harangue. . . . [It] acquires a hypnotic force. . . . You forget . . . the things listed; and you remember, instead, the *form* that holds them together and gives them meaning.[60]

Moretti's remarks pertain to our reading of Guo—and not only because Guo cites "Song of the Open Road" in one of his letters, as I will discuss in a moment. "Good Morning" is also based on the constant invocation of places and proper nouns; the repetition of "good morning" serves a formal (and ideological) function of hypnosis in a free-verse poem. If the ideology of Whitman's form means a "hypnotic force" of listing, then what is the ideological effect of Guo's poem? After the three callings of Whitman's

59. Moretti, *Modern Epic*, 64.
60. Ibid., 65–66; emphasis in original.

name, "Good Morning" descends into Guo's locality and ends with the poet awakening Japan by calling its ancient Chinese name, *Fusang*:

> Good morning! The Pacific Ocean! Islands on the Pacific! Fusang on the Pacific!
> O Fusang! Fusang still wrapped in dream.
> Awake! *Mésamé* [*sic*]!
> Hasten to share and enjoy this millennial dawn![61]

In this fictive personification of a young Chinese student-poet as an awakening call, as a herald of the dawn, Guo's lyrical mission manifests its own rhetorical-ideological dialectics. What the poet's apostrophic sequence is supposed to acquire is not a "hypnotic force" but an awakening one, in which the modernized lyrical form recognizes its potential global territory. More precisely, this poem is supposed to "hypnotize" the imagined readership of Chinese New Poetry into a moment of "awakening." From the morning breeze to the dawn light, this poem provides its apostrophic mode as a method of participating in the demarcation of May Fourth China's ideological space. Culler suggests that "one [should] distinguish two forces in poetry, the narrative and the apostrophic, and that the lyric is characteristically the triumph of the apostrophic."[62] "Good Morning" is a case in point. Devoid of a diachronic narrative temporality, the poem offers a singular event, that is, the externalization and internalization of a new Chinese lyrical voice. Every addressee becomes the voice's own image. The lyrical voice reaches its highest note by way of the magic of the proper name, by way of invoking the name of Whitman. Via this tour of global mapping, lyric poetry reveals itself as an organ open to any content of cultural-political imagination. It gives rises to a new subjectivity whose amorphous potentials become visible through the apostrophic act of addressing. The "millennial dawn" serves as a visionary (and fictive) synchronization of every addressee into a dawning moment—a moment that is not only a "now" of poetic discourse but also a horizon of new historical time. This poem is thus a Chinese "world text,"

61. *N*, 96; *SPG*, 22.
62. Culler, "Apostrophe," 149.

lyrical rather than narrative: the poet salutes the openness of a world-historical possibility.

Translating Shelley's Winds: Translatability and "Poetic Monism"

The invocation of Whitman also forms an apostrophic relationship with Guo's translation of Shelley's poetry. In this regard, a book called *Kleeblatt* demands our special attention. *Kleeblatt*, meaning "shamrock" or "the trifoliate leaf," is the German title given to *San ye ji* 三叶集, a collection of correspondences between Guo, Tian Han, and Zong Baihua in 1920. The German title is more proper than pretentious, for it is indicative of the translingual nature of this small volume. All three young writers had the tendency to insert English, German, or Japanese passages in their letters. Moreover, this German word symbolizes their shared interest in German literature, especially Goethe's work. *Kleeblatt* is thus a botanical (and therefore Goethean) symbol of a growing friendship, which Guo fantasized as the embryo of a "Goethe Studies Association."[63] In this sense, the book of letters also exhibits a dialectic between private friendship and public openness: the sense of intimacy created by the letters calls effectively for a public communicability of their experience. For example, Zong, at the time an editor who published Guo's poems, praises Guo's "*Lyrical* genius" in his letter and claims: "The world of your poems is the world of my heart. . . . I recognize your poems as my own. Will you permit?"[64] In his response, Guo not only "permits" Zong to claim a shared ownership of his poems but also goes one step further by stating that the poems Zong did not manage to write "must have also been recognized as my poems."[65] In this conversation, a lyrical romanticism is taking shape: it assumes, on one hand, that poetry is the expression of one's inner self, and on the other hand, this interiority is simultaneously an open community or a collective event.

63. Guo, Tian, and Zong, *San ye ji*, 75.
64. Ibid., 3.
65. Ibid., 5.

Guo's letters provide an intertextual and translingual field in which his confessional narrative is intertwined with moments of poetic readings, citations, creative writings, and translations. That explains why Xie Kang 谢康, one of the earliest commentators of Guo's work, proposed to read *Kleeblatt* as an "introduction" to *The Goddesses*.[66] In a lengthy letter to Zong Baihua, dated March 3, 1920, Guo relates the visit Tian Han paid to him in Kyushu. According to this letter, Guo took a walk of several miles to find Tian at a railway station, which called to his mind Whitman's "Song of the Open Road." Translating some passages from Whitman's poem, Guo tells Zong that on his way back with Tian, he heard beautiful sounds from unseen birds and improvised a short poem: "Where are you singing? / What is your name, my bird? / How beautiful is your song!"[67] Two things about this moment of improvisation need our attention: the first is that this fragment is written in purely modern vernacular Chinese, in line with the Literary Revolution; the second is that this apostrophic praise of heavenly music is actually a recurring theme in the romantic tradition.

This apostrophe does not stop with such an impromptu. As soon as Guo went back home from this trip, he hastened to read Shelley's "Ode to a Sky-Lark": "O! It feels as if [Shelley] developed the germ cell of my own actual feeling into a superb lyrical piece!"[68] Notably, Guo sees poetic inspiration and writing as an open source, claiming for his own a share of Shelley's originality. More interestingly, Guo singles out an apostrophic moment from Whitman's "Song of the Open Road" and uses it to make an apostrophic gesture toward Shelley: "Reading Shelley, I want to borrow two lines from Whitman to express my gratitude to Shelley: *You express me better than I can express myself; / You shall be more to me than my poem.*"[69]

This Guo-Whitman-Shelley circuit of apostrophic invocation is significant, first because it embodies an impulsive act of identifying with a higher poetical power: "You shall be more to me." Furthermore, this apostrophic logic of identification also figures prominently in Shelley's "To a

66. Xie Kang, "Du le Nüshen zhihou," 17.

67. Guo, Tian, and Zong, *San ye ji*, 148.

68. Ibid.

69. Ibid., 149 (emphasis in original); Whitman, "Song of the Open Road," 299.

Sky-Lark." The invisible heavenly voice is evidently a metaphor for the higher poetical power:

Like a Poet hidden
  In the light of thought,
Singing hymns unbidden,
  Till the world is wrought
To sympathy with hopes and fears it heeded not.[70]

In other words, Guo identifies his own inspiration with Shelley's creativity, which is identified with the poetical spirit as such. This cycle of identification fulfills itself with an act of translation. In the letter Guo shares with Zong his translation of this ode, though at the same time he repeatedly expresses the idea that "poetry is untranslatable," echoing Shelley's comment about the "vanity of translation" in *A Defence of Poetry* (*Defence* hereafter).[71] This act of invoking and translating the foreign can be categorized as a prime example of rewriting as the "manipulation" of literary authority: according to André Lefevere's theory of translation, "rewriters created images of a writer, a work, a period, a genre, sometimes even a whole literature."[72] Between the music of singing birds and Shelley's praise of a skylark, Guo's "manipulation" as both a writer and rewriter creates an "*Embiologie* [*sic*; it must be a typo for the German word *Embryologie*] of poetry."[73]

However, in Guo's original fragment the apostrophic "you" is a vernacular Chinese pronoun, *ni* 你, whereas in the same letter, Guo translates Shelley's apostrophic equivalent "Thou" as *ru* 汝, a pronoun that comes from classical Chinese. The poetic form Guo invents in this translation is also noteworthy. He transforms Shelley's five-line stanza into a three-line stanza in Chinese, with every line composed of two *wuyan* 五言 or five-character (therefore pentasyllabic) clauses. The pentasyllabic punctuation shows Guo's recourse to the traditional poetic tradition,

70. Shelley, *Shelley's Poetry and Prose,* 305.
71. Guo, Tian, and Zong, *San ye ji*, 157; Shelley, *Shelley's Poetry and Prose*, 514.
72. Lefevere, *Translation, Rewriting and the Manipulation of Literary Fame*, 5.
73. Guo, Tian, and Zong, *San ye ji*, 157.

though he does not follow the classical tonal rules. Below is Guo's translation of the stanza I have just cited above:

> 宛如一詩人，藏在智光中。
> 靈感自天來，曠渺頌歌起。
> 歡恐意外生，世人爲悲喜。[74]
>
> [Like a poet, hidden in the light of wisdom. / The inspiration comes from the heaven, and odes are sung from faraway. / Joy and fear emerge unexpectedly, and humans have sadness and happiness.]

Due to Guo's embrace of a traditional poetic diction, this passage registers an exquisite and sentimental note. Such abstract nouns as "thought," "hopes," and "fears" are rendered into one-syllable lofty nouns of classical Chinese, *zhi* 智, *huan* 歡, and *kong* 恐. "Sympathy" is missing in the translation, and instead is paraphrased into an indication that the human world is full of "sadness and happiness." Guo leaves aside almost all the grammatical and prepositional markers such as "till," "to," and "with"; instead, he offers a translation that is neither formally faithful nor syntactically literal. It involves a rewriting that is nothing less than a reversification. Guo's letter thus mingles together, as if effortlessly, his own poetic fragment in vernacular free verse, his citation of Whitman in English, and his translation of Shelley in a quasi-classical form. Apostrophizing each other, these different poetic elements form an "embryology" or phenomenology of the lyrical.

Besides "To a Sky-Lark," Guo translated Shelley's "Ode to the West Wind," two poems titled "Mutability" ("We are as clouds" and "The Flowers that smiles today"), "Song" ("Rarely, rarely, comest thou"), "Stanzas written in Dejection—December 1818, Near Naples," "Invocation to Misery," and "On Death." Guo's translations of those of Shelley's best lyrical works appeared (alongside a chronology of Shelley's life he prepared) in *Creation Quarterly* (*Chuangzao jikan* 創造季刊) in spring 1923. For "Mutability," he mobilizes the classical *wuyan lü* 五言律 (eight pentasyllabic lines) to render each and every stanza of Shelley's. Yet a closer look shows that this recycling of a classical form is merely an appearance, for no tonal rule of *wuyan lü* is observed. Translating "Invocation to Misery,"

74. Ibid., 152.

Guo explicitly tells the reader in a note that "this poem personifies Misery and calls upon it, the tone saddening, the rhyme melodious; so the most appropriate is to express it in our *sao* 騷 style."[75] The *sao* style originates from Qu Yuan's poetry and represents an ancient Chinese tradition of poetic invocation. In other cases, Guo's language of poetical translation continues to be hybrid, combining the vernacular with the classical and using traditional diction with a modernizing tinge. For example, the apostrophic line of "rarely, rarely, comest thou" becomes: 罕哉，罕哉，你之来 [How rare, how rare is your coming].[76] The combination of ancient Chinese grammar and a modern vernacular pronoun is experimental, if not overdone. Guo's language in such translations, to echo Shengqing Wu's observation, is "pitched at a level between the vernacular and the classical."[77]

The hybridity of Guo's poetic language suggests a peculiar vision of translatability. His translations of Shelley's poems include "Mutability" ("We are as clouds"), an 1816 poem that, according to Earl Wasserman, signals the "true" beginning of Shelley's poetic career: "The only enduring principle in the world that he now admits is not the Spirit of Nature but mutability."[78] Guo translates this key concept "mutability" into *zhuanxi* 轉徙, a word that literally means turning, transformation, and mobility.[79] The analogy between poetry and "morning clouds" in Guo's "Good Morning" may also derive from Shelley's line in "Mutability": "We are as clouds."[80] The unstable language and form in Guo's translations of Shelley's works can be seen as poetry's own mutability or *zhuanxi*.

Tracing the birth of New Poetry, Michelle Yeh has emphasized "the revolutionary nature of modern Chinese poetry" and explored "how it is distinct from the classical norm in key aspects."[81] Guo's experiments in *The Goddesses* have been seen as a pioneering example of this struggle against the "heritage of three millennia of classical poetry," testifying to

75. Guo, trans., "Zhao buxing ci," 28.
76. Shelley, *Shelley's Poetry and Prose*, 467; Guo, trans., "Huanle de jingling," 24.
77. Wu, *Modern Archaics*, 339.
78. Wasserman, *Shelley*, 5.
79. Guo, trans., "Zhuanxi," 31.
80. Shelley, *Shelley's Poetry and Prose*, 91.
81. Yeh, *Modern Chinese Poetry*, 2.

a "new language in the making."[82] In the eyes of supporters of the vernacular literary movement, his return to classical prosody in translations may then seem to be a superficial, if not mannered, stylization. Yet this style is reminiscent of what Shengqing Wu calls "ornamental lyricism" in the persistence of classical-style poetry as a "hybrid field consisting of the modern and the archaic" in twentieth-century China.[83] Wu's study also shows how some traditionalist poets, such as Su Manshu 蘇曼殊 (1884–1918) and Ma Junwu 馬君武 (1881–1940), used classical forms to translate Shelley and Lord Byron. In her account of this "neglected but significant phenomenon" of "using the classical form to render Western poetry," Wu finds that such translators' "shared concern for domestic intelligibility and acculturation outweighed their interest in fidelity to the foreign texts."[84] Here one can discern the dichotomy between foreignization and domestication—a paradigm that can be traced to Friedrich Schleiermacher's theory of translation and is further developed in Venuti's argument for linguistic and cultural difference.[85]

But the approach of domestication only has a limited relevance for the early Guo's case. When Sun Mingchuan 孫銘傳, a Tsinghua University student, criticized Guo's translation of "Stanzas Written in Dejection," Guo refused to accept the corrections Sun offered, arguing: "I never agree with word-for-word literal translation. . . . I believe for the sake of aesthetic air and rhythm [*qi yun* 氣韻], the translator has every right to rearrange words and sentences."[86] So Guo's ideal of translation is in conflict with the approach of literalism. Nor does it fall into the category of sensible translation as domestication that prioritizes fluency. The emphasis on aesthetic transmogrification indicates an approach of translation that is oriented toward what Eugene Nida calls "dynamic equivalence" rather than linguistic "formal equivalence."[87] Guo's use of certain classical poetic conventions does not necessarily lead to the homogeneity of language, but in fact raises the translator's visibility in the lyrical-lingual formation.

82. Ibid., 10, xi.

83. Wu, *Modern Archaics*, 11.

84. Ibid., 345, 346.

85. See Schleiermacher, "On the Different Methods of Translating," 49–63; Venuti, *The Translator's Invisibility*, chapter 1.

86. Guo, "Da Sun Mingchuan jun," 205.

87. See Nida, "Principles of Correspondence."

Concerned with the creative freedom of lyrical translation, his practice draws closer to Ezra Pound's experimentalism, according to which the translator is "definitely making a new poem, falls simply in the domain of original writing."[88] What lies behind Guo's unstable language is a model of translation as rewriting, based on an ideological vision of the affinity between the creator and translator, of the open translatability of poetic inspiration, and of the external (lingual/formal) mutability of the inner dynamic.

Herein comes the metaphor of "winds" in Guo's pantheistic interpretation of Shelley. Anticipating that the contrast between his linguistic hybridity and the vernacular Literary Revolution may create controversy, he preemptively defends such poetic mutability in "A Short Preface" ("Xiao xu" 小序) to his Shelley translations. He first expresses his admiration for Shelley as a true pantheistic poet: "He is the beloved son of Nature, a believer in pantheism, and a pioneer of revolutionary thought."[89] Guo compares the morphological diversity of Shelley's works to a pantheistic cosmos, with the wind as a central metaphor:

> [Shelley] is a great unfinished work. The universe is also an eternal, great, and yet unfinished work. The ancients compare poetry to wind. There is *Orkan*, which tears down houses; *Sturm*, which shatters big trees; *Stark*, which shatters small trees; *Frisch*, which waves big branches; *Maessig*, which waves small branches; *Schwach*, which touches on grasses and leaves; and *Still*, which does not even disturb any chimney smoke. The will of the universe flows into those different kinds of winds. Shelley's poetic winds are as diverse as they are. Winds do not come from outside the universe. Poetry does not come from outside the heart.[90]

Guo seizes on a "characteristic of Shelley's imagination": "He conceived many of his poems in cosmic terms."[91] With Guo's own cosmic terms and his obsession with German words for various winds, "Preface" marks a crucial yet long overlooked moment in the development of his

88. Pound, "Guido's Relations," 91.
89. Guo, "Xiao xu," 19.
90. Ibid.
91. Wasserman, *Shelley*, 328.

pantheism. At this point, pantheism becomes a "pan-poetism."[92] Moreover, this pantheism/pan-poetism provides a radical vision of lyrical translation:

> To translate Shelley is to let me become Shelley, and to let Shelley become myself. Translating is not imitating like a parrot. . . .
>
> I love Shelley, I can hear the voice of his heart, I resonate with him, and thus I marry him.—Shelley and I become one. His poetry is then my poetry. I translate his poetry as if I were myself versifying.[93]

His identification with Shelley's work results in the identity between creation and translation. Translation becomes legitimate versification.

We encounter here again the translator's ideological "manipulation," leading to an image of poetic originality as an open community. Guo's translation of Shelley thus occasions his insistence on a poetic essence open to any possible form: "It does not matter whether poetry is written in classical or vernacular language, in rhyme or in free verse, as long as it is poetry."[94] The lingual and formal mutability obviously refers to his varied translations of Shelley. In this dialectic between a unitary poetic spirit and formal diversity, he no longer differentiates the poet from the translator:

> Who says the ancient forms are like a dead skeleton? Who says free verse is the crazy moderns' incantation? The poetic form is an issue of *Sein*, not an issue of *Sollen*. The poeticizing one is absolutely free. . . . When his poetry flows into an ancient form, he is not necessarily a classicist. When his poetry flows as a blow struck to all the given rules, he is not necessarily merely following the current fashion. . . . The monist spirit, as the essence of poetry, remains unchangeable forever.[95]

92. I borrow this term from György Lukács's famous reading of German early romanticism. See Lukács, *Soul and Form*, 65.

93. Guo, "Xiao xu," 19–20.

94. Ibid., 20.

95. Ibid.

Whereas in Wu's account the line between the modern and the archaic is blurred because of the continuation of classical-style poetry, here Guo deconstructs the evolutionist preference of vernacular verse over classical form by idealizing a "poetic monism." This poetic monism is nothing but the obverse side of his pantheism, in which the diverse and mutable manifestations are united in a universal spirituality. On another occasion, the early Guo defines poetry directly in English: "The poetic spirit is the *Intrinsic Rhythm*," which allows utmost external mutability and indicates a free translatability.[96] According to this lyricism, literary creation is already an act of inspired translation, a translation of the poetic-cosmic spirit into "winds." If the poetic cosmos is considered as the constant transmutation of the inner spirit, then Guo's "monism" is a poetic pantheism of creation/translation.

Interestingly, the figure of wind also appears in Guo's proposal for an alternative method of poetic translation. In 1920, on the occasion of publishing his rendering of Goethe's poems, Guo stated that "a poem's life lies in that ungraspable *fengyun*, and therefore I think in addition to literal translation and sensible translation there should be a method of *fengyun* translation." *Feng* literally means "wind." In classical poetics, it also designates metaphorically the aesthetic style. *Yun* means rhythm. Thus *fengyun* refers to the internal aesthetic mood, aura, or style of a given work. In 1922, Guo expressed his distrust for both literal translation and sensible translation, and proposed again "*fengyun* 風韻 translation." He gave two examples for further consideration: "Read, for example, Shelley's translation of the 'Prologue in Heaven' of *Faust*, in which the translator practices free translation and offers literal translation as footnotes; read also Edward Fitzgerald's rendering of *The Rubáiyát of Omar Khayyám*."[97] Fitzgerald's *Rubáiyát* is a famous example of poetic "rewriting." According to Lefevere, "ideologically Fitzgerald obviously thinks Persians inferior to their Victorian English counterparts. . . . Poetologically he thinks they should be made to read more like the dominant current in the poetry of his own time."[98] As one of the earliest Chinese translators of *Rubáiyát*, Guo's blindness lies in his neglect of the imperialist

96. Guo, "Lun shi san zha," in *GQJ/W*, 15:337; emphasis in original.
97. Guo, "Pipan Yimenhu yiben ji qita," 28.
98. Lefevere, *Translation, Rewriting, and the Manipulation of Literary Fame*, 8.

power structure behind this rewriting; his insight lies in the transformation of this example into a case for the translator's subjectivity.[99] As Li Chun's study has indicated, *fengyun* translation suggests that the translator functions as a receiver of the "intrinsic rhythm" of an original poem, and then reexpresses it in his or her own language.[100]

Critics have long been attempting to analyze the early Guo's pantheism as an intellectual outlook.[101] Yet as I have shown, this pantheism is first and foremost a pan-poetism, a lyrical ideology centered on and driven by a conception of translatability. It is comparable to what Antoine Berman discovers in the early German romantic discourse of poetry: " 'Versability' . . . is equivalent to the *principle of translatability of everything into everything*."[102] Throughout this book, I demonstrate that this logic of translatability or versability was central to the romantic productivity of China's long cultural revolution.[103]

Invoking Goethe: "The Creative Spirit" and the Macrocosm

To understand the early Guo's conception of pantheism, it is also necessary to interrogate the beginning of his decades-long engagement with Goethe's work during the May Fourth period. While I leave a full discussion of the translation of *Faust* to chapter 3, here I intend to pinpoint Guo's initial reading of Goethe as a translingual moment of May Fourth cultural politics. Guo first attempted to translate *Faust* in 1919–20. In a special 1919 issue of *China Times* (*Shishi xinbao* 時事新報) on the occasion of the anniversary of the 1911 revolution, Guo published his translation of an excerpt of the first scene from *Faust I*, "Night." In the "Translator's Preface," Guo manipulates the image of Goethe by invoking the Ger-

99. See Guo, trans., *Lubai ji*. Guo's translation is solely based on the fourth edition of Fitzgerald's *Rubáiyát*. Also see Guo, trans., *Moruo yi shi ji*.

100. Li Chun, *Wenxue fanyi yu wenxue geming*, 118.

101. See Chen Yongzhi, *Guo Moruo sixiang zhengti guan*.

102. Berman, *The Experience of the Foreign*, 82; emphasis in original.

103. I borrow the phrase "romantic productivity" from Schmitt, *Political Romanticism*, 159.

man poet as an original authority, an inspiration, and a higher spiritual power: "Whenever I started to translate, I called upon the spirit of Goethe: please bestow on me the heavenly light of divine wisdom, so that I would have a complete understanding as an assistance to my clumsy and inferior writing [*shoubi* 手筆]."[104] The invocative gesture is clearly a ritual of the early Guo's work as translator. Some passages from his later remembrances seem to indicate that the intensive labor of translating Goethe in 1920 was a "bad influence" that confined Guo's own poetic writing to rhyme.[105] But that account does not reveal the whole picture of his relationship with Goethe. In fact, amid his self-claimed Whitmanian fever, Guo had already translated thirteen lyrical poems by Goethe by 1920. It was on the occasion of the publication of these early translations that Guo first proposed the ideal of *fengyun* translation.[106]

Guo also translated *Sorrows of Young Werther* in 1922. As Leo Lee notes, "soon after Guo's translated version was published, *Young Werther* reaped such popularity as to become almost the bible of modern Chinese youth."[107] The theme of "the contradiction between personality and society" determined the novel's appeal to the May Fourth generation.[108] However, my reading is more concerned about the role of this translation in Guo's formulation of pantheism. Guo's "Translator's Introduction" contains the following definition: "Pantheism is atheism. Everything in nature is the expression of God, and I am the expression of God, and therefore I am God, and everything in nature is my expression. . . . It is with this spiritual totality that Werther loves, revels, agonizes, and dies!"[109]

This definition of pantheism corresponds secretly to an important mechanism of mirroring between subjectivity and Nature in Goethe's original:

> My friend, when everything grows dim then before my eyes, and sky and earth rest in my soul like the image of a beloved being—I am often

104. Guo, trans., "*Faust* chaoyi."
105. See *GQJ/W*, 12:76–77.
106. See Vuilenmier, "Guo Moruo 20 niandai baihua shixuan li de Gede yi shi."
107. Lee, *The Romantic Generation of Modern Chinese Writers*, 283.
108. See Lukács, *Goethe and His Age*, 35–49.
109. Guo, "Shaonian Weite zhi fannao xuyin," 2–3.

> overcome by longing and by the thought: could you only breathe upon paper all that lives so full and warm within you, so that it might become the *mirror* of your soul, as your soul is the *mirror* of the infinite God!—My friend—but it is more than I can bear.[110]

This is a "specular moment"—to use David Wellbery's term—in a double sense.[111] First, one's soul is the mirror image of the infinite Nature; second, the textuality—of Werther's drawing or "paper" or ultimately the novella itself—is imagined to be, but often fails to be, the mirror of one's soul and therefore of Nature. Literary translation follows a similar logic of spiritual mirroring/identification. By extension, if Goethe's novel is a mirror of a liberated self that is in turn the "mirror of the infinite God," then Guo's translation of *Young Werther* functioned as a specular moment in which a new cultural subjectivity/collectivity would recognize a primordial self-image.

With this mirroring effect in mind, let us return to Guo's early reading of *Faust* and his creative translation of *geschäftiger Geist* as *chuangzao jingshen* (creative spirit), on which I briefly touched in the introduction. Faust's invocation of the Earth Spirit takes place in the opening scene in Faust's studio. Faust turns first to "the Sign of Macrocosm." Yet the Macrocosm is merely a "show" that mirrors boundless Nature. Unsatisfied, he invokes the Earth Spirit by the magic word: "He seizes the book and mysteriously pronounces the sign of the [Earth Spirit]. A reddish flame flashes."[112] Faust identifies himself with this spirit as the true power of the universe, the "geschäftiger Geist": "I am Faust, your match, I am the same!" (line 500). Yet after singing the song that Guo cites, the Earth Spirit rejects Faust's embrace: "Close to the wraith you comprehend, / Not me!" (lines 512–13; see fig. 3) As Cyrus Hamlin remarks, "the distinction between the Sign of the Macrocosm and the Earth Spirit also introduces a crucial contrast between two opposing forms of semiosis; a pictorial sign in the case of the former . . . ; and a verbal sign in the latter instance."[113] So the Macrocosm is similar to a mirroring image of the Infinity, whereas

110. Goethe, *The Sorrows of Young Werther*, 6; emphasis added.
111. See Wellbery, *The Specular Moment*.
112. Goethe, *Faust*, 14, 15.
113. Hamlin, "Interpretative Notes," 351–52.

FIGURE 3 Goethe's drawing for Faust's encounter with the Earth Spirit in the scene "Night," ca. 1810–12 or 1819. Courtesy of Klassik Stiftung Weimar, Germany.

the call for the Earth Spirit comes closer to an invocative mode of poetry. Adding to this interpretation, I suggest that the theme of mirroring and likeness is in fact inseparable from the logic of invocation and identification. After the Earth Spirit's rejection, Faust is left to ponder: "What, I, / Made in God's likeness, / Yet like—not even thee?" (lines 514–17). In Guo's 1919 translation, "likeness" is *xiezhen* 寫眞, meaning "copy" or "photograph."[114] There seems to be a failed mirroring or a blocked passage into the primordial sign.

The opening of Goethe's *Faust*, of course, is itself deeply related to the theme of translation, as exemplified by the famous early scene: Faust encounters a difficulty in his translation of a line from the New Testament, "In the beginning was the Word." Eventually, Faust translates the Greek "logos" as deed or act—"Im Anfang war die Tat" ("in the beginning was the Deed"; line 1237). The choice of *Tat*, which commentators consider as the most Faustian, is prefigured already in a key phrase of the Earth Spirit's song: the storm of doing (*Tatensturm*, line 501). Guo's letter is then his own reenactment of a translation scene. Translating the song of the Earth Spirit is Guo's own "specular moment," in which he as the translator is seduced by and then draws close to a sign/song that he (mis) recognizes or (mis)translates as the "symbol" of creation, creativity, and "creative spirit."

The ideological magic power of this word is borne out by the name Guo came up with for the literary society he cofounded in 1921: *Chuangzao she* 創造社—the Creation Society. The Creation Society was one of the most important cultural groups in modern Chinese history. The society, composed primarily of overseas students in Japan, represented an experiment in collective formations and functioned as a free labor force in the burgeoning market of the New Culture.[115] It is precisely these literary "proletarians" who produced the most densely divine aura of the romantic ideology. In the first issue of *Creation Quarterly*, Guo published a manifesto poem. Titled "The Creator" ("Chuangzao zhe" 創造者), it is a hymn to the creative spirit:

114. Guo, trans., "*Faust* chaoyi."

115. See Guo, *Chuangzao shinian*. For a compilation of the early Creation Society's journals, see Ito, ed., *Sōzōsha shiryō*.

Blow, blow, the autumnal wind!
Write, write, my pen!
I know the inspiration has come,
I will be busy with my creation![116]

In the poem, Guo refers to a number of "creators" in world civilizations as part of an imagined community of creativity, including the ancient Chinese and Indian poets, Dante, Milton, and Goethe. Such creators form a "great stellar galaxy."[117] Then appears the creative spirit/*chuangzao jingshen*: "He is the creative spirit, / . . . / Substance is him, God is him; . . . / Out of himself he creates a bright world."[118] The last product of such creation is a newborn infant, who embodies the ambitions of the Creation Society. The wind and the skylark "sing the hymn," and clouds come to the site of birth to pay homage. The ending returns to the scene of writing:

You, the flame-like, blood-like
Creative pen,
Please lend yourself to me to write this hymn "The Creator,"
For I want to praise highly the first infant;
For I want to praise highly the grand self [*da wo* 大我] breaking the ground.[119]

This apostrophic address not only confirms the action or event of writing, it also serves as an interpellation toward a new collectivity. This poem and other similar editorial poems Guo wrote for the journals of the Creation Society address an amorphous collectivity of the New Culture that comes into being only through such acts of addressing. The ending apostrophe embodies a gesture of scattering the words across this imagined/addressed community. If "the first infant" refers to the establishment of the Creation Society, then the "grand self"—which would later become a key word of collectivism in revolutionary ideologies—calls

116. Guo, "Chuangzao zhe," 1.
117. Ibid., 2.
118. Ibid.
119. Ibid., 3.

on this imagined collectivity to launch its cultural and potentially political agenda. Almost all the editorial poems published in the society's periodicals share this self-referential gesture meant to propagandize a new literary and social interactivity.[120]

Eventually, Guo's invocation of the creative spirit turns into a drawing of the Macrocosm in "Starry Sky" ("Xinkong" 星空), which reads like a serene and beautiful show of the stars and constellations: "Full of boundless love, my gaze! / There are only the stars and me in this universe."[121] The starry sky amounts to a "mirror image" that idealizes the May Fourth cultural-political cosmos. So in these moments of translation and versification, the signs of the cosmos and the "creative spirit" produce the magic mirror for an identification, in which Guo and his peers recognize a sublimated image of their selfhood. The pantheist Macrocosm he draws fulfills an ideological interpellation for the imagined collectivity and its age, even though the "likeness" between its cultural-political potential and actual history may remain blocked.

The Spirit of the Age: From "History's Lyre" to Revolution's "Gramophone"

To end this chapter, I return to the metaphor of wind, and by so doing extend the perspective of lyrical politics to Guo's transition from romanticism/pantheism to revolutionary politics in the mid-1920s. Lyrical or "windy" translation, as an indispensable moment of this pantheistic versability, solicits the Spinozan question of subjectivity and determinism: is the expressive subject an active, free agency or a passive recipient of the invisible power?[122] I would suggest asking it more historically in the context of Guo's case: what is the historical wind—or "the spirit of the age," as we will see—that Guo as poet-translator eventually invokes, enters, and yields to?

120. Also see Guo, "Women de huayuan."

121. Guo, "Xin kong," 139.

122. The philosophical problem of expression in the context of Spinozan pantheism is powerfully laid out in Deleuze, *Expressionism in Philosophy*.

The early Guo's overemphasis on the unified subjectivity of the poet-translator is strikingly justified by another metaphorical move: the instrumentalization of this lyrical sovereignty. If Shelley's "poetic heart" is considered as a "piano," then the translator's subjectivity serves also as a musical instrument that resonates with the Shelleyan winds.[123] In European romanticism, the instrument of musical resonance usually appears paired with the metaphor of wind. M. H. Abrams's study demonstrates the centrality of the images of the wind, the wind-harp, and the "Aeolian lyre."[124] Guo's combination of pantheism and monism is itself a reminder of Coleridge's renowned poem, "The Eolian Harp," in which the British philosopher-poet famously contemplates:

> And what if all of animated nature
> Be but organic Harps diversely fram'd,
> That tremble into thought, as o'er them sweeps,
> Plastic and vast, one intellectual Breeze
> At once the Soul of each, and God of all?[125]

Guo's comparison of Shelley to a piano may as well come from Shelley's defense of the poetic potential of humanity: "Man is an instrument over which a series of external and internal impressions are driven, like the alternations of an ever-changing wind over an Aeolian lyre, which move it by their motion to ever-changing melody."[126] Guo's ideal of the poet-translator's self-expression shows a similar paradoxical romantic mechanism: poetic expression is an active affirmation of subjectivity, but it is also a passive process automated by an inspiring power.

This mechanism leads us to Shelley's "Ode to the West Wind" and Guo's translation of it. The "Ode" opens with a famous apostrophe to the west wind, a seasonal natural force, a shapeless spiritual power: "O wild West Wind, thou breath of Autumn's being."[127] Earl Wasserman sees the west wind as "an appropriate symbol of Power," the "immediate

123. Guo, "Xiao xu," 19.
124. See Abrams, *The Mirror and the Lamp*, chapter 3.
125. Coleridge, "Effusion XXXV [The Eolian Harp]," 18–19.
126. Shelley, *Shelley's Poetry and Prose*, 511.
127. Ibid., 298.

cause" or "unseen presence" that drives the "cycle of mutability," which is both natural and historical, and the "cause" or spirit that "cannot be experienced empirically."[128] The true crux of the issue raised by this apostrophe is how to understand and interpret the poet's identification with the west wind as the "fierce spirit," historical change, and poetry itself, especially when this identification becomes complicated toward the end of the poem:

> Make me thy lyre, even as the forest is:
> . . . .
> . . . Be thou, Spirit fierce,
> My spirit! Be thou me, impetuous one!
>
> Drive my dead thoughts over the universe,
> Like withered leaves to quicken a new birth!
> And, by the incantation of this verse,
>
> Scatter, as from an unextinguished hearth
> Ashes and sparks, my words among mankind!
> Be through my lips to unawakened Earth
>
> The trumpet of a prophecy! O Wind,
> If Winter comes, can Spring be far behind?[129]

Written in the verse of a terza rima sonnet, this final part of "Ode" has solicited numerous readings on the lyre and the Spirit. One can surely read "Be thou, Spirit fierce, / My spirit! Be thou me" as the poet's self-empowerment by invoking and identifying with a higher spiritual force, "for a final, cosmological voyage."[130] But one can also argue that rather than empowering himself, the poet actually yields himself to the wind. Wasserman, for example, emphasizes the "passivity" of being a lyre: "Should the poet willfully submit himself to the Power, he would of necessity be the passive lyre over which the Spirit blows . . . , and the Spirit would 'touch' him for the 'hymns' it sings."[131] Harold Bloom elabo-

128. Wasserman, *Shelley*, 239.
129. Shelley, *Shelley's Poetry and Prose*, 300–301.
130. Bloom, "The Art of Reading Poetry," 18.
131. Wasserman, *Shelley*, 248.

rates on this complexity of the poet's stance in the following way: "He can either surrender himself to the wind as an object for it to experience, as the leaf, cloud, and the wave . . . , or else he can attempt to call upon the wind to take up a stand in relation to him, to enter into him and he into the wind."[132]

Notably in the criticism of Guo's pantheist poetry, a problem of self-empowerment versus passivity is likewise acutely felt.[133] It becomes difficult to determine whether such an identification with the sublime means a self-expansion or self-cancellation in, say, "Morning Snow": "A universe all of silver! / My whole being is ready to melt into light and flow forth!"[134] Or: "The hands [of countless pine trees] tremble in awe against the sky, / Every fiber of my nerves trembles in awe within me."[135] In fact, this paradox is not a dilemma to be resolved but represents the essential feature of romantic apostrophic politics. James Chandler's reading of "Ode" as his final case study of "Romantic historicism" is pertinent in this regard. Carrying further Wasserman's attention to the "lyre" in both Shelley's "Ode" and *Defence*, Chandler comes to the conclusion that "it is precisely at the moment in the text when writers seem to be reduced to the status of objective instrumentality in the service of higher laws and powers that they are suddenly given the status of subjects, agents, and lawmakers."[136] Subjectivity and instrumentality are fused into a lyrical dialectic. Guo translates "lyre" as *yaoqin* 瑤琴, referring to the ancient Chinese heptachord decorated with jades. When Shelley aspires to become the west wind's lyre, Guo becomes a Chinese instrument that transmutes the "Ode" into a highly unstable poetic language: the poem is by and large rendered into vernacular Chinese, yet the ending question again carries a classical flavor: 陽春寧尚迢遙? [Will the spring full of sunshine be far away?][137] He empowers and instrumentalizes the translator's role in the cycle of lingual/formal mutability.

Echoing Shelley's "Ode," Guo's lyricism calls into being an active experience of passive determination. His turn to revolutionary politics in

132. Bloom, *Shelley's Mythmaking*, 84.
133. See Wang Furen, "Shenmei zhuiqiu de maoluan yu shicuo," 153–58.
134. Guo, "Xue zhao," in *N*, 121; *SPG*, 33.
135. Guo, "Ye bu shili songlin," in *N*, 141; *SPG*, 38.
136. Chandler, *England in 1819*, 544.
137. Guo, trans., "Xifeng song," 23.

the mid-1920s must be understood in this lyrical dialectic of activism and determinism. Here I hope to touch on two conceptions that Guo offered on the relationship between revolution and literature. Let me return to his definition of "revolutionary literature" that came in the form of a "mathematic equation" in a 1926 article titled "Revolution and Literature" ("Geming yu wenxue" 革命與文學): "Revolutionary literature = Function (Zeitgeist). Or simply: literature = Function (revolution)."[138] I argued in the introduction that this formula reproduces a pantheist dialectic between the historically mutable manifestations and the unitary revolutionary spirit. The term *shidai jingshen*, more specifically, resonates with the discourse in Shelley's *Defence*: "[Poets] measure the circumference and sound the depths of human nature with a comprehensive and all-penetrating spirit, and they are themselves perhaps the most sincerely astonished at its manifestations; for it is less their spirit than the spirit of the age."[139] Guo pushes to the extreme Shelley's message. Revolution is now the pantheist-monist "wind," the universal power or cause. Since every age is revolutionary, all true literature is likewise revolutionary literature.

Chandler reads "Ode" as the dramatization of Shelley's idea of "the spirit of the age." He argues that Shelley is a Spinozist rather than a Platonist. On the one hand, "the spirit of age is understood to animate the poet's work," or "the power that moves the writer irrespective of his will or system is directly identified as 'the spirit of the age.'"[140] But on the other hand, Shelley's theory of "the spirit of age" also indicates that the poet is someone who "aims to represent in words and figures the power that moves him, but who understands . . . that he cannot finally understand the power he represents."[141] In Shelley's words: "Poets are the hierophants of an unapprehended inspiration, the mirrors of the gigantic shadows which futurity casts upon the present, the words which express what they understand not, the trumpets which sing to battle, and feel not what they inspire: the influence which is moved not, but moves."[142] Chandler then contends that the "spirit of the age" designates "the very

138. Guo, "Geming yu wenxue," in *GQJ/W*, 16:39.
139. Shelley, *Shelley's Poetry and Prose*, 535.
140. Chandler, *England in 1819*, 544, 548–49.
141. Ibid., 548.
142. Shelley, *Shelley's Poetry and Prose*, 535.

kind of *historical determination* that Shelley claims a poet must *not* be able to recognize."[143] In other words, history is an absent cause beyond comprehension or representation, but it produces poetical traces in the poet's subjectivity as a vehicle or instrument. Chandler characterizes this "Romantic historicism" as "history's lyre."[144]

The lyrical politics in Guo's early work can also be characterized as inventing new subjective ways of experiencing the invisible spirit of the age. Two years after his formulation of "revolutionary literature," Guo provided the metaphor of the "gramophone" (*liushengji* 留聲機) in 1928. Proposing a slogan—"be a gramophone"—Guo gave a to-do list for young revolutionary writers in the wake of the National Revolution of 1925–27:

> Be a gramophone—this should be the best mantra for literary youth.
> Do you think this is too easy? Here are some conditions:
> First, you must draw yourself closer to that voice,
> Second, you should be ego-less,
> Third, you should be active.[145]

This view of literature appears to be a significant departure from Guo's early romantic celebration of selfhood. But the metaphor of the gramophone actually was a further modernized/mechanized version of the figure of the lyre in the age of party politics. As Cheng Kai's recent book has demonstrated, most May Fourth writers, including Guo, had used the metaphor of the gramophone in a negative sense of mechanical reproduction.[146] But when the CCP started to search its revolutionary path after the failure of its first coalition with the GMD in 1927, Guo turned this metaphor into a positive use. For him, "the revolution found its own voice. . . . At the moment of one's identification with the proletarian revolution, the gramophone was no longer a negative image, because the revolutionist . . . only needed to transmit that voice."[147]

143. Chandler, *England in 1819*, 532; emphasis added.
144. Ibid., chapter 10.
145. Guo, "Yingxiong shu," in *GQJ/W*, 16:46.
146. See Cheng Kai, *Geming de zhangli*, 237–43.
147. Ibid., 243.

The assertion of ego is replaced by a leftist act of self-erasure. In this regard, Kirk Denton discusses the general difficulty involved in modern Chinese writers' acceptance of Western romantic conception of absolute ego, due to a legacy of an "organic cosmology."[148] Guo's proposal for self-negation also reminds us of the repression of self in the "sublime figure" in modern Chinese aesthetic and politics, as is analyzed by Ban Wang.[149] That "a poet should function like a phonograph broadcasting the mandate of revolution," as David Wang points out, is the thesis of leftist political lyricism.[150] I seek the deeper dynamic of this image of revolution's gramophone from the perspective of "Romantic historicism" and hope to reach a more dialectical understanding of the revolutionary-romantic ego. Within the lyrical logic of self-instrumentalization, becoming an "active" organ of the revolutionary consciousness is self-empowerment and self-cancellation at one and the same time. Whereas for Shelley the spirit of the age is the invisible "wind" or "absent cause" of history, for Guo the revolutionary "voice" is identifiable as a historical power present in the communist revolution. In contrast to Shelleyan historicism, Guo's ideology of Zeitgeist prioritizes the representability and translatability of a historical momentum, and entails a Faustian step of constantly identifying oneself with that momentum, as we will see more clearly in following chapters.

Here I have tried to argue that an apostrophic and invocative mode not only defined the interfusion of lyrical writing and translation in the early Guo, it also shaped a lyrical politics. I have also indicated that with the mechanism of identification, internalization, expansion, empowerment, and transformation, the lyrical subjectivity prefigured the making of a political subjectivity. These apostrophic instances call on the "now" as a moment of historical participation/determination. In this sense, an original contact between the lyrical and the political in revolutionary China lies in the very act of imagining, experiencing, and translating the historical "wind" as an open-ended determinism.

Guo's early career therefore evokes the controversial question about the revolutionary-romantic subjectivity and political lyricism. Through-

148. Denton, *The Problematic of Self in Modern Chinese Literature*, 105.

149. Ban Wang, *The Sublime Figure of History*, 1.

150. David Wang, *The Lyrical in Epic Time*, 77.

out the rest of this book, I come back to this issue time and again and continue to contend that the logic of translatability/mutability enables a dynamic of cultural imagination and political intervention. In the following chapters I also touch on other domains of Guo's early work as origins of his later developments. Yet the urgent task of the next chapter is to follow Guo's visionary tour to an actual revolutionary caesura.

CHAPTER 2

Translingual Practice and a "Caesura of the Revolution"

"Leafing through [the first issue of] *Cultural Critique*, I composed a poem before going to bed."[1] Thus Guo Moruo started his diary entry for January 16, 1928. Titled "To Seize" ("Zhanqu" 战取), the political lyric in his diary book was the last poem he composed while hiding in Shanghai in late 1927 and early 1928. Written on a date of no apparent significance, it attests to a reversal of Guo's fate, a moment of crisis in China's long revolution, and a turning point in modern Chinese literature.

The poem starts with a characterization of the "current situation": on one hand, it is "depressing" and "chaotic," and on the other hand, it is the "eve" of a storm of revolutionary blood.[2] What was the historical conjuncture that Guo tried to address? It is noteworthy that the inaugural issue of *Cultural Critique* (*Wenhua pipan* 文化批判), the Creation Society's new journal, which seems to have triggered the composition of this poem, contained a newly coined Chinese term for Marxist enlightenment: *aofuhebian* 奥伏赫變. This bizarre term was a transliteration of the Hegelian-Marxian concept *Aufheben*. Highlighting the philosophical and even political untranslatability of this German word, the younger Creationists' transliteration dramatized a self-justification of the group's turn to the radical left. Moreover, the poem "To Seize" was to be included as the concluding piece of *Huifu* 恢復, Guo's fifth book of poetry. He later

1. Guo, "Li Hu zhiqian," in *GQJ/W*, 13:275.
2. Ibid.

gave this book of poetry an English title: *Reconvalescence* (an idiosyncratic word for convalescence; he probably got it from the German word *Rekonvaleszenz*). In what sense was his poetic eruption a convalescence in the wake of a revolutionary crisis? Most interestingly, at the closing of this final poem in *Huifu*/*Reconvalescence*, the poet cautioned against the "wine from the Rhineland" (*laizi laiyin de putao* 來自萊茵的葡萄) as the fake revolutionary blood.[3] In Guo's seemingly straightforward outcry for the revolutionary storm, this foreign image stands out as an obscure reference that begs further interpretation. What did the Rhine wine mean—allegorically—at that moment of a personal, poetic, and political convalescence?

Revolving around the precarious fate of Guo and the Creation Society in late 1927 and early 1928, this chapter revisits that brief period as a critical moment in the making of China's revolutionary literature and culture. With a symptomatic reading of the various forms of discursive production—such as theoretical debate, poetic writing, and literary translation—that were condensed in that moment, I draw particular attention to a translingual dimension of the displacement of the frustrated revolutionary desire. In particular, I single out three translingual instances of "revolutionary literature": the Creation Society's scandalous transliteration of *Aufheben* into *aofuhebian*, Guo's lyrical practice under the idiosyncratic title "Reconvalescence" intended as a rehabilitation of the traumatized political unconscious, and a long neglected intertextual image of Rhine wine (*Rheinwein*/*laiyin de putao*) circulated from Guo's *Faust* translation into the political-lyrical rhetoric.

A scrutiny of these translingual figures will provide a new narrative about how the initial configuration of revolutionary literature was shaped by the experience of a revolutionary crisis and caesura. It is such a translingual rhetoric that codified an ambivalent dynamic of revolutionary imagination that was shared and contested by literary practice, theoretical warfare, and even party politics. The three seemingly marginal translingual fragments thus constitute, as I argue, a "dialectical image," which captures a standstill of both revolution and rhetoric.[4] With the rediscovery of these translingual symptoms, the making of China's revolutionary

3. Ibid.
4. I borrow this term from Walter Benjamin; see below.

literature can come to relief and be restored as an "occasion" (*jiyuan* 機緣) and a "caesura" (*duncuo* 頓挫)—both in Guo's words—that is, a dialectical standstill of new cultural-political possibilities and impossibilities.

"Tragedy," "Occasion," and "Caesura"

On April 2, 1927, the right-wing faction of the GMD held an emergency meeting in Shanghai. Usurping the title of GMD Central Supervision Committee, the participants of this meeting passed a resolution that required the arrest of 197 revolutionary politicians. Guo Moruo's name was listed in the same company as Mikhail Borodin (1884–1951, the leading aide sent by Moscow in support of the GMD-CCP coalition), Chen Duxiu 陳獨秀 (1879–1942, the communist leader who later became a Trotskyite), Mao Zedong, and Zhou Enlai.[5] The first "wanted warrant" that included Guo as a political criminal, this document was a glaring indicator of the widening fissure of the GMD-CCP united front, which had been the political basis for the 1925–27 National Revolution (*Guomin da geming* 國民大革命). "The tragedy of the revolution, in all probability, is about to happen."[6] This sense of foreboding, shared by Guo and many others, was soon confirmed as a reality. At that time, Guo was the vice director of the Political Department of the National Revolutionary Army, a key organ of propaganda and activism in the GMD-CCP joint effort of the Northern Expedition (see fig. 4). Only recently, GMD military leader Jiang Jieshi had tried to lure Guo to his side by appointing him the director of the Political Department of the Commander-in-Chief's Camp. Having escaped from Jiang's camp, Guo immediately finished a pamphlet titled "Look at Today's Jiang Jieshi" ("Qing kan jinri zhi Jiang Jieshi" 請看今日之蔣介石), which exposed his former political boss's anticommunist stance and warned of the looming possibility of a military coup. Ten days after the demand of the arrest of leftist activists had been issued, Jiang openly severed the coalition with the CCP and orchestrated

5. Guo, *Guo Moruo yi wen ji*, 2:401.
6. Guo, "Tuoli Jiang Jieshi yihou," in *GQJ/W* 12:174.

FIGURE 4 Guo Moruo (front row, second from left) as a commissar of the National Revolutionary Army during the Northern Expedition, 1927. Courtesy of Guo Pingying.

a massacre of the communists and workers in Shanghai, later known as the April Twelfth Purge. What followed was the GMD's nationwide anticommunist campaign.

On May 7, the GMD Central Executive Committee forwarded a report prepared by Jiang's secretariat to the National Government that Jiang had newly established in Nanjing. The report requested a manhunt for Guo: "We received and ratified a report by the GMD Committee of the General Headquarters: Guo Moruo ingratiated himself with the CCP, and became a self-willed traitor. So please purge him of the GMD membership and have him wanted and arrested. . . . Please act accordingly as soon as possible."[7] Hu Hanmin 胡漢民 (1879–1936), who had been warmly welcomed in Moscow only one year earlier and now was the head of this new government, wrote the following instruction on this document:

7. Di'er lishi dang'an guan, ed., *Minguo shiliao dang'an huibian*, 5 *ji*, 3 *bian*, *wenhua* 1 *juan*, 401.

"Proceed accordingly."[8] Three days later, the arrest warrant, bearing Jiang's signature, was circulated to every army corps and every province.

While the "white terror" was falling on the land of China, Guo reached his own political resolution. He went to Nanchang to take part in the Nanchang Uprising that Zhou Enlai was organizing to counter the GMD's betrayal of the revolutionary cause. Then on the way of retreat, he decided to join the CCP—when a CCP membership meant the risk of life. At that time, Lu Xun, a veteran May Fourth writer who would later become the spiritual leader of the leftist literary movement, observed from a critical distance the chaotic development of "revolution, counter-revolution, re-revolution."[9] Shen Yanbing 沈雁冰 (1896–1981), a CCP member who would soon emerge as a major leftist novelist under the pen name Mao Dun 茅盾, decided not to participate in the uprising. The uprising was defeated; Guo and his comrades were on the run. With the assistance of some communists in the countryside of Guangdong, he managed to flee to Hong Kong and then to Shanghai by sea. Upon his arrival in Shanghai in early November, he went into hiding and started a secret life with his family in an apartment on Darroch Road, which was located in the International Concession of the semi-colonial metropolis. In December, he fell severely ill and was hospitalized for ship fever. With the revolution at its low ebb, his body finally collapsed.

Guo's experience in 1927—"one of the most important years in modern Chinese history"—was an integral part of the "tragedy" of the 1925–27 National Revolution.[10] Led by the first coalition of the GMD and CCP, it was the first armed revolution in the non-European world in which a communist party played a vanguard role. Its climactic "tragedy" in 1927 has long been considered a political baptism for every social class of modern China.[11] The initial success of the Northern Expedition went hand in hand with the radicalization of the peasants, the proletariat, and even the petit bourgeoisie. It seemed that eventually a united, independent bourgeois republic was on the horizon for China. But meanwhile, not only the imperialist powers but also the Chinese bourgeoisie felt

8. Ibid., 402.
9. Lu Xun, "Xiao zagan," 556.
10. Wong, *Politics and Literature in Shanghai*, 5.
11. See Isaacs, *The Tragedy of the Chinese Revolution*.

threatened by the proletariat's activism in the urban regions and the peasants' movements in the countryside. The ensuing collapse of the united front dealt an unexpected blow to the revolution-minded youth across the country. In less than a year, they witnessed the military victory of the united front, Jiang's betrayal of the revolutionary cause, and the nationwide massacre of communists. Guo was lucky enough to have survived the campaign of terror.[12]

It is also clear that Guo was at the center of the vortex of revolutionary party politics. The National Revolution catapulted this May Fourth poet into the status of a revolutionary politician. Though a lot of attention has been paid to the leftist turn of Guo's intellectual outlook in the mid-1920s, I want to put more emphasis on the transformation of his social existence, which is indicative of a tectonic reconfiguration of the New Culture as a social space. The New Culture movement has long been seen as a preparation for the political movements that led to the National Revolution. From a perspective of social mobility, it is evident that since the anti-imperialist May Thirtieth Movement in 1925, a great number of the literary youths—the very products of the May Fourth culture—joined the current of revolution and became the political youths, providing important human resources for the first GMD-CCP coalition. Guo's sudden rise as a political activist encapsulated this social change, which can be characterized as a "revolutionization" of the May Fourth literary community.[13]

More interestingly, insofar as Guo's case is concerned, there seems to have been a revolving door between the domain of literature and that of revolutionary politics. While Guo engaged himself in a political effort to resist Jiang's anticommunism, a series of his literary works and translations were published in Shanghai. One day after he wrote "Look at Today's Jiang Jieshi"—a pamphlet that the GMD later denounced as "a crazy calumny launched by an evil traitor"—Guo's collection of love poems, *The Vase* (*Ping* 瓶), was published by the Creation Society.[14] On the same day, amid growing fear of a coup, Guo drafted an announcement to his

12. For an estimate of "how many persons were massacred during the purges," see Eastman, *The Abortive Revolution*, 7–9.

13. See Cheng Kai, *Geming de zhangli*, especially chapters 1, 2, and 6.

14. Di'er lishi dang'an guan, ed., *Minguo shiliao dang'an huibian*, 5 *ji*, 3 *bian*, 1 *juan*, 401.

armed comrades on the front to win over to the revolution's side as many as possible military troops. When he was trying to escape from the GMD's suppression in Guangdong, Guo resumed fictional writing in October. His translation of a set of German poems—in collaboration with another Creationist, Cheng Fangwu—came out in print around the same time.[15] Predicting the tragic ending of the revolution, Guo had reflected on his double-sided social existence: "The tragedy of the Revolution is . . . about to take place. . . . This outcome may become an occasion (*jiyuan* 機緣) that will turn me into a litterateur (*wenxue jia* 文學家) for the rest of my life, but I will fight to the last drop. The career as a revolutionary can be dismissed, but the revolutionary spirit will never be."[16] Guo's case testified to an emerging social space in which the revolutionary spirit oscillated between literature and politics. Immediately following his narrow escape, this political provocateur picked up his translation of *Faust I* in Shanghai. My revisiting of this historical moment starts with this imbrication of culture and politics: Guo's case can help us perceive of the tragedy of the National Revolution not only as a political crisis but also a cultural "occasion."

Just as the remaining CCP-controlled military force had to retreat deep into the countryside, so did a great number of revolutionary youths, now disenfranchised, retreat into the semi-colonial metropolis Shanghai, the center of print media where they could make a living without giving up the "revolutionary spirit." With a generational experience of "disillusionment," "oscillation," and "search," their political coming of age suddenly turned into a traumatic event.[17] Their reactions to this dramatic change, ranging from fatalist self-abandon to hysterical putschism and melancholic depression, were symptomatically channeled into the space of literary, cultural, and ideological productions. Since late 1927, what was later known as the "revolutionary literature debate" took a feverish turn, which "signified a tip in the direction of mainstream Chinese letters to

15. In late 1927, Guo's name also appeared in a lot of political gossips produced by newspaper media: one paper even reported that he was already executed. See Gong Jimin and Fang Rennian, *Guo Moruo zhuan*, 118, 138.

16. Guo, "Tuoli Jiang Jieshi yihou," in *GQJ/W*, 13:174.

17. *Huanmie* (disillusionment), *Dongyao* (oscillation), and *Zhuiqiu* (search) are the three titles in Mao Dun's famous novella trilogy about the Chinese youth in the age of the National Revolution. See *Mao Dun quanji*, vol. 1.

the left."[18] The "social character and social history controversy" (*shehui xingzhi he shehui shi lunzheng* 社會性質和社會史論爭) started to germinate as well. Therefore, Leo O. Lee notes: "when the leftist writers began to clamor for revolutionary literature, revolution was at its lowest ebb."[19] Arif Dirlik echoes such an observation in his study of Marxist historiography in China. He mentions that "between 1925 and 1927, in fact, most of the future Marxist historians joined the revolutionary movement in some capacity or other"; then he adds: "Ironically, in the years when the fortunes of communism in China were at their lowest ebb, Marxism emerged as the most dynamic current in Chinese social thought."[20]

The symptom of this transfer of the political to the cultural domain was vividly captured in Lu Xun's poignantly satirical entry into the "revolutionary literature debate." In an essay titled "Befuddled Woolliness" ("Zuiyan zhong de menglong" 醉眼中的朦朧), he wrote of the new year of 1928:

> This year—by the old calendar as well as by the new—seems to be having a strangely stimulating effect on Shanghai writers, for both lunar and solar new year have seen a spate of new periodicals, which have lavished all the attentions on big impressive topics not caring how deadly dull the contents are. Even magazines more than one year old are thrashing about in desperation and undergoing sudden metamorphoses. Some of the writers are new, but many of them are old acquaintances, though a number seem like strangers because they have written nothing for a year or so. What were they doing all that time, and why have they taken up their pens again simultaneously? Well, that is a long story. Suffice it to say they did not have to write then, but now they have to.[21]

The beginning of 1928 witnessed the explosion of literary polemics and the proliferation of leftist theories. Lu Xun's sharp comments touched on the actual dynamic hidden behind the proposed teleological transition "from literary revolutionary to revolutionary literature."[22] When the

18. Laughlin, *Chinese Reportage*, 9.
19. Lee, *The Romantic Generation of Modern Chinese Writers*, 253.
20. Dirlik, *Revolution and History*, 48, 20.
21. Lu Xun, "Befuddled Woolliness," 11.
22. Cheng Fangwu, "Cong wenxue geming dao geming wenxue," 130–37.

direct political participation was all but impossible, the frustrated collective revolutionary desire had to figure itself as a discursive or theoretical hysteria.[23]

Among that "spate of new periodicals" was *Cultural Critique*, a journal the Creation Society founded in January 1928. The appearance of this journal represented the society's turn to Marxist theories. It is also with this journal that the later Creationists brought to the debate a dimension of theoretical warfare or *Kampf* (a German word the later Creationists preferred) and escalated an ultra-leftist criticism of such veteran writers as Lu Xun. What did the new year of 1928 mean for Guo, the spiritual leader of the Creation Society, whose fate hung in the balance precisely because he had leapt from literature to revolution? In an interview in 1959, Guo tried to retrospectively downplay the "contradictions" or antagonisms between the Creationists and Lu Xun during the debate, and he simply explained away that chaotic moment with a vague reference to leftist infantilism.[24] But his autobiography leaves us a record of his diary entries from January 15 to February 23, 1928. During his convalescence, Guo was preoccupied with the issue of revolutionary literature and tried to keep pace with his new followers' theoretical turn. On January 15, he finished a new book of poetry and gave it a bilingual title: *Huifu/Reconvalescence.* On February 1, his translation of *Faust I* eventually saw the light of the day. On February 10, a comrade named "Wu Hao" 伍豪 (Zhou Enlai's pseudonym as an underground party leader), for whom Guo had been anxiously waiting, finally visited Guo's apartment. Reportedly Zhou approved Guo's plan to go into exile in Japan. On February 24, Guo embarked for Japan, also under an alias. This was a new year about the entanglement of culture and politics. He Ganzhi 何干之 (1906–69), the first compiler of the "social character and social history controversy," saw the emergence of Marxist theory in 1928 as a result of the "standstill" (*tingdun* 停頓) of the revolution.[25] Later, Guo used the following phrase to describe that moment: "a caesura [*duncuo* 頓挫] of the revolution."[26]

23. Also see Wong, *Politics and Literature in Shanghai.*
24. Guo, "Guo Moruo tongzhi da qingnian wen," in *GZL*, 346.
25. He Ganzhi, *Zhongguo shehui xingzhi wenti lunzheng*, 1.
26. Guo, "Guo Moruo shizuo tan," in *GZL*, 215.

Aufheben/Aofuhebian*: Transliteration and the Creation Society's Turn to Theory*

Even though—or precisely because—the political battle was lost, the revolutionary periodicals and pamphlets mushroomed in Shanghai at the beginning of 1928, carrying out a bombardment of new discourses of Marxism-Leninism and social theories. Among them, *Cultural Critique* pioneered a turn from literature to theory, fueled a series of debates throughout the year, and annoyed Lu Xun and some other veteran May Fourth writers. For many outsiders, the Creation Society's transformation from a *l'art pour l'art* group into a Marxist study group seemed to take place almost overnight.

The Creation Society's ten-year history is commonly divided into two phases, with the National Revolution as a watershed. In the early 1920s, the Creationists positioned themselves as the young outsiders of the literary establishment and the true guardians of the temple of art.[27] Guo's romantic-pantheistic poetry and translations, Yu Dafu's 郁達夫 (1896–1945) naturalist-sentimentalist fiction, and Cheng Fangwu's provocative criticism were all trademarks of the early Creation Society. Since the May Thirtieth Incident in 1925, some Creationists started to call for revolutionary literature and later participated in the National Revolution, during which, in Lu Xun's words, they "did not have to write." In the wake of the GMD's "white terror," the Creation Society initially planned to form a united front with Lu Xun. On December 3, 1927, an advertisement was published, announcing that the new *Creation Weekly* would be in print on New Year's Day 1928 with such contributors as Lu Xun, Guo Moruo (under the pseudonym of Maike Ang 麥克昂, literally meaning "Maker I"), and Jiang Guangci 蔣光慈 (1901–31; the rising "revolution plus love" writer and a CCP member).[28] Unfortunately, this plan never materialized. In October, Cheng Fangwu went to Japan and met with some overseas Chinese students who were involved in a study group of the works of Marx, Engels, and Lenin. Such young radicals as Feng Naichao, Peng Kang 彭康 (1901–68), and Li Chuli 李初梨 (1900–1994) came back to

27. See Tang with Hockx, "The Creation Society."
28. See Rao Hongjing et al., ed., *Chuangzao she ziliao*, 1139.

China and became the new face of the Creation Society. These later Creationists argued for the urgent need of theory at this moment of crisis, seeing the intellectual struggle as indispensable to both the revolutionary movement and the intelligentsia's self-transformation. While enjoying a communal life at the Creation Publishing House and starting to seek contact with the CCP, they persuaded the collective to abandon the initial plan and instead created a theoretical journal. Guo eventually conceded this turn to theory.[29]

Congratulating the inaugural issue of *Cultural Critique*, Cheng Fangwu declared that "this is a great enlightenment": "*Cultural Critique* will provide the revolutionary theory as a whole, and bring illuminations to every front of the revolution."[30] This Marxist enlightenment was meant to overcome the May Fourth enlightenment, now seen as an outmoded bourgeois project. In "Art and Social Life" ("Yishu yu shehui" 藝術與社會), the first article of the inaugural issue, Feng Naichao commented on five May Fourth veteran writers, including Lu Xun and Guo, characterizing all of them as being limited by the "class nature of petit bourgeoisie."[31] This journal therefore presented the later Creationists as vanguard theoretical warriors. What they brought to the ongoing revolutionary crisis was nothing less than a discursive putsch. The first issue of *Cultural Critique*, in my view, was the most theoretically provocative and rigorous among the five issues of this short-lived periodical. It includes—in addition to "Art and Social Life"—such titles as "What Is the Task of Philosophy?" ("Zhexue di renwu shi shenme" 哲學底任務是什麼), "Scientific View of Society" ("Kexue de shehui guan" 科學的社會觀), "Critique of Religion" ("Zongjiao pipan" 宗教批判), and "Theory and Practice" ("Lilun yu shijian" 理論與實踐). Constituting a well-orchestrated display of theoretical novelty and a well-rounded critique of social thought, these essays appropriate a philosophical terminology ranging from Hegelian idealism to Marxism-Leninism. At least on a stylistic level, the later Creationists tend to resort to German terms and concepts without translating them, and they interject into their articles long German quotations

29. For a detailed account of the Creation Society's turn to leftism and theory, see Zhiguang Yin, *Politics of Art*, chapters 4 and 5.

30. Cheng Fangwu, "Zhuci," 1.

31. Feng Naichao, "Yishu yu shehui," 6.

from Marx, Engels, and other revolutionary thinkers. Their gesture of assuming a vantage point of class consciousness is based on the fetishistic emphasis on Marxist theory as such. The journal referred to Lenin's famous line: "There is no revolutionary action without revolutionary theory."[32] The major impact *Cultural Critique* produced was on the dimension of its theoretical language.

This explosive impact propelled Lu Xun to disapprovingly point out, as we have seen, that some journals "lavished all the attentions on big impressive topics, not caring how deadly dull the contents are." If the early Creation Society was infamous for its excessive sentimentalism, then the late Creation Society was infamous for churning out a flurry of slogans for its newly attained class consciousness. Lu Xun, who had once been attacked by the Creationists for being too realistic in fictional writing and was now labeled by the same group as a leftover of the bourgeois literature, gave a quite negative characterization of the group in 1930. Although the society had by then been banned by their common enemy, the GMD regime, he still denigrated the typical Creationist as a "scholar-*cum*-hooligan."[33] The indication of Lu Xun's words is clear: on the Shanghai scene of print culture, the Creationists were an aimless intellectual labor force whose incantation of "revolutionary literature" was yet another effort to seize discursive symbolic capital. Qu Qiubai 瞿秋白 (1899–1935), an important leftist intellectual and CCP leader who was a friend of Lu Xun and Guo, echoed Lu Xun's comments in his own criticism of Guo and other like-minded supporters of revolutionary literature as a band of Chinese "Bohemians" (transliterated by Qu as *bohaimin* 薄海民). Those Chinese intellectual Bohemians were cut off from the traditional society, yet also alienated from the socioeconomic reality in semi-colonial and semi-feudal China. Repressed in their cultural and political life, they leaned toward revolution by nature; meanwhile, their revolutionary fervor was unreliable and disconnected from the masses. Qu's account of "wandering petit-bourgeois intellectual youth" can be used as a diagnosis of the collective ethos of the Creation Society (even though Qu, executed by the GMD in 1935, did not live long enough to see that most

32. Cheng Fangwu, "Zhuci," 1.
33. Lu Xun, "A Glance at Shanghai Literature," 132.

Creationists later did become reliable CCP cadres).[34] In 1928, most pro-revolution writers found the Creationists' Marxist turn suspicious and questionable. Mao Dun, for example, stated: "The Creation Society's manifesto about their change of attitude does not include any confession about their past, but continues to show off a pioneering, omniscient gesture, at which anyone who is not forgetful cannot help laughing."[35]

But in this chapter I propose to understand the late Creation Society via its own theoretical language. The Creationists proclaimed time and again that the group's transformation was not an opportunistic turn but an *Aufhebung*, based on the Hegelian-Marxian dialectic. As Zhiguang Yin points out, their attempt to "legitimize the class transition of intellectuals" rests on the "key concept" of "Aufheben."[36] Most remarkably, this self-understanding involves a moment of transliteration. In the first issue of *Cultural Critique*, Peng Kang's article, "The Task of Philosophy," reads more like a commentary on—or even paraphrase translation of—Marx's "Introduction to a Critique of Hegel's Philosophy of Right" (but no reference to this title is to be found). Peng's essay stresses that critique is also a weapon. The model for critique should derive from the Hegelian-Marxian conception of *Aufhebung*. Peng did not bother to translate either *Aufhebung* or *Aufheben*; instead he chose to use a transliterated word: *aofuhebian* 奥伏赫变. Functioning as a catchword of the later Creation Society's discourse, this transliteration marked the emergence of critical theory as a space of political praxis.

The editing collective was extremely self-aware of their theoretical language. In the "Editors' Notes," they admitted that their first issue might cause difficulties of comprehension for readers. So they set up a special section in the journal called "New Lexicon" ("Xin ciyuan" 新辞源). In the first issue's "New Lexicon," nine terms were introduced and explained, with Chinese equivalents side by side the German or English originals: dialectic, dialectical materialism, materialist dialectics, *Aufheben*, bourgeoisie, the bourgeois, proletariat, the proletarian, and finally *Ideologie*. The Creation Society published five issues *of Cultural Critique*

34. Qu Qiubai, "Lu Xun zagan xuan ji xuyan," 113.
35. Mao Dun, "Du 'Ni Huanzhi,'" 854.
36. Zhiguang Yin, *Politics of Art*, 163.

in total, and introduced more than fifty "new" Marxist terms.[37] Apart from *Aufhebung/aofuhebian*, bourgeoisie, proletariat, and ideology were also rendered into Chinese by way of transliteration. Creating a flood of theoretical neologisms, the Creationists' preference for transliteration pointed to a peculiar translingual mode of their political transformation.

The entry of *aofuhebian* (see fig. 5) states that "*aofuhebian* is the transliteration of the German word *Aufheben*," and explains that it is difficult to find a consistent Chinese equivalent of this term "characteristic of Hegelian philosophy."[38] *Aufheben/Aufhebung* is a prime example of philosophical "fetishes of the untranslatable."[39] The fetishistic status of the term *Aufheben* can be traced to Hegel's account—"it is certainly remarkable to find that a language has come to use one and the same word for two opposite meanings. . . . The German language has a number of such [words]."[40] *Aufheben* "constitute[s] one of the most important notions in philosophy" precisely due to its "double meaning": this German verb means "to preserve," "to maintain," but also "to cause to cease" and "to put an end to."[41] The Creationists rightly noted in their entry of *aofuhebian* that this word signifies a "dialectical process."[42] The negative "annihilation" of certain aspects of a contradiction, on one hand, and the positive "preservation" and "development" of rational aspects, on the other, merge into a "process that can be called as *aofuhebian*."[43] In addition, these young Chinese Marxists emphasized that this process does not merely concern speculative thinking but actually originates from the "necessary development" of the objective world.[44] Later on, Cheng Fangwu also seized on the newly coined word *aofuhebian* in another manifesto-like statement: "With the efforts of critique we will *aofuhebian* the old ideology and the old forms of expression—we carry out a

37. For a complete list of the terms introduced in the "New Lexicon" sections, see Zhiguang Yin, *Politics of Art*, 182–84.

38. "Aofuhebian," 100.

39. Büttgen, "Aufheben," 71.

40. Ibid., 72.

41. Ibid., 72, 73.

42. "Aofuhebian," 100.

43. Ibid.

44. Ibid.

100　新　辭　源　第一期

向——分析與綜合——的研究之中，發見這對象的構成及運動法則的，就叫做唯物辯證法。總之，這個方法是在全體與部分及普遍與特殊的關係上去觀察事物，對於事物的運動方面，則採取歷史的考察方法，對於觀察特殊的個體，則顧慮這個體與環境的關係。

4.奧伏赫變

奧伏赫變為德文 *Aufheben* 的譯音，其意譯是抑揚，然亦有譯作棄揚或止揚的，頗不一致。牠本是黑格爾哲學的特有的用語，用以表示辯證法的進程的。就是一個思考必然地包含與牠相矛盾的思考，對於這二個相反的矛盾的思考，丟棄了矛盾的不合理的部分，表揚牠的合理的部分，形成一個較高級的綜合的思考，這個丟棄、蓄積及表揚的過程，就叫做奧伏赫變。不過在辯證法的唯物論上，所謂思考，當然不是絕對精神的發現，這是事物自身的必然的發展，由此發展，反映到人的頭腦，纔形成種種的思考。所以思考發生與牠自己相矛盾的思考時，就是物質自身的發展的發現，有了這個物質自身的矛盾發現，纔發生兩者的鬥爭而反映於人的思考上，使人們有不得不奧伏赫變二者間的矛盾而形成一個較高級的綜合思考了。

5.布爾喬亞汜

布爾喬亞汜是 *Bourgeoisie* 譯音，其意譯為資產者階級，換言之，就是近世的資本家階級，佔有社會的生產底手段，雇傭着勞銀勞動者的階級的簡稱。

FIGURE 5 The page containing the entry of *Aufheben* in *Cultural Critique*, no. 1 (1928).

revolution consciously."[45] The transliterated term *aofuhebian* was thus not simply a concept imported from Hegelianism but signified, in a self-referential way, the logic of the Creationists' practice of "total critique." For all its estrangement effects, the bombardment of German terms and quotations in *Cultural Critique* was fashioned as the very sign of the group's own *Aufhebung/aofuhebian*.

To better understand this discursive style and theoretical gesture, it is worth undertaking a detour through what is called "Fukumotoism" in the Japanese communist movement. Fukumoto Kazuo 福本 和夫 (1894–1983) was an important Marxist theorist and activist in 1920s Japan. After studying with Marxist philosopher Karl Korsch (1886–1961), he came back to Japan in 1924 and launched his theoretical war against the mainstream of Japan's Communist Party. As Li Huoren notes, "Fukumoto's way of expression is to cite Marx and Lenin excessively, and add some brief commentary of his own. These Marxist-Leninist works were not yet translated into Japanese, so their appearance in Fukumoto's writings came as a huge shock to Japanese leftist intellectuals."[46] When this "Fukumoto whirlwind" raised the theoretical issue of class consciousness during the mid-1920s, the late Creationists were all in Japan and submerged themselves in the reading of the theories of Fukumoto, Korsch, and Lukács. Most essays in the first issue of *Cultural Critique* were written under the Fukumotoist spell. Both such German quotations and their transliterations of Marxist theoretical terms indicate the Creationists' imitation of Fukomoto's cult of theoretical-political break. As Lawrence Wang-Chi Wong has pointed out, the Creationists' pursuit of the theoretical struggle "was taken from Fukumotoism."[47]

45. Cheng Fangwu, "Quanmian de pipan zhi biyao," 179.

46. Li Huoren, *Lukaqi dui zhongguo wenxue de yingxiang*, 28.

47. Wong, *Politics and Literature in Shanghai*, 19. It is also worth mentioning that Fukumoto's theoretical style turned into a political success: "Within two years and a month, Fukumoto, formerly an unknown contributor to [a communist journal], was elevated to the status as the leader of the Japanese Communist Party." Li Huoren, *Lukaqi dui zhongguo wenxue de yingxiang*, 28. The late Creationists had a different political trajectory, though. When the Creation Society was eventually banned by the Nationalist government, most of its members had already been recruited by the CCP Jiangsu Provincial Committee and later transformed themselves into reliable party cadres over the course of the long march of the revolution. But that is a story beyond the scope of my study.

Unsurprisingly, this Fukumotoist style exasperated some other writers concerned with the issue of "revolutionary literature." Lu Xun was very critical of the Creationists' incantation of dogmas and slogan-shouting of German concepts. In his essay "Befuddled Woolliness," he did not hesitate to poke fun at the transliteration of *Aufheben*: "This is the Creation school's phonetic translation for *Aufheben*, [which means] 'annihilate' [*chudiao* 除掉]. I do not know why they chose such a difficult phonetic version, which must be harder for one of [the proletarians] to write than the original."[48] Here, Lu Xun translated *Aufheben* into *chudiao* (annihilate). He meant to show how alienated these so-called revolutionary writers were from the proletariat in the first place. The Creationists' practice of transliteration was thus considered to be a testimony of their political inconsistency.

Lu Xun only put this brief translation criticism between parentheses. But this fleeting comment immediately solicited the Creation Society's counterattack. In the fourth issue of *Cultural Critique*, Peng Kang published "Annihilate Lu Xun's 'Annihilate' " ("Chudiao Lu Xun de chudiao" 除掉鲁迅的除掉). Thus, this untranslatable philosophical concept of *Aufheben* became a battleground between a veteran May Fourth writer and a young Marxist critic. Denouncing Lu Xun's understanding of *Aufheben* as "annihilate," Peng referred Lu Xun back to the Creationists' definition of *Aufheben* in the "New Lexicon" and provided further elucidation (again, his interpretation is dotted with German words). He argued that initially *Aufheben* was a Hegelian concept used to characterize the dialectical *Werden*/becoming of the Absolute Spirit. But Marxism developed this term, and as a result, *Aufhebung* of one's consciousness should be viewed as determined by historical contradictions. He justified their choice of the transliteration by stating that all the available Chinese translations were unable to deliver its condensed meaning for Marxism. Peng maintained that "*Aufheben* contains three meanings"—"to negate," "to preserve," and "to elevate."[49] A translation of the aspect of negativity in *Aufhebung*, such as Lu Xun's, missed the dimension of positivity in this concept and showed a lack of dialectical understanding. He not only

48. Lu Xun, "Befuddled Woolliness," 20 (translation modified); Lu Xun, "Zuiyan zhong de menglong," 64–65.

49. Peng Kang, "Chudiao Lu Xun de chudiao," 59.

doubted Lu Xun's German capabilities but also suggested that the misunderstanding was precisely an indicator of the imprisonment of Lu Xun in the undialectical bourgeois thinking. To translate *Aufheben* as "annihilate," in other words, would miss the core significance of this philosophical concept in historical practice. Peng went on to contend that what Chinese intellectuals and writers needed was nothing but an *Aufhebung* of their own class consciousness. "To *aufheben* his [own petit-bourgeois class nature] one has to consciously understand *Aufhebung/aofuhebian*."[50] He concluded: "the historical necessity and the conscious effort are one and the same process of actual social change, and are the process of *Aufhebung* itself."[51]

Now it becomes clear that Peng's criticism of Lu Xun's philosophical "mistake" was intended for a self-positioning of the Creation Society in a conjuncture of revolution and theory. Peng indicated that the development of the Chinese Revolution determined and demanded a conscious *Aufhebung*. The Creation Society's turn to theory was a process of superseding their own petit-bourgeois past, a process necessitated by the dialectical movement of history itself rather than a show of theoretical ebullience or complacency. Contrary to Lu Xun's observation of the society's leftist "metamorphosis," Peng posited his group at a vantage point of historical necessity and revolutionary consciousness.

The transliteration of *Aufheben* was then supposed to be part and parcel of the actual *Aufhebung* of history. Peng once again quoted—without mentioning the name—the famous line by the young Marx: "Criticism . . . is a weapon."[52] The battlefield of "ideology" (*yidewoluoji* 意德沃羅基), according to him, was an internal division of revolutionary practice, without which the Chinese Revolution could not advance any more. In the same issue, the section "New Lexicon" of *Cultural Critique* listed another German phrase: *Theoretischer Kampf* (theoretical struggle). Thus the Creation Society's embrace of a new theoretical language can be seen as a transliteration/transformation from a halted revolution into a discursive

50. Ibid., 60.

51. Ibid., 61.

52. Ibid., 62. The line is from Marx, "Towards a Critique of Hegel's *Philosophy of Right*: Introduction."

battle, that is, a socially symbolic act aimed at overcoming the tragic failure and reorienting the traumatized political unconscious.

Seen from this round of theoretical arguments, the term *aofuhebian* was interwoven deeply into the fabric of the cultural-political tensions at that conjuncture. Bringing four Chinese characters into an incomprehensible word accented with the German-ness of Hegelian philosophy, *aofuhebian* was a linguistic-fetishistic emblem of the Creation Society's historicity, that is, their dialectic at standstill. This polemic triggered by a transliteration was only a small ripple on the vast waves of the debates and discursive proliferations that raged in the Chinese literary community in 1928.[53] But this mode of transliteration was a symptom of the disorder and displacement of the whole lingual-philosophical-political signification system. Though the coinage of the German-sounding *aofuhebian* had only a fleeting valence, its transitory nature nevertheless captured the moment at which the leftist theoretical struggle emerged within modern Chinese literature. As Yin indicates, the making of a "battlefield of ideology" was key to the Creationists' positioning as writers of revolutionary literature "in the new era."[54] According to the analysis of Xiaobing Tang and Michel Hockx, "embedded in [the Creation Society's] notion of a 'transitional period' was a profound millenarianism that acknowledged an objective condition capable of defying the human will, but at the same time pointed to a moment of potentiality that demanded extraordinary subjective efforts."[55] Lu Xun called that historical moment "an age of fluctuations and change."[56] Peng saw it as a moment of inevitable *Aufhebung*. In one word, the symbolic *Aufhebung* of the signification system was a desperate search for the actual *Aufhebung* of history.

53. In his study of the Europeanized language in 1920s–1930s Chinese translations of Marxist theories, Lawrence Wang-Chi Wong briefly mentions the Creationists' practice of transliteration. See Wong, *Fanyi yu wenxue zhijian*, 226. His insightful discussion also covers the ensuing debates among leftist writers on the issue of translation and language in the 1930s, which are beyond the scope of my study here.

54. Zhiguang Yin, *Politics of Art*, 170.

55. Tang with Hockx, "The Creation Society," 128.

56. Lu Xun, "Befuddled Woolliness," 13.

The Convalescence of the Political Unconscious

In his apology for the Creation Society's transliteration of *Aufheben*, Peng mentioned in passing that "Maike Ang translated *Aufheben* as *tuibian* 蛻變 [molting or metamorphosis], but it cannot fully deliver the term's positive meaning either."[57] Maike Ang was Guo's pseudonym. It is likely that as a senior member of the group, Guo proposed this translation during their internal discussions. Peng, whom Guo praised as a "rising talented junior" (*hou qi zhi xiu* 後起之秀), refused Guo's translation of *Aufheben* as well as Lu Xun's.[58] This fact implies the delicate nature of Guo's relationship with the later Creationists. For the young radical theorists, the word *tuibian* must have been too metaphorical, showing the lack of conceptual labor on Guo's part. The difference between Guo and the latecomers surfaced more obviously in their disagreement about another metaphor I discussed in chapter 1: the "gramophone" of the revolutionary "voice." For Guo, that "voice" was a fixed one of the proletarian revolution and its vanguard organization, and as a result the revolutionary writer should simply identify that "voice" and instrumentalize him- or herself as a "gramophone." For the theory-minded later Creationists, the attainment of the proletarian consciousness had to be a dialectical process of intellectual struggle.[59]

In early 1928, Guo was in fact unable to be a gramophone of the revolution but had to experience his own *tuibian*. After escaping to Shanghai, he fell seriously ill and was hospitalized from December 12, 1927, to January 4, 1928. After returning to his home, he started a daily life similar to house arrest: politically, he was in hiding; physically, he was extremely weak, "unable to walk, and also deaf."[60] This made an occasion for his diary writing: "I have had no perseverance for diary writing

57. Peng Kang, "Chudiao Lu Xun de chudiao," 58.

58. Guo, "Li Hu zhiqian," in *GQJ/W*, 13:296.

59. For Li Chuli's resistance to the gramophone metaphor, see "Zenyang de jianshe geming wenxue," 17–20. Guo was concerned about any possible internal schism and tried to reconcile the two approaches. See Maike Ang (Guo Moruo), "Liushengji de huiyin." For a discussion of the Creation Society's internal disagreement in the context of the rise of revolutionary discourses, see Cheng Kai, *Geming de zhangli*, 224–67.

60. Guo, "Li Hu zhiqian," in *GQJ/W*, 13:272.

throughout my life, . . . and keeping a record of my everyday life for more than a single month like this was a rare thing to me."[61] Guo's diary from January 15 to February 23, which was later published as an autobiographical piece titled "Before Leaving Shanghai" ("Li Hu zhiqian" 離滬之前), gives us an intimate account of the physical, psychological, and social conditions of a revolutionary writer who was just thrown off from the epicenter of the political struggle.

I draw particular attention to the heterogeneity of both the content and form of this rare document. The symptoms of neurotic depression, the personal details of libidinal economy, the tensions in Guo's marriage, the internal schisms in the Creation Society, and the obscure references to party politics—all are exposed on a naturalistic textual surface. Seen from the diary, Guo was surrounded by secret party members, Trotskyists, and young activists—while his heart was sometimes torn apart between his family and an extramarital platonic (or comradely) lover. The diary chronicles his unhappy preparation for exile and the escalation of the debates on the strategy of the Chinese Revolution. He was pressed by the new members of the society to read Marxist theory, and he sometimes participated, in an absent-minded fashion, in the social science reading group held at the Creation Society's publishing house (whereas his Japanese wife complained that the communal life of the younger members consumed most of the income the society's publications had made). Guo declined an invitation to form another leftist party, and in the meanwhile, he regretted the missed opportunity to travel to Soviet Russia.

This diary book is not just a running account of personal life; it is also a writer's or translator's notebook, used for drafting of a series of poems, translations, and critical essays. Composed of a number of reading journals, the diary offers a reading list during the short period of Guo's recovery, featuring Marx's *Capital*, Engels's *Anti-Düring*, Gabrielle D'Annunzio's plays, Ernst Toller's expressionist works, Abram Deborin's study of Kant, some works of traditional and modern Japanese literature, and more. In addition, the diary book occasions Guo's practice of theoretical translation. The entry of January 17 consists solely of his excerpt translation of the famous "formula of the materialist con-

61. Ibid.

ception of history" in Marx's "Preface to *A Contribution to the Critique of Political Economy*." The passage about the conditions of "social revolution" was to have great relevance to the "social characterization and social history controversy," and shaped Guo's Marxist outlook of history (see chapter 4). Finally, the entry for February 18 includes his draft of a synopsis titled "A Review of My Life as a Writer." After sections such as "my poetic formation," "my poetic awakening," "my development into drama," the last section is devoted to "the transformation of thought." The textual hybridization of Guo's diary can be recognized as a pathological snapshot of the self-styled *aofuhebian*/*Aufhebung*, preserving a moment of individual, collective, and intellectual-political fluctuations.

"January 15, Sunday" is the first entry of this diary, and it starts with the following sentence: "Finished transcribing *Huifu*." *Huifu* was his latest volume of poetry, which he gave to Cheng Fangwu for publication on the same day. It was a collection of more than twenty poems he wrote during his recovery in early January 1928. In his 1933 preface to this diary, Guo emphasized the English title given to this book, *Reconvalescence*: "After I composed those more than twenty poems—they were written with a pencil on a notebook while I was lying in bed or sitting on a wicker chair—and put them together as [a book titled] *Reconvalescence*, I started to write my diary on the same notebook."[62] The notebook for both poetic writing and diary writing embodied a body politics of convalescence. In a 1936 interview, Guo described *Reconvalescence* as a by-product of "a caesura of the revolution." In 1947, Guo's autobiographical writing offered a retrospective self-portrait of a recovering poet:

> Surviving the severe illness, I nevertheless won the happiness of rebirth. . . . During my convalescence, the symptoms of insomnia occurred to me. . . . Poetic inspiration started to flow continuously. No, it was not flowing; it was more like being invaded from outside. I lay in my bed and put a notebook under my pillow; whenever under spell of poetic inspiration, I immediately recorded it with a pencil. That grew into the book *Reconvalescence*, which was published and then banned. I only experienced such constant invasions of inspiration three times in my whole life: the first was when

62. Ibid.

> I was composing *The Goddesses* during the May Fourth period, the second was when I was writing *The Vase*, and the third was when writing *Reconvalescence*.[63]

Just when the revolutionary cause seems to have abandoned him, the muse replaced it at Guo's bedside. It was indeed an inspired moment: all twenty-four poems were written in a short time span, from January 5 to January 16. Similar to what we have seen in Guo's remembrances of his writing of *The Goddesses*, Guo once again described his own experience of poetic inspiration in a pathological language. The very fact that his last occasion of being possessed by a poetic inspiration overlapped with the "caesura" of the revolution deserves our attention. This neurotic event, in other words, concerns the recovery of his body, the restoration of poetic writing, and eventually the convalescence of a traumatized revolutionary subjectivity. His translation of *huifu* into *reconvalesence* reinforces the metaphoric of revolutionary body politics. While commentators tend to assume the political plainness of this verse book, I want to seize upon the intensity of its poetic rhetoric: what corresponds to the "caesura" and "convalescence" of the body/revolution is actually a semantic and semiotic neurosis.

All the poems in *Reconvalescence* are composed of quatrain stanzas with loose rhymes. The lyrical dynamic in this book manifests itself as an oscillation between two thematic-rhetorical poles: one is the internalizing reconstruction of a poetic self; the other is an externalizing impulse toward political protest and provocation. The first poem, also titled "Convalescence" ("Huifu" 恢復), records the poet's sick sleep-talk: "I said, I want to piss with the radical attitude, / I said, I want to shit with the power of will."[64] Here the linguistic delirium combines a political-propagandist speech act with a sick man's daily reality.

The second poem, "Expressing My Feeling" ("Shu huai" 述懷), is a self-reflection set up by an apostrophic gesture toward an imaginary "friend":

63. Guo, "Kua zhe Donghai," in *GQJ/W*, 13:313.

64. Guo, "Huifu," in *GQJ/W*, 1:356. The following references to this book of poetry are noted in parentheses, with the page numbers.

> Friend, you don't know me, and sometimes I don't either,
> In the sunshine of the white day sometimes I am annoyed by myself;
> But in this unfathomable night, in this sick bed,
> My deep heart, my deep heart, lifts his veil. (359)

This complication of pronouns—"I," "you," and "his"—is interestingly related to a moment of self-revelation. The lyrical self, moreover, is always bound up with a defiant political gesture bordering on self-glorification. "I will sing about our new proletarian life" (359), Guo exclaims in the same poem.

In other words, this recovery of the lyrical self is also meant to fulfill the hysterical incantation of a collective ego and a ready-made propagandist language. In another poem, "A Manifesto of Poetry" ("Shi de xuanyan" 詩的宣言), he cries out: "I hope one day I will roar like a storm!" (375). In many places, this lyrical mood gives way to political ranting, in which the poet condemns capitalism and calls for the "red terror" to counter the "white terror." As a result, the "you" is no longer an imaginary friend or the ghost of a martyred comrade, but suddenly becomes the target of the poet's class hatred in "The Gossip" ("Chuanwen" 傳聞):

> Who cares about you? You go on fighting with each other!
> We have our iron axes and sickles.
> When the day of turning-upside-down arrives,
> We'll beat you down, even if you are the sun! (385)

Amid this mood of political hysteria, the third poem in this book contains an uncanny recovery of the erotic drive that takes form as a creative translation of "The Ospreys Cry" ("Guan ju" 關雎—the first poem from *Shi jing*)—into vernacular modern Chinese. This translation rewrites an ancient classic into a typical modern love poem, referring to the poet-translator's insomnia:

> Ah, the night is too long, long, long,
> I toss and turn relentlessly and yet can't fall asleep.
> The waterfowl on the river, you are still crying sadly,
> So are you also in search of your lover, as lonely as I? (361)

Yet the next poem is even more surprising. Titled "Hysteria" ("Xiesidieli" 歇斯迭里), it reads like a highly unfriendly valediction sung to an extramarital lover: "Girl, I'm simply unable to love you!" (362).

In poems like "Homecoming" ("Guilai" 歸來), "Resting in Peace" ("De le anxi" 得了安息), and "The Magic Power of Money" ("Jinqian de moli" 金錢的魔力), the poet laments the sacrifices his wife Satō Tomiko has made. In his hymn to this rediscovered love, he returns to the symbol of womanhood as the pure love that cures everything: "This is the tie of love, flesh in flesh, bone in bone, / This is the natural key of the universe" (373). But the sentimental note about family love also leads to venting his blames on capitalism:

Everything, everything has been crashed,
Our love, our family.
You crash everything, everything,
You the evil of capitalism, your wheels! (371)

The poet vacillates between political provocation and remembrance of the past. In "I Think of Chen She and Wu Guang" ("Wo xiangqi le Chen She Wu Guang" 我想起了陳涉吳廣), he turns to one of the first ancient peasant rebellions, preaching about the strategic importance of Chinese peasantry in the ongoing uprisings. In a poetic dialogue titled "The Dialogue between the Yangzi River and the Yellow River" ("Huanghe yu Yangzijiang duihua" 黃河與揚子江對話), the two personified symbols of China's reality turn to Chinese "peasants" and "workers" for hope. In the meantime, he encounters his older sisters in the dreams about his flight, and the homesickness starts to haunt him in "Awakening from a Dream" ("Meng xing" 夢醒), "The White Snow on the Mountaintop of Emei" ("Emei shan shang de bai xue" 峨眉山上的白雪), and "The Memory of Wuxia" ("Wuxia de huiyi" 巫峽的回憶). The poet tries to transform the memory of his Sichuan hometown into a national-geographic metaphor:

Ah, life advances like a boat navigating between the Three Gorges;
Today does not know tomorrow's destiny, and the last moment does not know the next moment's whereabouts.

Right now I am as if imprisoned in a gorge surrounded by high stiff mountains—
But as soon as I leave the Kuimen Gorge behind, I will break the waves with fair wind! (398)

This internalization of the traumatic memory as a necessary step toward self-overcoming is in fact closer to the true meaning of *Aufhebung.*

Guo's book of poetry thus showcases an unstable poetic experience of the revolutionary crisis, in which the political desire is displaced in the domain of poetic language. The image of a convalescence is the mediation of this sudden displacement. The "gorge surrounded by high stiff mountains" is nothing but a metaphor of poetic writing itself, since the poet is in fact "imprisoned" in the lyrical language. On the rhetorical level, this impasse bears an imprint of the historical time at caesura.

"Rheinwein/Rhine Wine" between Political Lyric and Translation

As I mentioned at the beginning of this chapter, on January 16, 1928, Guo wrote in his diary: "Leafing through [the first issue of] *Cultural Critique*, I completed a poem before going to bed."[65] Guo's notebook for poetic writing had become his diary book on January 15. Drafted one day after his transcription of the other poems from the notebook, "To Seize" was later added to *Reconvalescence* as a concluding piece. Its dual appearance attests to a textual overlap between Guo's book of poetry and diary:

My friend, do you think the current situation is too depressing?
This is the harbinger of the storm about to come.
My friend, do you think the current situation is too chaotic?
This is the eve before the new society is born.

65. Guo, "Li Hu zhiqian," in *GQJ/W*, 13:275.

The pain of contractions has gradually reached the climax,
The Mother's body, lying there for too long, can no longer bear it,
We have prepared a glass of blood-red wine for celebration,
But it must not be the wine from the banks of the Rhine.

We have prepared a glass of blood-red wine for celebration.
My friend, it is my warm blood surging in my heart.
Let us brew a violent storm of blood in this dark night,
In order to seize this newborn sun, this newborn universe! (409)

The words "depression" and "chaos," used in the poem to characterize "the current situation," not only testify on a personal level to the poet's physical and psychological status but suggest a larger context: calling on "my friend," Guo's poem addresses a social group of like-minded youths and refers to their experience of the defeat, disorientation, and "caesura." The whole poem then weaves together two metaphorical threads. One thread concerns the body politics of social revolution as birth pangs, while the other focuses on the image of wine as the celebration of revolution. The link between them is the blood-wine analogy: the only revolutionary wine is a "storm of blood." Situating the reader ("my friend") on "the eve before the new society is born," and evoking a revolutionary "climax," this poem exhibits a desperately prophetic gesture.

Consequently, this poem has long been read as a typical—if not stereotypical—political lyric, a "prophetic poem about the revolutionary storm" that "has no particular artistic nuances."[66] But in this straightforward outcry for a "newborn" society, one image stands out as something obscure, and merits further interpretation: the image of the wine from the Rhineland, ensconced between the two references to the blood-red wine of celebration. Denounced by the poet, the wine from the Rhineland is supposed to be a mere analogy of red blood, counterfeiting the true revolutionary blood. No commentator pauses over the strange appearance of "Rhine wine" here. It is worth noting, in addition, that the most famous Rhine wines are not the color of blood—they are white wines. Then Guo's sudden mentioning of a foreign land and its wines seems even more idiosyncratic.

66. Zou Jianjun, "Geming fengbao de yuyan shi—du 'Zhanqu,'" 237.

The Rhine is itself an overloaded cultural-historical reference. Linking the historical fates of Germany and France, it is associated with the impact of the French Revolution on the German lands. It reminds us of Friedrich Hölderlin's poetry, in which the river is the symbol of the spiritual origin of Germany.[67] As Marx's homeland, the Rhineland also recalls the powerful chronicles of the 1848 uprisings in *Neue Rheinische Zeitung*, the ban of which led to Marx's exile. The river also appears in the musical mythmaking of Richard Wagner: his epic opera opens with *Das Rheingold*. Given Guo's immersion in German culture since his student years, what did he mean by referring to the Rhine at a moment of China's political crisis?

Guo's fleeting reference to the Rhine actually embodies a more complicated intertextual rhetoric than a reader might initially assume. A fact that has escaped critical attention so far is that this "wine from the banks of the Rhine" in fact comes from his translation of the German "Rheinwein," a figure that looms large in the scene "Auerbach's Tavern in Leipzig" in Goethe's *Faust I*. Guo resumed his translation of *Faust* in November 1927 in Shanghai. "Generally speaking, the work of translation went very fast and smoothly this time," he said in "Postscript" ("Houji" 後記) to his translation, "in only ten days, I completed the rendering of Part One, based on my previous work."[68] He also said: "It was my true delight that when I lost my freedom, I was able to finish my translation."[69] Later Guo's composition of *Reconvalescence* followed in suite and overlapped with his copyediting of the Chinese version of *Faust I*. His diary entries show how anxious he was while preparing and waiting for its publication. On February 1, his *Faust I* (*Fushide* 浮士德) was eventually published.[70] Both his practice of translation and his writing of poetry marked a moment of a return to literature when the revolution was halted.

In this 1928 Chinese version of *Faust I*, Guo translates *Rheinwein* of line 2264 as *laiyin de putao* 萊茵的葡萄.[71] We find in his own "To Seize": "the wine from the banks of the Rhine" (*laiyin hepan de putao* 萊茵河畔的葡萄). In other words, Guo used almost the same phrase in his translation,

67. See Hölderlin, "Der Rhein."
68. Guo, "Houji," 5.
69. Ibid., 1.
70. Guo, "Li Hu zhiqian," in *GQJ/W*, 13:288.
71. Guo, trans., *Fushide*, 175.

which was completed in November 1927, and in his own lyric poem, which was composed on January 16, 1928. Though ostensibly a trivial intertextuality, this transference of a translation detail into the lyrical domain actually constitutes a symptom of the political unconscious.

"Auerbach's Tavern in Leipzig" is a comic satire about the self-indulgent lifestyle of German academics and students. Set between the tragedy of scholarship and the tragedy of love, the scene is a complicated temporal-spatial combination. As Cyrus Hamlin, a commentator of Goethe's *Faust*, points out,

> "Auerbach's Tavern in Leipzig" is the only scene in *Faust*, Part One, located with geographical specificity in an actual place. The drinking locale also joins together the widely disparate eras separating the historical Dr. Faustus from the author of the drama. According to tradition, Faustus actually visited Auerbach's Tavern when he was in Leipzig in the year 1526; Goethe, as student at the University of Leipzig during the mid-1760s, also frequented the place.[72]

In this scene, Mephistopheles leads Faust—who is not yet rejuvenated—to Auerbach's Tavern in Leipzig, where the drinkers represent "academic stereotypes," with Frosch as a "freshman," Brander as a "sophomore," Altmayer as an "alumnus," and Siebel as the bartender ("sieve").[73] Faust, interestingly, refuses to participate in their debauchery, whereas Mephistopheles becomes a main actor of dramatic development. At the beginning, Goethe sets up a parallel between Frosch, who sings of love, and Siebel, who has just lost his love, indicating that the freshman has stolen Siebel's mistress. Then Brander sings a song of the rat, mocking the convention of love. Mephistopheles joins the drinkers and sings about a flea of which the king is fond ("There ruled a king among us, / who had a mighty big flea," lines 2211–12), poking fun at the "politics of the ancien régime."[74] The students and Mephistopheles want to raise their glasses to Freedom. When Mephistopheles promises to "provide each honored guest a fine drop from my own cellar," Frosch makes his request:

72. Hamlin, "Interpretative Notes," 369.
73. Ibid., 368.
74. Ibid., 369.

Gut! Wenn ich wählen soll, so will ich Rheinwein haben.
Das Vaterland verleiht die allerbesten Gaben. (lines 2264–65)

(Good! If I am to choose, I choose the Rhine wine. / One's native land bestows the finest dower.)[75]

好的，我便要萊茵的葡萄。
葡萄酒中我們的國產最好。[76]

[Good, then I'll choose the Rhine wine. / Among wines our national one is the best.]

So Mephistopheles, by way of magic, makes *Rheinwein* out of the "fire of hell." When the drinkers spill the wine, it turns into flame. At the end of the scene, when they realize they have been fooled by Mephistopheles, Frosch says: "I surely thought that I drank wine" ("Mir däuchte doch als tränk' ich Wein," line 2334).[77] In his translation of this line, Guo specifies the *Wein* once again as the "Rhine wine" (*laiyin de putao* 萊茵的葡萄).[78]

In Goethe's satire, the Rhine wine is associated with the devil's magic and points toward the self-indulgence of German intellectuals. Guo's reference to the Rhine wine, first, complicates the temporal-spatial configuration of a sociopolitical caesura. The Rhine wine is incorporated figuratively as a comparative point of reference for the revolutionary blood. His negation of the Rhine wine as the fake blood is then a key trace—or even a fissure—of this condensed historical time in which the Chinese Revolution had to be reoriented, restrategized, and reimagined.

Second and more specifically, with the *Rheinwein*/*laiyin de putao*, Guo's poem performs on an allegorical level a self-critique of the tragic National Revolution. The "pastime" (line 2151) of these academic types in Leipzig—a "lesser Paris" (line 2172)—shows Goethe's characterization of the social life of German intellectuals or academics ("The people here make every day a feast," line 2161). Guo is fully aware of Goethe's satirical force directed at the young intellectuals. He translates Frosch as *Hulexu* 胡樂虛; *hu* has a connotation of confusion and chaos, *le* means

75. English translation modified.
76. Guo, trans., *Fushide*, 175.
77. English translation modified.
78. Guo, trans., *Fushide*, 181.

enjoyment, and *xu* denotes emptiness or vanity.[79] In his own poem, the refusal of the *Rheinwein* serves as a symbolic criticism of China's revolutionary youth. Due to their political naïveté, they were fooled by a "devil"—Jiang's GMD—and this devil's promise of revolution turned into the "fire of hell": the ensuing white terror. The failed National Revolution, at least for Guo and his comrades, proved to be the fake *Rheinwein*. The expectation was high, the magic was played, and the masses were deceived by the counterrevolutionary forces under the revolutionary disguise. Just as Siebel finally realizes the trick and calls the wine "a juggler's game" (line 2332), so does Guo find Jiang Jieshi to be a "central force of hooligan's societies, wicked landlords, corrupted bureaucrats, warlords, and all other reactionary factors."[80] At the same time, after "leafing through" the inaugural issue of *Cultural Critique*, which includes such new lexicons as the transliteration of *Aufhebung*, Guo composed "To Seize." So the denunciation of the *Rheinwein* as the fake blood seems to also contain a preemptive criticism of his fellow Creationists' obsession with the "German-ness" of revolutionary theories and their detachment from the actual revolutionary blood spilled for China. Hence, Guo's reference to "Rheinwein" is a political reminder whose meaning is multifaceted, if not unstable.

Such ambiguity leads us to the third and final implication of this intertextual detail. Goethe's initial version of the "Tavern" scene already appears in *Urfaust*. But the scene undergoes a significant change in *Faust: A Fragment* (1790). In *Urfaust*, it is still Faust who performs the magic in front of the academic stereotypes. In contrast, in the *Fragment*, Faust, full of contempt, refuses to participate in the debauchery and assumes a detached position of observation, and Mephistopheles comes to the fore and leads the action of this scene. Goethe undertook to prepare *Faust: A Fragment* between spring 1788 and late 1789. In late 1789 he recast the "Tavern" scene into verse. The timing of its revisions is of great significance. György Lukács, in his "*Faust* Studies," has emphasized the concurrence of Goethe's conception of *Faust* with the world-historic event of the French Revolution.[81] It is thus interesting to note that between singing the satiri-

79. Ibid., 157.
80. Guo, "Qing kan jinri zhi Jiang Jieshi," in *GQJ/W*, 13:129.
81. Lukács, *Goethe and His Age*, 171–72.

cal song about the courtly life and conjuring up better wine, Mephistopheles calls on "Freiheit":

> Ich tränke gern ein Glas, die Freiheit hoch zu ehren,
> Wenn eure Weine nur ein bißchen besser wären. (lines 2245–46)
>
> (I'd gladly raise my glass to freedom, let it clink, / If just your wines were halfway fit to drink.)
>
> 我也想爲自由浮一大白，
> 只可惜你們的酒過於蹩脚。[82]
>
> [I'd like to drink one full glass for freedom, / But unfortunately your wine is too poor.]

Freedom, glorified in the French Revolution, is a major banner of modern political revolutions. It is in the name of freedom that the drinkers raise their glasses and then are duped by Mephistopheles; in fact, the drinking debauchery as the celebration of freedom among the scholars points precisely to the absence of any political revolution in the German context. While political freedom had dawned on France, Germany, a country of the delayed development of bourgeoisie, was still trapped in feudal absolutism and pettiness and had to experience what Marx once called the "German misery" (*die deutsche Misère*): as distanced spectators of the French Revolution from the other side of the Rhine, the Germans "are philosophical contemporaries [of the modern age] without being historical ones."[83] What marks the German experience of modernity, in Rebecca Comay's words, is "a repetitive failure of actuality and action."[84] The freedom left to the German intellectuals was the free development of knowledge and philosophy, the ivory tower lifestyle that Faust can no longer endure. The drinking students only poke fun at the old regime; their feast reveals their political inaction. Guo recycled the image of "Rhine wine" in his poem at a historical moment when the opportunity of a Chinese revolution was missed or suspended. The negation of "Rhine

82. Guo, trans., *Fushide*, 173.

83. Marx, "Towards a Critique of Hegel's *Philosophy of Right*: Introduction," 75. For a Marxist account of the delayed "bourgeois-democratic revolution" in Germany, see Lukács, *The Destruction of Reason*, 37–94.

84. Comay, *Mourning Sickness*, 3.

wine" then indicates his anxiety about the political impotence of Chinese intellectuals in this situation: no one should indulge in the fake wine and fake freedom.

However critical of the students' feast, Faust only remains an inactive observer. Goethe's change of Faust from an active role to a detached observer is itself characteristic of what Franco Moretti generalizes as the main structural and thematic symptom of *Faust*, that is, Faust's "inaction," despite his motto "Im Anfang war die Tat."[85] In early 1928, Guo was also an inactive observer. Ironically, poetry was Guo's own fake wine, a substitute for political action. The refusal of fake wine and the call for actual revolutionary blood remained nothing more than a symbolic-prophetic performance of overcoming the anxiety inherent in revolutionary literature. This translingual moment can be seen as a symptomatic self-reference of the political lyric, which, as a "preparation" for revolution, is an imaginary solution to the halted revolutionary time.

Therefore, the transference of "Rhine wine" from Guo's translation to his revolutionary lyric is more complicated than the mere borrowing of a word. His translation of *Faust* ultimately becomes the ambivalent and self-referential allegory of a modern Chinese writer's life in revolutionary times. His convalescence, on one hand, is something similar to the restoration of Faust's spiritual energies after the Gretchen tragedy. Like Faust, Guo was eager to leap forward into the larger world of social action. On the other hand, as he had been forced back into a literary life, Guo saw his resumption of this translation project as a homecoming. Later Guo retrospectively compared his return to translation in a Shanghai *longtang* apartment with Faust's return to his little world of a "restricted cell":

> Ach wenn in unsrer engen Zelle
> Die Lampe freundlich wieder brennt,
> Dann wird's in unserm Busen helle
> Im Herzen, das sich selber kennt. (lines 1194–97)
>
> (Ah, when in our restricted cell / The lamp resumes its kindly blaze, / It lights the inner self as well, / The heart aware of its own ways.)

85. Moretti, *Modern Epic*, 16.

嗟我小齋中，燈火今復燃，
胸底生光明，深心知內觀。[86]

[O in my little study, the lamp is rekindled today, / Light emerges from the bottom of my bosom, and my deep heart attains the introspective knowledge.]

Thus, he described his retreat "from the battlefield struggles to a tiny room" as a meaningful Faustian one: "My life was limited, but my hope was green and rich. . . . The feelings with which my translation is impregnated [*hanyun* 含孕] are richer than what Goethe composed."[87] He also claimed: "[The translation] is impregnated [*hanyun*] with the experience and moods of the past ten years, which makes the translation text grow."[88] "Impregnation" or "growth" via translation constitutes the logic of Guo's own internalization of his experience of the revolution as a missed opportunity, a temporary failure, and an interrupted project.

In other words, Guo's translation of *Faust I* and his writing of *Reconvalescence* were two literary eruptions in response to one single political standstill. *Aufhebung/aofuhebian,* convalescence/*huifu*, and "impregnation" are the same process of a cultural-political disorientation/reorientation. The idiosyncratic figuration of the Rhine wine, as a rhetorical implosion between translation and poetry, allegorizes the contradictions intrinsic to a revolutionary caesura.

The Translingual-Dialectical Caesura of Time

From *Aufhebung/aofuhebian* through *Reconvalescence/huifu* to *Rheinwein/laiyin de putao*, I have analyzed some translingual fragments rediscovered from a brief period of political uncertainties and emergencies. They contain a series of traces of a sudden displacement of political energies into cultural or discursive production and bear testimony to the halt, interruption, postponement, and reconfiguration of historical time. From our hindsight, they look like some frameworks abandoned by the revolutionary

86. Guo, "Kua zhe Donghai," in *GQJ/W*, 13:306–7.
87. Ibid., 307.
88. Ibid., 306.

history itself. Having no time to be fully developed, these rhetorical moments, redeemed in this chapter, nevertheless represent an emerging and open-ended "occasion" (*jiyuan*). As self-references of a revolutionary caesura, they embody a mode of translation that is as historical-temporal as translingual. In the diary entry of January 29, 1928, the same day he was proof-reading his *Faust*, Guo offered a comparative point of reference for China's situation, arguing that "China's current situation is very much like Europe of 1848": "The February Revolution in France had a pan-European influence, but the revolutions failed one by one in Germany, Austria, Belgium and France, and when the White Terror took over and became pervasive, Marx and Engels had to flee into exile in other countries."[89] Just as Guo's demand for true blood in "To Seize" was an unmistakable echo of the demand of "revolutionary terror" that the young Marx had made in response to the counterrevolution in 1848, so here Guo established a translational relationship between China's current situation and the failure of the 1848 revolutions across Europe, between his fate and Marx's.[90] Less than a month later, Guo embarked on his own exile.

In other words, different historical-temporal frameworks were synchronized into a precarious self-understanding of the Chinese Revolution. In a sense of the "recognizability of now-time," I contend that the translingual moments discussed in this chapter constitute a series of dialectical images of the Chinese Revolution and its caesura.[91] As is well known, the dialectical image is a key concept in Walter Benjamin's later work. For Benjamin, dialectics does not mean a teleological narrative of *Aufhebung*; he pays critical attention to history's own standstill (rather than synthesis), in which different historical moments or epochs coexist and recognize each other through remote yet deep correspondences. The uncertain now-time into which different historical experiences and memories collapse is a moment of the dialectical image: "Image is dialectics at a standstill. . . . Only dialectical images are genuine image (that is, not archaic); and the place where one encounter them is language."[92] In a

89. Guo, "Li Hu zhiqian," in *GQJ/W*, 13:286.

90. Marx, "The Victory of Counter-Revolution in Vienna," 505–6.

91. The quote is from Benjamin, "Paralipomena to 'On the Concept of History,'" 405.

92. Benjamin, *The Arcades Project*, 462.

series of translingual acts, we encounter the dialectical images of the Chinese Revolution's standstill. The sudden figurations of *Aufhebung/aofuhebian*, *Reconvalescence/huifu*, and *Rheinwein/laiyin de putao*, as strange signs of China's rising "revolutionary literature," give us a glimpse of a critical moment in which the temporal frame of sociopolitical experience was constantly evoked and contested. It was the moment that historical dialectics encountered its own caesura. Such dialectical images soon disappeared in the depth of history, but their fleeting existence flashed into a translingual codification of revolutionary time.

CHAPTER 3

Poetics, Thematics, and Time

Translating *Faust* in Revolutionary China

In 1947, on the occasion of the final completion of his rendering of Goethe's *Faust,* Guo Moruo congratulated himself by emphasizing the time span of his translation project: "Just as it took sixty years for Goethe to compose *Faust* intermittently, so it took almost three decades for me to finish my translation. The fact that this time span equals half of that of [Goethe's composition] is a coincidence I find interesting and meaningful."[1]

Faust has been considered an allegorical epic about modernity.[2] Goethe himself called it an "incommensurable production," and the Marxist philosopher-critic György Lukács read it in the 1940s as a "drama of human species," a work comparable to Hegel's *Phenomenology of Spirit.*[3] A tragedy in two parts, *Faust* narrates Faust's search for the true meaning of human striving under a wager with Mephistopheles, the devil. Unsatisfied with knowledge, Faust is rejuvenated by the magic and experiences the tragedy of love with Gretchen. Then he leaps from the "small world" (*kleine Welt*) into the "large world" (*grosse Welt*), with more journeys that lead to the disillusionment from court politics (shown in the paper money scheme), the exploration of natural philosophy (represented in the metamorphosis of Homunculus), and the downfall of ideal beauty (symbolized in the scenario of Helen and Euphorion). After helping the

1. Guo, "Di er bu yi hou ji," 387.
2. See Moretti, *Modern Epic*, 77–99.
3. Lukács, *Goethe and His Age*, 157, 175–76.

emperor crash the peasants' uprising, Faust, in old age again, finds the highest moment of satisfaction in the industrial-urban project of land reclamation, being blind to its brutal human cost. When Mephistopheles finally has the chance to claim Faust's soul, Faust receives redemption from the angels, including Gretchen. Jane Brown, a Goethe scholar, finds in this "German tragedy" a "self-conscious" mode of "world theatre."[4] As Franco Moretti argues, *Faust* encompasses a wide-ranging literary representation of the uneven developments of a burgeoning capitalist world-system and exemplifies the genre of the "world text."[5]

What dominated Guo's work as a translator was his decades-long effort to translate *Faust* into Chinese. It started as early as 1919, and in 1928, his rendition of *Faust I* appeared in print. He eventually turned to *Faust II* in 1947, another year full of uncertainties and "fundamental changes" for China: the post–World War II peace negotiations between the GMD and CCP had failed, and the civil war reached a deadlock.[6] The GMD had lost its upper hand, and the triumph of a CCP-led "people's China" was not yet on the horizon. Over twenty-eight years, Guo kept returning to a project of rendering *Faust* into Chinese. This duration of time was surely "meaningful."

More important, time itself constitutes a central theme of this translation of *Faust*. In 1947, Guo claimed that "[Goethe's *Faust*] is a developmental history of Zeitgeist [*shidai jingshen*]."[7] The term "Zeitgeist," obviously, points to Goethe's own era, that is, the age of European modernity. In the meantime, it is also a thinly veiled reference to the Chinese Revolution that was still under way while Guo was bringing his translation project to an eventual finish. After all, the "three decades" he devoted to translating this masterpiece corresponded to the three decades of the so-called New Democratic Revolution, a period running from the May Fourth Movement in 1919 to the founding of the People's Republic in 1949. This periodization of the Chinese Revolution was not merely the

4. Brown, *Goethe's* Faust, 25.

5. "World text" is a term coined by Franco Moretti for the epic representations of the capitalist world system. See Moretti, *Modern Epic*, part 1.

6. Mao Zedong, for example, described the significance of 1947 as witnessing a "fundamental change" taking place in the war. Mao Zedong, "Carry the Revolution through to the End," 300.

7. Guo, "Fushide jian lun," 3.

CCP's retroactive historical narrative; rather, as I demonstrated in the introduction, it was rooted in a self-periodizing act from within a continuous revolutionary process.

The making of Guo's *Faust* (*Fushide* 浮士德, *Fushide* hereafter) was interwoven into the cultural-political fabric of that revolutionary period. Just as Chinese intellectuals' obsession with *Faust* during revolutionary times was an uncanny event in modern Chinese culture, so Guo's translation amounts to a translingual-allegorical periodization of the long Chinese Revolution and its bargain with the historical necessity/negativity. Put differently, the historicity of this translation of *Faust*—not only in terms of the project's duration but in terms of its poetic language and thematic interpretation—was intrinsic to the historicity of the Chinese Revolution. I have touched on Guo's initial attempts at translating *Faust* and pinpointed his resumption of this project in the wake of a failed revolution. In this chapter, my discussion of Guo's translation and interpretation of *Faust* will come full circle. Drawing on the peculiar linkage between translation and historical time, I focus on the poetics and thematics in Guo's engagements with *Faust* as a whole.

Many have commented on Goethe's influence on Guo; critical attention has also been paid to the reception of Goethe's *Faust* in modern China in general and the translation styles of Guo's *Fushide I* in particular.[8] However, the textual formations and historical conditions of *Fushide* in its totality deserve a more focused examination from the perspective of translation as a poetic, cultural, and political practice of interpretation. Such an examination also entails a critical survey of the genealogy of the critical receptions of Goethe's masterpiece in revolutionary China. Consequently, this chapter strives to combine the approach of translation studies with a broader perspective of literary, intellectual, and cultural politics. According to André Lefevere, translation as an act of rewriting is always motivated or constrained by the "ideological and poetological

8. See Jiang Zheng, *Ren de jiefang yu yishu de jiefang*. For a critical account of the reception of Goethe in China, see Yang Wuneng, *Gede yu zhongguo*. Also see Ye Jun, "Die Veränderung der Faustrezeption als Spiegel der Entwicklung des nationalen Aufbaus im modernen China (1920–1940er Jahre)." The latest discussion of Guo's translation of *Faust I* comes from Bartels, "Goethes *Faust* bei Mori Rintarō und Guo Moruo."

currents of [its] time."[9] So first, on the "poetological" level, my reading will show that Guo's translation text turns out to be a working site for the borrowed, recycled, and reinvented forms, rhymes, meters, and styles, resulting in an unstable poetic language. Second, the "ideological" constructions embedded in the rewritings of *Faust* in revolutionary China are to be found in a variety of thematic interpretations. Paul de Man observed that "thematic criticism" was characteristic of *Faust* commentary.[10] The Chinese reception confirms this observation. My discussion therefore turns to the domain of thematics and compares Guo's rendition of *Faust* with other interpretations made by his contemporaries, such as Zong Baihua (an aesthetician), Hu Qiuyuan (a nonpartisan quasi-Marxist intellectual), Feng Zhi (a Heidelberg-trained scholar and modernist poet), and Lukács (whose study of Goethe was penned in the age of antifascism). An analysis of such instances of thematic criticism demonstrates how Guo's translation of *Faust* becomes an allegorical periodization of China's revolutionary modernity. Contextualizing Guo's case in revolutionary China's fascination with the "German ideology" (to use Marx's term), I contend that this long journey of translation encoded the experience of the ongoing Chinese Revolution as a condensation of historical temporalities.

An Unstable Poetic Language in Guo's Fushide I

As I mentioned in chapter 1, in 1919, Guo published his excerpted translation of the first scene from *Faust*, "Night" (see fig. 6). On March 20, 1920, in *China Times* appeared Guo's translation of the opening of *Faust II*, "Charming Landscape" ("Anmutige Gegend"). As Marián Gálik notes, however, little attention has been paid to these fragments and their differences from the 1928 edition of *Fushide I*.[11] Now let us turn to the 1919 translation, which is in fact a free translation bordering on paraphrasing:

9. Lefevere, *Translation, Rewriting, and the Manipulation of Literary Fame*, 8.
10. See de Man, "Thematic Criticism and the Theme of Faust."
11. Gálik, "Gothic Chamber in Goethe's *Faust* and a Tiny Room in Hakozaki," 410.

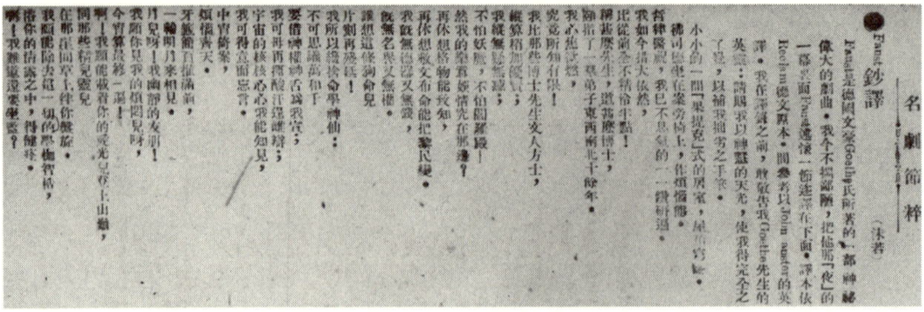

名劇節粹

Faust鈔譯 （沫若）

Faust是德國文豪Goethe氏所著的一部神秘偉大的劇曲。我今不揣謭陋，把他第「夜」的一幕裏面Faust述懷一節迻譯在下面。譯本依Reclam德文原本，間參考以John auster的英譯。我在譯述之前，敢敬告我Goethe先生的英靈：請賜我以神靈的天光，使我得完全之了解，以補我拙劣之手筆。

小小的一間「果提克」式的居室，屋頂穹隆。佛司德坐在案旁椅上，作煩惱態。

哲律醫祝，我已不息氣的一一鑽研遍。

我如今措大依然，

比從前全不精伶半點！

FIGURE 6 Guo Moruo's "*Faust* chaoyi" in *China Times*, October 10, 1919 (detail).

In einem hochgewölbten, engen, gotischen Zimmer FAUST *unruhig auf seinem Sessel am Pulte.*
FAUST
Habe nun, ach! Philosophie,
Juristerei und Medizin,
Und leider auch Theologie!
Durchaus studiert, mit heißem Bemühn.
Da steh' ich nun, ich armer Tor!
Und bin so klug als wie zuvor. (lines 354–59)

(*In a narrow, high-vaulted Gothic chamber,* FAUST, *restless in his armchair by the desk.*
FAUST. I have pursued, alas, philosophy, / Jurisprudence, and medicine, / And, help me god, theology, / With fervent zeal through thick and thin. / And here, poor fool, I stand once more, / No wiser than I was before.)

小小的一間"果提克"式的居室，屋頂穹隆。佛司德坐在案旁椅上，作煩惱態。
哲律醫祝，我已不息氣的一一鑽研遍。
我如今措大依然，
比從前全不精伶半點！[12]

[*In a small Gothic apartment with a high vault. Faust sits in his chair by the desk, showing the expression of anxiety.*
Philosophy, law, medicine, theology, I have studied one by one without rest. / Now I am still foolish, / Not a single bit smarter than before.]

In the translator's note, Guo suggested that his translation was based on a Reclam edition of *Faust*, and he also kept John Auster's English trans-

12. Guo, trans., "*Faust* chaoyi."

lation as a reference.[13] What the young Guo had in hand may have been Auster's 1835 translation. Just as Auster elongated Goethe's verse, Guo rearranged Goethe's lines. Discussing this style of translation, Gálik emphasizes that "the reading and translating of *Faust* at that moment was also connected with" Guo's personal crisis in 1919.[14] Gálik goes so far as to argue that the young Guo misrecognized the *gotisches Zimmer* as his own "tiny room in Hakozaki."[15] This does not come as a surprise. So far we have been familiar with the figuring of the translator's subjectivity in Guo's work. The preceding two chapters have drawn attention to his predilection of describing his own sentimental or social conditions by using Goethe's lines.[16] One can even see the whole translation of *Faust I* as an occasion for Guo's self-portrayal. After all, he remembered his experience of translating *Faust I* in the following way: "It felt as if I had been creatively writing it by myself."[17]

What merits more scrutiny is the poetic language that was formed in such a practice of translation as creative rewriting. It should be kept in mind that although there had been a long history of literary uses of vernacular Chinese, as a modern national language newly proposed by May Fourth writers, it was still under construction throughout the 1920s.[18] Through the lens of translation, Lawrence Wong has perceptively examined the fast transformation of China's written language from classical Chinese or *wenyan* 文言 to vernacular Chinese or *baihua* 白話, and to a controversial Europeanized form.[19] Yet the poetic language is not a main focus in Wong's account. I suggest that the forgotten 1919 translation fragment contains some missing links of this evolving poetic language, and the differences and continuities between these early attempts and the 1928

13. Guo, trans., "*Faust* chaoyi."

14. Gálik, "Gothic Chamber in Goethe's *Faust* and a Tiny Room in Hakozaki," 410–11.

15. Ibid., 419.

16. For additional examples, see Guo, "Li Hu zhiqian," in *GQJ/W*, 13:297.

17. Guo, "Di er bu yi hou ji," 384.

18. For a discussion of the construction of vernacular Chinese as a "modern written language," see Wang Feng, *Shi yun tuiyi yu wenzhang xingti*. Also see Kaske, *The Politics of Language in Chinese Education*.

19. Wong, *Fanyi yu wenxue zhijian*, 189–228.

edition of *Fushide I* embody the itinerary of an unstable, hybrid, and flexible poetics in translation.

While Guo translates *gotischen* by the way of transliteration (*guotike*), he finds classical terms—*zhe*, *lü*, *yi*, *zhu*—for the four disciplines mentioned, rather than using the modernized Chinese translations of those branches of Western knowledge. Similarly, some grammatical elements of classical Chinese are reused in vernacular sentences, such as *zai* 哉 (a rhetorical question word): "我怎能把你擁抱哉?" ["How could I embrace you?"][20] This poetic-linguistic malleability is also partly due to the fact that the 1919 fragment was Guo's earliest effort to reproduce Goethe's rhymes in translation. Starting from the first line of Faust's soliloquy cited above, Guo uses one single rhyme (*-ian/üan*), alternating with other minor rhymes, until the translation of line 429 (the moment when Faust is about to turn to Nostradamus's book). To sustain a rhyming structure, he sometimes chooses to use Chinese words remote from the originals, to rearrange or distort the syntax, or to overstretch the rules of word- or phrase-building:

> Drum hab' ich mich der Magie ergeben,
> Ob mir, durch Geistes Kraft und Mund,
> Nicht manch Geheimnis würde kund. (lines 377–79)
>
> (So I resorted to Magic's art, / To see if by spirit mouth and might / Many a secret may come to light.)
>
> 我所以才捨命學神仙 [*xian*]:
> 不可思議萬和千 [*qian*]
> 要借神權神舌爲我宣 [*xuan*];
>
> [So I learn from the immortals at the cost of my life: / Thousands of incomprehensible things / Need to be articulated by the power and tongue of the spirit.]

Shenxian 神仙, referring to the Daoist immortals or deities, is a loose rendering of *Magie*; the phrase *wan he qian* 萬和千 is built to maintain a rhyme similar to traditional Chinese opera.

20. Guo, trans., "*Faust* chaoyi." It responds to line 455 in the original: "Wo fass' ich dich . . . ?" (How . . . seize you in my clasp?)

Guo also tried to combine a new vernacular literary language with metrical forms recycled from classical poetry. In this short piece of translation, one encounters vernacularized *siyan* 四言 (four-syllable), *wuyan* 五言 (five-syllable), *liuyan* 六言 (six-syllable), and *qiyan* 七言 (seven-syllable) patterns. It must be noted again that before the vernacular Literary Revolution, it had been a common practice of using traditional poetic forms to translate Western poetry.[21] But in this translation excerpt, just as in Guo's translation of Shelley's pieces, the classical elements are creatively mingled with the vernacular flexibility. For instance, the two four-character lines—"中宵倚案, / 煩惱齊天" ["Being wakeful at the desk at midnight, / My anxiety is as high as the sky"]—are Guo's paraphrasing of the lines following Faust's octosyllabic apostrophe toward the moon: "Den ich so manche Mitternacht / An diesem Pult herangewacht" ("Who many a midnight vigil through / Have found me wakeful in this chair," lines 388–89). This translation is closer to Auster's equally free rendition: "Oft by this desk, at middle night, / I have sat gazing for thy light, / Wearied with search."[22] Yet amid a number of quasi-classical couplets, we find a vernacular and even Europeanized version of the apostrophe of "trübsel'ger Freund" (line 391): "月兒呀！我幽靜的友朋！" ["The moon, my silent friend!"]. Then two five-character lines appear in Guo's translation of Faust's praise of the sign of the Macrocosm: "萬象本一如，/全盤動著在" ["Thousands of phenomena are actually one essence, / all are acting in a total cycle"]. They correspond to: "Wie alles sich zum Ganzen webt, / Eins in dem andern wirkt und lebt" ("How all one common weft contrives, / Each in the other works and thrives," lines 447–48). Whereas Guo recycles ancient vocabulary in the first line, in the second line he uses *zuozai* 着在 as a vernacular verb complement to express the present tense in Chinese. It is partly because he needs to keep the *ai* rhyme running, but another reason may be that there are so many verbs that this stanza has a strong mood of activity. Auster's translation also reinforces this atmosphere of the present tense: "Floating, mingling, interweaving— / Rising, sinking, and receiving."[23]

21. See Wu, *Modern Archaics*, chapter 6.
22. Goethe, *The First Part of Goethe's Faust*, trans. Auster, 30.
23. Ibid., 34.

To sum up: Guo's translation fragment puts into Faust's mouth a diction that mixes old fashions and neologisms and mingles the highbrow and the popular. The heterogeneous poetic language as a whole can be characterized as an inventive yet sometimes forced combination of an overstretched flexibility of the vernacular Chinese, a residue of classical poetic forms, and a rhyming effect reminiscent of traditional popular drama.[24]

The 1928 edition of Guo's *Faust I* is expected to demonstrate a substantial improvement. Concluding his retranslation in 1927, Guo wrote: "Rereading the remnant manuscript, I felt deeply ashamed of my [earlier] work. . . . I now feel lucky that the manuscript was gnawed by the rats. . . . The current product is a completely modified and improved translation."[25] A combination of poetic fluency and faithfulness was his aspiration in this new translation: "In my translation I have pursued fluency as much as possible, and I believe I have achieved a great deal of poetic effectiveness. But I am as faithful to the original, and anyone who has German will realize how much effort I have made for accuracy as soon as he reads one or two pages."[26] To reach this vision of literary translation, Guo insisted on the approach of verse translation: "I offer verse translation wherever the original is in verse. This is an experiment in China, and some verse translations of mine may seem to be non-sense. But I have made my utmost effort. Sometimes I had to spend half a day in searching for the right word or rhyme."[27]

Let us compare the new version of Faust's opening lines with the 1919 rendering of the same lines cited above:

莪特式的居室，狹隘，屋頂穹窿，
浮士德坐案旁靠椅上，呈不安態。
浮士德：
哲理啊，法律啊，醫典 [*dian*]，
甚至於神學的一切簡篇 [*bian*]，

24. It is noteworthy that in 1932 Guo briefly compared Goethe's dramatic verse with the combination of rhymed verse and vernacular prose in traditional Chinese drama. Guo, *Chuangzao shinian*, in *GQJ/W*, 12:75.

25. Guo, "Yi hou," 4.

26. Ibid., 5.

27. Ibid., 4.

我如今，啊！都已努力鑽研遍 [*bian*]。
畢竟是措大依然 [*ran*]，
毫不見聰明半點 [*dian*]。[28]

[*Gothic chamber, narrow, high-vaulted, / Faust sits in his armchair by the desk, looking restless.*
Faust: Ah philosophy, ah law, medicine, / And even theology: all their books / I have, alas, painstakingly studied by now. / But I'm still dumb, / Not a single bit smarter.]

The rhyme remains the same, but the stage description and Faust's monologue are translated differently from his earlier fragment. Not only is the 1928 version a line-by-line translation, Guo also adheres to a more vernacular mode of expression.

Also consider, for example, his new translation of Faust's lines in another scene:

Vom Eise befreit sind Strom und Bäche
Durch des Frühlings holden, belebenden Blick,
Im Tale grünet Hoffnungs-Glück;
Der alte Winter, in seiner Schwäche,
Zog sich in rauhe Berge zurück. (lines 903–7)

(Freed from the ice are brooks and rivers / By spring's enchanting, enlivening gaze; / The valley is blithe with hope's green haze; / Hoary winter with senile shivers / Back to his mountain lair withdrew.)

阳春的和惠而甦人的眼光
把河水与溪流从冰冻解放，
山谷中翠绿着希望的欣幸；
老了的残冬已向荒山逃遁。[29]

[Sunny spring's harmonizing and enlivening gaze / Liberated rivers and brooks from the ice, / In the valley hope's delight is green; / The aged winter is fleeing to the empty mountain.]

The language is vernacular yet elegant, and the tone is lyrical yet spoken. This passage is a showcase of Guo's poetic skillfulness in translation.

28. Guo, trans., *Fushide*, 1.
29. Ibid., 70.

But the combination of faithfulness and fluency, of accuracy and poetic effectiveness remains at best an ideal. As Nora Bartels's study of the 1928 edition of *Fushide* reminds us, Guo translated *Faust I* in a "historical circumstance" in which "paraphrases, omissions and additions were prevalent" in Chinese translations; Bartels is also right to see in the 1928 rendition "a combination of omissions, Sinifications, and comments."[30] Such practices in modern Chinese translation history do not necessarily mean the existence of what Venuti criticizes as a hegemonic "regime of fluent domestication," especially given the competition of different approaches to literary modernity in China.[31] The poetic language in Guo's translation in 1928 was bound to be inventive and unstable. In the 1920s New Poetry was still a literary experiment; no metrical rules were well established or standardized. In this sense, the textuality of Guo's translation embodies the historicity of a new poetic language, and I further suggest that a similar heterogeneous poetics also dominates Guo's later rendering of *Faust II* and constitutes a central characteristic of his translation as a whole from 1919–20 to 1947. Before doing that, I need to account for the time gap between Guo's 1928 rendition of *Faust I* and his 1947 rendition of *Faust II* by reviewing the genealogy of the critical receptions of *Faust* in China.

The Genealogy of Faust *Commentary in Revolutionary China*

May Fourth Chinese intellectuals' interest in Goethe's work is perhaps best shown in the 1920 correspondences between Guo, Zong Baihua, and Tian Han.[32] The catalyst of the three young men's friendship was their shared love of Goethe, pantheism/romanticism, and German culture. Liang Luo has pointed out the "Faustian trope" in the early Tian, who

30. Bartels, "Goethes *Faust* bei Mori Rintarō und Guo Moruo," 141.

31. The quote is from Venuti, *The Translator's Invisibility*, 184.

32. My survey of Chinese interpretations of *Faust* is only framed in the context of revolutionary China's intellectual politics in parallel to Guo's translation project from the May Fourth era to the 1940s. For more details about the *Faust* reception in China, see Yang Wuneng, *Gede yu zhongguo*.

also "discussed the spiritual and socialist implications of Goethe's romanticism with Guo Moruo and Zong Baihua."[33] Zong suggested to Guo in a letter that he was planning to write an essay to be titled "The German Poet Goethe's Outlooks on Life and the Universe."[34] In response, Guo wrote a long letter, in which he claimed that there are two types of "the development of genius," one being the "linear development," the other "the globular development." This idea of "the globular genius," suggesting a full development of personality, is akin to the ideal of the Renaissance man. Guo drew an analogy between Goethe and Confucius, arguing for their similar "globular development": "For this type, I only find two living examples: one is Confucius of our nation, the other Goethe of Germany."[35] He praised Goethe's scientific discoveries, political successes, and intellectual contributions: "[Goethe] is Faust . . . ; he is also simultaneously Mephistopheles." He characterized Confucius and Goethe as "Menschlichste aller Menschen" (the most human of all the men).[36]

The full development of humanity in a liberated individuality was without doubt a crucial ideal shared by Guo, Zong, and their intellectual peers—a new social group that bore the mark of May Fourth individualism. In the 1920s, Guo's translations of *Young Werther* and *Faust I* linked the image of Goethe decisively with the Wertherian personality and the Gretchen tragedy. The tragic conflict between free individuality and a repressive society preconditioned the initial reception of Goethe in China. With his turn to revolutionary activism, Guo was eager to take a Faustian step to plunge into "time's on-rushing tide, / Events' on-rolling stride" (lines 1753–54, translation modified). However, in the 1920s he still found himself alien to *Faust II*.[37] While he authored the first Chinese translation of *Faust I*, the first complete translation of *Faust I and II* was to be accomplished by Zhou Xuepu 周學普 in 1935.

The year 1932, the 100th anniversary of Goethe's death, saw a surge of critical interest in Goethe in China. Zong, for instance, wrote a long essay called "Goethe as an Illumination of Life" ("Gede dui rensheng de qishi" 歌德對人生的啓示). This essay, composed after Zong's study abroad

33. Luo, *The Avant-Garde and the Popular in Modern China*, 34.
34. Guo, Tian, and Zong, *San ye ji*, 9.
35. Ibid., 14.
36. Ibid., 15–16.
37. Guo, "Di er bu yi hou ji," 384.

in Germany, shows a strong influence of *Lebensphilosophe* (philosophy of life) as a critique of nineteenth-century modernity. The essay opens with an ultimate questioning about life: "What is life? What is the truth of life? What is the meaning of life? What is the purpose of life?"[38] Zong then situates Goethe in the historical-philosophical condition of modern man:

> Insofar as European culture is concerned, Goethe represented the inner life of modern man [*jindai ren* 近代人]. . . . Modern man has lost the harmony between humanity and universe of the Greek culture, and also lost the pious faith in transcendental God of Christianity. The human spirit was liberated and received its freedom; but in the meantime, it lost its anchor and had to search aimlessly in ennui, aspiring in its own effort to find the meaning of life. Goethe was the great representative of this Zeitgeist [*shidai jingshen*], and his masterpiece *Faust* is a total reflection of such a life and a solution to its problems (the contemporary philosopher Spengler in his *Decline of the Western Civilization* calls modern culture a "Faustian culture"). The life-content of Goethe and his persona of Faust is to experience this specific spiritual meaning of modern life as much as possible, to understand modern man's tragic striving, and to find a solution.[39]

With such a totalizing perspective and an idealistic vocabulary, Zong attempts to develop a dialectic of life and even a spiritual critique of modernity in his reading of *Faust*. For him, *Urfaust* is purely tragic because "life is the highest desire, and yet is also the biggest problem."[40] But in *Faust II*, he argues, Goethe's thought has a qualitative development. The tragedy of life receives a "reevaluation in Goethe's own development. The condemnable eternal flux of life now becomes the noblest value and meaning of life."[41] Citing Goethe's famous couplet—"Whoever strives in ceaseless toil, / Him we may grant redemption" (lines 11936–37)—Zong concludes: "[Faust] moves from the disillusionment with knowledge to the guilty conscience of love, and then moves from the dream of true beauty to a practical career. None of the experiences melt into

38. Zong Baihua, "Gede zhi rensheng qishi," 36.
39. Ibid., 36–37.
40. Ibid., 45.
41. Ibid., 46.

air; rather they are all stepping stones of the advancement of personality."[42] This interpretation was one of the early attempts of Chinese critics to capture the dialectical dimension of *Faust* as a totality, that is, "the vision of a human experience that continues and expands by passage through the necessary sorrow of negation."[43]

In contrast to this idealist dialectic of life was the appearance of a Chinese Marxist reading of Goethe. By 1932, left-leaning literary critics were familiar with Engels's comments on Goethe centered on the belated development of capitalism in Germany. In 1847, Engels criticized Goethe's "liberation from within":

> Goethe is thus at one moment a towering figure, at the next petty; at one moment an obstinate, mocking genius full of contempt for the world, at the next a circumspect, unexacting, narrow philistine. Not even Goethe was able to conquer the wretchedness of Germany; on the contrary, it conquered him, and this victory of wretchedness over the greatest of Germans is the most conclusive proof that it cannot be surmounted at all "from within."[44]

In his critique of German classical philosophy, Engels drew a parallel between Hegel and Goethe and famously underscored their shared limitation: "Hegel was a German, and like his contemporary Goethe had a bit of the philistine's queue dangling behind." Engels thus stated: "Each of them was an Olympian Zeus in his own sphere, yet neither of them ever quite freed himself from German philistinism."[45]

It was on this note of philistinism that Guo once denounced Goethe in the 1930s:

> Goethe . . . was a poet living in the age of Germany's transition from feudalism to capitalism. During his early years, he was a herald of the bourgeois revolution, but since he became the Weimar privy-councilor, he actually retreated into the camp of feudalism, and his aristocratic taste and worship of emperors and kings really had a strong stink. Heine castigated

42. Ibid., 47.
43. De Man, "Thematic Criticism and the Theme of Faust," 84.
44. Engels, "German Socialism in Verse and Prose," 259.
45. Engels, *Ludwig Feuerbach and the End of German Classical Philosophy*, 600.

> him, saying that he only knew how to kiss women—if we put it in the language of *Dream of the Red Chamber* [*Hong lou meng* 紅樓夢], it means "eating the rouge on the young girls' lips"; our old Mr. Goethe can be called a Jia Baoyu 賈寶玉 of Germany.[46]

This unexpected comparison of Goethe to Jia Baoyu, the protagonist of the classical Chinese novel *Dream of the Red Chamber* who is a teenager in an aristocratic family and a prototypical sentimental womanizer, shows an exaggerated change of Guo's attitude toward Goethe, which seems attributable to the dogmatic leftist position assumed in many of his 1930s works.

As a result, in 1930s China a more engaging Marxist reading was provided by Hu Qiuyuan, a quasi-Marxist critic who was not affiliated with the CCP. In 1932, Hu tried to gauge both Goethe's greatness and limitation in "Goethe in the Marxist Light" ("Makesizhuyi suojian de Gede" 馬克思主義所見的歌德). His interpretation of *Faust* shifts the focus from the theme of the individual development to the relationship between Faust and Mephistopheles (in Zong's essay, Mephistopheles is almost absent) and links the power of the devil to a Marxist schema of historical development. Of particular interest is Hu's synopsis of Part II and his characterization of the world that Faust eventually builds: "Faust metamorphoses from a thinker in the study room to a lover, then to an artist, and to a builder of actual life." The world Faust builds is a new bourgeois society developed out of the Middle Ages. The brutal demolition of the home of Philemon and Baucis during Faust's land reclamation project is then "an allegory of the transition from the agricultural feudal life to the industrial-commercial culture."[47]

It is noteworthy that Hu viewed Faust as a capitalist developer. The process of development is simultaneously a process of destruction: " 'Good' [*shan* 善] is born out of 'Evil' [*e* 惡]. . . . The individual sin is paid off by the happiness of the multitudes, and Good triumphs over Evil. The development of humanity is progressive. But without 'Evil,' the progress is impossible. The personification of Evil is the 'spirit of negation'—Mephistopheles, who . . . always hopes for Evil but arrives at the con-

46. Guo, *Chuangzao shinian*, in *GQJ/W*, 12:78–79.
47. Hu Qiuyuan, "Makesizhuyi suojian de Gede," 40.

verse of Evil, and therefore creates 'the spirit of Good.' "[48] Though Hu's interpretation of Mephistopheles is largely based on his translation of V. M. Fritche, a Soviet critic, his essay points to a new dialectical conception of history, a theme that, according to Lukács's 1940s studies, binds Goethe's *Faust* with Hegel's philosophy: "So for Goethe and Hegel both, the unceasing progress of the human species results from a chain of individual tragedies."[49]

While Zong's thematic reading of *Faust* offered a dialectic of life, Hu's demonstrated a dialectic of history. These two approaches were developed in more significant ways in the works of Feng Zhi and Guo. Feng expanded the approach of philosophy of life in response to the spiritual problems confronting Chinese liberal intellectuals in the 1940s, whereas Guo's interpretation overcame the dogmatic leftist reading and translated *Faust* into an allegorical drama of modern Chinese history.

Feng Zhi versus Guo: Bildung, *Metamorphosis, and Wartime China*

As Paul de Man summarizes, "the first part of [*Faust*] presents the history of a singular and individual consciousness (Goethe's *kleine Welt*) while the second presents the history of an intersubjective, universal consciousness, preoccupied with the *grosse Welt*."[50] In the meantime, however, Part II resists any easy thematization because it lacks a consistent plot line that corresponds to a thematic sequence. De Man points out that in Part II, "zones of the imaginary, degrees of surreality, and multiple temporalities are superimposed on one another to make a tangle of indescribable complexity."[51] In 1932 Guo complained that "the construction of the whole drama [of *Faust II*] is too fragmented [*zhili* 支離]."[52] He fell short of continuing his translation in the 1930s, but in the early 1940s

48. Ibid., 41.
49. Lukács, *Goethe and His Age*, 181.
50. De Man, "Thematic Criticism and the Theme of Faust," 84.
51. Ibid., 85.
52. Guo, *Chuangzao shinian*, in *GQJ/W*, 12:75.

Feng Zhi, another Chinese poet and scholar, criticized this neglect and called for a true encounter with *Faust II*.[53]

Feng and Guo have long been considered two crucial figures in Chinese scholarship on German literature, but their life paths had more divergences than convergences. Twelve years younger than Guo, Feng was a prolific poet, translator, and scholar. While Guo is famous for his revolutionary-romantic poetry, Feng is known for his Rilkean modernist sonnets. While Guo translated *Young Werther* and *Faust*, Feng rendered into Chinese *Wilhelm Meister's Apprenticeship* and Schiller's *On the Aesthetic Education of Man*. While Guo was an "amateur" scholar of German culture, Feng attended the University of Heidelberg and received his doctoral degree in 1935 with a dissertation on Novalis's poetry. While Guo was a Marxist, Feng's mind was rooted in the European tradition of humanism and idealism. In the 1940s, their sociopolitical positions were equally different. Working in the wartime capital Chongqing, Guo was a leader of the Chongqing progressive cultural movement and "democratic movement" (*minzhu yundong* 民主運動), and in the postwar years he performed as an activist solidarizing with the CCP. Feng was a professor at the National Southwest Associated University in Kunming (also known by its acronym as Xinan Lianda 西南聯大), an institution composed of three prominent universities in exile—Peking University, Tsinghua University, and Nankai University—which had fled from northern China. The Kunming intellectual community was an enclave of the independent intellectuals who generally refused to side with either the GMD or CCP but were equally concerned with China's national survival and spiritual revival. In this wartime atmosphere, Feng composed a series of essays on Goethe, among which two were devoted to *Faust*: "On the Devil in *Faust*" ("Fushide li de mo" 《浮士德》里的魔) and "Goethe's Philosophy of Nature Seen from the Character of Homunculus" ("Cong Fushide li de renzaoren luelun Gede de ziran zhexue" 從《浮士德》里的人造人略論歌德的自然哲學).

In Feng's reading, the dialectic of life was developed into a dialectic of *Bildung*. The opening of "On the Devil in *Faust*" addressed the neglect of *Faust II* among Chinese readers, and its emphasis on the totality of the two parts of *Faust* was an implicit response to the fact that Guo

53. Feng Zhi, "Fushide li de mo," 25.

had expressed his dislike of Part II in the 1930s. Feng, instead, saw the whole poem as being composed of a series of interlocking tragedies: first, the tragedy of the scholar; second, the love tragedy with Gretchen; third, the tragedy of beauty with Helena and Euphorion; last, the tragedy of career, with the conquest of nature.[54] Referring to the Chinese idiom "ceaseless self-striving" (*ziqiang buxi* 自強不息), Feng would agree with Lukács that the central theme of *Faust* is man's progress through self-creativity.[55] From the Faust-Mephistopheles duel, Feng and Lukács concluded in the 1940s that "the struggle between good and evil engenders the forward direction of evolution."[56] The similarity between Feng's and Lukács's perspectives indicated a shared intellectual politics in the age of antifascism. Whereas Lukács emphasized "the partially capitalist basis of Mephisto's character," Feng saw in this theme a philosophy of *Bildung* of individuality rather than any materialist conception of history.[57] His idealist reading described Mephistopheles as the embodiment of the aberrant development of the enlightenment Reason: "This negative spirit originated from the one-sided Reason. The mid-eighteenth century was the Age of Reason in Europe. Reason, on the positive side, liberated humans from the superstitions that had hindered progress, and helped build a well-developed humanity. But on the other side, it limited the radium of human activity, banishing feeling and understanding."[58] One can read this characterization of Mephistopheles as a mild self-critique of China's own enlightenment intellectuals, as their social radius became more and more confined in wartime China dominated by the competition between the GMD and CCP.

More symptomatic is Feng's obsession with the character of the man-made life, Homunculus. Though his essay on Homunculus is supposed to be about Goethe's natural philosophy, the discussion of water as the original element of the world formation is in fact only a preparation for a larger argument about "metamorphosis." As Xiaojue Wang's study has pointed out, for Feng, "this principle of [metamorphosis or *bian* 變]

54. Ibid., 26.

55. The idiom is derived from the *Book of Change*. Feng Zhi, "Fushide li de mo," 28, 33. Also see Lukács, *Goethe and His Age*.

56. Lukács, *Goethe and His Age*, 197.

57. Ibid., 200.

58. Feng Zhi, "Fushide li de mo," 35.

applies to the development of not only plants and insects but also human beings and society."[59] In his essay on Homunculus, Feng views Wagner (Faust's former disciple) as the representative of enlightenment. Homunculus, the product of Wagner's knowledge, is thus the offspring of the enlightenment reason, and therefore is "body-less": living in a flask, Homunculus needs to find an "actual life."[60] His journey (with Thales) of finding the true form of life should then be read in relation to Goethe's "Metamorphosenlehre" (*tuibian lun* 蜕變論; theory of metamorphosis). The passage Feng refers to is the lines Thales speaks to Homunculus:

> Espouse the recommended part,
> Begin creation from the start.
> For swift enactment gird your will!
> You move there by eternal norms,
> Through thousand, countless thousand forms,
> There's time enough for manship still. (lines 8321–26)

Thales describes, according to Feng, an organic process of evolution through stages of metamorphosis. This is an allegory of human *Bildung* toward the true form of "manhood." The moment of the crashing of the crystal container and the scattering of Homunculus into the ocean does not mean death but is the metamorphosis of Homunculus's formless and purely spiritual existence into a more universal body, or in Jane Brown's language, a "union of ideal and real."[61] The marriage of Homunculus and the water element, symbolizing the reunion with the actual life, means an overcoming of the enlightenment reason and pure spirituality. By reading Homunculus's journey, Feng proposes a "*Metamorphosenlehre* [theory of metamorphosis] of human."[62]

Feng's particular interest in Homunculus's search for true life points to a deeper spiritual and political anxiety shared by many Chinese intellectuals at that historical moment. In fact, the situation of the indepen-

59. Xiaojue Wang, *Modernity with a Cold War Face*, 235.

60. Feng Zhi, "Cong Fushide li de renzaoren lue lun Gede de ziran zhexue," 53–54.

61. Brown, *Goethe's* Faust, 175; also see Feng Zhi, "Cong Fushide li de renzaoren lue lun Gede de ziran zhexue," 55–56.

62. Feng Zhi, "Cong Fushide li de renzaoren lue lun Gede de ziran zhexue," 59.

dent intellectuals—including Feng—can be easily caricatured by the image of Homunculus as "a shining little dwarf" (line 8245). For all their spiritual splendor as the offspring of the May Fourth enlightenment, the independent intellectuals were nevertheless imprisoned in their spiritual world. During wartime, these intellectuals acutely realized that as a social group they did not have an "actual life" and remained politically "body-less." Like Homunculus, they were anxious to overcome the abstractness of their social existence and enter the ocean of sociopolitical change. As David Wang points out in his analysis of Feng's "born-again lyricism," "Feng Zhi insinuates that the Chinese intellectual has also lived in an insular world and must throw himself into 'the sea of life.' "[63]

The praise of Homunculus's metamorphosis from spirituality to actuality was thus emblematic of the political implications of Feng's *Bildung* of the "New Man." In another essay, titled "Goethe and the Education of Man" ("Gede yu ren de jiaoyu" 歌德與人的教育), Feng combined his readings of *Faust* and *Wilhelm Meister*. Arguing that an understanding of Goethe based on Guo's translations would be partial, if not misleading, Feng emphasized the moment of interiorization (that is, the overcoming from within, as Engels notes) in Goethe's life and work. Then he suggested that when one strives for the whole "human species," Mephistopheles will lose his power.[64] The *Bildung* of the individual, he concluded, has the goal of creating the "New Man" (*xinren* 新人) as a type. This idea of the New Man meant the full development and education of the individuality as the preparation for a higher "collectivity" and "new society," and in the meantime was supposed to differ from the political New Man proposed by the communist revolutionaries.[65] This essay, concluding Feng's wartime Goethe studies, was written immediately after the collapse of Hitler's regime. When all the major political forces of China started to draft their blueprints for a postwar "New China," Feng's ideal of metamorphosis contained the independent intellectuals' social-democratic vision of the reconstruction of China based on the "education of man."[66]

63. David Wang, *The Lyrical in Epic Time*, 144.

64. Feng Zhi, "Gede yu ren de jiaoyu," 85.

65. Ibid., 86.

66. How such independent intellectuals as Feng Zhi negotiated their political visions with CCP's agenda of "people's democracy" has been an issue that attracts the

Feng's avoidance of Faust's final social-industrial project is thus not surprising. Nor is the absence of any mention of Germany's social development in Goethe's age. In contrast to this was Guo's rediscovery of Goethe as a symbol of German modernity. Guo's new perspective should be situated in a global context of the leftist reflections on fascism in the 1940s. Like many critics of German fascism (such as Ernst Bloch, see below), during World War II he considered the remnants of feudalism to be the soil of fascism: "Japan, Germany and Italy are countries that had rapid modernization without getting rid of the feudal forces."[67] He used a rhetoric of bestiality versus humanity, attributing fascism to bestialization of humanity. In 1937, he argued: "We must continue this war of reason against bestiality, and unite all the nations and individuals of reason to destroy all the beasts in the human form."[68] On the occasion of the republication of *Fushide I* in 1944, Guo's invocation of the spirit of Goethe formed a hidden dialogue with Feng's view of human *Bildung*:

> The individuality should not be negated, but a high purpose should be established in order to orient its development. . . .
>
> Goethe had wisdom in self-understanding, knowing that there were two opposing spirits fighting constantly in his heart; so he strove to reconcile them and develop himself to redeem humanity. Though he failed to rid himself of his medieval vestment, his lifelong striving was about the externalization of this ideal. He externalized this ideal in his work, and also in his personality, and thereby pursued a synthetic unity.
>
> The German nation did not follow the instruction of this man of labor, and was misguided into bestiality.[69]

Despite a shared humanistic vision, Guo's historical consciousness and Marxist commitment determined a significant difference from Feng's perspective. With a critique of German modernization, Guo embraced a

critical attention of many scholars. See, for example, He Guimei, *Zhuanzhe de shidai*, 134–204. Similarly, for Xiaojue Wang, the issue of the "relationship between the individual and society" was key to Feng's "transition from poetry to politics in socialist China." Xiaojue Wang, *Modernity with a Cold War Face*, 203.

67. Guo, "Xin wenyi de shiming," in *GQJ/W*, 19:379.
68. Guo, "Lixing yu shouxing zhi zhan," in *GQJ/W*, 18:155.
69. Guo, "Ren hu, ren hu, hun xi guilai," in *GQJ/W*, 19:411.

historicist alternative to the individualist perspective and eventually found his own way into the thematic world of *Faust II*. After calling on the soul of Goethe as the spirit of humanity—"human, human, your soul come back"—Guo indicated his wish to translate *Faust II*: "Last year my desire to continue my work and translate Part II was aroused, but I accomplished nothing yet."[70] He explained the continued postponement: "I am also a man of labor, . . . and what I need to work on [right now] seems to be more important than [the translation project]."[71] From 1943 to late 1946, he submerged himself in the actual *grosse Welt* of China's politics, fighting for a coalition government as proposed by the CCP. It was the failure of the postwar negotiations for peace and democracy that gave him the "leisure to repay [this] debt."[72]

The Poetic Bricolage in Guo's Translation of Faust II

"The range and variety of verse forms in *Faust* is more complex than in any other work of literature," thus states Cyrus Hamlin. Commenting on the composition of *Faust*, he continues: "Goethe undertook to imitate and adapt forms from the entire tradition of Western poetry. The variety of verse forms is especially great in Part II, which contains several scenes depending sometimes on a sense of earlier poetic structures, sometimes on quasi-musical effects."[73] The coexistence of different verse forms also corresponds to the vast historical landscape synchronized into this modern epic. As Moretti compellingly argues, "*Faust* is a kind of Europe in verse, full of ruined castles and pointless conflicts, and literally invaded by the past: characters, places, meters, stories, allegories, and phantasms."[74] *Faust*, especially Part II, is thus recognizable as a "storehouse of poetical and historical memories."[75] Moretti discerns in

70. Ibid., 412.
71. Ibid.
72. Guo, "Di er bu yi hou ji," 385.
73. Hamlin, "The Composition of *Faust*," 505.
74. Moretti, *Modern Epic*, 40.
75. Ibid.

Goethe's composition a poetics of "*bricolage*: old materials, and new treatment."[76]

This dazzling phantasmagoria of diverse forms had once alienated Guo from Part II. In the early 1930s, Guo explained why he had only translated Part I: "Part II is even lengthier and more difficult to translate. The reason for this difficulty is that there are even more plays of words than in Part I."[77] By "plays of words" (*wenzi youxi* 文字遊戲), Guo meant the verse digressions that seem unrelated to the main storyline of Faust's adventures. This phenomenon also prompted Guo to reflect on the role of verse in drama: "The Western verse drama, as a form, deserves our consideration, for it is highly unnatural to have all the dialogues in rhyme. . . . If I translate all the [plays of words in *Faust*] into prose, then they become senseless skeletons. If I translate them into verse forms, they are nevertheless still a number of plays of words in Chinese."[78]

Guo's complaint showed his sensitivity to the issue of poetic form. So in 1947, how did he deal with this variety of verse forms and poetic heterogeneity in his translation of *Faust II*? His solution was a Chinese bricolage, characteristic of anachronistic improvisation and makeshift formal hybridity. Consider, for example, the extreme case where Guo resorts to a five-syllable form of doggerel to translate Pulcinelli's playful lines in the scene "Spacious Hall":

> Ihr seid die Toren
> Gebückt geboren.
> Wir sind die Klugen
> Die nie was trugen;
> Denn unsre Kappen,
> Jacken und Lappen
> Sind leicht zu tragen.
> Und mit Behagen
> Wir immer müßig,
> Pantoffelfüßig,
> Durch Markt und Haufen
> Einher zu laufen. (lines 5215–26)

76. Ibid., 41.
77. Guo, *Chuangzao shinian*, in *GQJ/W*, 12:75.
78. Ibid.

(You are the zanies, / For drudging sent. / We are the brainies / Who never bent; / For our caps, / Jackets, and flaps / Are feather-light wraps. / We take our pleasure / As market trippers, / In constant leisure / And floppy slippers, / On saunters bent.)

你們大傻子,
生成駝背子,
我們聰明子,
決不背啥子;
頭上小帽子,
身上短打子,
一身輕便子,
躡上拖鞋子,
無憂無慮子,
市上逍遙子,
呆著吊膀子。[79]

[You idiots, / Born to be hunchbacks; / We are smart kids, / Never learning by rote. / On our heads are small caps; / We wear shorts, / Easy to move; / Wearing slippers, / We are carefree dandies, / Wondering in the market, / Doing nothing with our arms.]

Guo's excessive use of *–zi* 子, a Chinese noun suffix that usually has a strong colloquial effect, refunctionizes it into a rhyming marker of light verse.

In general, Guo has to mobilize all the formal techniques available to him and redevise them into new forms. For instance, he uses a particular kind of five-character metric form reminiscent of the *yuefu* 樂府 style in classical poetry, and redevises it as a vernacular form to deal with the choruses in the Helena act and the closing scene. The following lines are a sensible translation that rearranges the choral ode in "Before the Palace of Menelaus at Sparta":

Werfet o Schwestern, ihr
Traurig gefangenen,
Alle Schmerzen ins Weite;
Teilet der Herrin Glück,

79. Guo, trans., *Fushide di er bu*, 32.

Teilet Helenens Glück,
Welche zu Vaterhauses Herd,
Zwar mit spätzurückkehrendem,
Aber mit desto festerem
Fuße freudig herannaht. (lines 8610–18)

(Cast any suffering / Far away, sisters, you / Dolefully captive ones; / Share in our lady's bliss, / Helena's happiness, / Who joyously, on feet / Returning belatedly, to be sure, / But all the firmer for that, / Nears her paternal hearth.)

嗟我諸姊妹，
被俘誠可哀，
請將苦痛事，
一律都拋開；
海倫今已歸，
福社與之偕。[80]

[Oh my sisters, / Being captives are truly lamentable. / Please cast any suffering / Away altogether; / Today Helen has returned, / And coming with her is the paternal hearth of happiness.]

In the closing scenes, the lines of Care (Sorge) are consistently rendered into the six-character verse, in which the border between the classical and the vernacular disappears:

Wen ich einmal besitze
Dem ist alle Welt nichts nütze,
Ewiges Düstre steigt herunter,
Sonne geht nicht auf noch unter. (lines 11453–56)

(Once I mark him and assail him, / Nothing earthly will avail him, / Neverending gloom descending, / Sun his rise and fall suspending.)

誰若被我佔有，
世界化爲烏有，
永恆之夜罩臨，
日不沒兮不昇。[81]

[Whoever you are, if you are owned by me, / Your world will become nothing. / The eternal night is descending, / The sun will not set nor rise.]

80. Ibid., 205–6.
81. Ibid., 350.

In a similar fashion, the central thematic couplet is translated into a seven-character pattern of the vernacular:

> Wer immer strebend sich bemüht,
> Den können wir erlösen. (lines 11936–37)
>
> (Whoever strives in ceaseless toil, / Him we may grant redemption.)
>
> 凡是自強不息者,
> 到頭我輩都能救。[82]
>
> [Whoever strengthens himself ceaselessly, / Him we will at the end be able to save.]

Compared with the use of classical prosody in some twentieth-century traditionalist poets' translations of Western poetry, what Guo provided is a combination of make-do formality and vernacular flexibility. This poetic heterogeneity is further complicated by a vocabulary ranging across ancient Chinese terms, Buddhist concepts, and vulgar slang.[83] Similar to what we have seen in chapter 1, some of Guo's translation choices seem to lead to what Lawrence Venuti calls "domestication" in Anglo-American translations. Yet Guo's strategies are not intended for homogeneity of the "dominant target-language cultural values."[84] In his case, the foreignness of the German tragedy is rendered with the recycled classical remnants and the provisionally fixed semantic or semiotic choices. Although at first glance it goes against the approach of foreignization that Venuti valorizes, his attempt is experimental in its own right and produces a defamiliarizing rather than naturalizing effect. The poetic heterogeneity in his *Fushide* is not only a "locus of difference"[85] between the original and the target culture; it also contains the differences within

82. Ibid., 373.

83. For example, Guo translates the titles of the courtiers in Part II consistently into ancient Chinese official titles, such as *Schatzmeister* into *hubu shangshu* 户部尚書 [minister of population], and *Astrolog* into *qintian jian* 欽天監 [minister of heaven measurement]. He uses the Buddhist concept of Avīci (*abi diyu* 阿鼻地獄) to translate the hell and underground. He also takes liberties to use *biesan* 癟三, a Shanghai slang word for personal denigration. See Guo, trans., *Fushide di er bu*.

84. Venuti, *The Translator's Invisibility*, 23.

85. Ibid., 42.

modern Chinese literature. It is not my task to judge whether this poetic heterogeneity in Guo's translation is successful or counterproductive. Suffice it to say that his bricolage represents a unique possibility of the poetic language, a possibility which at that historical moment kept a marked distance from a Europeanized vernacular among modernist writers (such as Feng Zhi) and yet was also obviously different from the use of local dialects and national-popular forms among leftist writers. This poetic heterogeneity, in turn, renders *Faust* even more phantasmal, as the German masterpiece is now invaded by a wide range of Chinese poetic patterns, dictions, and even temporalities—both ancient and modern.

Corresponding to this poetic medley is the speed with which Guo executed his translation project. According to Guo, he finished his rendering of *Faust II* almost miraculously within forty days.[86] It inevitably solicits the question as to what strategies the translator adopted to accomplish this huge project over such a short course of time. In this regard, the relationship of his translation to the Japanese rendition of *Faust* by famous Japanese writer Mori Ōgai 森鷗外 (1862–1922) is worth mentioning in passing. While Bartels's study compares Mori's 1913 translation and Guo's 1928 translation of *Faust I* (one of her conclusions is that their translations bear a "seal of two important historical personalities"[87]), Guo himself informs the reader that when working on Part II in the 1940s, he kept handy for reference Mori's Japanese translation, Bayard Taylor's English version, and Zhou Xuepu's Chinese one.[88] My analysis is not concerned about the extent to which Guo's version relies on these preexisting translations.[89] In what follows I illustrate how his *Fushide II*, which at some points incorporates Mori's version, fulfills a revolutionary allegorization of *Faust*/*Fushide*. Hence, we need to move from the level of poetics back to the level of thematics.

86. Guo, trans., *Fushide di er bu*, 385.

87. Bartels, "Goethes *Faust* bei Mori Rintarō und Guo Moruo," 141.

88. Guo, "Di er bu yi hou ji," 387.

89. Some of the above-cited passages are actually examples showing that Guo's treatment of Goethe's poetic style diverges significantly from Mori's.

A Thematic Translation: Zeitgeist, Nonsynchronism, Synchronization

Guo attributed his earlier "repulsion" (*yanwu* 厭惡) from *Faust II* to the remote distance he had from the mature Goethe's spiritual world.[90] But after a twenty-year hiatus, he finished its Chinese translation in a short period of time. Again, the timing was significant. The post-1945 peace negotiations for a coalition democratic government failed, temporarily frustrating Guo's hope for a new China. Such a retreat from direct political participation was what enabled Guo to concentrate on the work of translation. More important, he referred to his own spiritual growth in China's revolutionary struggles: "My current age and life experience have drawn me closer to the Goethe writing Part II from 1797 to 1832; Goethe satirized Germany's reality—the reality in which even the immense antifeudal effort could not expel the dense mist due to the heavy suppression of the feudal residue. This tragic atmosphere resembles our situation in today's China."[91] In the 1940s, consequently, Guo's alienation from *Faust II* gave way to a new historical consciousness propelled by a kinship between Goethe's Germany and "today's China." The "dense mist" of *Faust II* that had once frustrated Guo on the formal level now manifested itself as the historical content occupying his mind in the 1940s. While Feng's account of Part II revolved around the theme of cultivation, Guo moved to a perspective of historicism.

Just as Goethe's poetic language is a combination of various verse forms, so *Faust* is a world text famous for anachronistic coexistence of different temporalities. Another Chinese translator of *Faust*, Zhou Xuepu, whose interpretation echoed Zong's and focused on the "struggle between the centrifugal and centripetal forces in humanity," had observed in his 1936 rendition: "The opening scenes of Part I are medieval"; "the Gretchen tragedy is about the real civil society"; the Helen scenario in Part II is "classical"; the scenario of Faust's colony is "modern"; and the ending is

90. Guo, "Di er bu yi hou ji," 384.
91. Ibid., 385.

"catholic and mystic."[92] Even more specific is Moretti's characterization of the "multiple temporalities" in Part II:

> It starts off from the Renaissance of the Imperial Court, then moves from there to the Mothers who exist before and outside time; it goes back to the Renaissance, where French Revolution *assignats* crop up; then it goes back to the Classical Walpurgis Night, on the anniversary of Pharsalus; farther back—between Homer and the Tragedians—with the "Helen" Act; forward to the Crusades; back to Arcadia; two millennia forward in the vision of Byron, then again to the Renaissance; the ghosts of mediaeval wars are evoked; it moves forward to Holland, and then to the industrial visions of the dying Faust; and ends in a Marian-Catholic atmosphere, between Middle Ages and Counter-Reformation.
>
> This is a sequence which—as a sequence—has no meaning.[93]

This anachronistic sequence reminds us of Ernst Bloch's famous definition of modern Germany as "the classical land of non-contemporaneity, i.e. of unsurmounted remnants of older economic being and consciousness."[94] Moretti argues that Goethe's *Faust II* embodies a "rhetorical figure" of "contemporaneity of the non-contemporaneous."[95]

Guo was painfully conscious of this rhetoric of nonsynchronism. At the very beginning of "A Concise Interpretation of *Faust*" ("Fushide jian lun" 浮士德簡論), a 1947 text of central importance, he noted: "In Part II any consistent sequence [*lianguan xing* 連貫性] of a storyline is all but abandoned, and as a result [the text] is obscure to an astonishing degree."[96] Commenting on the "episodic nature of the play" and the "discontinuities in the plot," Jane Brown observes that "there is a distinguished history of defences of the unity of the play in conceptual or thematic terms."[97] Like Lukács, Guo of the 1940s came to find in the fragmented nature of *Faust* a totality, an "abbreviated reproduction of the stages traversed by

92. Zhou Xuepu, "Yizhe xu," 33.
93. Moretti, *Modern Epic*, 52.
94. Bloch, *Heritage of Our Times*, 106.
95. Moretti, *Modern Epic*, 52–91.
96. Guo, "Fushide jian lun," 3.
97. Brown, *Goethe's* Faust, 23.

the consciousness of men in the course of history."[98] He turned to the concept of *shidai jingshen*: "But [*Faust*] is a whole [*zhengti* 整體]. In forming a whole, it has a consistent thematic thread. It . . . is a developmental history of Zeitgeist [*shidai jingshen*]. Which epoch [*shidai*] is it? What is its development? How has it developed? The more than sixteen thousand lines of *Faust* are all about this actual history."[99]

A catchword of modern historical teleology though it is, "Zeitgeist" here nevertheless becomes an organizing metaphor of incomplete modernization, belated revolution, and epochal anachronism. With a focus on Germany's feudal remnants, Guo constructed a dialectical relation between the phenomenon of "multiple temporalities" and the thematic unity of Zeitgeist. He reimagined this murky temporal "heterogeneity" as a tragic unfolding of Zeitgeist:

> [*Faust*] is clothed in a medieval vestment, but what is inside is the fire of the modern man's insatiable impulse. It seems to be a contradiction, and this ostensible contradiction determines the immense heterogeneity [*pangzaxing* 龐雜性] within *Faust*. But we should not be shocked by the appearance of this immense heterogeneity. . . . [The murkiness] . . . is actually . . . a faithful record of the development of the age. So I venture to argue that this is a work of reality, not only filled with the appearances of reality, but also with the soul [*hun* 魂] of reality. A macro-soul [*da hun* 大魂] of reality, that is, the Zeitgeist, embodies a wide variety of micro-souls of reality, i.e. individualities. . . . [Goethe] . . . revealed the truth of the development of the world, and grasped this dialectical spirit.[100]

The critique of noncontemporaneity in German modernity can be traced to—as I mentioned in chapter 2—Marx's observation that the Germans were not historical "contemporaries" of the modern age. It became a consensus among Marxist thinkers to see the "retarded development of capitalism" and the postponement of the "bourgeois-democratic revolution" as a general characteristic of German modernity.[101] "Unlike England,

98. Lukács, *Goethe and His Age*, 176, 178.

99. Guo, "Fushide jian lun," 3.

100. Ibid., 9–10.

101. For a Marxist account of the delayed "bourgeois-democratic revolution" in Germany, see Lukács, *The Destruction of Reason*, 37–94.

and especially France," Bloch noted in 1932, "Germany . . . had managed no bourgeois revolution."[102] I have little evidence about whether Guo had read the related works of either Lukács or Bloch, but his verdict was strikingly similar: "Britain had harvested the success of the Glorious Revolution, and France was seeking the fulfilment of the Revolution in the bloody Terror. Germany was lagging behind."[103]

The issue of late development, as Harootunian suggests, had been haunting many Chinese Marxists since the early 1930s, leading to a series of debates on historical time and periodization (also see my chapter 4).[104] Guo now saw the "murkiness" or heterogeneity of Part II as historically conditioned: "Germany's metamorphosis from a feudal society to a capitalist society was belated, and its feudal remnants, difficult to be superseded, persisted until the recent destruction of Nazism." The theme of Zeitgeist thus has to figure—tragically and dialectically—in the "strange scenes in which different epochs meet and mingle."[105] Guo urged Chinese readers to read *Faust II* in this historical context: "You will clearly feel a fleshly kinship in the seemingly chaotic density."[106] Hence the thematic resonance of *Faust II* in Guo's translation: "Just as I was inspired by Germany's *Sturm und Drang* spirit when translating Part I, I now resonate with Part II on [the theme] of the difficulty of transformation [*tuibian jiannan* 蛻變艱難]."[107] It is worth recalling in passing that *tuibian* had also been Guo's proposal for a Chinese translation of *Aufheben* (see chapter 2). More interestingly, Feng had used the same term in his translation of Goethe's idea of *Metamorphosenlehre* (theory of metamorphosis) as *tuibian lun* 蛻變論. While for Feng the term *tuibian* signifies the human metamorphosis as a process of education, for Guo *tuibian* denotes sociohistorical modernization as a "difficult" revolutionary change.

Guo's translation/interpretation in this sense was deeply embedded in the culture and politics of China's transformation in the 1940s. By 1945, the question about China's modernization and postwar reconstruction—summarized by Mao as "Whither China?"—had dominated the intel-

102. Bloch, *Heritage of Our Times*, 106.
103. Guo, "Fushide jian lun," 8.
104. See Harootunian, *Marx After Marx*, chapter 4.
105. Moretti, *Modern Epic*, 55.
106. Guo, "Di er bu yihou ji," 386.
107. Ibid., 385–86.

lectual community.[108] In Guo's words: China represented "the sickness of the heaven and the earth."[109] The dramatic sequence of the postwar CCP-GMD negotiations and the all-out civil war was experienced as chaotic, confusing, and tragic as Goethe's anachronistic sequence. Moretti reads *Faust II* as a "poem of the state of exception."[110] Guo's China, overshadowed by all the uncertainties of a civil war, similarly found itself in a state of exception.

Interrogating the reimagination of world history in late Qing China, Rebecca Karl shows "how a diachronically Darwinian staged world could be constituted as an active site of global reimaginings," which turned "global unevenness" into a "shared moment."[111] In the context of China's revolutionary century, we saw in chapter 2 how different temporal frameworks were mobilized and synchronized into a shared moment of crisis in 1928. This dialectic between diachronic unevenness and synchronic "shared moments" was central to the imaginaries of the Chinese Revolution. The "fleshly kinship" with the German phenomenon of noncontemporaneity thus points us back to an experience of China's "tragic epoch" (*beiju shidai* 悲劇時代). In 1946, when he was involved in the CCP-GMD negotiations, Guo returned to the keyword *shidai* (epoch): "The present is a tragic epoch, but it is also an epoch of the rebirth of gods." The epoch was a transition in which the wretchedness of the old and the political (or quasi-theological) hope of people's democracy simultaneously coexisted: "The arrogant, aggressive ghosts of the old age permeate every place, but every place is also shining with the solemnly innocent and selfless morning stars of the new epoch."[112] The young leftist writer Lu Ling 路翎 (1923–94) expressed a similar consciousness of historical time and its "difficulty": "A new epoch [*shidai*] will be born in the baptism of blood. Time is advancing haltingly and difficultly."[113] Guo's preoccupation with the theme of Zeitgeist/*shidai jingshen* in his 1947 translation thus shows

108. Mao Zedong, "On New Democracy," 339.
109. Guo, "Tian di xuan huang," in *GQJ/W*, 20:6.
110. Moretti, *Modern Epic*, 43.
111. Karl, *Staging the World*, 16.
112. Guo, *Nanjing yinxiang*, in *GQJ/W*, 14:533.
113. Cited in Qian Liqun, *1948: Tian di xuan huang*, 299.

a drive of self-periodization in such a state of emergency.[114] It is a symbolic act of synchronizing the shared experience of nonsynchronism into a figuration of the ongoing Chinese Revolution. Such a translation is not only subjective-interpretative, it is also historical and thematic, conditioned in an imagined translatability of Zeitgeist.

In fact, this tendency to use translation as an allegorical representation of contemporary conditions was already commonly manifested in late nineteenth-century and early twentieth-century Chinese translations. Michael Hill's study, for instance, shows how some of Lin Shu's late Qing translations of Charles Dickens's works made "it possible for readers to begin to see 'our China' as an entity that can be represented in fiction."[115] Moreover, Mark Gamsa's two books about Russian literature in twentieth-century China demonstrate that many translations were concerned about how to transform China by imitating Russia. " 'Word' became identical to 'Deed,' " as Gamsa argues, and Russian/Soviet literature became a manual of practice in China.[116] In Guo's leftist career, literary translations started to contain more and more allegorical interpretations of China's sociopolitical affairs. In the mid-1930s, for example, when translating Schiller's depiction of the Thirty Years' War in the opening of the Wallenstein trilogy, Guo found a "teaching for [our] epoch" (*dui shidai de jiaoxun* 對時代的教訓).[117] By the "epoch" Guo meant to refer to China's historical situation, which had not stripped itself of "the skin of the feudal epoch": "Isn't the situation [Schiller described] what is present before our eyes?"[118] As Joseph Levenson has observed, Guo's translation of Schiller's plays "prescribed a revolutionary medicine for the Chinese body politics": "[Guo] made both the 'periodization' case for

114. The CCP–GMD negotiations eventually fell apart in late 1946. Before his departure from the GMD capital Nanjing, Zhou Enlai, the chief CCP negotiator, wrote Guo an intimate farewell letter. With the civil war escalating, Guo finished his translation before leaving Shanghai for Hong Kong in 1947. The complete translation was published in November 1947, the same month as his arrival in Hong Kong. For his other cultural activities in Hong Kong, see Guo, *Yingjie xin Zhongguo*.

115. Hill, *Lin Shu, Inc.*, 114.

116. Gamsa, *The Reading of Russian Literature in China*, 116. Also see Gamsa, *The Chinese Translation of Russian Literature*. Guo's translation of Turgenev's *Virgin Soil* is a case in point, though Gamsa does not discuss it.

117. Guo, "Yi wan le 'Hualunsitan' zhihou," 474.

118. Ibid., 475.

Schiller's relevance to China and the 'pattern case,' the universal play of people-*versus*-antipeople."[119]

I would further suggest that this tendency was developed into a translation as historical thematization in Guo's *Fushide II.* To illustrate this, one example may suffice. It comes from his creative rendition of the scene of the peasants' uprising in act IV:

> Die Tüchtigen sie standen auf mit Kraft
> Und sagten: Herr ist der uns Ruhe schafft.
> Der Kaiser kanns nicht, wills nicht—laßt uns wählen,
> Den neuen Kaiser neu das Reich beseelen,
> Indem er jeden sicher stellt,
> In einer frisch geschaffnen Welt
> Fried' und Gerechtigkeit vermählen. (lines 10278–83)
>
> (The most resourceful rose with one accord / And said: "He who can give us peace is lord. / The Emperor cannot, will not—let us choose, / Let a new Emperor new life infuse, / Make fresh the world and safe for men / So none will suffer, none abuse; / And peace and justice wed again.")
>
> 有爲者已經把義旗高舉在手,
> 他們的宣言是:要和平才要領袖。
> 如今的當局不想和平,也不能夠——
> 讓我們重新選舉一個新主。
> 重新要把靈魂向國家賦與,
> 要這樣每個人才能夠得保安寧,
> 在新造的社會和平與正義結婚。[120]
>
> [The active ones have raised the flag in hand, / And their manifesto is: only by giving peace can one be a leader. / The current government does not want peace, nor can it achieve it— / Let us elect a new master. / Let us endow the nation with a new soul, / And only by so doing can everyone have safety; / In this newly created society peace and justice wed.]

Notably, Guo avoided the word *Kaiser* (emperor) in his translation of this passage; instead he translated it as *rujin de dangju* 如今的當局 (the current government), and *neuen Kaiser* (new emperor) as *xin zhu* 新主

119. Levenson, *Revolution and Cosmopolitanism*, 15.
120. Guo, trans., *Fushide di er bu*, 288–89.

(new master). In like manner, he rendered *Reich* (empire) as *guojia* 國家 (nation), and *frisch geschaffnen Welt* (a freshly built world) as *xin zao de shehui* 新造的社會 (a newly created society). This symptomatic move points to the translator's political undertone: the true subject matter of this passage is the Chinese Civil War, which, for Guo, was a revolutionary war rather than a fight for the emperorship. With the promise of new *guojia* (nation) and new *shehui* (society), Guo's rendering of Goethe's lines overlapped with the CCP's ideological rhetoric in its clarion call to arms (also in the name of peace and justice). Thus it is particularly interesting to note that Guo translated the phrase "Und sagten" (and said) as "他們的宣言是" [Their manifesto is]. This change of expression shows Guo's reference to Mori's Japanese rendition, in which the same phrase is rendered as: "こんな宣言をしました" [It was the manifesto like this].[121] Yet Guo's reliance on Mori's version was turned to an allegorical intervention. Not only did Guo use a peasants' war depicted in a feudal background to refer to the CCP-led revolution; he also transformed this passage into a political manifesto in support of the "people's war" against the GMD regime. More precisely, Guo's translation activated a political language with which Mao would soon proclaim: "The Chinese people will win the final victory in the great War of Liberation."[122]

In Goethe's original, as is well known, Faust sides with the emperor and helps him crash the peasants' rebellion for the reward of a piece of land. That had led Guo in 1932 to conclude that *Faust II* "contains royalist thought and is counterrevolutionary."[123] In 1947 this limitation did not undermine but actually reinforced Guo's interpretation of the "allegorical meaning [*yuyi* 寓意] of the whole sequence."[124] On one hand, the whole effort of Faust, "from the individual liberation to the utopian project of land reclamation," was interpreted as a "tragedy" of history: "[Faust] is still blinded . . . by the forces of feudal remnants. This is indeed a tragedy."[125] This insight is in line with what we have seen in Engels's critique of Goethe's "liberation from within."

121. Goethe, *Fausuto*, trans. Mori Ōgai, 748.
122. Mao Zedong, "Carry the Revolution through to the End," 299.
123. Guo, *Chuangzao shinian*, in *GQJ/W*, 12:75.
124. Guo, "Fushide jian lun," 8.
125. Guo, "Di er bu yi hou ji," 386.

On the other hand, Guo synchronized this tragic sequence into a Chinese allegory of the revolutionization of consciousness:

> Individualism is the core of capitalism. Capitalism represents a progress compared to feudalism. . . . But the consciousness of Faust does not stop there; rather, it moves forward. Though it is a fantasy, Faust nevertheless wants to "open land to live millions" and hopes to see "free people living on the free land." This is a step from individualism toward people-centrism [*renmin benwei zhuyi* 人民本位主義]. . . . This is . . . a leap forward beyond Goethe's own epoch [*shidai*]; though Goethe, together with his Faust, does not finish this leap, he dreams of it. . . . So the whole tragedy, one can say, is a spontaneous development toward the awakening of the consciousness of the people [*renmin yishi* 人民意識].[126]

This interpretation effectively transformed the thematic itinerary of *Faust* into a historical trajectory of what the CCP called "the New Democratic Revolution" from the May Fourth Movement to the civil war. In this allegorical reading, Faust represents the progressive bourgeois individuality, which is also the insignia of the May Fourth spirit; Mephistopheles is then the personification of the negative force of self-centrism in history. Most important is Guo's invocation of the concept of "the people" (*renmin*). Since the CCP's call for "New Democracy" and the intellectuals' active participation in the democratic movements in the GMD-controlled region, the idea of "the people" (*renmin*) and "people's democracy" had emerged as a political discourse under heated contestation.[127] At the highest moment of his striving, Faust has a final utopian vision of "free people" living on the "free lands" (line 11580). In addition to *Volke*, Guo translated both *Völkerschaft* (nation; line 11568) and *Gemeindrang* (communal spirit; line 11572) in Faust's final monologue as "the people" (*renmin*).[128] Politicized and "Sinicized" in this fashion, Faust's

126. Guo, "Fushide jian lun," 12.

127. See Mao Zedong, "On New Democracy," 339–84. For the relevant debates among Chinese intellectuals during the first half of the 1940s, see Cai Shangsi ed., *Zhongguo xiandai sixiang shi ziliao jianbian*. Also see Guo, "Minzhu yundong zhong de er san shi," in *GQJ/W*, 20:182–93. For Chinese intellectuals' responses to the agenda of people's democracy, see Qian Liqun, *1948: Tian di yuan huang*.

128. Guo, trans., *Fushide di er bu*, 355–56.

final vision was no longer a bourgeois-industrial project, as Hu's reading once suggested. The "moment" (*Augenblick*, line 11586) anticipated by the "Chinese Faust" amounted to a utopian imagination of the people's triumph: "The Chinese Faust shall never grow old, never be blind, and never die. He will not be satisfied with gaining land from the sea shore, or bestowing democracy in a feudal manner; rather he wants China to become the ocean of democracy, and the people to really be the master and take command."[129]

"People-centrism" or "the consciousness of the people" was a major ideological contribution of Guo's work to China's leftist culture in the 1940s. I leave a fuller discussion of Guo's discourse of "the people" to chapter 5. Notably, in preexisting scholarship on Guo's idea of people-centrism, the translation/interpretation of *Faust* has rarely been mentioned. In a way, this Chinese speculation on the meaning of Faust's final fate is reminiscent of Lukács's perspective of Faust as both "individual and species," which "enables [Lukács] to look beyond Faust's individual death to a future which is not Faust's immortality but the future growth and progress of the human species."[130] Written in the same year as Lukács published *Goethe and His Age*, and predating the socialist assessments of *Faust* in East Germany influenced by Lukács's interpretation, Guo's 1947 vision of a Chinese Faust was a mediation between the May Fourth legacies and the fight for "people's China."[131] On one hand, it was a leftist response to Feng's social-democratic idea of the "New Man"; on the other hand, it encapsulated a creative utopian transcoding of CCP's political agenda.[132]

With this historical-thematic metamorphosis from feudalism via individualism to people's democracy, the whole translation synchronized the "immense heterogeneity" of *Faust* into the "developmental history" (*fazhan shi* 發展史) of China's revolutionary "Zeigeist/*shidai jingshen*." As

129. Guo, "Di er bu yi hou ji," 386.

130. Farrelly, *Goethe in East Germany*, 109.

131. See ibid., 88–129.

132. For the CCP's orthodox definition of "the people," see Mao Zedong, "On the People's Democratic Dictatorship," 417: "Who are the people? At the present stage in China, they are the working class, the peasantry, the urban petty bourgeoisie and the national bourgeoisie." Guo's idea of Faustian striving toward the people underscores the historical consciousness in a larger sense—also see chapter 5.

Andrew Jones's study of evolutionary thinking points out, the key discourse of "development" (*fazhan*) in twentieth-century Chinese culture functioned as "a way of knowing, narrating, and attempting to manage processes of radical historical change."[133] It gave rise to a "narrative structure," and even a "historiographic template": "History . . . became 'developmental history'" in twentieth-century China.[134] In Guo's translation of *Faust* into a "developmental" narrative of the Zeitgeist, one can discern a complicated dimension behind the homogenization of history, as this evolutionary/revolutionary teleology is conditioned in a perspective of temporal confusion and intensification. The Zeitgeist figured as a dialectical (and tragic) interaction between a conjuncture of anachronistic temporalities and a project of historical progression. A translation of *Faust* turned into a Faustian act of constant self-periodization, in which the Chinese Revolution would find its own thematic.

Conclusion: "The Eternal-Feminine," Translation, and Revolution

To conclude this chapter, let me turn to Guo's translation of the final couplet in *Faust*:

> Das Ewig-Weibliche
> Zieht uns hinan. (lines 12110–11)
> (The Eternal-Feminine / Draws us on high.)
>
> 永恆之女性，
> 領導我們走。[135]
> [The Eternal-Feminine / Leads us to advance.]

Jane Brown stresses that Goethe's ending is not synthetic: "there is really no eternal realm, only the eternally varying flux of temporality."[136] This

133. Jones, *Developmental Fairy Tales*, 3.
134. Ibid., 9.
135. Guo, trans., *Fushide di er bu*, 380.
136. Brown, *Goethe's* Faust, 245.

couplet, as a poetic closure sung by a Chorus Mysticus, has attracted the attention of generations of *Faust* commentators. Locating the Eternal-Feminine in a series of "festive epiphanies" in *Faust*, Cyrus Hamlin has argued that this figure follows the logic of "moment" or *Augenblick*.[137] Another scholar, Ellis Dye, states that "woman in *Faust* symbolizes mediation—indeed symbolism itself."[138]

This chorus appeared in Guo's epigraph to the earliest version of "Rebirth of the Goddesses" (1921), a work envisioning the creation of a new China and a new world.[139] It was a symbolic moment for Guo in 1947 to come back to his earlier translation of this chorus, marking the full circle of his engagement with *Faust*. More important, in 1947 Guo considered the "Eternal-Feminine" as the incarnation of "the people," "democracy," and "peace."[140] He did not erotize the Eternal-Feminine but elaborated on the political meaning of the gender. He argued that *Faust* starts with a patriarchal God but ends with the matriarchal holy mother. "A male-centered universe is turned into a female-centered universe," and "this fantasy is nothing more or less than a symbol [of revolution]." He thus imagined a hermaphrodite ideal of new politics: "Generally speaking, the symbol of masculinity means independence, but also means autocracy and absolutism; the symbol of femininity means love and forgiveness, and the ideal is democracy and peace. To subordinate the male to the female is to nurture independence and autonomy with love and grace, and to develop an anti-absolutist peaceful democracy."[141]

For Lukács, Faust's union with the Eternal-Feminine symbolizes Goethe's ideal of the "boundless progress of human species," according to which "growth of the discrete and dominant capacities should be accompanied rather by a harmonious growth of the whole man."[142] For Guo, this feminine politics embodies the rule of "the people" (*renmin*): "The people (*renmin*) are the God of the new age. To respect the people, one has to overcome selfhood, and that [spirit] develops into forgiveness, into graceful love, and into rational self-sacrifice. This anti-Christian poem

137. Hamlin, "Tracking the Eternal-Feminine in Goethe's *Faust II*," 153.
138. Dye, "Figurations of the Feminine in Goethe's *Faust*," 116–17.
139. Guo, *N*, 1.
140. Guo, "Fushide jian lun," 13.
141. Ibid.
142. Lukács, *Goethe and His Age*, 230.

has a Christian head and a Christian tail, which seems a structural contradiction but is actually a reconciliation in terms of the poet's ideal."[143] Such a secular theology, which again could be seen as a precursor of secularizing readings of Goethe's final lines in socialist countries during the Cold War, was an obvious intervention into China's revolutionary politics.[144] When the reunion of Faust with the Eternal-Feminine was viewed as the marriage of the creative individuality with "the people," the translation of *Faust* became a historical narrative of the Chinese Revolution leading from the May Fourth Movement to a moment Guo characterized as the tragic "rebirth of gods."[145]

This trajectory of the Eternal-Feminine in Guo's poetry, translation, and interpretation affords an occasion for concluding my discussion of Guo's *Fushide* and other translingual engagements during the three decades in China's revolutionary century. From the *geschäftiger Geist* to the Rhine wine, to Zeitgeist and the Eternal-Feminine, I have demonstrated how Guo's translation—as a text, as a journey, and as an allegory—was inscribed in the Chinese Revolution. It is not only a linguistic, interpretative, and intellectual transference, it also distills the historical experience of revolution. If in the May Fourth Movement Guo's translation of *geschäftiger Geist* as "creative spirit" represented an identification with a new creativity/collectivity, then the "difficult" figuring of Zeitgeist in 1947 testified to the Chinese Revolution as a dialectical translation of confusing temporalities into an urgent momentum of sociopolitical change.

On this note I would draw a tentative conclusion for part I of this book. Aiming to complicate our understanding of twentieth-century Chinese culture as translingual practice, my discussion stresses the affinity between translation and revolution. I argue that the cultural-political subjectivity of revolutionary translation resides in the historical imagination of the now-time. This translingual mode of cultural production embodies

143. Guo, "Fushide jian lun," 13.

144. For the reading of this Catholic ending in the Eastern bloc, see Farrelly, *Goethe in East Germany*.

145. It needs to be noted that months later, when the CCP's military turned offensive in 1948, the tragic thematic gave way to the discursive violence Guo used in his verdicts on "reactionary literature." See Guo, "Chi fandong wenyi." Also see Guo, *Yingjie xin Zhongguo*. In 1949, the figure of the feminine did not appear in his official hymn of a "New China." See Guo, "Xin hua song."

a vital agency in the emerging historical periodization and configuration, pointing to a translation between different temporalities, between different moments of crisis or standstill, between different forms of nonsynchronism in a state of exception that is China's continuous revolution and incomplete modernization. The experience of translation, in this sense, is intrinsic to the experience of revolution.

As we have seen how Guo wrestled with the temporal heterogeneity and tried to transform it into a revolutionary thematic of "developmental history," in the next three chapters I deal directly with the issue of historical interpretation—which constitutes a translation between revolution and antiquity—and move across the watershed year of 1949.

PART II
Translating Antiquity into Revolution

CHAPTER 4

Autobiography and Historiography

If Guo's rendering of *Faust* as the "history of Zeitgeist" offers translingual poetics and thematics of the Chinese Revolution, then his reinterpretations of Chinese antiquity in lyrical, dramatic, and scholarly forms represent another mode of cultural-political transcoding. Whereas a lot of attention has been paid to the renarration of ancient past into a linear history of the nation-state in modern China, I hope to raise the question as to how the Chinese Revolution unfolded itself as a productive/destructive historical imagination.[1] In a study of Chinese Marxist historiography, Arif Dirlik points out: "Chinese historical consciousness in the twentieth century has evolved in a dialectical relationship with the revolutionization of Chinese society."[2] Revolution means the making, unmaking, and remaking of historical consciousness: "As long as the problem of revolution persists, so will the problem of history."[3] Chinese civilization is famous for its long practice of historical recording. Exhibiting a degree of historical nihilism, the revolutionary era has been widely seen as the most antihistorical period in Chinese history. But in the meantime, from the May Fourth reevaluation of traditions to Mao's slogan "make the past serve the present," the revolution constantly reimagined modern China's relationship with ancient heritage and actively negotiated with

1. See Duara, *Rescuing History from the Nation*, 17–50.
2. Dirlik, *Revolution and History*, 259.
3. Ibid., 268.

West-originated conceptions of history, especially the Marxist outlook of social development.

No discussion of the interaction between antiquity and revolution can afford ignoring the work of Guo Moruo. He was not only a poet of the "Zeitgeist of the twentieth century," he was also known to have an "antiquarian addiction" (*lishi pi* 歷史癖).[4] It is no exaggeration to assert that his rewritings of Chinese history occupied a central place in the "revolutionization" of historical consciousness. Dirlik's 1978 book situates Guo's early historical scholarship in the context of the emergence of Marxist historiography. Yet Guo did not merely work as a pioneering Marxist historian in 1920s–1930s China. The early Guo's romantic career was already inseparable from his creative use of the ancient. His later adventure into Marxist historiography went hand in hand with his pathbreaking contributions to the archeological-paleographical interpretation of oracle bones and bronze inscriptions. In the 1940s, Guo's writings in historical drama and his studies in ancient Chinese intellectual history were complementary. Moreover, he made a series of attempts to translate classical Chinese poetry into modern vernacular from the 1920s through the 1970s, creating an almost forgotten genealogy of lyrical modernization and revolutionary interpretation.

Few other Chinese writers or intellectuals ever brought history and revolution together on a wider scale or in a more controversial fashion. Covering Guo's whole career from the May Fourth period to the Cultural Revolution, my inquiry in part II is not limited to his historical studies; it also deals with his archaeological-philological studies, historical plays, historical short stories, vernacular translations of ancient poetry, theoretical polemics, and autobiographical writings. As his historical "reversal of verdicts" sometimes followed the ever-changing wind of revolutionary politics of the day, it is no wonder that scholars have complained about Guo's creative (ab)use of history. It is, however, precisely this tendency of antihistorical historicism in the leftist culture that leads me to have a closer look at his fusion of the ancient and the present, through which I aim to unveil how the Chinese Revolution constituted

4. Guo, *Lishi renwu*, 1.

a rhetorical, ideological, and epistemological crisis of the new "historical significance" as permanent reversal.[5]

Part II thus tackles three major dimensions of Guo's historical interpretations in a broader cultural-political context: the romantic-scientific patterns of the historical narrative; the political imagination of an ancient revolutionary Zeitgeist; and the modernizing vernacular translation of classical poetry as a creative rediscovery of national legacies. What runs through the next three chapters is an issue of historical rewriting that in Guo's case is intertwined with the acts of intralingual translation, such as deciphering ancient pictographs in light of the materialist conception of history, interpreting the ancient concept of *min* (the people) amid the struggles for a "people's democracy," and rendering classical poetry into the poetic-political vernacular. The historical rewritings in different genres thus form a network of discursive production that I characterize as a translation of antiquity into revolution. Rather than evaluating the legitimacy of this network according to any kind of historicism, my inquiry means to problematize a rhetoric of the translatability/reversibility of historical time.

In this chapter I experiment with a counterintuitive task of discovering and interrogating the parallelism between autobiography and historiography in Guo's career. One of the first works Guo completed during his exile in Japan was *My Childhood* (*Wode younian* 我的幼年). Finished in April 1928 and published in book form in April 1929, this initial attempt later grew into an autobiography of four volumes, *The Autobiography of Moruo* (*Moruo Zizhuan* 沫若自傳; *Autobiography* hereafter). This work as a whole is a rare monument in the writings of autobiography in modern China. Almost three months after writing *My Childhood*, Guo finished an essay originally titled "The Epochal Background and Spiritual Production in *The Book of Changes*" ("Zhou Yi de shidai beijing yu jingshen shengchan" 周易的時代背景與精神生產); it was his first attempt to interpret ancient Chinese classics from a Marxist perspective and was later included as a chapter in *Studies of Ancient Chinese Society* (*Zhongguo gudai shehui yanjiu* 中國古代社會研究; *Studies* hereafter). Also in 1928, Guo

5. The phrase is borrowed from Levenson, *Confucian China and Its Modern Fate*, vol. 3.

embarked on the archeological-paleographical study of Shang-Zhou inscriptions.

In other words, Guo's political exile was marked by the initiation of his autobiographical production and his historiographical-paleographical scholarship. This chapter aims to discover the hidden isomorphic relationship between autobiography and historiography. His *Studies* applies historical materialism and locates three revolutionary transitions in Chinese history: the "social revolutions" (*sehui biange* 社會變革) from primitive society to slavery, from slavery to feudalism, and from feudalism to capitalism.[6] While *Studies* focuses on the first revolutionary transition, Guo claims that his first installments of *Autobiography* deal with the third "revolutionary epoch" in China via a portrayal of his lived experience. Positing autobiography vis-à-vis historiography and vice versa, my reading here traces their mutual configurations within a new historical consciousness. I demonstrate that the narrative strategies in Guo's autobiographical writings and the intellectual innovations in his historiographical writings share the same authorial voice, and participate in the same production of a revolutionary-scientific authority. Just as his autobiography establishes an immediate equivalence between social history and personal life, his archeological-philological works rediscover the prehistorical Chinese pictograph as the particular emblem of a universal sequence of historical stages. Then I show how Guo translates into his autobiographical composition not only the Marxist discourse but a pictographical thinking about historical time. By unearthing this relationship between historiography and autobiography, we can finally reconstruct a romantic-scientific strategy of translating between the particular and the universal in China's revolutionary imagination.

6. See Guo, *Zhongguo gudai shehui yanjiu*, in *GQJ/L*, 1:13–18.

Narrative Strategies from Shishōsetsu *Fiction to Autobiography*

David Roy observes: "[Guo's] entire literary output is little more than an autobiography in a variety of modes, and even in his scholarly work his personal prejudices and private obsessions obtrude themselves at every turn." He then turns to Guo's properly "autobiographical writings," seeing them as "one of the most illuminating documents available to the students of modern China."[7] Notably, there exist two registers within the concept of autobiography as the word is used in Roy's account. On one hand, "autobiography" designates a tendency toward self-exposure, a mode at work underneath all of Guo's writings, including scholarly work. On the other hand, it refers to a body of literature that is produced by Guo and can be used as a presumably reliable record of this author/subject's life. In the former case, autobiography can be viewed as a mode; in the latter, it means a literary genre that can even be used for historical evidence. However, as Paul de Man demonstrates, autobiography is "not a genre or a mode." Not only is "the distinction between fiction and autobiography" impossible, but more important, one can say that "all texts are autobiographical" and at the same time "none of them is or can be."[8] De Man's argument pertains to my inquiry in a delicate way. One may notice that Roy, like many other commentators, has to rely on Guo's autobiography as a "document." But Roy's words are pointed in reminding us of the autobiographical aura (or the "obtrusion" of the authorial voice) that pervades all forms of Guo's writings. This autobiographical aura is a literary effect rather than anything verifiable or reliable. It reflects a romantic ideology emphasizing the priority, spontaneity, and authenticity of self-expression. From this point on, we should stop (for the time being) viewing Guo's autobiography or any autobiographical obtrusions as simply a record of an identifiable lived history. Instead, I try to dissect the autobiographical affect in his work as a tropological construct of authorship and self-knowledge.

7. Roy, *Kuo Mo-jo*, 1.
8. De Man, "Autobiography as De-facement," 70.

Before continuing to problematize autobiography along these lines, I need to briefly discuss the early Guo's autobiographical fiction to locate one of the origins of the ideology of autobiography in modern Chinese literature. Critics have analyzed the early Guo's fictional writings from both the perspective of psychoanalysis as a cosmopolitan discourse and that of masochist masculinity as a nationalist complex.[9] Here I limit my discussion to the autobiographical trait of these works. "Almost all of Kuo Mo-jo's [early] stories are autobiographical to a greater or lesser extent."[10] These stories include "Lingering Spring" ("Can Cun" 殘春, 1922), "The Eclipse" ("Yue Shi" 月蝕, 1923), "The Tomb of Ye Luoti" ("Ye Luoti zhimu" 葉羅提之墓, 1924), "The Trilogy of Wandering" ("Piaoliu sanbuqu" 漂流三部曲, 1924), "The Fallen Leaves" ("Luo ye" 落葉, 1925), "Donna Karméla" ("Kaermeiluo guniang" 喀爾美蘿姑娘, 1926), and other sketches.

Guo's fictional style in such works cannot be truly understood without taking into account the Creation Society's remaking of the Japanese *Shishōsetsu* (I-novel). The May Fourth New Literature had as its mantra the discovery of individuality and the liberation of personality. In this literary and cultural movement, the Creation Society's appropriation of the Japanese *Shishōsetsu* promoted an image of the subversive self and defined a fashion of self-exposure in China. According to Christopher Keaveney's characterization, as a self-referential approach in modern Japanese literature, "the *Shishōsetsu* narrative is a world reduced to that of an individual and contains no value systems other than the author's own." Consequently, fiction becomes "an incontestable and unpremeditated record" of the author's experience and "the result of spontaneity."[11] As Keaveney has shown, "the Creationists were heirs to the main currents of Taisho period literature."[12] Modeled on this *Shishōsetsu* ideal, Yu Dafu, a major Creationist writer, offered his own theory of literature as "autobiography" (*zixuzhuan* 自敘傳) in the 1920s: "Every literary work is the author's *zixuzhuan*."[13]

9. See Shih, *The Lure of the Modern*, chapter 3; and Tsu, *Failure, Nationalism, and Literature*, chapter 6.

10. Roy, *Kuo Mo-jo*, 75.

11. Keaveney, *The Subversive Self in Modern Chinese Literature*, 22.

12. Ibid., 20.

13. Yu Dafu, "Wu liu nian lai chuangzuo shenghuo de huigu," 180. Similarly, he states that "literary works all have an autobiographical coloring to some extent." Yu Dafu, "Riji wenxue," 261.

Guo's early fictional pieces are also part of this Chinese remaking of the *Shishōsetsu* narrative. Their main subject matter is sexual psychology and domestic life. "Lingering Spring," for example, plays with the theme of extramarital erotic desire. The first-person protagonist, Aimo, who like Guo is a medical student, is tortured by his erotic desire for a Japanese nurse (Miss S) and the ensuing feeling of guilt for his wife. This tension grows into a dream scene built on a medical-examination fantasy and a Medea scenario:

> "So, Mr. Aimo, could you please examine me?"
> "But I have not yet graduated and got my license!"
> "Ah, don't be reluctant!" Then she unclothed herself and came to my side. Her body was like a marble bust, her naked shoulders like a litchi fruit stripped off the shell, her breasts bending upwards like two flowers about to blossom. . . . As I warmed my hands and was about to do auscultation, Baiyang rushed in breathlessly, crying to me:
> "Horrible! Aimo! Aimo! Why are you still lingering here? Your wife killed your two children!"[14]

In "Donna Karméla" this theme is further developed into a detailed account of voyeurism. The protagonist, again the "I," has the unconscious split into his secret erotic desire for a young Japanese girl and his spiritual admiration for his Maria-like wife: "Ah, my split self, my doubled life."[15]

From "Lingering Spring" on, this sentimental obsession with the selfhood led to the writing of what I call a serial fiction. In those stories, the reader encounters a male protagonist called "Aimo," who serves as the author's alter ego, a common setup in the I-novel narrative; a female character called either Xiaofu or Ruihua, corresponding perfectly to Guo's common-law wife; and their children. Those stories deal with the protagonist's sexual frustrations, the family's economic instability, Guo's unsuccessful adventures in the Shanghai literary community, and the ensuing domestic tensions. On a representational level, Guo's fiction relies on confessional immediacy and seems to be always on the brink of

14. Guo, "Can chun," in *GQJ/W*, 9:31.
15. Guo, "Kaermeiluo guniang," in *GQJ/W*, 9:215.

collapsing into a spontaneous naturalistic accumulation of details. Novelist Shen Congwen 沈從文 (1902–88) was very critical of this tendency, harshly commenting that Guo "did not know restraint" in fictional writing. For Shen, the lack of self-restraint leads to "superfluity" (*feihua* 廢話), and superfluity leads to "triviality" (*suosui* 瑣碎).[16]

Such a style attests to the excessiveness of what Jaroslav Průšek calls "subjectivism and individualism" in modern Chinese literature: "an emphasis on the creator's personality . . . and a concentration of attention on the artist's own life."[17] Yet with a typical *Shishōsetsu* operation of "authorial intrusion," the exhibitionist/naturalist "obesity of details" is organized into a sentimental authorial voice. That voice, sometimes disguised as the protagonist's internal monologue, frequently intrudes and translates every detail of personal life into a sentimental critique directed at money, city life, capitalism, China's repressive social norms, and even the alienated civilization in general: "We are imprisoned by space, as well as by time, and we have to be tortured by all kinds of the inherited social norms and moral values, which make it impossible to enjoy any comfort in our brief life."[18]

This mechanism underwent a metamorphosis in Guo's later autobiographical project, which ushered in a different authorial contract. In the first place, Guo's writing of *zizhuan* 自傳 (autobiography) in 1928 was conditioned by the changes of his own social existence. We need to bear in mind the impact of the "tragedy" of the National Revolution in 1927. Shen Congwen, in his critique of Guo's work, satirically observed:

> That Guo authored [autobiographical works] *My Childhood* and *Around the Time of the 1911 Revolution* was such a surprise that many believe that this must be due to the commercial calculation of the publisher.
>
> Almost all the famous authors of the world, when they are admired by the public and yet their own creativity is in abeyance, will write an [autobiography] like this, for the reason of no other than "convenience."[19]

16. Shen Congwen, "Lun Guo Moruo," 9.
17. Průšek, *The Lyrical and the Epic*, 1.
18. Guo, "Piaoliu sanbuqu," in *GQJ/W*, 9:270.
19. Shen Congwen, "Lun Guo Moruo," 14.

Despite its dismissive (if not prejudiced) tone, there might be a kernel of truth in Shen's account. It is true that nothing other than Guo's fame warranted the publication of a purely autobiographical record of such a length (*My Childhood* alone has more than 100 pages). Secretly departing from Shanghai for Japan, Guo was not only a litterateur with a romantic halo, he was a revolutionary in exile (fig. 7). This legendary status made an autobiographical narrative appealing to the public and potentially lucrative. It seems also true that in 1928 Guo was forced to do so because, having no income during his political exile and being harassed by the Japanese police, he had to produce something marketable to make a living for himself, his wife, and their four children (with a fifth on the way).[20]

But more importantly, this autobiographical endeavor marks a development in his literary self-exposure, in which the sentimentalist perspective is joined by a new social-historical authorial voice. In a letter to Zong Baihua, dated February 16, 1920, Guo had once declared: "I often regret that I lack the genius of an Augustine, a Rousseau, or a Tolstoy, that I might write a naked 'confession,' and thus reveal myself to the world. If I do not rid myself completely of my burden of guilt, my pitiful soul will remain embroiled in a sea of tears, with no prospect of escape."[21] Seen from this statement, the impulse for confessional self-exposure meant, in the early Guo, a romanticized (and quasi-Christian) governance of self. The names of Augustine, Rousseau, and Tolstoy, joined by Goethe, reappeared in Guo's (quasi-poetic) preface to the first installment of *Autobiography*, but his self-positioning was changed significantly:

> My childhood took place in the transitional epoch [*shidai* 時代] from feudalist society to capitalist system,
> Now I unearthed it from the bottom of the dark coal mine.
> I don't want to imitate Augustine and Rousseau in expressing any confession whatsoever,

20. See his letters to Ye Lingfeng 葉靈鳳 (1905–75) in 1932, in which Guo discussed the editing and publication of his autobiographical pieces and demanded higher payments and the quick transaction of money. Guo, *Guo Moruo shuxin ji*, 380–92.

21. Guo, Tian, and Zong, *San ye ji*, 44; here I use Roy's translation, see Roy, *Kuo Mo-jo*, 87.

FIGURE 7 Guo Moruo in Japan. Courtesy of Guo Pingying.

> I don't want to imitate Goethe and Tolstoy in portraying any genius whatsoever.
> I just want to write about how a society produced such an individual,
> Or, such a life existed in such an epoch.[22]

22. Guo, *Wo de tongnian*, in *GQJ/W*, 11:7.

Apparently, Guo's transition from *zixuzhuan* fiction to a proper *zizhuan* not only involves the metamorphosis of the "second self" as a vehicle of authorship into a new narrative bound by an autobiographical norm; it also gives rise to the privileged vantage point of the author/subject in a panoramic view of a revolutionary "epoch." Summarizing the first volume of his autobiography in a 1947 preface, he reaffirms that the "consistent" motivation for his autobiographical writings is "to see an epoch [*shidai*] through myself."[23] The autobiographical "I" not only orients a narrative of personal history but also embodies a time frame of China's social-historical change.

Japanese sinologist Kawai Kozo finds the "close relationship between the individual and the epoch" as a general characteristic of Chinese autobiographical literature.[24] Seeing autobiography as a reflection of "an attitude or political position toward one's society," Janet Ng notes that "the May Fourth autobiographers all believed that they were in some ways representative of their contemporaries."[25] In Guo's case, the authorial perspective derives from a Marxist conception of history, combining the logic of self-exposure with the applicability of historical materialism. Therefore, his narrative strategies are transformed correspondingly into the production of a new discursive authority. In her study of autobiography in modern China, Wendy Larson raises the question of "literary authority" and observes that "Guo Moruo's acceptance of revolutionary literature and of the writer's responsibility toward the revolution reorients questions of self and work."[26] According to Larson, the first volume of Guo's *Autobiography*, like other Chinese autobiographies written in the 1920s and 1930s, depicts the subject/author's early years as a "divorce" from the "orthodox China" and demonstrates the author's search for "alternative authorities."[27] I would approach this issue of authority on the level of narrativization: what is the internalized authority of the autobiographical technique? I argue that Guo's autobiography not only involves a search for a socially meaningful role of the writer but also impersonates a self-claimed authority of the scientific historical narrative.

23. Guo, "Shaonian shidai xu," in *GQJ/W*, 11:3.
24. Kawai Kozo, *Zhongguo de zizhuan wenxue*, 3.
25. Ng, *The Experience of Modernity*, x.
26. Larson, *Literary Authority and the Modern Chinese Writer*, 138.
27. Ibid., 119.

Guo's *Autobiography* thus makes explicit an immediate correspondence or expressive causality between the author's life experience ("myself") and the social formation in modern China ("epoch"). The authorial I moves freely and constantly between self-exposure and sociohistorical commentary. In the first installments of his autobiography, it is as if every detail in his childhood and adolescence were an expression of the historical characteristics of social change in China. In *My Childhood*, Guo's remembrance starts with a reference to the 1900 victory of the Eight-Nation Alliance over the Qing empire: "The wild current of imperialist capitalism battered down the Great Wall of an age of feudal empire."[28] Then he moves to the subject of his early education: "Needless to say I was liberated from the yokes of examination poetry. . . . To whom should I have expressed my thanks? Probably to the imperialists."[29] A leftist historical narrative is interwoven retrospectively and seamlessly into personal remembrances. Later in the same piece, Guo sees in a map of East Asia hung on the classroom wall the "epochal force" and describes his oldest brother's taste for Su-styled calligraphy as a manifestation of "the collapse of feudalism."[30] In *Around the Time of the 1911 Revolution* (*Fanzheng qianhou* 反正前後), Guo switches between lengthy historical-political commentary on the delayed development of capitalism in China, on one hand, and a depiction of his prodigal life at a boys-only middle school in Chengdu, on the other. In a passage about the disappearance of traditional opera houses, a Marxist sociohistorical authority once again intrudes into a hometown memory. Guo first recalls: "It was a fashion of the students to cause trouble in traditional opera houses. . . . And I was there, nine of ten times, when trouble was there."[31] Then a Marxist historical vocabulary intervenes. The decline of the "feudal opera houses" and their "feudalist organizations in the age of capitalism" was "manifested on the opera stage": "The form, content, organization, and architecture for opera performance all accurately confirm a materialist outlook of history."[32]

28. Guo, *Wo de tongnian*, in *GQJ/W*, 11:41.
29. Ibid., 42.
30. Ibid., 45, 52.
31. Guo, *Fanzheng qianhou*, in *GQJ/W*, 11:108.
32. Ibid., 109.

This account, bordering on a kind of so-called vulgar sociology, reveals an assumption of the mechanical "relation of expression" that determines the very possibility of Guo's autobiographical narrative. I borrow the phrase "relation of expression" from the structuralist critique of "expressive causality." As Louis Althusser points out, such a concept of expression

> presupposes in principle that the whole in question be reducible to an *inner essence,* of which the elements of the whole are then no more than the phenomenal forms of expression, the inner principle of the essence being present at each point in the whole, such that at each moment it is possible to write the immediately adequate equation: *such and such an element . . . = the inner essence of the whole.*[33]

With a similar principle of equivalence, Guo's *Autobiography* rearranges every detail of lived experience into a "manifestation" of a scientific Marxist authority. This authority of "materialist outlook of history," in turn, finds immediate expressions on the "phenomenal" level of the self and epoch. In his "Prologue" ("Faduan" 發端) to *Around the Time of the 1911 Revolution*, Guo openly belittles the careful choice of subject matter and the necessity of formal sophistication: "Any subject matter is fine, any form is fine—the most important is consciousness!"[34] The naturalistic attitude toward subject matter is reminiscent of the *Shishōsetsu* model, and yet the sentimental authority in Guo's early fiction is updated with a new authority called "consciousness."

This is even discernible in Guo's dealing with the theme of sexuality in his autobiography. The sexual motive provides a degree of continuity from his early fiction to his autobiography. When reading *My Childhood*, one realizes that the short story "The Tomb of Ye Luoti" is in fact a distorted representation of Guo's infantile sex life. In that story, the young boy Ye Luoti's sexual desire for his *tangsao* (wife of one's cousin) is sentimentalized in the moment of the protagonist's fatal melancholia after learning of his *tangsao*'s death. *My Childhood* restores this plot to a "real" account of infantile sexuality: "Till now I am still puzzled; I don't know

33. Althusser and Balibar, *Reading Capital*, 206; emphasis in original.
34. Guo, *Fanzheng qianhou*, in *GQJ/W*, 11:164.

why I had such an early sexual awakening."[35] The sexual awakening of the authorial I takes place during his early life in a landlord-merchant's household at the turn of the twentieth century. It is a prime day of springtime, and Guo passes by a bamboo garden during a break at the clan school. The passage about his erotic encounter with his *tangsao* is almost identical with the one in "The Tomb of Ye Luoti": "In the air tinged with the color of milky chyle, the bamboo leaves swayed aimlessly. *Tangsao*'s two hands had a color of pink cherry-apple flowers. Suddenly a beautiful desire came to me. I really wanted to touch her pink and soft hands. But strangely I did not dare to go ahead and fulfill this desire. . . . I always feel that this memory was the first sign [*zhengzao*] of my sexual awakening."[36] He goes on to tell us that he soon started to be addicted to masturbation.

Interestingly, this remembrance of sexual awakening is framed in a spontaneous relation to a larger theme of historical change: "Just as the external society underwent fierce changes, so there were fierce changes within my body before I was ten."[37] This equivalence between the personal sexual formation and what Guo calls the epoch (*shidai*) is the authorial narrator's rhetorical maneuvering of the expressivity of history. What is more remarkable, then, is that in fact the same rhetoric finds its way into Guo's Marxist historiography:

> When a human reaches at the age of fifteen or sixteen and as an adolescent becomes sexually excitable, his or her body starts to change [*biange* 變革], or we can say, when his or her body starts to change, he or she becomes sexually excitable. But either way, the true reason is that the human body's vitalism is reaching a more advanced stage [*jieduan* 階段].
>
> Analogous to this is the period of the revolutionary change [*biange*] of a society. When the productive forces of a society reach a more advanced stage, class relations and intellectual expressions will undergo a profound change [*biange*].[38]

35. Guo, *Wo de tongnian*, *GQJ/W*, 11:52.
36. Ibid., 53–54.
37. Ibid., 52.
38. Guo, *Zhongguo gudai shehui yanjiu*, in *GQJ/L*, 1:170.

Whereas *My Childhood* was reportedly written in March and April 1928, the passage above is from "The Social Revolution and Its Reflection in Thought during the Epoch of the *Book of Songs* and *Book of Documents*" ("Shi Shu shidai de shehui biange yu qi zai sixiang shang zhi fanying" 詩書時代的社會變革與其在思想上之反映), which was written between August and October 1928. In the autobiographical piece, the analogy between sexual development and social change reinforces the authorial insertion of a temporal framework between the self and the "epoch." In the historiographical case, the same analogy is depersonalized and, similar to what Andrew Jones sees as the "narrative form" of "developmental thinking," serves to illustrate the "expressive causality" of social development, which presumes the superstructure as the expression of the base.[39] The double figuration of this analogy marks the beginning of an autobiographical-historiographical parallelism.

A Transnational "Romantic Science" of Historical Writing

Shidai (epoch), *biange* (revolutionary change), and *jieduan* (stage or phase) are the key words characteristic of Guo's historical works. His first major book in this regard was *Studies*, finished in 1929 and published in 1930. Responding to the "social history controversy" (*zhongguo shehui shi lunzhan* 中國社會史論戰) taking place at the turn of the 1930s, this influential work takes on two characteristics. First, applying Marxist conceptions of history, it periodizes Chinese history into a linear, progressive sequence of social-developmental stages. Second, focusing on the transition from primitive society to civilized society in Chinese history, *Studies* bears a decisive influence of Lewis Morgan's *Ancient Society* and Friedrich Engels's *Origin of the Family, Private Property and the State* (*Origin* hereafter).

Emphasizing the urgency of a scientific "liquidation of Chinese society," Guo's preface to *Studies* exhibits a rhetoric of enlightenment and

39. See Jones, *Developmental Fairy Tales*, 5. Also see Fredric Jameson's discussion of "expressive causality" in *Political Unconscious*, 26–32.

scientism that echoes the Creation Society's proposal of "Marxist enlightenment":

> We, trained and bound by the feudal thought for more than two thousand years, are all shortsighted. . . .
>
> For the blind, of course, sight cannot be retrieved. But for those who are shortsighted, we need to treat them with scientific methods.
>
> In this age of developed science, why do you still turn to magicians and sorcerers from remote villages when you have eye diseases?
>
> In this age of developed science, why do you still imprison yourself in feudalist thought?[40]

This intrusion of a voice of scientific authority bespeaks the ideology of social scientism in modern Chinese historiography. One of the most persistent legacies of Chinese modernity, "Mr. Science" (*sai xiansheng* 賽先生)—the famous May Fourth catchword—meant a modernizing project of "a scientific mentality that extended itself to the transformation of weltanschauung."[41] The May Fourth historiography, according to Q. Edward Wang, "acquires a transnational dimension, helping attest to the universal value (perceived at least at that time) of science."[42] Guo's approach to Marxist historiography further radicalizes this dimension of scientism. A well-known retrospection about the motivation behind his adventure into the historical profession can be found in his *Autobiography*: "Initially I mainly wanted to apply dialectical materialism in a study of the development of Chinese thought, Chinese society and Chinese history in general. I also intended to use Chinese thought, Chinese society and Chinese history to test the validity of dialectical materialism."[43]

The materialistic conception of history is what Engels calls one of Marx's "scientific discoveries."[44] Moreover, in Morgan's anthropological analysis of tribal societies, Engels finds the same law of history discovered by Marx: "Morgan in his own way discovered afresh in America the

40. Guo, *Zhongguo gudai shehui yanjiu*, in *GQJ/L*, 1:6–7.
41. Wang Hui, *The Politics of Imagining Asia*, 89.
42. Q. E. Wang, *Inventing China through History*, 5.
43. Guo, "Kua zhe donghai," in *GQJ/W*, 13:331.
44. Engels, *Socialism: Utopian and Scientific*, 416.

materialist conception of history discovered by Marx forty years ago."[45] In the introduction of *Studies*, Guo in turn states: "We have to express our gratitude to Engels and modern American scholar Morgan."[46] He defines his own work as "a sequel to Engels' *Origin*."[47]

The cornerstone—and perhaps the ultimate weakness—of Guo's application of Marxism then seems to be the periodization of Chinese history into a sequence of evolutionary stages of social development. The introduction of *Studies*, written in late October 1928 and titled "The Developmental Stages of the History of Chinese Society," periodizes the 3,000 years of Chinese history into a schema of four "stages" (*jieduan*): from primitive society (before the West Zhou dynasty) to slavery (the Zhou period), to feudalism (from the Spring and Autumn period onward), and to capitalism ("the recent one hundred years").[48] This four-stage periodization bears a clear influence of Marx's "Preface to *A Contribution to the Critique of Political Economy*," a text Guo once tried to translate in early 1928. The text contains what Guo called "the formula of the materialist conception of history."[49] That is Marx's classic exposition about the "progressive epochs in the economic formation of society": "the Asiatic, ancient, feudal, and modern bourgeois modes of production."[50] In contrast to many of his contemporaries, who showed a profound interest in the contentious concept of "the Asiatic mode of production," Guo simply equated it to primitive clan society.[51] His four-stage periodization also draws close to Engels's conclusion that after primitive society, there are three stages of civilization: slavery, serfdom, and wage labor.[52] This four-stage approach to the universal-historical sequence remained intact in his later works on Chinese history. Though Guo later revised his views of periodization a number of times since the publication of *Studies*, "these revisions . . . have been restricted to matters of timing."[53]

45. Engels, *Origin*, 71.
46. Guo, *Zhongguo gudai shehui yanjiu*, in *GQJ/L*, 1:13.
47. Ibid., 9.
48. Ibid., 30.
49. Guo, "Li Hu zhiqian," in *GQJ/W*, 13:275.
50. Marx, "Preface to *A Contribution to the Critique of Political Economy*," 183.
51. See Guo, "Gudai shehui yanjiu da ke nan," in *GQJ/L*, 3:416–17.
52. Engels, *Origin*, 234.
53. Dirlik, *Revolution and History*, 179.

This was an early example of Chinese communists' efforts to seek what Joseph Levenson has called the "equivalence" between Chinese history and universal history: Chinese history was driven by "the same dynamic principles" as Western history.[54] Yet the true emphasis of Guo's translation between the particular and the universal in *Studies* is not placed on the static existence of the four stages but on what Marx calls the eras of "social revolution" as the transitions between these stages. In parallel to the four-stage schema, Guo provides yet another periodization—the one about "three social revolutions" in Chinese history: the transition from the Yin (Shang) to the Zhou system; the feudal revolution from the Zhou dynasty to the Qin empire; and the capitalist revolution, during the late Qing period.[55] Marx's *Preface* defines the sociohistorical change thus: "At a certain stage of their development, the material productive forces of society come in conflict with the existing relations of production. . . . Then begins an epoch of social revolution."[56] This perspective of social revolution electrifies Guo's periodization and transforms the four stages into a dynamic historical time. Clearly, in both his works in autobiography and historiography, the term "epoch" prioritizes a diachronic dynamic rather than static temporality.

In his critique of Chinese Marxists' "commitment to the idea of social science," D. W. Y. Kwok sees in the scholarship of Marxist historians (including Guo) "an intensification of materialistic positive scientism" and "a built-in criticism of the past."[57] But here I want to further complicate this issue of Marxist scientism. I contend that Guo's impulse for social-scientific periodization and his reception of the Engels-Morgan perspective are actually rooted in a transnational genealogy of romantic visions of history. The first point I want to make is that Guo's focus on the transition from the primitive to civilized society actually can be traced back to his early romantic historical imagination. Second, Engels's periodization of historical progress is itself inextricably intertwined with a revolutionary-romantic critique of capitalistic modernity.

54. Levenson, *Confucian China and Its Modern Fate*, 3:50.
55. Guo, *Zhongguo gudai shehui yanjiu*, in *GQJ/L*, 1:31.
56. Marx, "Preface to *A Contribution to the Critique of Political Economy*," 182.
57. Kwok, *Scientism in Chinese Thought*, 169.

This revolutionary romanticism also preconditions Guo's reception of Engels's *Origin*.

In 1921, Guo published "A Pompeii in the Intellectual History of Our Nation" ("Woguo sixiang shi shang zhi Pengpai cheng" 我國思想史上之澎湃城). This unfinished essay shows the penetration of Guo's early romanticism into the historical imagination. Using Pompeii's glory and burial as a metaphor, he adopted to Chinese history an alternation of "golden ages" and "dark ages." The age of "Sage Kings," described in the Confucian classics, was a time of freedom and equality, and then the emergence of state politics (early dynasties, starting from twenty-first century BCE) was the first dark age; later, the age of "One Hundred Schools" (the "axial age" of Chinese civilization) was the Renaissance, only to be buried again by the second dark age, the unification of China by Qin Shi Huang in 221 BCE. Marking a beginning of Guo's obsession with the periodization of Chinese history, the essay suggests that the transition from "freedom" to "darkness" should be understood within two themes: communal egalitarian society and private property: "The state of our nation originated in a social contract, and the inherent thought of our nation was egalitarian idealism; so all individuals were equal, and the land of the state was communally owned by all. The *jingtian* system [*jingtian zhi* 井田制, also known as the 'well field' system] began with Huang Di, and that was the earliest history of communism practiced in our nation."[58]

This is one of the earliest references to "communism" (*gongchanzhuyi* 共產主義) in Guo's writings. Idealizing the Sage Kings era in terms of "social contract," "people's sovereignty," and "democracy," the early Guo rewrites the Confucian utopian idea of great universality in modern terms. In contrast, he sees the replacement of democracy by the Xia hereditary kingship as a sign of the rising private property, the "origin of all conflicts."[59] He concludes with a lamentation: "The transition from the sage kings to the Xia dynasty was one of immense importance in our national history: the ancient thought changed from a dynamic pantheism of cosmos to a static theology of religion; political organization changed

58. Guo, "Woguo sixiang shi shang zhi Pengpai cheng," 77.
59. Ibid., 78.

from communal ownership to private ownership, from democracy to theocracy."[60]

This condemnation of civilized society as a burial of primitive freedom, equality, and creativity finds its sentimental expression in Guo's poetic drama, "Two Princes of Guzhu" ("Guzhu jun zhi er zi" 孤竹君之二子, 1923). The play is based on the legendary princes Bo Yi and Shu Qi, who both refused to inherit the shrine. In his rewriting of this myth/history, these figures become the mouthpieces for Guo's nostalgia for a primitive society: "Humans before the age of sage kings, how free, how pure, and how heroic they were!"[61] In another passage, one of the princes extends a condemnation of private property to the whole civilized society: "From private property, . . . / Arise so many customs and so many laws, which plant immeasurable miseries."[62] This lyrical monologue is a thinly veiled intrusion of the romantic author.

Xiaoming Chen's study, which emphasizes the fusion of Confucian values and the communist revolution in modern China, views Guo's early romanticization of the ideal of *datong* as offering a May Fourth cosmopolitan version of the "pastoral/primitive paradise": "To save the world . . . from its sufferings and crises Guo, before 1924, held the goal of reaching an ideal that would be modeled after an ancient society that he believed to have existed in China."[63] Chen points out that Guo's critique of private properties is targeted at a modern capitalistic world. Based on Chen's observation, my inquiry would place this historical critique in a long tradition of global romanticism.[64] Guo's early egalitarian view was evidently in dialogue with the Rousseauist vision of the origins of human society. According to Rousseau's *Discourse on Inequality*, there existed a "nascent society" when humans "lived free, healthy, good and happy . . . and continued to enjoy the gentleness of independent dealings with one another."[65] With the birth of private property came the downfall of

60. Ibid., 81.
61. Guo, "Guzhu jun zhi er zi," 11.
62. Ibid., 12.
63. Xiaoming Chen, *From the May Fourth Movement to Communist Revolution*, 73.
64. Here I have no space to discuss the influences of late Qing Confucian philosophers—such as Kang Youwei 康有為 (1858–1927) and Liao Ping 廖平 (1852–1932)—on Guo's utopian historical imagination.
65. Rousseau, *The Discourses and Other Early Political Writings*, 167.

equality and human happiness. In their book on the romantic vision of history as a critique of capitalistic modernity, Michael Löwy and Robert Sayre argue: "The specificity of Romanticism is that it develops this critique from the standpoint of a value system—with reference to an ideal—drawn from the past."[66] Guo's early historical thinking fits this categorization.

His later reception of Engels's *Origin* does not necessarily mean a liquidation of his early vision. Engels's confidence in scientism comes from his reformulation of Morgan's anthropological research in *Ancient Society*.[67] *Ancient Society* follows a historical narrative of "progress," exhibiting a prototypical nineteenth-century enlightenment view of humankind: "Mankind commenced their career at the bottom of the scale and worked their way up from savagery to civilization through the slow accumulations of experimental knowledge."[68] Its scientific power is based on an anthropological maneuvering of temporality: taking the synchronic as the diachronic, taking the currently existing "savages" as the specimens of our primitive past. Reworking the diversity of cultures into a sequence, Morgan produces a teleological and unilinear history, a "natural as well as necessary sequence of progress," from savagery to barbarism to civilization.[69]

Engels's *Origin* translates Morgan's "ratio of human progress" into a conceptual Marxist language. This transcoding contains even more effusive words eulogizing the primitive communism exemplified in the Native American Iroquois tribe than Rousseau could afford to his praise of the primeval times: "And a wonderful constitution it is, this gentile constitution, in all its childlike simplicity! No soldiers, no gendarmes or police, no nobles, kings, regents, prefects, or judges, no prisons, no lawsuits—and everything takes its orderly course."[70] Engels's ode to primitive communism immediately leads to a revolutionary critique of modern capitalism, as is shown in an anachronistic figuration of the "proletarian." He continues: "An enormous gulf separates the present-day proletarian and small peasant from the free member of the old gentile

66. Löwy and Sayre, *Romanticism against the Tide of Modernity*, 28.
67. For his appraisal of Rousseau, see Engels, *Anti-Dühring*, 152–53.
68. Morgan, *Ancient Society*, 3.
69. Ibid.
70. Engels, *Origin*, 159.

society."[71] The hymn is finally transformed into an elegy of the loss of this innocent state: "The power of this primitive community had to be broken. . . . But it was broken by influences which from the very start appear as a degradation."[72]

Löwy draws attention to precisely these passages where Engels's historical science takes eruptive flights into poetico-political intrusions. In so doing, he aims to unravel a "revolutionary romanticism" (*romantisme révolutionnaire*) hidden in the Marxist historical outlook.[73] Löwy and Sayre further develops this thesis of Marxism and romanticism by discerning in Marx and Engels a "critical judgment of industrial-capitalist civilization as representing, in certain respects, a step backward, from the human point of view in relation to communities of the past."[74] Every "degradation" or "regression" is also seen as a necessary progress, and ultimately, this romantic dialectic propels Engels to join Morgan in celebrating a progressivist restoration of the primitive happiness: "*It will be a revival, in a higher form, of the liberty, equality, and fraternity of the ancient gentes.*"[75] Just as some of anthropologists believe that Morgan's study "committed the mortal sin of evolutionism," Engels's work attests to social scientism.[76] But scholars of romanticism like M. H. Abrams would recognize this Marxist conception of "return"—a revival on a higher level—as a typical "Romantic dialectics" of redemption, revolution, and the second coming, which "serves a secular theodicy," meaning "the conception of that end as a 'return' to the beginning, but at a higher level which has converted to 'conscious' knowledge, hence preserved, the values achieved during all preceding stages."[77] Or, to put it in Hayden White's language, Engels's grand historical narrative can be read exactly as a "Romance" of liberation and redemption.[78] Romanticism, scientism, and the revolutionary vision are interfused.

71. Ibid., 160.
72. Ibid., 161.
73. Löwy, *Marxisme et romantisme révolutionnaire*, 24.
74. Löwy and Sayre, *Romanticism against the Tide of Modernity*, 93.
75. Engels, *Origin*, 237; emphasis in original.
76. Terray, *Marxism and "Primitive" Society*, 9.
77. Abrams, *Natural Supernaturalism*, 315–16.
78. See White, *Metahistory*, 8–9.

The early Guo's rhetoric was clearly attuned to Engels's ode to primitive communism, his lamentation of its fall, and his prophecy of its return. Later, Guo the Marxist historian followed Engels as a guide. As a result, his earlier sentimental indignation is translated into a romantic-scientific authority on Chinese history: "What was manifested on the social level was the rise of patriarchal power, the establishment of private property, the use of slave labor, class division, and the appearance of kings and states. This was the beginning of civilization, but also the beginning of the tragedy of man's exploitation of man."[79] What Löwy calls revolutionary romanticism in Engels and what Guo and many other leftists see as science in Engels's theory in fact precondition each other in creating a narrative voice. This voice embodies a revolutionary-romantic subjectivity while legitimizing a claim to science. I propose to call this narrative mode a "revolutionary-romantic science," whose transnational making is manifest in Guo's case.

This revolutionary-romantic science of history is pregnant with an urgent projection of social change as a temporal telos, end, or "return." Guo begins his preface to *Studies* by situating his historical science in this way: "A desperate desire for a future society propels us to demand a liquidation of the society of the past."[80] A moment more emblematic of this condensed temporal framing can be found at the very end of part 4 of *Studies*. There, he dates his writing: "Night, November 7, 1929, sitting alone in my tiny study, while commemorating another thing."[81] This dating can be seen as an autobiographical moment intruded into his Marxist historiography, typical of his tendency for self-fashioning. The "thing" occupying his mind is not hard to be deciphered: November 7, 1929, was the twelfth anniversary of the October Revolution. While writing a scholarly work on ancient Chinese society, he was commemorating the first successful communist revolution. This self-dating therefore dramatizes a temporal dynamic of desiring revolution through history, whereby the rediscovery of prehistorical society, the critique of civilization, and the vision of a revolution become one and the same perspective.

79. Guo, *Zhongguo gudai shehui yanjiu*, in *GQJ/L*, 1:6.
80. Ibid., 9.
81. Ibid., 270.

The Visibility of the "Epoch": Translating Ancient Pictographs into Social History

Just as Guo's autobiographical composition is criticized for being superficial, so is his periodization of Chinese history vulnerable to criticism of dogmatism. The issue of periodization of Chinese history in fact was at the center of the epistemological breakthrough that a new generation of Marxists was trying to bring to Chinese historical thinking in the late 1920s and early 1930s. Dirlik's study lists thirty-four versions of the Marxist periodization of Chinese history proposed during the "social history controversy."[82] He also points out that Guo's "assumption of universality for the process of [social] development" is more rigid than that held by Engel.[83] However rigid the application of Marxism was in some of these periodizations, and however trivial the debate about them turned out to be, this interest in Marxist periodization led to a systematic transcoding of ancient Chinese history into a universal history. What Guo attempted was nothing less than a translation, as it were, between the Marxist science of universal history and the particular historical development of China. Dirlik's scrutiny of Chinese Marxist historiography has already offered a detailed discussion of Guo's case for slavery in the age of the Shang civilization (ca. 1600–1046 BCE). My study attempts to make a metahistorical argument about how Guo's narrative relies on his paleographical-philological breakthroughs. His deciphering of the oracle bone and bronze pictographs—as a modern translation of the unearthed archaic written system—serves as a new methodology of making a revolutionary epoch (*shidai*) not only knowable but even visible.

According to his *Autobiography*, after Guo finished two essays—which later became the first two parts of *Studies*—in August 1928, he started to shed doubtful light on his own research. He later claimed: "I don't need to hide the fact that the method of my initial study committed the crime of formulaic application. I imposed, in a rigid manner, the materialist conception of history on the texts which, moreover, are

82. Dirlik, *Revolution and History*, 180–91.
83. Ibid., 177.

unreliable."[84] He decided to base his Marxist study on the more reliable materials and submerged himself in the ancient inscriptions. Within two months, he "finished reading all the works of oracle bone inscriptions and bronze inscriptions, and Wang Guowei's *Collected Works*."[85] Guided by the groundbreaking scholarship of Wang Guowei 王國維 (1877–1927), Guo declared he had found the key to the scientific deciphering of oracle bone characters within two days: "[The deciphering] was not due to any particular talent of mine, but was indebted to a master who paved a way for us, and I must express my thanks to him. Who is this master? Wang Guowei, who . . . committed suicide in Beijing."[86] The discovery of oracle bone inscriptions (dated from ca. fourteenth century to ca. eleventh century BCE) was perhaps *the* most important archaeological event in twentieth-century China, and Wang Guowei was a pioneer in incorporating the interpretation of oracle bones into the study of early Chinese history, especially the Yin (Shang)-Zhou dynastic transition. Moreover, Guo extended his philological deciphering to the bronze inscriptions. Parts three and four of *Studies* are to a marked degree built on his archeological-paleographical endeavors, such as the works included in *Studies of Oracle Bone Inscriptions* (*Jiagu wenzi yanjiu* 甲骨文字研究, 1931). The output of his paleographical works of the whole exile period—including three major collection of scholarly essays and three cataloged collections of inscriptions—was phenomenal in quantity and quality. Chen Mengjia 陳夢家 (1911–66), a non-Marxist expert of oracle bone studies, acknowledged in the 1950s that Guo's contribution defined a new paradigm of "social historical science" in this field.[87] Kwang-chih Chang, a leading archeologist of ancient China in North America, stated in 1986 that although Guo was not a field archeologist, "his pioneer works on oracle bone and bronze inscription and on the evolution of bronze styles are still indispensable readings."[88]

At the heart of his contribution to oracle bone and bronze inscription studies is a new perspective of the pictograph. In "Pictographs in the Shang Bronze Inscriptions: An Interpretation" ("Yinyi zhong tuxing wenzi

84. Guo, "Wo shi Zhongguo ren," in *GQJ/W*, 13:357.
85. Ibid., 365.
86. Ibid., 363.
87. Chen Mengjia, *Yinxu buci zongshu*, 53.
88. Chang, *The Archaeology of Ancient China*, 19.

zhi yi jie" 殷彝中圖形文字之一解, 1930), the first essay of his multivolume studies of Shang and Zhou bronze inscriptions, Guo contends that traditional Chinese philology is inefficient in interpreting ancient inscriptions because it is alien to the "scientific" concept of "pictograph" (*xiangxing wenzi* 象形文字). Guo singles out some pictographs that a large number of scholars, including Wang Guowei, have failed to decipher. Wang and others have difficulty in understanding such pictographs, Guo argues, because they do not even know the anthropological and art-historical concept of "totem." He concludes: "In summary, according to the universal principle of general social development and the characteristic of bronze styles, all the pictographs of animal shapes must be totems of ancient clans or the remnants of such totems."[89]

Affirming the Marxist universal principle of history, his paleographical philology decodes ancient Chinese pictographs as the emblems of social history rather than mere characters. Consequently, in Guo's studies of oracle bone inscriptions, the logic or rhetoric of visibility emerges in the following fashion: "With the access to the oracle bone inscriptions, the actuality of ancient society is vividly and splendidly present to our eyes."[90] Deciphering an archaic written system means an act of interpretative translation. This philological translation is not simply a reproduction of the ancient signification but contains a profound hermeneutic dimension. In particular, Guo's philological deciphering of oracle bone and bronze "characters" involves a translation of the visuality of ancient pictographs into the visibility of the "stages" (*jieduan*) of social history. The formulaic catchword that sets this pictographic translation in motion is "epoch" (*shidai*) or "epochality" (*shidaixing*). In fact, Guo's interpretation of the *Book of Changes* already contains this perspective of pictographic visuality, as he describes the ancient trigrams as "the dances of the naked primitives."[91] He goes as far as to define the epochality of the *Book of Changes* as "the transition from primitive communism to slavery."[92] By the same token, in his view, the pictographs in ancient inscriptions are visual representations of an epoch and its social development. For

89. Guo, "Yinyi zhong tuxing wenzi zhi yi jie," in *GQJ/K*, 4:22.
90. Guo, *Zhongguo gudai shehui yanjiu*, in *GQJ/L*, 1:196.
91. Ibid., 38.
92. Ibid., 69.

instance, he suggests that two oracle bone pictographs, which later evolved into characters *shou* 狩 (hunting) and *yu* 御 (horsing), "vividly represent their epoch [*shidai*]." For "in *yu* we see the use of horse, and in its fourth visual part we even see the trace of taming an elephant. In *shou* we see the use of dogs. They must have been pictographs after the invention of livestock."[93] Crucial here is Guo's method of using ancient pictographs as the representational trace of social development.

Dirlik stresses that the perspective of "sexual relations and kinship," especially the category of the "punaluan family," plays a crucial role in Guo's periodization of early Chinese society in *Studies*.[94] This perspective is in fact closely associated with a major breakthrough of Guo's interpretation of the pictographs. The first essay in his enterprise of archeological philology was an interpretation of *zu* 祖 and *bi* 妣, two Chinese characters whose appearance in oracle bones had caused perplexity. In the Confucian tradition, *zu* is a ritual name for father, *bi* for mother, in close correspondence to *fu* 父 (father) and *mu* 母 (mother). Because of the traditional emphasis on the patrilinear kinship structure and familial piety in China, those characters had long been considered solemn kinship titles of high symbolic value. But in oracle bone inscriptions, the four characters were used widely in proper names. As a result, no traces could be found or restored for any patriarchal lineage of power succession or structure of kinship. Wang Guowei, in his masterpiece "On the Yin-Zhou Institutional Change" ("Yin Zhou zhidu lun" 殷周制度論), points out the "lack of formalized structures" (*wu ding zhi* 無定制) for inheritance rights, commemorative rituals, and marriage in the Yin culture, while praising the founders of the Zhou dynasty for institutionalizing the patriarchal kinship network, the patrilineal succession system, and the "taboo on sexual relations among the same patriarchal clan" (*tong xing bu hun* 同姓不婚).[95]

Following Wang's suite, Guo finds ample evidence in oracle bone inscriptions of the existence of multiple fathers and multiple mothers and the rarity of the father–son inheritance. But he questions Wang's Confucian assumption about sexuality and kinship. Guo's conclusion shows an

93. Ibid., 201.
94. Dirlik, *Revolution and History*, 173.
95. Wang Guowei, "Yin Zhou zhidu lun," 466, 472.

anthropological insight: "The ancestors of the Yin people practiced the ancient custom of the sub-consanguine marriage."[96] By "sub-consanguine marriage" he means "the punaluan family," a concept about "family formation" provided by Morgan's *Ancient Society* and developed in Engels's *Origin*. Morgan's definition of punaluan family is based on a series of accounts about the punaluan custom among native Hawaiians. In a punaluan group, "the husbands and wives were jointly intermarried."[97] The intermarriage between brothers and sisters was already a taboo, but brothers shared their wives and sisters shared their husbands. For Morgan, "the advancement of society out of the consanguine into the punaluan family was the inception of a great upward movement."[98] This explains Guo's renaming of this family formation as "sub-consanguine family." Morgan argues for the historical "necessity" of the existence of the punaluan family as a transition toward the monogamy and sees the "traces," "remains," and "survival" of this custom in multiple tribes ranging from the "Status of Savagery" through the "Middle Status of Barbarism."[99] Furthermore, for Engels, the punaluan family means the prevalence of descent in the female line: "the children of my mother's sisters are still her children, just as the children of my father's brothers are also his children; and they are all my brothers and sisters."[100] Engels then links its dominance with the "female right": "In all forms of group family, it is uncertain who is the father of a child; but it is certain who its mother is. . . . It is therefore clear that in so far as group marriage prevails, descent can only be proved on the *mother's* side and that therefore only the *female* line is recognized."[101]

In almost every chapter of *Studies*, Guo refers to the punaluan family. Imitating Morgan's vocabulary, Guo argues for the existence of "remains" (*jieyi* 孑遺) and "traces" (*henji* 痕跡) of the punaluan family in Chinese

96. Guo, "Shi zu bi," in *GQJ/K*, 1:30–31; Guo also investigates ancient mythology from an anthropological viewpoint and demonstrates that the legendary sage kings and many god-ancestors of ancient clans were married to a set of sisters, and moreover, they shared wives with their brothers.

97. Morgan, *Ancient Society*, 428.

98. Ibid., 429.

99. Ibid., 426–32.

100. Engels, *Origin*, 104.

101. Ibid., 106; emphasis in original.

mythology and Yin culture. Deciphering oracle bones, Guo substantiates his observation that "the sub-consanguine family did exist in ancient China."[102] Such a formation of sexuality, family, and kinship explains the seemingly strange abuse of the kinship titles of *zu* and *bi* in oracle bone inscriptions, for those ancients as adults "had multiple wives or husbands" and as children "had multiple father and multiple mothers."[103] *Zu* and *bi* were therefore not applied to actual father and mother but to a group of fathers and a group of mothers. Exposing this classificatory issue in a system of relationships, Guo further argues that since this group marriage preceded monogamy in ancient China, *zu* and *bi* must have pictographic origins that had nothing to do with monogamous conception of parenthood. He links the characters to the totems and ritual emblems of sexual genitals in oracle bone inscriptions and establishes a genealogy of worship of genitals.

In fig. 8, the left column shows the totemic/pictographic variety of female genitals, the right the totemic lineage of male genitals. The two Chinese characters on top are *zu* and *bi* in their current shapes. In other words, they originated from the worship of genitals and sexual fertility and became the emblems of two sexes under the group marriage system. That they started to mean the actual biological father and mother was a late phenomenon when the establishment of the Zhou dynasty gave rise to the system of monogamy.

As Kevin Anderson observes, Engels's combination of the Rousseauist note with the new data leads to the conclusion that "what was called civilization, with its hierarchies of class, property and gender, was an atypical . . . way of ordering human affairs." Engels thus places the issue of gender "at the center of his concerns."[104] He famously holds that "the overthrow of mother right was the world historical defeat of the female sex."[105] This revolution was "one of the most decisive ever experienced by humanity," yet Engels admits: "as to how and when this revolution took place . . . we have no knowledge."[106] But Guo translates the pictographs into the visibility of the first epoch of social revolution in Chinese

102. Guo, "Shi zu bi," in *GQJ/K*, 1:33.
103. Ibid., 31.
104. Anderson, *Marxism at the Margins*, 199–200.
105. Engels, *Origin*, 120.
106. Ibid.

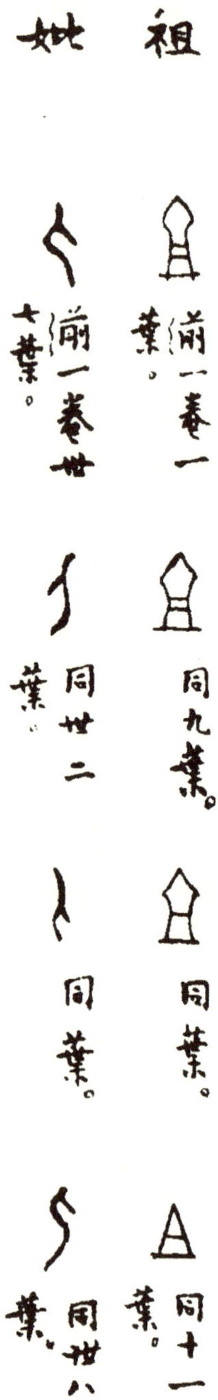

FIGURE 8 A chart of the genital totems/pictographs of the two sexes, Guo Moruo's calligraphy, used in *GQJ/K*, 1:37. Courtesy of Guo Pingying.

history, that is, the Yin-Zhou transition. With the discourse of epoch and epochality, I can thus summarize the vocabulary and syntax of Guo's historiography in his *Studies* and archeological-philological works: the ancient pictographs and inscriptions are representational emblems, or even visible expressions, of the epochality, the developmental stage, or the revolutionary transition from clan society to slavery. The Morgan-Engels perspective is thus combined with the paleographical translation of prehistorical pictographs into evidence of social development. More interestingly, the genealogy of marriage system is displaced and "restaged"—as an anachronistically condensed sequence—in Guo's autobiographical narrative.

The "Restaging" (Chongyan): *Translating "Ancient Society" into Autobiography*

In embodying a Marxist perspective of historical development, Guo's historiography and autobiography reach a marked degree of isomorphism. His transcoding of personal experiences into the exemplar signs of sociohistorical development forms an uncanny parallel to his transcoding of pictographs into sociohistorical emblems. The issue of sexuality and marriage offers an occasion whereby the autobiographical and the historiographical narratives form a mutual translation, and the autobiographical authorship and the Marxist analytical authority become identical to each other. Perhaps no other parts of Guo's *Autobiography* are more troubling than "The Black Cat" ("Hei Mao" 黑貓), the installment that relates his arranged marriage of 1912. A social custom practiced in late imperial China, the arranged marriage was seen as the glaring symptom of the backward and antihuman nature of "old China" in the May Fourth discourse of enlightenment. It was a biographical marker of certain important members of the May Fourth writers—such as Lu Xun, to name the most famous—who were forced by their parents to have arranged marriages and then grew up to be the advocates of its abolition. While others avoid this unhappy, if not traumatic, memory, Guo provides a detailed account of his own arranged marriage. He was arranged by his parents to marry Zhang Qionghua 張瓊華 in 1912. Soon after the wedding (and after "destroying my chastity," according to Guo's dubious confession to Tian Han), he went to Beijing and then to Japan to pursue higher education, permanently leaving behind his appointed wife in his hometown in Sichuan—to which he never returned except for his father's funeral.[107] Dealing with this personal and family trauma with a characteristic authorial spontaneity in this 1929 piece, Guo does not refrain from expressing his dislike for Zhang, a woman who was far more victimized than was Guo in that social norm. While this autobiographical piece seems to have only been able to satisfy readers' curiosity about the author's private life, I want to draw attention to a different aspect: the historical thinking of the epochs or stages and the Morgan-Engels discourse of sex and marriage are strangely and fully translated into Guo's autobiographical narrative in this piece.

At the outset, Guo frames his personal "tragedy" in the historical context of the 1911 revolution—a timeframe that is precisely what he periodizes in his *Studies* as the epoch of a failed "capitalist revolution"—and characterizes his arranged marriage not only as a "tragedy of the transitional epoch" but also as a sign of the failure of that revolution:

107. Guo, Tian, and Zong, *San ye ji*, 42.

> The year of 1912 is the first year of the Republic of China.
>
> This year is commemorative for me in a double sense: first, needless to say we Chinese had achieved a revolution; second, I had a marriage this year. That marriage of mine, as an interlude [in this autobiography], is now really a pain in my remembrance, a humiliation, a regret. . . . But it was also a social tragedy in that transitional epoch. The protagonist of that tragedy, strictly speaking, was not me. I was just an actor who happened to play a leading role.[108]

Clearly, this opening aims to historicize and also depersonalize this personal tragedy. From that moment on, Guo the author constantly immunizes the young Guo (the I) from any true agency. In other words, the arranged marriage is depicted in such a way that the young Guo always appears to be in a passive position. The pressure from parents is emphasized; the persisting custom of arranged marriage is described as being strengthened by the social chaos following the 1911 revolution. So one has to blame the backwardness of Chinese traditions. Before surrendering to his parents, the young Guo makes a single request, that is, the arranged wife should have no foot-binding. Foot-binding, as a custom related to sexual perversion in late imperial China, has been viewed or used by Chinese enlightenment intellectuals and Western observers as the Orientalist cultural-anthropological sign of "old China." A typical May Fourth symbolic narrative is prepared here: a young individual, with a modernized enlightened mind, struggles in vain with the persistence of the ancien régime.

Guo's negative depiction of his arranged marriage as a social tragedy fits neatly into Larson's reading of the "rejection of China" and the powerless position of the enlightened individual in the first volume of Guo's *Autobiography*. The bride is "an uneducated girl who belongs to the old 'China' the author is about to leave"; the marriage is in fact a divorce from China: "Rituals of marriage and revolution thus both appear strange and senseless and are unable to serve as self-validating ideologies."[109] More important, in Guo's description of the wedding, the narrative voice secretly transforms into a prosopopoeia of a retrospectively imposed his-

108. Guo, "Hei mao," in *GQJ/W*, 11:279.

109. Larson, *Literary Authority and the Modern Chinese Writer*, 129.

torical discourse. The descriptive account is invaded by the authorial intrusion from the analytical authority of the Morgan-Engels theory: "[Kowtowing to the titles of ancestors] is naturally the remnant of the primitive worship of genitals. In primitive times, gods are simply gods of fertility, so union before the gods means sexual intercourse before them. When the civilization advanced, kowtow replaced sexual intercourse."[110]

One can immediately discern the uncanny appearance of the issue of the worship of genitals that is central to Guo's Marxist interpretation of the oracle bone totems. He goes on to view the scenario of the groom leading the way for the bride as a "revival of the marriage by capture": "The bride following the groom is like a female trophy."[111] However, the furniture in the new bedroom of union is provided by the bride's family, and according to the authorial voiceover, it amounts to a "partial reappearance of the epoch [*shidai*] of matriarchy."[112] After recounting the ritual proceedings of the wedding, Guo offers the ultimate authorial intrusion:

> The whole old-styled wedding ritual is the remains [*jieyi*] of primitive epochs [*shidai*]. Within one day and a half, the descendants of primitive humans restage [*zaiyan*], in an interlocking way, the epochs of consanguinity or promiscuity, matriarchy, marriage by capture—the progress of which took thousands of years for their ancestors [*zu bi*] to achieve. These primitive customs are not necessarily barbarian; but what is restaged [*zaiyan*] here is only their residues [*caihai*], rather than essence. In the epochs of promiscuity and matriarchy, marriage is based on mutual willingness. In the marriage by capture, though it is unfair to women, this male-dominated choice . . . guarantees that the strongest warrior on the winning side will have the most beautiful woman. . . . But in the arranged marriage based on the order of parents and the words of matchmakers, both males and females . . . are now chained by the sheer matter of fate. It is our Chinese characteristic to become more and more lazy and hypercritical, . . . and for this our system of marriage should also be responsible.[113]

110. Guo, "Hei mao," in *GQJ/W*, 11:296.
111. Ibid.
112. Ibid., 297.
113. Ibid., 297–98.

A personal experience of arranged marriage is not only depersonalized as a social tragedy, but becomes an anthropological-historical site. Apparently, this commentary, slowing down the autobiographical narrative flow while controlling its ideological message, recycles the Morgan-Engels discourse and the analytical language of his paleographical endeavors (note the mention of *zu* and *bi* here). The vocabulary and syntax here are almost the same as I just summarized in Guo's historical writings: the details of the wedding ritual are representational "remains" of past epochs.

The word "restage" is of particular significance. It is suggestive of the temporal maneuvering Guo creates as an autobiographical author and as a historian. First, this "restaging" means the visibility of yet another form of "non-contemporaneity of the contemporaneous" (to borrow Bloch's phrase again): a series of the primitive epochs, taken from the Morgan-Engels chart of the humanity's progress, are condensed into the traditional wedding custom, which persists even in modern times. The visibility of these epochs then becomes the "exemplification" of "regression" and "stagnancy"—to put it in Morgan's language. The restaging can thus be recognized as a cross-genre translation of the historiographical categories into the autobiographical discourse.

Furthermore, with such a restaging, Guo the author completely detaches and defaces the character of the young Guo from the tragic marriage scene. The authorial voice comes from the Marxist author commenting on a past event, rather than from the I present in the wedding of that historical past. The bride Zhang Qionghua, as a character, is also depersonalized into an anthropological sample. The turn of fate comes when Guo notices that Zhang is actually foot-bound—a sexualized/gendered symbol of social stagnancy. Her ugliness reinforces her image as the national-allegorical "face" of a backward China. The foot-binding and the ugly face are the only two details Guo mentions about this bride. She eventually becomes what ethnographers call a "contemporary ancestor," a living fossil of the ancient society. Her existence in this autobiography is similar to a ghostly looking ancient pictograph awaiting the Marxist historian's interpretation. The first-person narrator then gives a final disclaimer of responsibility: "I cannot remember what happened exactly afterwards."[114] As a result, this defaced authorship not only occupies a

114. Ibid., 297.

retrospective vantage point of historical temporality, it also assumes the authority of a scientific-Marxist consciousness. Performing a narrative maneuvering of temporalities, the author/subject turns into an agency of the translation of "ancient history" into autobiography.

I can thus conclude my discussion of the isomorphism and even mutual translation between autobiography and historiography in Guo's work. These two modes of narrativization have their own translingual making in the global and national genealogies of both the romantic-sentimental critique of civilization and the scientific discourse of history. Mirroring each other, they form a series of cross-references while serving the same figuration of a revolutionized conception of history. Their isomorphism then reveals a deeper mechanism, that is, the relation of expressive translation between a universalized history (an epoch, a stage, or a social development), on the one hand, and the particular signs (a personal detail or a pictograph) on the other. This mechanism of equivalence/translatability conditions the "emplotment," "tropology," and "ideological implications"—to use Hayden White's metahistorical terms—in Guo's historiographical works and autobiographical writings: the "plot" of this autobiographical-historiographical network is a romance of fall and overcoming; its "tropology" is mechanical-metonymical expressivity; and its ideology is the exigency of social revolution.[115] De Man states that that "prosopopeia is the trope of autobiography, by which one's name . . . is made as intelligible and memorable as a face"; autobiography "deals with the giving and taking away of faces, with face and deface, *figure*, figuration and disfiguration."[116] To understand modern China's negotiation with the Marxist historical conception, I argue, one needs to take into account Guo's autobiographical-historiographical production of knowledge as a romantic science. In this parallelism, a self-fashioned authorial voice constantly discloses, deciphers, and defaces the particular—be it a genital-shaped pictograph or an arranged marriage—to transcode it into the staging, restaging, and displacement of a universal revolutionary history.

115. See White, *Metahistory*, especially 1–42.
116. De Man, "Autobiography as De-facement," 76.

CHAPTER 5

People's Democracy in Ancient Costume

In January 1942, Guo Moruo published a "historical play in five acts," *Qu Yuan* 屈原. This was the moment to be celebrated as the flowering of the historical drama in wartime China. The War of Resistance Against Japan (also known as the Second Sino-Japanese War) had entered its fifth year; the GMD had reinforced its authoritarian rule in its controlled region and resumed its anticommunist agenda. The Anti-Japanese United Front was on the brink of collapse, and the CCP was put on the defense by the GMD's campaigns. Zhou Enlai, then a CCP leader in charge of united front affairs and a political patron of Guo's cultural activities, saw this play as part and parcel of the ongoing political struggle.[1] Transforming the renowned Chu poet-politician Qu Yuan—who was exiled by his fatuous king—into a symbol of literary expression, patriotic loyalty, and political dissent, Guo's play allowed the CCP for a comeback, or indeed, a counterattack, on the cultural front. What he put on stage was an allegorical correspondence between a prosecuted ancient poet on one hand and a prosecuted CCP and its intellectual allies on the other. Even before the spectacular debut of *Qu Yuan* in Chongqing, China's wartime capital, Guo's poetic inspiration had flowed into another historical tragedy, *The Tiger Tally* (*Hu fu* 虎符), finished in February 1942. By mid-1943, Guo had produced three more historical tragedies; meanwhile, the exasperated GMD government hastened to censor his works.

1. See Shanghai shifan daxue zhongwen xi, ed., *Guo Moruo zhuan ji*, 2:3.

On the occasion of the staging of *The Tiger Tally*, Guo characterized four of his plays as a cycle of tragedies about the Warring States era (about 475 to 221 BCE; the era started soon after Confucius's death and ended with the Qin kingdom's violent unification of China), comparable to a cycle of four seasons. *Twin Flowers* (*Tang di zhi hua* 棠棣之花) represented the season of spring, *Qu Yuan* the summer, *The Tiger Tally* the autumn, and *Gao Jianli* 高漸離 (banned from staging) the winter. These plays, Guo said, embodied the cycle of that historical period: "The Warring States era, as a whole, was a tragic age. Our ancestors struggled to strip themselves of the bondage of slavery, trying to liberate themselves from that iron fetter, but the whole effort met with the result of changing it for another set of shackles."[2] The reinvention of "historical tragedy" (*lishi beiju* 歷史悲劇) as a genre was meant to develop a theme of people's liberation in response to a contemporary situation.

Commentators have long agreed that Guo helped create a leftist mode of "allegorization of the ancient for contemporary causes" (*yi gu yu jin* 以古喻今).[3] Central to the reception of Guo's historical drama, therefore, has been the controversy as to whether the modernization of the ancient adheres to historicism or spirals into antihistoricism. In a letter dated January 9, 1944, Mao Zedong viewed Guo's historical plays as a Marxist effort to "restore the historical truth" distorted by the ideologies of the ancient ruling classes.[4] In another letter dated November 21, Mao emphasized the service of Guo's work to the revolution: "Your historical plays are a great contribution to the people's cause."[5] In this sense, Guo's historical plays championed both a revolutionary historicism and an effort of "making the past serve the present" (*gu wei jin yong* 古為今用). Wang Yao 王瑤 (1914–89), a leading literary historian in socialist China, once praised Guo as "a talented romantic playwright, a . . . cultural fighter, and an accomplished Marxist historian," and characterized his plays as a "synthesis of popular appeal, scientific nature and artistic quality."[6] But this

2. Guo, "Xian gei xianshi de pantao," in *GZL*, 286.

3. See Wei Jian, "Guo Moruo lishi ju yanjiu shuping."

4. Mao Zedong, "Kanle *Bishang Liangshan* hou xie gei Yang Shaoxuan Qi Yanming er tongzhi de xin," 3.

5. Mao Zedong, "Mao Zedong tongzhi gei Guo Moruo tongzhi de xin," 140.

6. Wang Yao, "Guo Moruo de langmanzhuyi lishiju chuangzuo lilun," in *GHY*, 7:121.

"romantic approach to the historical drama" remains vulnerable to criticism.[7] It was associated with the political abuse of history that was later stigmatized as "innuendo historiography" (*yingshe shixue* 影射史學). It is, after all, tempting to follow C. T. Hsia's suite in stating that in Guo's wartime plays, "characters and events of the ancient Warring State period are freely distorted to make room for antigovernment and pro-Communist propaganda."[8] Moreover, his post-1949 historical plays, composed as an endorsement of the Maoist line, received a "reversed verdict" in post-Mao China and earned the playwright the posthumous infamy of "antihistoricism."[9]

Confronting such an "antihistorical historicism" in Guo's historical plays and historical studies from the 1940s to the early 1960s, in this chapter I delve into the precarious zone of historical knowledge, allegorical rhetoric, and political interventions. First, I trace the formation of Guo's dramatic poetics and situate it in a global itinerary of Marxist discourses on historical representation as well as in a national context of cultural-political struggles. In the 1930s and 1940s, Guo's dramatic practice also paralleled the global leftist debates about the antifascist popular front. In this respect, I limit myself to only mentioning Lukács's study of historical literature in the late 1930s as a defense of realism and "democratic humanism."[10] During the War of Resistance, Guo's historical plays went hand in hand with his controversial studies of the Warring States era. The historical-dramatic imagination of a tragic age of people's liberation was not just a poetic and intellectual matter but had its cultural-political determinations in a conjuncture about the "Sinification" of Marxism and the reevaluation of national antiquity.

Second and more important, Guo's historical poetics contained an alternative conception of "the people" (*renmin* 人民) within the leftist agenda of "people's democracy" (*renmin minzhu* 人民民主). This interpretation of the Warring States era as an epoch of a failed people's revolution, which, in contrast to other leftist readings, considered Confucian

7. The quote is from Wang Yao, "Guo Moruo de langmanzhuyi lishiju chuangzuo lilun," in *GHY*, 7:120.

8. C. T. Hsia, *A History of Modern Chinese Fiction*, 320.

9. See Zeng Liping, "Ping lishi ju chuangzuo zhong de fan lishizhuyi qingxiang (jiexuan)."

10. Lukács, *The Historical Novel*, 13.

humanism to be a progressive Zeitgeist, was an intrinsic yet contentious part of the articulation of "the people," a crucial political concept in 1940s China. The discourse of "people-centrism" in Guo's dramatic and scholarly interpretation of ancient China has been often reduced (by both his supporters and critics) to a one-dimensional partisan function. But on closer inspection, the staging of "people" in ancient costume presented the internal dynamic and dilemma of the revolutionary-popular project, and thus in an allegorical way contended for the "articulatory principles" of CCP-proposed New Democracy.[11]

Third, my discussion follows this parallelism between historical drama and historical scholarship to the socialist period. As Guo resumed his composition of the historical drama and continued to conduct subversive leftist historiography in the 1950s and 1960s, the question of historical literature became a central site of political contestations in Maoist China. My diagnosis of the metamorphosis and internal contradictions of Guo's later historical writings will be based on a larger problem of the socialist revolution as both a continuation and a supersession of "New Democracy."

China's long cultural revolution, supposedly an antitraditional period, translated itself into a "stage interpretation" of the ancient "spirits." This anachronism recalls to mind Karl Marx's thesis on history and revolution: "And just as they seem to be occupied with revolutionizing themselves and things, creating something that did not exist before, precisely in such epochs of revolutionary crisis they anxiously conjure up the spirits of the past to their service, borrowing from them names, battle slogans, and costumes in order to present this new scene in world history."[12] By analyzing the imagination of "people's democracy" in ancient costume, I aim to illustrate a permanent crisis of historical representation in a prolonged exceptional state of revolution.

11. The term is from Laclau and Mouffe, *Hegemony and Socialist Strategy*, 57.
12. Marx, *The Eighteenth Brumaire of Louis Bonaparte*, 97.

Origins of Guo's Historical Drama

Guo's experiment in the historical drama can be traced back to his lyrical period in the wake of the May Fourth Literary Revolution. The four opening pieces of *The Goddesses* are all poetic dramas. "The Rebirth of the Goddesses," for instance, mobilizes the ancient myth about the war between two titanic gods—Huang Di 黃帝 and Zhuan Xu 顓頊—and the subsequent reparation of the sky by Nüwa 女媧, the goddess or "eternal femininity" of creation, renewal, and redemption. "The Tragedy at the Xiang River" ("Xiang lei" 湘累, 1920) represents Guo's first attempt to dramatize, romanticize, and modernize the life tragedy of Qu Yuan, an ancient poet who became an archetype of poetic selfhood and political exile. Similarly, "Twin Flowers" (1920) was an initial dramatization of Nie Zheng 聶政 (an ancient assassin) and his twin sister, Nie Ying 聶嫈, but the work was unfinished. These early attempts remain mere "tableaux and scenes."[13] "Two Princes of Guzhu" (1923), based on the legendary flight of two brother princes of high virtue, Boyi 伯夷 and Shuqi 叔齊, then shows a continued experiment in the historical drama. As I analyzed in the last chapter, the aria of the whole play is found in Boyi's monologue, which condemns the corrupting effects of private property and civilization. Boyi is no longer a role model of Confucian morality or Daoist philosophy, but becomes a mouthpiece that vents the poet's political emotions and philosophical ideas.

It is beyond the scope of my study to inquire into Guo's foreign influences in the making of this allegorical mode of dramatization.[14] Suffice it to say that his early historical drama functioned as a lyrical device, rewriting the ancient into symbols of the May Fourth themes. This approach sparked criticism. Xiang Peiliang 向培良 (1905–59), one of the earliest reviewers of Guo's dramatic works, argued that "the characteristic of Guo['s plays] lies only in his pedagogy [*jiaoxun* 教訓]."[15] For Xiang, Guo's plays were allegories of this or that -ism. Indeed, Guo's first collec-

13. Roy, *Kuo Mo-jo*, 96.

14. According to Guo's own accounts, as a young dramatist he was under the influence of the Greek tragedy, German expressionism, and the works of Schiller, Goethe, Wagner, and Shakespeare.

15. Xiang Peiliang, "Suowei lishi ju," in *GZL*, 722.

tion of historical plays, *Three Rebellious Women* (*San ge panni de nüxing* 三個叛逆的女性, 1926) followed the May Fourth themes of women's liberation and individualist rebellion in a didactic way. According to Xiang, the three plays that treat three famous ancient females—Nie Ying, Zhuo Wenjun 卓文君, and Wang Zhaojun 王昭君, respectively—are little more than propaganda for the women's movement and thus have nothing to do with either drama or history.

Xiang's criticism also brings to the fore another feature of Guo's historical dramas, namely, his obsession with self-commentary. Guo "is worried about whether the reader understands his intention," and as a result his "pedagogy" exceeds the textual confines of the drama: "He preaches in his plays, and, unsatisfied with that, he continues his pedagogy outside the plays."[16] Starting with his earliest dramatic experiments, Guo was obsessed about writing notes, prefaces, postscripts, and interpretations for his own historical plays; during his mature period of dramatic writing, this format evolved into a systematic self-commentary. These pieces of commentary form a textual network involving self-congratulation, thematic explanation, scholarly justification, and countercriticism. This mode of self-commentary has a decisive "surplus value," without which Guo's later historical tragedies could never function fully as cultural-political interventions.

Some secrets of Guo's dramatic-pedagogic mechanism lie precisely in these supplementary texts. "The stage director" he puts at the very end of "The Rebirth of the Goddesses" is reminiscent of the "theater manager" appearing at the beginning of Goethe's *Faust* and prefigures Guo's habit of self-interpretation. A more suggestive case is "The Introductory Scene Before the Staging" ("Mu qian xu hua" 幕前序話) he wrote for "Two Princes of Guzhu." This introduction is itself a mini-play by design, with its own scene setting—a writer's study—and characters—a writer and his friend. The dialogue between the two revolves around the question as to whether we need the "historical drama" (*gushi ju* 古史劇) in the age of New Literature.

According to "the friend," there are two tendencies in composing the historical drama. One is to speak on behalf of the ancients, as in Shakespeare's histories. The other is to use the ancients as one's own

16. Ibid., 726.

mouthpieces, as shown in Goethe's *Faust*. "The writer," in turn, fends off the dilemma between historicization and modernization by resorting to a pantheistic flow of transformation: "The multitudes of phenomena in the universe are in constant motion of cycling, and in endless transformation, evolution, and revolution." Therefore, "the old" can and must be recycled and remolded into "the new": "In this world there's neither absolute new nor absolute old." By seeking an accurate interpretation of the ancients' psyche, we can reach a "profound sympathy and an intrinsic accordance [between the ancient and the modern]," which will endow the poet with an irrepressible impulse toward self-expression.[17] Lyrical self-expression is in accordance, rather than in conflict, with historical representation.

"The writer" then provides an eccentric reading of the legend of the two princes: "They are the ancient antimilitarists, anarchists. Their spirit is in deep correspondence [*qihe* 契合] to that of our moderns; writing about them has no difference from writing about Kropotkin, Bakunin, and so on." Reading ancient legendary figures on the same footing with modern European anarchists is definitely a bold move. In the statement that "such ancient individuals are the new men [*xin ren* 新人] forever," one can discern the antihistorical "newness"—the absolute modern—that Guo accords to the historical imagination. To end this introductory scene, Guo names the stage "The Theater of Freedom," and requires playing Beethoven's "Moonlight Sonata."[18] For Guo, the dramatist's freedom is intended to create correspondences between the ancient and the modern. The later maturation of his historical drama was a development of this problematic.

"Translation," Lyrical "Unification," and Political Catharsis

When restarting his composition of historical drama, Guo arrived at a new definition of the dramatist's task: "The task of the dramatist is to grasp the *spirit of historical times* rather than be confined by the historical

17. Guo, "Guzhu jun zhi er zi," 2.
18. Ibid., 4.

facts. The dramatist has his creative freedom: he can reverse the traditional conclusions, give the facts new interpretations, and concretely *translate* the real spirit of ancient times into modern times."[19] This idea of historical drama as translation was voiced on the occasion of the staging of *Twin Flowers*—newly revised and extended—in 1941. As early as 1940, the GMD, based in Chongqing, decided to reshuffle the Third Department of the Central Propaganda, headed by Guo, which had been a symbol of the patriotic unity of the GMD, the CCP, and the progressive intelligentsia. Guo was then appointed to lead the Committee of Cultural Work, an institution the GMD invented to keep in check Guo's leftist circle.[20] The tension within the GMD-CCP United Front soon escalated into the Wannan Incident in January 1941, during which the CCP suffered a substantial loss because of the offensive of the GMD army in Jiangsu. In the GMD-controlled region, the CCP had to concentrate on the arena of culture. The staging of *Twin Flowers* was part of an orchestrated promotion of Guo's status as a flag-bearer of progressive culture, with which the CCP hoped to counter the GMD's anticommunist policy and win over the public.[21]

This play is based on the story of Nie Zheng and his twin sister, Nie Ying. In the Warring States era, when China's fate was controlled by seven powerful kingdoms, Nie Zheng supports an alliance of the six kingdoms in the east against the military hegemony of the Qin kingdom in western China. He volunteers to assassinate a minister of the Han kingdom who wants to surrender to Qin, and in doing so he sacrifices his own life. His sister commits suicide to follow his footsteps. While the earliest May Fourth version of this play struck a pacifist note (in response to the warlords' rule of China in the early 1920s), the newly completed version resonated with the Chinese patriots' anxiety as to whether the GMD would sever the united front and surrender to Japan. In "How I wrote *Twin Flowers*" ("Wo zenme xie Tang di zhi hua" 我怎樣寫棠棣之花), Guo attributed the play's warm reception to its political theme of "promoting solidarity and opposing disunity." He conceded: "Needless to say, this is a subjective interpretation inserted [into history]." He added that the wish

19. Guo, "Wo zenme xie Tang di zhi hua," in *GQJ/W*, 6:277; emphasis added.

20. Cai Zhen, *Guo Moruo shengping wenxian shiliao kaobian*, 66.

21. For details about other related cultural activities, see Zeng Jianrong, ed., *Guo Moruo zai Chongqing.*

of unification was a political faith "shared by both ancient and modern" Chinese: "We can study the ancient from a modern viewpoint, and also reflect upon the present by using the ancient materials, and in this sense, this insertion is not unnatural."[22]

Such a translation of the spirit of ancient times into modern times determined the "bright prospect" of the historical drama in wartime literature.[23] Other leftist writers, such as Yan Hansheng 陽翰笙 (1902–93) and Qian Xingcun (A Ying 阿英), joined the effort and offered historical plays. Because this genre embodied two domains where the CCP could sustain its voice in the GMD-controlled region—historical scholarship and theatrical practice—Guo was prompted to compose a new play, *Qu Yuan*. Written and staged in early 1942, *Qu Yuan* represented the pinnacle of Guo's dramatic career. Qu Yuan (340?–278 BCE), an aristocrat of the Chu kingdom during the Warring States era, was the first great poet of China. The author of the long poem "On Encountering Trouble" ("Li sao" 離騷), Qu Yuan used the southern language and shamanistic style to create a lyrical image of a righteous man in political exile, of a melancholy poet-madman, and of an unpolluted soul enmeshed in a corrupted world. In the Warring States era, the southern kingdom Chu was a major contender for China's unification, and Qu Yuan as a courtier advised King Huai to unite other kingdoms to resist the expansionist Qin kingdom. Attacked by other pro-Qin ministers, Qu Yuan lost the king's favor. He spent most of his late life in exile until committing suicide by drowning himself in the Miluo River on hearing the news of his kingdom's defeat by Qin.

Qu Yuan's status as a founding political lyric poet took its root in traditional Chinese lore, rituals, and customs. As Laurence Schneider has shown, the legend of Qu Yuan always embodied the tensions of "loyalty and dissent," and therefore invited a series of reinterpretations among modern Chinese intellectuals who imagined themselves as the enlightened "mad men" for the national survival.[24] According to Michelle Yeh, modern Chinese poets found in Qu Yuan a "self-image" of "the poet as

22. *GQJ/W*, 6:277.

23. See Zhang Ying, "Cong Tang di zhi hua tandao ping lishi ju," in *GZL*, 769–73.

24. See Schneider, *A Madman of Ch'u*.

tragic hero."[25] Monica E. M. Zikpi's article focuses on the transformation of Qu Yuan's image in twentieth-century China, observing that his "primary bond shifted from personal loyalty to his king to solidarity with the common people and dedication to an abstract ideal of the Chinese nation."[26] Wartime Chinese intellectuals' renewed interest in Qu Yuan was conditioned by the increasing cultural, ideological, and political importance of national antiquity.

Guo originally conceived this play as a two-part long drama, structurally similar to Goethe's *Faust*. This plan was intended to solve the difficulty of how to cover Qu Yuan's tragic life of more than thirty years. However, when Guo started writing on January 2, 1942, the plan was immediately set aside. In "How I Wrote *Qu Yuan*" ("Wo zenyang xie wu mu shi ju Qu Yuan" 我怎樣寫五幕史劇屈原), Guo once again offered a self-fashioned myth about literary spontaneity. According to this account, the composition only took ten days. The whole plot and structure underwent changes. The outcome, "an unexpected accomplishment," was more in observance with the classicist law of unity of place and time than with the epic structure of *Faust* or Wagnerian theater: "Originally I planned to write about the whole life of Qu Yuan, but it turned out to be about just one day in his life."[27]

With the concentration of Qu Yuan's tragedy into the duration of a single day, a number of characters and events are fictional in Guo's play. At the beginning, Qu Yuan discusses poetry, history, and self-cultivation in his garden with Song Yu 宋玉, his pupil and another important Chu poet. The maid Chan Juan 嬋娟, a fictional character, informs Qu Yuan that Zhang Yi 張儀, Qin's prime minister, is visiting Chu. Qu Yuan is invited to direct the rehearsal of the singing and dancing rituals of *Nine Songs* (*Jiu ge* 九歌; a religious and mythological work attributed to Qu Yuan) at the palace, without knowing that Queen Zheng Xiu 鄭袖 and other pro-Qin courtiers are plotting a conspiracy against him. During the rehearsal, the queen frames Qu Yuan and unjustly accuses him of sexually molesting her. Humiliated by King Huai and betrayed by his

25. See Yeh, *Modern Chinese Poetry*, 32–36.

26. Zikpi, "Revolution and Continuity in Guo Moruo's Representations of Qu Yuan," 176.

27. Guo, "Wo zenyang xie wu mu shi ju Qu Yuan," in *GQJ/W*, 6:401, 404.

pupils, Qu Yuan is seen as a demented man. But Chan Juan and some other plebeian people remain deeply supportive. In the hope of preventing Chu's capitulation to Qin, Qu Yuan confronts King Huai and Zhang Yi in public. But the king orders his imprisonment in the Temple of the Eastern Emperor (the sun god in the Chu culture). Chan Juan comes to his rescue; by mistake, she drinks the poisoned wine prepared for him and dies in Qu Yuan's place. A guard decides to escort Qu Yuan to flee to the northern part of the kingdom. With the temple on fire, Qu Yuan departs in deep sorrow, indignation, and love. The curtain falls with a mourning song.

Much has been said about how the publication and staging of this play became an "unprecedented" theatrical-political event.[28] What I want to analyze here in particular is the lyrical rhetoric of this historical "translation" that produces a moment of theatrical-political catharsis. For such a rhetorical analysis, one has to concentrate on Qu Yuan's soliloquy during his imprisonment in act five. This soliloquy—the longest in this play, often called by critics the "Ode to Thunder and Lightning"—testifies to Guo's poetic power and political passion. I view the lyrical dynamic of this soliloquy as emblematic of the whole mechanism underneath his form production of the historical tragedy. Its importance warrants a lengthy quote:

> Qu Yuan (*addressing the wind, thunder and lightning*):
>
> Wind! Roar, roar! Roar with all your might! In this pitchy darkness without the light of day everything is asleep, wrapped in deep slumber or dead; it is time for you to roar, for you to roar with all your might!
>
> Yet, however you roar, you cannot awake them from their dreams, you cannot bring to life what is dead. . . . But you . . . can rouse the Dongting Lake, the Yangtze River and the Eastern Sea to roar in concert with you.
>
> Ah, I long for the Dongting Lake, I long for the Yangtze River, I long for the Eastern Sea, that mighty and boundless expanse of waves, that mighty and boundless expanse of strength! That is liberty, dancing, music, poetry!
>
> Ah, the great poem of the universe! You wind, thunder, lightning, you who roar in the darkness, brightening all things, you are all poetry, all music, all dancing. Great artists of the universe, express your utmost power,

28. Qin Chuan, *Wenhua juren Guo Moruo*, 340–41.

vent your boundless wrath and smash to atoms this dark universe, this gloomy universe!

Thunder! Is your rumbling the sound of your chariot wheels? Carry me to the edge of the Dongting Lake, to the bank of the Yangtze River, to the shore of the Eastern Sea! . . .

Ah, lightning! Keenest sword of the universe! . . . Lightning, sword of the universe, you are also the sword of my heart. Pierce, pierce, pierce through this darkness which is heavier than iron! . . .

Oh, light, I adore you! . . . For I know your element is fire, the greatest element in the universe. . . . I know that you are the life of the universe, my own life. You are myself! My blazing life, my smoldering wrath, will they not burst into a blaze?

Burst, my body! Burst, universe! Let the red flames leap forth like this wind, like the plunging sea, until all material things, all filth, are consumed in your flames; and let this darkness be consumed, the cloak of all evil![29]

The setting of Qu Yuan's imprisonment in the Temple of the Eastern Emperor, which has no historical evidence, comes as a stroke of Guo's genius. The Eastern Emperor, a deity of Chu mythology, figures prominently in Qu Yuan's *Nine Songs*. The imprisonment helps portray Qu Yuan as a visionary priest while being isolated physically and politically. Before this monologue, Guo uses other characters' words to forecast the coming of a storm: "What changeful weather. There will probably be a storm."[30] In the romantic theatrical tradition, a fierce precipitation has long been a favorite setting for the catharsis of psychological and sociopolitical collisions. The romantic meteorology and national geography merge into a cosmological view, with the wind, thunder, and lightning internalized as the universe's poetry. Here, the reappearance of the apostrophic motives and rhetoric of Guo's early pantheist verse is quite apparent, returning us to the discussion of his translation of Shelley's "Ode to the West Wind." The addressees of Qu Yuan's lines range from the natural forces to light and fire. The apostrophic gap between "you" and "I" disappears into a unification of the self and the universal revolution: "You are myself!" It is also reminiscent of Faust's embrace of the Earth

29. Guo, *Qu Yuan*, 180–81.
30. Ibid., 175.

Spirit. The lyrical subjectivity reaches its climax in a now of catharsis through the cosmic-revolutionary Heraclitean element of fire.

Xu Chi 徐遲 (1914–96), a modernist poet, was the first to discern an echo of *King Lear* in this soliloquy. In Shakespeare's masterpiece, Lear vents his wrath against the backdrop of a storm: "Blow, winds, and crack your cheeks!"[31] His monologue continues:

> Let the great gods,
> That keep this dreadful pudder o'er our heads,
> Find out their enemies now. Tremble thou wretch,
> That hast within thee undivulgèd crimes,
> Unwhipped of justice.[32]

Xu nevertheless proposed some changes for Qu Yuan's soliloquy to keep Guo's portrayal more in attune with actual history: "[Qu Yuan] did not have a personality of storm."[33]

In his response, Guo elaborated on his difference from Shakespeare: "Fortunately there is a huge difference [between Qu Yuan and Lear], that is, in my play Qu Yuan is unified [*tonghua* 同化] with the thunder, while Lear is still in a position alienated [*yihua* 異化] from the thunder."[34] Guo uses the concept of *tonghua* to suggest a self-expansion into or identification with the sublime force of permanent change. In this sense, "unification" (*tonghua*) in the historical drama is a continuation of the apostrophic politics in Guo's early lyricism. It transforms the setting of a Chu polytheist temple into an occasion of political protestation and theatrical catharsis. Thus, catharsis is not grounded in Aristotelian poetics of recognition or horror but revolves around the apostrophic instant of identification. Culler argues that apostrophe carries the "uncalculable force an event."[35] The true poetic event in this play is that Qu Yuan is identified as a "mouth" (visible and audible) of revolutionary politics. On the stage, Qu Yuan eventually takes off his persona and reveals his true

31. Shakespeare, *King Lear*, 99.
32. Ibid., 101–2.
33. Xu Chi, "Xu Chi xiansheng laixin," in *GQJ/W*, 6:413.
34. Guo, "Qu Yuan yu Liya Wang," in *GQJ/W*, 6:408–9.
35. Culler, "Apostrophe," 152.

identity as a revolutionary subjectivity oppressed by the GMD's rule, or a superman-like "Prometheus bound."[36] Kun Qian notes that "Qu Yuan lives in Guo's present."[37] This moment of catharsis, as a *mise-en-abîme* of the whole play, embodies a now-time of the lyrical, whereby the unification (*tonghua*) of Guo's poetic voice, national antiquity, and revolution becomes theatrically possible.

Marxist Literary Theory and the Poetics of Historical Representation

In translating or modernizing the ancient, Guo's terminology of *tonghua* (unification) and *yihua* (alienation) hints at a Hegelian-Marxian vocabulary. Recalling their exchange of ideas, Xu Chi later emphasized that Guo had been using the terminology of *The German Ideology*.[38] In the mid-1930s, Guo translated excerpts of the youthful work of Marx and Engels into Chinese.[39] On the other hand, the lyrical mode of catharsis in Guo's tragedy production causes a degree of tension with the Marxist insistence on realism and historicism. At this point it is worth engaging in the problem of the historical drama in Marxist theory. One should keep in mind that the Marxist conception of realism is at least partly based on Marx's criticism of a historical play. In a letter from 1859, Marx writes to Ferdinand Lassalle about the latter's play, *Franz von Sickingen*. Criticizing that play's representation of the German Peasants' War, he lays out the opposition between "Shakespearism and Schillerism" in literary representation of history: "You would then have *Shakespearized* more; at present, there is too much Schillerism, which means making individuals into mere mouthpieces of the spirit of the times, and this is your main fault."[40] For Marx, Schiller stands for a tendency of intellectual abstraction in the historical drama, whereas Shakespeare is a true "dramatic poet" with a

36. Schneider, *A Madman of Ch'u*, 117–20.
37. K. Qian, *Imperial-Time-Order*, 134.
38. Xu Chi, "Guo Moruo, Qu Yuan he Cai Wenji," 320.
39. See Guo, "*Deyizhi yishixingtai* xu," i; "Yizhe bianyan," 1–7.
40. Marx, "Marx to Ferdinand Lassalle," 108; emphasis in original.

deep understanding of historical circumstances. Similarly, Engels comments: "In my view of drama, the realistic should not be neglected in favor of the intellectual elements, nor Shakespeare in favor of Schiller."[41] Realism in literature requires a characterization of historical individuals under historical circumstances, as opposed to an intellectual abstraction of characters into allegories.[42]

The Shakespeare-Schiller dichotomy recalls to mind the historicization versus modernization binary in the aforementioned discourse of the young Guo. The Schillerian abstraction can be seen as something similar to the lyricization in Guo's historical drama from his early attempts all the way to the wartime plays. But Guo's early romantic idea about the "correspondence" between the ancient and the modern should not be dispensed with easily in Marxist poetics. Even though Marx discredits Lassalle's play for too much dehistoricization, Marx's historicism is also concerned with a "spiritual" correspondence between the past and the present. That is why he is interested in a dramatization of the German Peasants' War in the first place: "The conflict chosen is not only tragic but is the tragic conflict which unerringly caused the wreck of the revolutionary party of 1848–1849."[43] A parallel between a past revolutionary moment and a tragic revolution of modern times is clearly drawn. According to Marx, the more historically the play depicts the truly revolutionary elements of the past moment, the more it can represent the current revolutionary situation: "Then you could have expressed in much greater measure the most modern ideas in their purest form."[44] Marx's mention of "the spirit of the times" should be underscored in particular.

This Marxist approach to historical literature is carried further by Lukács in his seminal book *The Historical Novel*. "Composed during the winter of 1936–1937" in Soviet Russia, Lukács's defense of realism was a response to the new leftist cultural situation marked by the consolidation of Stalinism (and its espousal of "socialist realism"), the antifascist agenda, and the issue of the "popular front." His criticism stresses the "peculiarity of dramatic characterization" and objects to any "abstracting

41. Engels, "Engels to Ferdinand Lassalle," 110.

42. For a detailed account of Marx's and Engels's discourses on the historical drama, see Lukács, "Die Sickingendebatte zwischen Marx-Engels und Lassalle."

43. Marx, "Marx to Ferdinand Lassalle," 107.

44. Ibid., 108.

methods." One mode of dramatic abstraction, for Lukács, is lyricism. He argues that when the "collision is enacted exclusively in the hero's soul" rather than in social interactions, "its mode of expression, therefore, can only be that of lyricism or of didactic rhetoric."[45] In line with Marx, he finds abstract types overgeneralized and insufficient.

In the context of the leftist debates on aesthetics and politics in 1930s Europe, Lukács's emphasis of historical characterization was an antidote to the abstract tendency in both socialist realism's production of the "literary type" and the modernist discourse of symbolic archetype.[46] Around the same time, the polemic of characterization versus typification was also played out in the debate on historical representation in China. In 1935, Lu Xun wrote a preface to his collection of historical stories, *Old Stories Retold* (*Gushi xin bian* 故事新編); in 1936, Guo wrote his preface to a collection of his historical sketches, *Pig's Trotters* (*Shi ti* 豕蹄). As Ito Toramaru suggests, their prefaces contained an implicit debate about the idea of type (*dianxing* 典型) introduced from Soviet socialist realism.[47]

On the surface, Lu Xun's and Guo's approaches seem similar. But Ito stresses that their divergence in literary outlook is equally decisive. In his preface, Lu Xun indicates the necessity of historicism: "And on the subject of historical fiction: those very detailed works, stuffed with research, every fact checked, that some deride as scholarly fiction—they're no picnic to pull off. If instead you take one tiny scrap of fact, add a bit of colour, then extrapolate it into a story of sorts: this doesn't take much out of a person."[48] Ito indicates that Lu Xun's criticism of the "extrapolation from a tiny scrap of historical fact" is targeted precisely at Guo's historical fiction. Guo's preface to his own collection, in turn, is titled "To Start with Type" ("Cong dianxing shuo qi" 從典型說起): "The abstraction and synthesization of characters' physical, psychological, social and professional traits are the secret of type-making."[49] Therefore, his method has little to do with individuation and characterization proposed by Lukács

45. Lukács, *The Historical Novel*, 108–9.

46. See Jameson, "Introduction," 1–8.

47. Ito Toramaru, *Lu Xun, Chuangzaoshe yu riben wenxue*, 191–207. For a detailed study of the theory of "type" in Chinese aesthetic modernity, see Button, *Configurations of the Real in Chinese Literary and Aesthetic Modernity*.

48. Lu Xun, "Preface to *Old Stories Retold*," 296.

49. Guo, "Cong dianxing shuo qi," in *GQJ/W*, 16:196.

and Lu Xun. "Types are pre-given" in Guo's work; his historical characters are only extrapolations of those pregiven concepts, categories and types.[50] Drawing on pathology and psychology, Guo believes that "Confucius must be large, Mencius must be thin, Qin Shi Huang must be of an introvert personality, and the Ba King of Chu must be of an extrovert personality."[51] In his sketches, Mencius is a caricature of religious mania and repressed sexual libido; the portrayal of Qin Shi Huang amounts to a pathological illustration of hypochondria.[52]

It is noteworthy that this mode of type making receives a belated justification displaced in Guo's post-1949 historical scholarship. In 1956, he finished his punctuation of *Discourse on Salt and Iron* (*Yan Tie Lun* 鹽鐵論), a Han dynasty document about imperial political economy. The text records heated debates during a court conference. In his introduction to this ancient text, Guo shifts his role of historian to that of literary critic, arguing that this text is "a historical novel in dialogic form" and shows "a development towards dramatic literature."[53] Then arises the issue of type: "Notably in particular, Huan Kuan 桓寬 [the author of the *Discourse*] creates characterological types in this text. He uses the technique of generalization, generalizing more than sixty conference attendants of no official ranks into two characters, called 'Righteous Man' and 'Man of Letters,' and all courtiers and bureaucrats into two characters, too, called 'Prime Minister' and 'Minister of Supervision.' "[54] This comment, buried in Guo's historical scholarship, reaffirms a preference for the "generalization" of historical characters as social or spiritual mouthpieces.

Moreover, in his 1936 preface to his historical sketches, Guo links this mode of typification to "an interpretation of historical materials and an allegorical critique [*fengyu* 諷喻] of the present."[55] *Fengyu* is a mode of literary expression rooted in ancient Chinese poetics, and in the 1930s, some of Guo's contemporaries were already setting up an equivalence of *fengyu* with the Western poetic concept of "allegory." For example, Xia Yan 夏衍 (1900–1995), in his 1936 defense of the historical drama, put "al-

50. Ito Toramaru, *Lu Xun, Chuangzaoshe yu riben wenxue*, 203.
51. Guo, "Cong dianxing shuo qi," in *GQJ/W*, 16:196.
52. See Guo, *Shi ti*, in *GQJ/W*, 10:143–234.
53. Guo, "*Yan tie lun duben* xu," in *GQJ/L*, 8:478, 477.
54. Ibid., 474–75.
55. Guo, "Cong dianxing shuo qi," in *GQJ/W*, 16:196.

legory" in the parentheses as the English translation of *fengyu*: "In order to make the reader see in the ancient characters the activities of the modern people, and in order to fulfill the function of *fengyu* (allegory), I decided to . . . reinforce those phenomena that can correspond to our actual life and arouse imagination."[56] Responding to the same debate, Guo similarly commented: "The present situation can be taken as the clue to our representation of the ancient, and in fact, allegory [*fengyu*], by nature, is motivated by the present in the first place, and then is built on the past; but this process should not be vulgarized to a level of anachronism."[57]

The allegorical generalization is readily discernible in Guo's 1940s cycle of tragedies on the Warring States era. This poetics seems to run the risk of what Lukács once called "decorative archeologism," using the historical facts as the cosmetics.[58] Yet Guo's theatrical practice goes back forcefully to Marx's term: "the spirit of the times." He believes that his allegorical plays are based on a Chinese practice of Marxist historicism and successfully represent the Zeitgeist of the Warring States era. With this in mind, we turn to his wartime historical studies.

A Historical Imagination of "the People"

As Huang Xiaowu's study of wartime Chinese Marxism has shown, the Marxist intellectuals in the GMD-controlled region were propelled to engage in a reappraisal of national history to confront the rise of nationalism, neo-Confucianism, and irrationalism in the first half of 1940s.[59] In a time of war and national crisis, the intellectual community turned to the pre-Qin history, especially the Spring and Autumn era and the Warring States era. These two consecutive eras have long been considered a "splendid golden age of Chinese culture," witnessing the rise of Confucian schools, Daoist schools, Mo Zi factions, legalists, logicians, and

56. Xia Yan, "Lishi yu fengyu," 249.
57. Guo, "Cong dianxing shuo qi," in *GQ J/W*, 16:198.
58. Lukács, *The Historical Novel*, 251.
59. See Huang Xiaowu, *Makesizhuyi yu zhutixing*, chapters 2 and 3.

more.[60] It is a part of what Karl Jaspers has called the "axial age" in world history: "The spiritual foundations of humanity were laid simultaneously and independently in China, India, Persia, Judea, and Greece. And these are the foundations upon which humanity still subsists today."[61] In the meantime, that time period also saw the profound transformation from the final collapse of the Zhou civilization, through chaos and violence, to the unification of China. A leftist reading of the founding traditions of Chinese civilization was in demand when the cultural, ideological, and political strategies of the Chinese Revolution became an open question in the early 1940s.

Guo's resumption of historical studies was in every sense a response to this situation. His works in the late 1920s and 1930s "unquestionably established [him] as a giant in the study of ancient China," but were not immune to a dogmatic application of the materialist conception of history.[62] In contrast, his scholarship in the 1940s, concerned with a "clearing" (*qingsan* 清算) of the history of pre-Qin China, took a unique position in the leftist agenda of "articulating" a new cultural-political leadership of "the people."[63]

He wrote a monograph "A Study of Qu Yuan" ("Qu Yuan yanjiu" 屈原研究) in February 1942, right after the completion of the play *Qu Yuan*. This work was Guo's contribution to the wartime debate on Qu Yuan's work and showed his disagreement within the Marxist camp. As Huang Xiaowu emphasizes, Guo's study formed a "peculiar" yet long neglected debate with his "Marxist comrade," Hou Wailu 侯外廬 (1903–87).[64] In Qu Yuan's thought, Hou discovered a "contradiction" between the progressive "method" and the conservative "worldview," between a realistic observation of history and a reactionary nostalgia for "the Asiatic ancient tribal society."[65] The tragic nature of Qu Yuan's art was then the "tragedy" of Chinese antiquity, that is, the "dystocia of a new age" caused by

60. Guo, "Qu Yuan yanjiu," 68.

61. Jaspers, *The Way to Wisdom*, 98.

62. Chang, *The Archaeology of Ancient China*, 19.

63. I use the terms "articulation," "leadership," and "hegemony" in the sense of Laclau and Mouffe's theorization of class alliance and popular front in leftist politics. See *Hegemony and Socialist Strategy*, chapter 2.

64. Huang Xiaowu, *Makesizhuyi yu zhutixing*, 43.

65. Hou Wailu, "Lun Qu Yuan sixiang," 347.

the residue of the "Asiatic mode of production."[66] Eager to incorporate Chinese antiquity into a "universal model" (*gong li* 公例), Guo in the 1940s dismissed the particular existence of "the Asiatic mode of production."[67] His study was instead intended to portray Qu Yuan as a "revolutionary poet" whose lifework represented the Zeitgeist (*shidai jingshen*) of the Warring States era. His analysis of Qu Yuan soon merges into a disproportionate "digression" devoted to his periodization of a revolution from slavery to feudalism in ancient China.[68] Guo concludes: "The significance of that golden age is nothing but the ideological reflection of the transition from slavery to feudalism. Qu Yuan was born in the second half of that age; in this light, the social-historical significance of his life and work presents to us like a relief."[69]

Here Guo's modification of his earlier periodization of Chinese antiquity is in fact a minor issue, for the basic logic remains the same: every transition from one mode of social formation to another means a revolutionary epoch, and the revolutionary spirit is to be expressed in that epoch's cultural development. In his account of that revolutionary tragic epoch, the figuring of "the people" (*renmin* 人民) as a concept is a more suggestive and symptomatic moment. Guo states: "As early as thirteen or fourteen years ago, I already said that the slaves of production in ancient China were the people [*renmin*]."[70] The scholarly piece of "thirteen or fourteen years ago" is the essay I mentioned in chapter 4, "Interpreting *Chen* and *Zai*" ("Shi chen zai" 釋臣宰), included in *Studies of Oracle Bone Inscriptions*. According to Guo's paleographical analysis, the character *chen* 臣, originating from a pictograph showing the shape of an eye, designates a captive-turned-slave; *zai* 宰 is an image signifying a domestic slave. Guo finds no character *min* 民 in oracle bone inscriptions, but in Zhou bronze inscriptions, *min* starts to appear. The pictograph *min* represents a blinded eye and therefore signifies the more rebellious slaves crippled by the slave owners. His conclusion in the 1930s was thus:

66. Ibid., 343.
67. Guo, "Gudai shehui yanjiu da ke nan," in *GQJ/L*, 3:417.
68. Miao Yue, "Du Guo Moruo zhu Qu Yuan yanjiu," in *GHY*, 9:431.
69. Guo, "Qu Yuan yanjiu," 68.
70. Ibid., 79.

> *Chen* and *min* are both ancient slaves, *zai* is a similar case. *Chen* and *zai* are superior to *min*, which generally can be seen in Zhou bronze inscriptions. The reason for this is perhaps that *min* are those captives who refuse to surrender to the status of slave . . . , while *chen* and *zai* are those who show obedience to the victorious clans. . . . After a long genealogy, *chen-zai* became the name of the administrators, and *shu-min* became the designator of those being governed. . . . A history of class oppression has its inkling in one or two characters—this is what a philologist has to be acutely aware of.[71]

Built on his earlier analysis of *min*, Guo's 1942 study on Qu Yuan argues that the Warring States era witnessed "the huge change of the significance of the people [*renmin*]," and therefore was an age of the collapse of slavery.[72] Living amid such a "revolution," Qu Yuan used the local vernacular language in poetry and showed sympathies with *min* (people/slaves): "Qu Yuan profoundly grasped the Zeitgeist of his own age. . . . I would rather call him a revolutionary poet."[73]

Guo's use of *renmin* in 1942 was of particular importance because even though the pictograph *min* had already been deciphered to be the emblem of class warfare, the term *renmin* had not surfaced in the 1929 essay. Nor was *renmin* widely used in historical documents of the Warring States era. So why did *renmin* suddenly appear in his social analysis of the Warring States era? What was the valence of this concept in Guo's historical scholarship and China's intellectual politics of the 1940s?

The perspective of people/*renmin* also informed *Ten Critiques* (written in 1944–45), which accomplished an ideological critique of the Warring States era. A key section of the first critique in this book, "Self-Critique of Studies of Antiquity" (Gudai yanjiu de ziwo pipan 古代研究的自我批判), is devoted to "Evolution of the People's Social Status" (Shenshu renmin shenfen de yanbian 申述人民身份的演變). Again Guo mobilizes his paleographical insights for an intralingual translation/interpretation. Putting *min* under his analytical microscope, he contends that it originally meant a slave with one eye blinded by the slave owner: "[The char-

71. Guo, "Shi chen zai," in *GQ J/K*, 1:75–76.
72. Guo, "Qu Yuan yanjiu," 87.
73. Ibid., 98–99.

acter] is a sign of a horizontal eye with a thorn, and that is because a blinded eye was one of the emblems of slavery. . . . According to ancient phonetics and linguistics, *min* means blindness. This shows the cruelty of slavery. . . . Musician-slaves, with both eyes blinded, existed for a long time."[74]

He then extrapolates that in the Shang and West Zhou dynasties, "the people [*renmin*] were slaves of production," and sees "the people" as the agency or drive of social change.[75] Whereas the very visibility of the pictograph *min* is an emblem of class struggle under slavery, he notes that in the Warring States era, the rising class of landlords and the decadent class of slave-owning aristocrats were competing in "winning over *renmin*": "Herein lies a key moment of social change, and it is on this condition that *renmin* liberated themselves from the shackles of slavery."[76] He defines the epochal change as a popular revolution: "The people were making a revolution."[77] To sum up, from the deciphering of *min* as slaves to the interpretation of slaves as ancient *renmin*, Guo's 1940s perspective on Chinese antiquity contained a maneuvering of intralingual translation and indicated a profound turn in the leftist discourse toward a rising concept of "the people."

The political concept of people originated from Rousseau's theory of social contract. Rousseau described the "the moment" (*l'instant*) in which the political collectivity "assumes the name of *people*" and emerges as a sovereignty.[78] Ever since the American and French Revolutions, the figure of the people has been central to modern democratic politics. As Giorgio Agamben observes, "what we call people was actually not a unitary subject but rather a dialectical oscillation between two opposite poles: on the one hand, the People as a whole and as an integral body politic and, on the other hand, the people as a subset and as fragmentary multiplicity of needy and excluded bodies."[79] At the center of the historical unfolding of this "oscillation" was the international communist movement, which since the time of Marx sought repeatedly to combine the unitary subject

74. Guo, *Shi pipan shu*, 34.
75. Ibid., 33.
76. Ibid., 53.
77. Ibid., 92.
78. Rousseau, *The Social Contract and Other Later Political Writings*, 50–51.
79. Agamben, "What Is a People," 31.

of class struggle with a democratic class alliance of "excluded bodies." Lenin, for instance, prescribed the class alliance of the people for the 1905 Russian Revolution. This conception of people's democratic revolution was rekindled in the 1920s and 1930s when the prospect of a proletarian revolution beyond the borders of the Soviet Union seemed dim. For example, the slogan of "the democratic dictatorship of the workers and peasants," proposed in Lukács's "Blum Theses," already contained a program of people's democracy.[80] Also in the interwar period, Antonio Gramsci's conception of "hegemony" as an alternative to class warfare was defined by a new significance attributed to the "national-popular."[81] In an entry devoted to the national-popular in his prison notebooks, Gramsci directly compared the "more restricted meaning" of the "national" and "popular" in Italian with the "three principles of Sun Yat-sen's national-popular politics."[82] The Comintern endorsed this approach of a multiclass formation in the struggles against fascism, and during the 1930s and 1940s, a great number of leftists called for the strategy of the popular front. Stalin subsequently prescribed "people's democracy" in the postwar era as a tactical pathway toward socialism. The cultural-intellectual correlative for the articulation of the people was the discourse of the "popular character" and "democratic humanism."[83]

A similar search for the new articulatory logic of the national-popular was acutely felt and debated within the anti-Japan united front. A seminal text in this regard was Mao Zedong's "On New Democracy" ("Xin minzhuzhuyi lun" 新民主主義論, 1940). This essay addressed the crisis of the united front and responded to the widespread sense of uncertainty that had occupied the mind of the Chinese intellectuals: "Of late, however, the dust and din of compromise and anti-communism have once again filled the air, and once again the people are thrown into bewilderment. . . . The question once again arises: What is to be done? Whither China?"[84] The answer of Mao and the CCP to this question was a revolutionary agenda of "people's democracy" as "new democracy." This agenda

80. Lukács, "Blum Theses 1928–1929," 251.

81. Laclau and Mouffe, *Hegemony and Socialist Strategy*, 59.

82. Gramsci, *Prison Notebooks*, 2:362.

83. See Lukács, *The Historical Novel*, 282–99. For a discussion of the discourse of the popular character (*renminxing*) in Chinese literary criticism, see my chapter 6.

84. Mao Zedong, "On New Democracy," 339.

called for a revolutionary alliance of all four progressive classes: workers, peasants, petit bourgeoisie, and national bourgeoisie. This CCP-led alliance would assume the name of "people/*renmin*." Mao thus periodized the ongoing revolutionary movements since the May Fourth movement as a New Democratic Revolution.[85] The CCP carried out this struggle for "people's China" throughout the 1940s and succeeded in establishing the People's Republic, with the people's democratic dictatorship as its constitutional cornerstone.

Instead of accepting the teleological narrative that the CCP retrospectively imposed on the New Democratic Revolution, I want to argue that in the 1940s the project of people's democracy was an emerging configuration, in which different political groups (including many nonpartisan intellectuals, as I indicated in chapter 3) and ideological approaches were contesting the articulation of "the people" as a subjectivity-in-making. Viewed from Ernesto Laclau and Chantal Mouffe's theory of political "articulation," at that time, the conception or construction of *renmin* as a hegemony/leadership meant a "field of historical contingency" rather than a predetermined structure.[86] This new historical bloc was "a precarious articulation among a number of subject positions," and therefore was replete with tensions and ambiguities.

In this sense of articulation and contestation, Guo developed a unique discourse of *renmin* in the 1940s. In his reinterpretation of Chinese antiquity, the keyword *renmin* had at least three meanings. First, it was used as a general naming of ancient slaves; second, it was a concept used to identify ancient class oppression and struggle, thereby providing a new perspective on sociohistorical development; third, by designating a driving force of history, the narrative of *renmin* legitimized the political subjectivity of the ongoing Chinese Revolution. Built on a philological sleight of hand, his wartime historical scholarship constructed a genealogy of people/*renmin* and contained a historical imagination of people's liberation.

85. Ibid., 347.
86. Laclau and Mouffe, *Hegemony and Socialist Strategy*, 58.

Articulating/Contending the People: The "Tragic Spirit" of the Warring States Era

In this genealogy Guo aimed to sketch out, *renmin* of the Warring States era was imagined to be, to use Agamben's language again, both a "unitary subject" of history and a multiclass alliance of "excluded bodies." The most peculiar characteristic of this imagination was then his argument for the role of Confucian humanism in the ancient revolution of *renmin*. In *Ten Critiques*, Guo suggested that the liberation of *renmin* as slaves led to the rise of a largely independent, mobile, and potentially progressive social class of *shi* 士(sometimes translated as "gentlemen"). Among the emerging class of *shi*, he argued, to almost everyone's surprise, that the Confucians were the most revolutionary.

In the first half of the 1940s, the GMD ideologues tried to revive the Confucian political thought to reinforce their version of nationalism at the service of the one-party system; they went as far as to propose the Confucian practice of "instituting rites and music" for GMD's nation-building.[87] Many leftist intellectuals mounted their attacks on this conservative turn by criticizing the role of Confucianism as an ancient reactionary ideology.[88] The communists in Yan'an, the center of the CCP-controlled region, took this critique of Confucianism as a struggle against the GMD.[89] What distinguished Guo from the mainstream communist voice was an argument that in fact Confucian humanism was the revolutionary spirit of the Warring States era. He contended: "Confucius spent his life amid the torrent of revolution."[90] His characterization of Confucius's thought reads thus:

> Confucius' basic position was in accordance with the tendency of the social change at the time. . . . Generally speaking, he stood on the side of

87. See, for example, Dai Jitao, "Zhonghua min guo li zhi zhi jiben guannian," 950–51.

88. See Du Guoxiang, "Lue lun li yue qi yuan ji zhongguo li xue de fazhan (jielu)," 952–57.

89. See Qi Xuemin, "Zai lun Shi pipan shu de zhuanzhu dongji yu lunxue zongzhi," in *GHY*, 9:373.

90. Guo, *Shi pipan shu*, 92.

> the people's interest, and he wanted to positively utilize the power of culture to advance the people's happiness. He partly accepted and reorganized the ancient culture, and partly transformed it critically, in hope of creating a new system as a bond of the newly rising feudal society.[91]

In a way this praise of Confucius even echoes Mao's proposal of the "national, scientific, and popular culture" of New Democracy.[92] If in Guo's interpretation the *shi* becomes a metaphor for the progressive leftist intelligentsia, then Confucian humanism could be seen as a coded reference to his proposal of democratic humanism within the leftist articulation of people's democracy.

He then laments the failure of the struggle for people's liberation in the Warring States era. This liberation was "usurped by a group of the new nobles," because "the landlords and industrial-commercial titans replaced the ruling position of the slave-owners, and monopolized the class of *shi*. . . . Thus the new feudal order took form." What *renmin* gained in return was "invisible shackles in the place of the former visible ones."[93] To use Hayden White's language of metahistorical analysis, the "emplotment" and "ideological implication" of Guo's historical narrative assume a "Tragic vision" of the people's revolution and its incompleteness: a historical collision reaches its peak and yet no solution is on the horizon.[94] This tragic mode leads us back to Guo's cycle of four historical tragedies. As mentioned earlier, he suggested that "the Warring States era as a whole was a tragic epoch": "In *The Tiger Tally*, I grasped relatively better the Zeitgeist [*shidai jingshen*] of that age. But essentially it was also a tragic spirit. If we really want to treat humans as humans, history has to progress further, and more people have to sacrifice their blood in order to water this peach tree of our reality."[95]

Guo used "this peach tree of our reality" to refer to the ongoing CCP-led struggle for people's democracy. This tragic perspective corresponds to his anxiety about the unfulfilled project of people's liberation. With the

91. Ibid., 74.
92. Mao Zedong, "On New Democracy," 380–82.
93. Guo, *Shi pipan shu*, 61.
94. See White, *Metahistory*, 9–10, 313.
95. Guo, "Xian gei xianshi de pantao," in *GZL*, 287.

four plays revolving around the theme of democratic humanism, a tragic pattern that pervades all of them is symptomatic of Guo's coded intervention into this unfolding politics of people's democracy. This pattern is embryonic in *Twin Flowers*, matures in *Qu Yuan* and *Tiger Tally*, and deteriorates into an unsuccessful form in *Gao Jianli*. It can be schematized as follows: first, the tragic figure is always a male hero representing an enlightened progressive patriotism in struggle with internal absolutism and/or external militarism. Nie Zheng, Qu Yuan, Lord Xinling (Xinling jun 信陵君), and Gao Jianli all belong to this type. The tragic fates of these male heroes (or *shi*), however, are mediated by the self-sacrifice of another set of characters, that is, the female figures whose actions are largely based on Guo's fictionalization rather than actual history. This group of female characters, represented by Chan Juan in *Qu Yuan* and Ru Ji 如姬 in *The Tiger Tally*, willingly accept the fate of death and destruction to support the male heroes in their cause of progressive struggles.

In this regard, *Qu Yuan* bears resemblance to Goethe's *Egmont*, a historical play in which the sacrificial death of Claire—Egmont's mistress from a humble background—symbolizes the popular support for Egmont, an open-minded aristocrat.[96] Just as Egmont is loyal to the court and yet mistreated, so is Guo's Qu Yuan. Whereas in Goethe's play Egmont tries to reconcile the political collision between the rulers and the citizens, Guo's Qu Yuan takes a more defiant attitude toward persecutions and evolves into a fighter of patriotic enlightenment. Still, Qu Yuan's final decision to struggle on behalf of the people is conditioned by Chan Juan's self-sacrifice. At the end of the play, Guo lets Chan Juan unknowingly drink the poisoned wine that a priest treacherously prepares for Qu Yuan. She dies in deep love for Qu Yuan: "But I . . . I am very happy . . . I am going to die for you, to save your life—how lucky I am. . . . I have served you faithfully, for you are the soul of our country. . . . I love our country, so I cannot but love you."[97] While Qu Yuan stands as a cultural hero on the stage, Chan Juan embodies the tragic in the political struggle for people's democracy.

96. See Goethe, *Early Verse Drama and Prose Plays*, 83–152.

97. Guo, *Qu Yuan*, 187–88.

In *The Tiger Tally*, this theme of popular support for the intelligentsia/*shi* leads to the central dramatic action that is carried out by the female character Ru Ji, rather than by the male protagonist, Lord Xinling, a progressive noble. In this renowned play set in 257 BCE, Lord Xinling of Wei argues against his half-brother king's foolish concession to the Qin kingdom that is now ready to conquer one more neighboring kingdom of Wei's, the Zhao kingdom. Faced with the Wei king's refusal to aid Zhao, Ru Ji, the king's concubine coming from a plebeian background, helps Xinling by stealing the tiger tally that is needed to authorize the royal army to advance. When the news of Xinling's victory in aiding Zhao against Qin finally arrives in Wei, it is time for Ru Ji to commit suicide.

Ten Critiques ends with a critique of Qin Shi Huang, who eventually united the warring states into an absolutist Chinese empire. The last critique sees this achievement as a usurpation of the people's liberation, a historical regression interrupting the transition from slavery to feudalism: "The epoch of the First Emperor was a regression into slavery—a momentary recovery from death. Only one year after his death, China exploded [with peasants' uprisings]."[98] Here, to put it in White's terms, Guo's "tragic mode" of historical narrative merges into an "ironic" one, traceable to Marx's famous discussion of repetition/regression as farce in history.[99] In *Gao Jianli*, Qin Shi Huang finally becomes visible on stage as a character, and Gao Jianli is a blinded musician—a fact that reminds us of the pictograph of *min*. Both Gao and his female supporter die in a heroic attempt to assassinate the emperor, and it is interesting to note that Guo depicts Qin Shi Huang as a pervert and rapist. This amounts to a caricature of the GMD autocrat Jiang Jieshi as an internal enemy of the people (whereas in other plays the Qin kingdom's aggression symbolizes Japanese militarism as an external threat).[100]

The image of femininity, similar to Guo's political worship of Eternal-Feminine in his translation of *Faust*, was a symbol of what he later called "the good will and just nature of people, in which the not-yet-awakened class consciousness is impregnated."[101] Yet the theme of self-sacrificial

98. Guo, *Shi pipan shu*, 404.

99. See White, *Metahistory*, 320.

100. *Gao Jianli* was banned for staging by the GMD for its obvious innuendo. See Guo, "Jiao hou ji zhi er," in *GQJ/W*, 7:129.

101. Guo, "Zhu Tang di zhi hua de yanchu," in *GQJ/W*, 6:283.

femininity concealed an impasse of the political imagination and articulation of people/*renmin*. In Mao's "articulatory logic" of people's democracy, the intellectuals did not count as a class in the four-class alliance of people/*renmin*, and the leadership belonged to the vanguard party. In his talk on literature and art in Yan'an, Mao urged "intelligentsia" to fulfill "a change from one class to another" and to "truly serve the masses of revolutionary workers, peasants and soldiers."[102] In other words, the intelligentsia had to receive reeducation to be part of "the people." Given Guo's cultural and political positioning, *renmin* as the true focus was actually unrepresentable in his wartime historical writings. A theatrical solution to this contradiction was the solidarity between the male hero and the female tragic protagonist, the correlation between the sacrifice of the latter and the redemption of the former. In this gendered allegorical politics, Guo was concerned about whether the intellectuals could continue to function as a hegemonic (allegorically and problematically male) force in this articulatory politics of people/*renmin*. On one hand, he glorified the pioneering role of the revolutionary intellectuals (costumed as ancient Confucians). On the other hand, revealing their inaction on the stage, he was eager to propose a solidarity with the new unitary subject of the Chinese Revolution. Only through the active sacrifice of *renmin* or femininity could the intellectuals overcome their own limitations and become a part of this popular leadership.

Chan Juan therefore has to die in place of Qu Yuan. Symbolizing this political bond with the lower classes, Qu Yuan decides to depart for the north, which is a thinly veiled reference to Yan'an, the CCP mecca. Guo used Qu Yuan's eventual determination to express the identification of the leftist intellectuals with the CCP's revolutionary line. But on a northern path, would the intellectuals be reeducated by the party and people or continue to play the role of the pioneering hero of enlightenment? The "tragic" in Guo's 1940s historical works was this impossibility to overcome the anxiety as to whether there would be an "articulatory principle" of leftist intellectuals within *renmin*.

Scholars have long characterized the main theme of Guo's cultural work and political activism in the 1940s as "people-centrism" (*renmin ben-*

102. Mao Zedong, "Talks at Yenan Forum on Literature and Art," 73, 77.

wei zhuyi 人民本位主義).[103] In Guo's historical drama and historical scholarship, the imagination of people/*renmin* formed a coded political intervention into the ambiguity, complexity, and contingency of people's democracy. Representing a non-Yan'an leftist approach, the poetics of Guo's historical imagination transcoded Mao's proposal and participated in the redefinition of that national-popular agenda. His reevaluation of the Warring States era and Confucianism was an answer of democratic humanism to the "whither China?" question. Its hidden concern with the role of progressive intellectuals formed a critical negotiation with the emerging Maoist strategy. This political intervention and its impasse were the true content of Guo's antihistorical historicism. The staging of *renmin* thus pointed to a conjunctural imbalance, a neglected heterogeneity, and a missed dialogue within the CCP-led articulation of people's democracy. Later it came back to haunt not only Guo himself but also the Maoist party in general during the Cultural Revolution (see the conclusion).

Allegorical Reversals in People's China

Referring to Guo's wartime historical drama and the Yan'an reform of old-styled opera, Mao remarked in an aforementioned 1944 letter: "History is created by the people [*renmin*], but on the stage of old-styled drama . . . the people are presented as dregs, and the stage is dominated by lords, madams, young masters, and young misses—this is the up-side-down reversal of historical truth. Now your works reverse this reversal, thereby restoring the true face of history."[104] Such a "reversal of the verdict," supposed to be both scientific and revolutionary, was no doubt the main drive of leftist historicism in China.

Guo's dramatic and scholarly practice of such reversals embodied this combination of a Marxist search for truth and a contemporary "contribution to the people's cause." When Dong Zuobin 董作賓 (1895–1963),

103. See Lin Ganquan and Huang Lie, eds., *Guo Moruo yu zhongguo shixue*, 115–23. Also see Fang Shiming and Liu Xiuming, "Minzhu yundong yu renmin benwei sixiang," in *GHY*, 9:230–59.

104. Mao Zedong, "Kanle *Bishang Liangshan* hou xiegei Yang Shaoxuan Qi Yanming er tongzhi de xin," 3.

another leading expert on oracle bone inscriptions, questioned Guo's Marxist approach by indicating that Guo's conclusion about slave society was only based on two ideograms—*chen* and *min*—Guo's response was very suggestive. He insisted on the sociohistorical linkage between the ancient emblem of *min* as a blinded slave and the modern term *renmin* and condemned Dong's criticism as unscholarly: "It is due to this unscholarly attitude that Dong had to flee to Taiwan and prepared to be a live sacrifice [for Jiang's regime]."[105] For Guo, the lack of the Marxist consciousness made Dong—a former friend of his—intellectually vulnerable and politically reactionary; a scholarly reply was complemented by a political verdict. Guo's overconfidence on science and revolution came from the actualization of the agenda of *renmin*. This defiant confirmation of the importance he had attached to the pictograph *min* was delivered in 1950, shortly after the founding of the People's Republic of China.

Yet as I mentioned at the outset, since the curtain of Maoism finally fell at the end of the 1970s, a number of critics have leveled provocative criticism against Guo, condemning in particular an antihistorical tendency in the historical writings he composed in "people's China." In the early 1950s, Guo defended the importance of tragedy to the historical experience of revolution: "When the newly born force of social progress is not strong enough, and the dying force that deters social progress is not yet weak, the genre of tragedy will emerge."[106] This definition of the tragic spirit reverberated with his 1940s vision of the tragic in both his translation of *Faust* and his historical drama. But the tragic perspective largely disappeared in his historical writings after 1949. Rather, Hou Wailu carried further his own tragic perspective—which had been partly rooted in the Qu Yuan debate. In cooperation with Du Guoxiang 杜國庠 (1889–1961) and other historians, he continued to lament the "tragic" stillbirth of a social revolution in ancient China's Asiatic mode of production in a series of intellectual-historical studies before and after 1949.[107]

Guo's revised poetics of historical imagination is instead to be found in his two final historical plays—*Cai Wenji* 蔡文姬 (1958) and *Wu Zetian*

105. Guo, "Xiyi de canmeng," in *GQW/L*, 3:76–77.

106. Guo, "You Hu fu shuodao beiju jingshen," in *GQJ/W*, 17:257.

107. See Hou Wailu, Zhao Jilin, and Du Guoxiang, *Zhongguo sixiang tongshi, di yi juan*, 6, 149. The writing of this volume started before the founding of the People's Republic.

武則天 (1960)—which also count as a last monument of his literary output. Now as a leader of New China's cultural front and a high-ranking scholar-official, he focused on two ancient periods of restored peace and prosperity when the Maoist leadership initiated a search for China's path of socialism. In 1956, China accomplished the "socialist transformation"; the rule of people's democratic dictatorship seems to have reached its peak. The same year, Mao encouraged the intellectuals to criticize the party cadres. The movement soon spiraled into the widespread questioning of the whole state bureaucracy. In 1957, Mao's democratic approach to the "contradictions among the people" suddenly gave way to the dictatorial "Anti-Rightist" movement, which had many intellectuals as its target of class struggle. In 1958, Mao confidently started the Great Leap Forward, accelerating the transition toward communism.[108] Like many other literary uses and abuses of ancient history in this period, Guo's new historical plays were responses to the dramatic, and often traumatic, social-political change.

As Hong Zicheng's study has demonstrated, in Maoist China literary production was "homogenized" into a subsystem of the revolutionary party-state.[109] In this process of radicalization and homogenization, drama emerged as an important component of socialist cultural life, preparing the way for the "revolutionary model plays" during the Cultural Revolution.[110] The revival of the historical drama in the late 1950s and early 1960s was then a significant development on the literary scene. When the relationship between the party and the intellectuals was strained in the aftermath of the Anti-Rightist movement, the focus on history rather than reality gave writers more interpretative freedom, and the theatrical experience enabled a "resonance" between "a narrative and a contemporary historical condition."[111] As Paul Cohen summarizes, "the shift toward historical drama therefore resulted in an extended—and highly contentious—debate . . . on the relationship between historical drama and the whole involved question of how the past could be made to serve

108. See Shen Zhihua, *Zhonghua renmin gongheguo shi, di san juan*; Hong Zicheng, *1956: baihua shidai*.

109. Hong Zicheng, ed. *Zhongguo dangdai wenxue shi*, IV.

110. See, for example, Tung and Mackerras eds., *Drama in the People's Republic of China*; Xiaomei Chen, *Acting the Right Part*.

111. Cohen, *Speaking to History*, xvii.

the present."[112] As Hong Zicheng points out, under the influence of modern historicism and especially Marxist conception of history, most revolutionary writers and intellectuals assumed that history could be faithfully represented: "However divergent their views were, they had consensus on the refusal to recognize the 'narrative nature' of 'history.' "[113] On the other hand, they also believed that such representations of history should simultaneously offer didactic meanings. Their commitment to historical truth produced its own political ambiguity, lending itself to conflicting interpretations of the present situation.[114]

According to Rudolf Wagner, the historical plays of that period demand a "deciphering" of the deeper implications underneath the esoteric meaning.[115] He observes: "In the political struggles that preceded the Cultural Revolution during the years 1958 through 1966, the stage became a hotly contested battleground. A number of historical plays appeared. Some of them were apparent attacks both on members of the Party leadership including the Chairman and on policies advocated during the Great Leap Forward, whereas others supported these very leaders and policies."[116] Attaching more importance to the critical voices in Tian Han's and Wu Han's plays, Wagner indicates that Guo's two plays belonged on the side of those advocating the party line and functioned as a defense of Mao's leadership. To end this chapter, I venture a brief discussion of the complexity of Guo's post-1949 historical interpretation in a context of historical knowledge in socialist China.

In the two plays, the gendered allegorical politics takes yet another twist. *Cai Wenji* retells the famous story of the female musician-poet Cai Wenji's return from a nomadic tribe of the Huns to the central dynasty of China during the late East Han dynasty. The first half of the play is reminiscent of Goethe's *Iphigenia in Tauris*. Like Iphigenia, Cai Wenji is forced to go into exile in a faraway land due to the political chaos in the wake of the decline of the East Han empire in central China. Having married a nomadic leader, she is urged by a messenger sent by Cao Cao,

112. Ibid., 137.

113. Hong Zicheng, *Zhongguo dangdai wenxueshi*, 172.

114. For a relevant discussion of historiography and politics in socialist China, see Unger, ed., *Using the Past to Serve the Present*.

115. Wagner, *The Contemporary Chinese Historical Drama*, 3.

116. Ibid., 236.

who has reunited northern China and restored the dynastic order. After a series of moments of mistrust, hesitation, and misunderstanding, she decides to go back to the homeland to carry on her cultural career; the cost is that she has to bid farewell to her husband and abandon her children—similar to Iphigenia's fate.

Guo explicitly stated: "Cai Wenji is myself!"[117] Cai Wenji's decision to return to her fatherland is depicted with Guo's experience of abandoning his children and leaving Japan for China in 1937. *Cai Wenji* thus serves as an autobiographical-allegorical narrative of the intellectuals' patriotic dream of constructing a new China. Yet in the second half of the play, Cao Cao occupies the spotlight as a highly cultivated, open-minded ruler who cherishes the national culture and appreciates Cai Wenji's artistic talent. As Guo told us, this play's aim was to "reverse the traditional verdict against Cao Cao."[118] The play was in this sense a by-product of his scholarly essays intended for a restoration of Cao Cao's image as a national hero and a rediscovery of Cai Wenji as a forgotten female poet.[119] More interesting are the changed gender dynamics. The intellectual is allegorized as a female figure that identifies herself with a fatherland, in contrast to the male cultural heroes glorified in the 1940s historical plays; the party, invisible in Guo's earlier plays, is now depicted as an ancient male ruler.

Wu Zetian, in turn, focuses on the only female emperor in ancient Chinese history, whose reign prepared for the glorious heyday of the Tang dynasty. In this sense, the play is also a reversal of the traditional verdict against this leader, whose achievements were overlooked in historical accounts largely due to a gender bias.[120] The play shows how Wu Zetian (624–705) is misunderstood by her subjects because of a series of conservative aristocrats' conspiracies against her rule. After crushing all those conspiracies, she wins the popular support as her subjects realize her policies are good-willed and far-sighted at the service of the lower classes.

117. Guo, "*Cai Wenji* xu," in *GQJ/W*, 8:3.

118. Ibid., 4.

119. For Guo's essays on Cai Wenji's poems, see *GQJ/W*, 17:334–92; for Guo's new verdict of Cao Cao, see "Ti Cao Cao fan'an," in *GQJ/L*, 3:457–76. Tan Qixiang, a Shanghai-based historian, offered a major criticism of Guo's approach. See Tan Qixiang, "Lun Cao Cao," in *GHY*, 9:445–57.

120. For other Marxist historians' views, see Wang Jian, "Wu Zetian."

On one hand, this play seems to contain a feminist dimension, highlighting the historical progress carried out by a female ruler and her female disciples (such as Shangguan Waner 上官婉兒).[121] On the other hand, the presence of such a progressive yet unjustly disputed female is a symbolic advocacy for the CCP's leadership, which according to Guo was also unjustly criticized by some intellectuals in 1956–57.[122]

The allegorical politics in these two plays is more complicated than one may assume at first sight and is indicative of the crisis of historical representation in socialist China. The two plays seem to conceal a new anxiety—within the party politics—about the relationship between the intellectuals and the CCP, and by extension, about the tension between democracy and dictatorship. Written shortly after Guo's party membership resumed, *Cai Wenji* was intended to be a showcase or much needed celebration of the solidarity between the intellectuals and the CCP in the aftermath of the Anti-Rightist campaign, highlighting the mutual appreciation between Cai, a poet returning from abroad, and Cao, a statesman rebuilding a nation. *Wu Zetian* demonstrated Guo's endorsement of the party's dictatorial criticism of the intellectuals, who according to him misunderstood the party due to the influence of the reactionary forces. Pei Yan 裴炎, a courtier, is portrayed as a conspirator who wants to usurp the throne and thus is a caricature of those whom the CCP called "the Rightists"; Luo Binwang 駱賓王, a Tang poet who opposed Wu's reign, is depicted as a fooled intellectual. Guo makes Luo confess his own guilt on stage, presenting the intellectual as a target of reeducation rather than as a cultural hero.

The reversal of traditional verdicts, the response to the contemporary situation, and the affirmation of Maoist rule actually coexisted inseparably in these post-1949 historical writings. Guo's subversive reappraisal of Cao Cao, for example, simultaneously catered to Mao's admiration for this ancient ruler and poet.[123] While the almost unconditional praise of Cao Cao's achievements has long been interpreted as a thinly veiled hymn to Mao's rule, in the play Guo also lets Cai Wenji criticize Cao Cao's hasty decision to execute Dong Si 董祀, a loyal and cultivated diplomat. This

121. See Boar, "Images of Women in the Dramas of Guo Moruo."
122. See Feng Xigang, *Wenge qian de Guo Moruo*, 179–95.
123. For Mao's praise of Cao Cao, see Mao Zedong, "Peitaiho."

plot design shows Guo's own caution against the party's dictatorial attitude toward intellectuals and implicitly urges the party to accept criticism from below.

Consequently, on stage the party occupies the symbolic position of the ancient sovereign rulers, even though the ancient ruling classes are routinely ridiculed or condemned in Marxist historical writings (including Guo's). Correspondingly, although the aim of Maoist historical reversal was to restore the people's history and all the historians in these debates assumed a perspective of the people, the people/*renmin* remained unrepresentable in Guo's socialist historical drama. In people's China, the CCP was not only a revolutionary vanguard but also a ruling party, a sovereign dictator. How does one combine revolutionary energies and sovereign powers in one ancient persona? Guo's theatrical presentation of Cao Cao and Wu Zetian as progressive heroes was a move bordering on a cult of personality. This linkage between the ancient sovereignty and the contemporary revolutionary supreme leader became even more contentious with the implosion of the Cultural Revolution (see the conclusion).

Hence a revolutionary party dressed as an ancient sovereignty: "The tradition of all dead generations weighs like a nightmare on the brains of the living."[124] Marx's comments also pertain to the case of revolutionary China. In the parallelism of historical drama and historical scholarship, I have tried to disclose a series of allegorical traces of antihistorical historicism. The poetics of the "translation" between the Zeitgeist of ancient times and that of modern times concealed the potential of cultural-political articulation and encapsulated the permanent crisis of historical representation within the Chinese Revolution. This crisis eventually pointed to a crisis of people's democracy itself. Kun Qian touches on the difficulty of "defining the people" in Guo's efforts to reevaluate Cao Cao and Wu Zetian.[125] I further argue that in fact the allegorical ambiguity of his reversal of verdict shows a new predicament of staging "the people/*renmin*" and the revolutionary sovereignty in the context of the Maoist search for a socialist path beyond "people's democracy." By the mid-1960s, it was the Maoist critique of "emperors, kings, generals and ministers"

124. Marx, *The Eighteenth Brumaire of Louis Bonaparte*, 97.
125. Kun Qian, *Imperial-Time-Order*, 171.

on the socialist theatrical stage that laid the ground for the Cultural Revolution as the continued class struggle.[126]

Commenting on the return of the ancient in the revolutionary age, Marx also used the metaphor of language and translation: "In like manner, the beginner who has learnt a new language always translates it back into his mother tongue."[127] When the Maoist party leaped from the New Democracy to a socialist path, it was disoriented in its search of a new language amid tensions between democracy and dictatorship. The continued Chinese Revolution had to translate itself into even more idiosyncratic poetics of historical interpretation—an issue I tackle in the rest of this book.

126. Jiang Qing, "Tan jing ju gaige," 514.
127. Marx, *The Eighteenth Brumaire of Louis Bonaparte*, 97.

CHAPTER 6

Modernizing Translations of Classical Poetry

In 1923, *Cockleburs* (*Juan'er ji* 卷耳集) appeared in print, consisting of Guo's vernacular translations of forty poems from *Shi jing*, the earliest anthology of Chinese poetry, supposedly edited by Confucius. This "tiny experiment" was in fact not so tiny, as it marked the emergence of modern vernacular translation of classical literature in China—a textual practice that spoke to two crucial projects of the May Fourth New Culture.[1] First, the May Fourth Movement promoted the vernacular language (*baihua* 白話) as a literary language, an intellectual medium, and even an institution of modernization; as a result, it became necessary to "popularize" or "immortalize" the ancient literary works through vernacular translation.[2] Second, such practice of vernacular translation was also a logical extension of the May Fourth reevaluation of traditional values.

If *Cockleburs* was one of the earliest efforts to translate ancient Chinese poetry into modern vernacular, then Guo's 1924 essay "The Issue of Modernizing Translation of Ancient Works" ("Gu shu jinyi wenti" 古書今譯問題) can be seen as a milestone in the theorization of "modernizing translation" (*jinyi* 今譯). Written as an accompaniment to *Cockleburs*, the essay requests that *jinyi* liberate ancient literary legacies from the "fetishism of the antiquarian."[3] *Jin* means modern, contemporary, or present, and *yi* denotes translation. Guo was not the only one using the concept

1. Guo, "*Juan'er ji* xu," 2.
2. Guo, "Gu shu jinyi wenti," 7.
3. Ibid., 8.

of *jinyi* in May Fourth China. Zhou Zuoren 周作人 (1885–1967), a major modern Chinese writer, discussed the issue of *jinyi* in his first published vernacular essay in 1918, yet what he meant by *jinyi* was primarily his translation of ancient Greek poetry, a translingual rather than intralingual undertaking.[4] In 1925, Gu Jiegang 顧頡剛 (1893–1980), a modern Chinese historian, published his annotated *jinyi* of several pieces from the *Book of Documents* (*Shang shu* 尚書), attempting to disperse the "mystery" of ancient history.[5] In addition to carrying out a similar enlightenment agenda of vernacularization, Guo posed the question as to "whether ancient poetry is translatable."[6] Underscoring the literary nature of vernacular translation, he particularly used the English word "modernize" and interpreted it as *xinhua* 新化 (to renew).[7] The presentist ethos behind this translingual definition of an intralingual translation deserves emphasis: it draws close to Ezra Pound's modernist motto "make it new," which is derived from Pound's modernization/translation of another Confucian classic, "Great Learning" ("Da xue" 大學).[8] In this chapter, I render *jinyi* as "modernizing translation" to highlight the problematic of modernity versus antiquity in revolutionary China: in what sense is ancient poetry translatable/modernizable?

Modernizing translation reappeared in Guo's later work. In 1953, he finished *Modernizing Translations of Qu Yuan's Poetic Works* (*Qu Yuan fu jinyi* 屈原賦今譯). Partaking in the socialist knowledge production of national heritage, this tribute to the ancient Chu poet as a "people's poet" concluded Guo's decades-long reinterpretation of Qu Yuan. Equally important, it furnished another occasion for his theoretical reflections: his view of poetic translation as creative rewriting was finalized in this intralingual rendition. From 1923 to 1953, Guo's two major achievements in modernizing translation corresponded to two important origins of traditional Chinese poetry: *Shi jing* and *The Songs of the South* (*Chu ci* 楚辭). On closer inspection, Guo's scholarly works also conceal many significant traces of modernizing translation of ancient poetry. For example, his penchant for vernacular translation seeps into his Marxist stud-

4. Zhou Zuoren, "Gu shi jinyi Apologia."
5. Gu Jiegang, "Shang shu Pangeng zhong pian jinyi," 7.
6. Guo, "Gu shu jinyi wenti," 8.
7. Ibid., 7.
8. Pound, trans., *Confucius*, 36.

ies of ancient Chinese society. In particular, his essay "Understanding the Zhou Society by Reading the Zhou Georgics" ("You Zhoudai nongshishi lun dao Zhoudai shehui" 由周代農事詩論到周代社會; "Nongshishi" hereafter), written in 1944, contains complete translations of ten poems from *Shi jing*. Nor did *Modernizing Translations of Qu Yuan's Poetic Works* conclude Guo's versed translation of classical poetry. In his last major scholarly output, *Li Bai and Du Fu*, published in 1971 as a rare monument of scholarship of the Cultural Revolution, one can find the rhymed line-by-line renderings of Du Fu's most famous narrative poems. This final act of vernacular translation was crucial to Guo's doubled reversal of the verdict, which refuted the traditionalist worship of Du Fu as the "sage of poetry" and the socialist crowning of Du Fu as a "people's poet."

Consequently, modernizing translation forms an underrepresented genealogy from the May Fourth period to the Cultural Revolution and solicits the question as to what was the role of translation in historical reinterpretation. Such vernacular renditions of ancient poetry belong to what Roman Jakobson calls "intralingual translation": "Intralingual translation or rewording is an interpretation of verbal signs by means of other signs of the same language."[9] But the case of modernizing translation of ancient poetry is far more complicated than what a rewording within the same language (or a linguistic update in accordance with the language's historical development) seems to indicate. The ancient classical Chinese, or *wenyan* 文言, used over a long historical period in high literature and culture, was declared a dead language during the May Fourth Movement. The vernacular, having its own history in ancient popular literature, was promoted as the living language by the Literary Revolution. This construction of a new national language thus presumed an evolutionary logic on the transition from *wenyan* to *baihua*, whereas the tradition of *wenyan* continued to crystalize a rich classical heritage no one could afford to neglect.[10] In this sense, the differences between ancient and modern Chinese involve a complex linguistic politics. Critics seem to have agreed that "it is not an easy thing to translate ancient

9. Jakobson, "On Linguistic Aspects of Translation," 127.

10. For relevant discussions of linguistic politics in modern China, see Hill, *Lin Shu, Inc.*; and again, Wang Feng, *Shi yun tuiyi yu wenzhang xingti*. For a reflection on the "literary governance" of the national language in the Sinophone context, see Jing Tsu, *Sound and Script in Chinese Diaspora*, chapter 1.

Chinese verse," and perhaps it is as difficult as translating foreign poetry.[11] Between the ancient original and its modern translation, there also stands a rich classical tradition of poetic interpretation (which can be seen as a cultural history of "intralingual translation").[12] Guo's engagement within it, more often than not, is subversive. In vernacular translation, an ancient Chinese poem sometimes has to undergo nearly as much metamorphosis as in its translation into foreign languages; in Guo's hands, this metamorphosis is even more radical. Although sometimes oversimplified as a cognitive intralingual transmission, modernizing translation is actually an act of poetic, cultural, and political interpretation.

Guo's case therefore prompts us to look beyond the taken-for-granted mission of popularization in vernacular translation. Modernizing translation was in fact a medium of literary innovation, a rhetorical device of knowledge production, and a polemical mode of political transcoding. Together with other modern intellectuals' reexamination of ancient classics, the traces of overinterpretation in Guo's rewritings of classical poetry helped demarcate a nebulous zone of intervention at the center of the tension between the Chinese Revolution and national antiquity. Tracing the literary, rhetorical, and intellectual politics hidden in this case, my study problematizes modernizing translation as a permanent construction/deconstruction of the interpretative subjectivity.

Poetic Translation, Shi jing*, and a Reinvention of Chinese Lyricism*

The vernacular, versed, and subversive renditions in *Cockleburs* should be situated in the making of a Chinese lyricism during the May Fourth period. Ever since the rise of Confucianism as a prevalent ideology in dynastic China, *Shi jing* ranked as one of the five classics. Accumulated over a course of more than 2,000 years, the commentaries on these 305 poems

11. Ding Xiaohan, "Ping Guo Moruo zhu Qu Yuan," in *GHY*, 9:410; Tian Hua, "Du Guo Moruo zhu Qu Yuan yanjiu guanjian," in *GHY*, 9:437.

12. For a relevant discussion of the history of *Shi jing* interpretation, see Saussy, *The Problem of a Chinese Aesthetic*.

formed a rich tradition in the "classical learning" (*jing xue* 經學), a main arena of scholarship in Confucian China. Any modern interpretation of *Shi jing* has to negotiate with this long exegetic tradition and raise the issue of poetic interpretation as such. In the 1923 "Preface," Guo describes his modernization/translation as "discarding the classics and deviating the Way" (*li jing pan dao* 離經叛道), asserting: "My interpretations of these poems are very bold. Except using ancient and traditional exegeses as a general reference, I rely purely on my own individual intuition [*zhiguan* 直觀] in an attempt to directly seek in each and every poem its own life."[13]

To see in what sense Guo's translation is bold and intuitive, I suggest concentrating on "The Cocklebur, a Poem from the South of Zhou" ("Zhounan juan'er" 周南卷耳), a translation of the third poem of *Shi jing*, which serves as the opening piece of Guo's book. The original poem is from "South of Zhou," the first section of "The Airs of the States" in *Shi jing*. Typical of ancient folk poetry, this poem is composed of four independently rhymed stanzas, with four lines per stanza. Guo's vernacular translation effectively reinvents its language, form, and lyrical unfolding. First, Guo develops this three-stanza lyric into a much longer poem of forty-eight lines and six stanzas (running more than six pages in the first book edition), composed in free verse. One can hardly recognize the poem's original shape any more.

Second, Guo replaces the simplicity of the original with a sophisticated and even Westernized mode of lyrical expression. Below is the first stanza of this translated poem:

> 一片碧綠的平原,
> 原中有卷耳蔓草開著白色的花。
> 有位青年婦人左邊肘上掛著一隻淺淺的提籃,
> 她時時弓下背去摘取卷耳,
> 又時時昂起頭來凝視遠方的山丘。[14]
>
> [On a green plain, / There are cockleburs blossoming with white flowers. / A young woman has a shallow basket hanging on her left elbow. / From time to time she bows down to pick the cockleburs, / And from time to time, she rears her head to gaze into the faraway mountains.]

13. Guo, "*Juan'er ji* xu," 2, 3.
14. Guo, trans., *Juan'er ji*, 1.

These five lines loosely correspond to the first couplet of the original: "采采卷耳，不盈頃筐" ("Thick grow the cocklebur; / But even a shallow basket I did not fill").[15] The couplet is traditionally considered as typical of the ancient Chinese figure of "arousal" (*xing* 兴). Arousing the feeling of sadness and longing through a reference to a daily scene of labor in a natural setting, this opening shows the power of rhetorical simplicity in ancient Chinese poetry. By creating a detailed depiction of the landscape and the female protagonist, Guo transforms the traditional rhetoric of *xing* into a descriptive mode. The third line of his version is as long as nineteen characters—a length unimaginable in traditional metrics.

Third, Guo's rendition decisively turns the whole poem into an internal drama of the young woman's mind, offering a strongly subjective perspective on its lyrical plot. The inward turn takes place in the second stanza, where the young woman sees the handsome face of her faraway lover in the cocklebur flower, and by extension she believes that the "faraway mountains" see her lover's "sorrowful face."[16] The difficult journey of the male character now becomes the young woman's worrisome thoughts. Guo adds a concluding stanza that does not exist in the original. The subjective drama of longing comes full circle:

> 旅途中的一山一谷，
> 便是她心坎中的一波一瀾。
> 卷耳草開著白色的花，
> 她淺淺的籃兒永沒有采滿的時候。[17]
>
> [Every mountain and valley in the journey / Is a ripple and torrent in her heart. / The cockleburs are blossoming with white flowers. / Her shallow basket will never be filled.]

This creative translation ignited a series of discussions on this ancient poem. Yu Pingbo 俞平伯 (1900–1990), a scholar of traditional culture, stated that "the general meaning of this piece is very obscure, resulting

15. Cheng Junying and Jiang Jianyuan, *Shi jing zhu xi*, 9–11; Waley, trans., *The Book of Songs*, 7.

16. Guo, trans., *Juan'er ji*, 2–3.

17. Ibid., 6–7.

in an entanglement of debates."[18] The main ambiguity lies in the relationship between the first stanza (which reads like a lady's words of longing) and the following three stanzas (which reads like a man's account about his sorrowful journey). Yu listed four traditional readings, and to redress their weaknesses he offered two alternatives: one indicates that this poem is about "a woman missing her faraway lover," written solely from the woman's perspective; the other holds that the poem is composed of two parts or two perspectives—the singing of "longing woman" (*si fu* 思婦) and the sad words of the "traveling man" (*zheng fu* 征夫).[19]

Accepting the second approach, Arthur Waley (1889–1966), a renowned English translator of *Shi jing*, comments that "in the first verse it is the lady left at home who speaks; in the remaining verses it is the man away on a perilous journey."[20] In accordance with this interpretation, Ezra Pound (1885–1972) translates "The Cocklebur" in a more dramatic setting, inventing a theatrical dialogue between "He" and "She" as two personae.[21] One the other hand, Guo's rewriting draws closer to the first approach and produces a poem of a longing woman's self-expression: "The last three stanzas are the longing woman's own imagination of the traveling husband's difficult journeys."[22] This psychologizing move reinforces the experience of love and longing as a lyrical theme, and makes possible a close description of a subjective interiority. Promoting the individualized sentimentality in a modern poetic form, the translated poem can be easily read as a piece of Chinese New Poetry.

Commenting on the May Fourth emancipatory atmosphere, Leo Lee observes that "for almost a decade, the keynote of this youthful emotional outburst was summarized in the amorphous word, love."[23] The "Airs of the States," the first and largest section of *Shi jing*, includes a great number of love poems. Reading the poem from the perspective of free love,

18. Yu Pingbo, "Qizhiliaoheng shi du shi zha ji: Zhounan Juan'er," 7.

19. Ibid., 11.

20. Waley, trans., *The Book of Songs*, 7.

21. Pound, trans., *Shih-ching*, 3.

22. Guo, "Wo duiyu 'Juan'er' yi shi de jieshi," 21. This essay was written as a response to Cao Juren's criticism. Cao suggested that in this poem it is the woman who rides the horse, climbs the mountains, and drinks wine to relieve her sorrows. See Cao Juren, "Du Juan'er," 17.

23. Lee, "Literary Trends: The Quest for Modernity," 168.

all the May Fourth intellectuals participating in "The Cocklebur" debate reached a consensus that its subject matter is "a woman missing her faraway lover."[24] The forty poems Guo selected for translation are all "love songs about the erotic desire between females and males," coming exclusively from the "Airs of the States."[25] The theme of free love served as a bridge between an ancient tradition and a modern lyrical liberation.

Yet as Cao Juren 曹聚仁 criticized, Guo's "intuitive" translations in fact still drew on the "Mao, Zheng, and Zhu commentaries," the major traditional Confucian interpretations.[26] By the same token, Guo's book was mocked in some reviews for boasting "creative genius" and simultaneously falling back on classical exegesis.[27] In what sense does his modernizing translation "discard the classical scholarship and deviate from the Way?" Where does the translator's "individual intuition" exactly lie? As a matter of fact, Guo did not "discard" traditional commentary with regard to the literal meanings of the originals. What he abandoned was the ideological horizon of traditional *Shi jing* scholarship. In the Han classical scholarship (*han xue* 漢學), some love poems were interpreted as teachings about the sovereign's righteousness and the consort's virtue. According to the Mao commentary, "The Cocklebur" expressed "the consort's intention" to support the king and offered a model of the bond between the sovereignty and his subjects.[28] With regard to the same poem, the neo-Confucian commentary of Zhu Xi 朱熹 (1130–1200) maintained that a consort "must have missed the absent husband and composed this poem."[29] Therefore, the traditional Confucian commentaries, despite the differences among them, tended to impose their political and moral pedagogy on *Shi jing*.

24. See Cao Juren, ed., *Juan'er taolun ji*.

25. Guo, "*Juan'er ji* xu," 3. It then comes as no surprise that fourteen poems among the chosen ones are from the "Airs of Zheng," a section famous for "music of excessive lust" (*yin sheng* 淫聲).

26. Cao Juren, "Du Juan'er," 18.

27. Xiaomin, "Juan'er ji de zanci," 12.

28. Ruan Yuan, ed., *Shi san jing zhu shu*, 1:277.

29. Zhu Xi, *Shi ji zhuan*, 3. In his reading of some other love songs Zhu uses the moral label of *yin* 淫 (excessive lust); see 52–57. Zhu Xi's exegesis nevertheless abandons the Mao prefaces. His contribution is commonly characterized as a "commentary of the poems based on the poems themselves" (*jiu shi lun shi*). See Cheng and Jiang, *Shi jing zhuxi*, i.

The May Fourth critics protested in eager agreement that such classical readings are "unreasonable."[30] It is to this tradition of "poetic education" (*shi jiao* 詩教) that the young Guo opposed his translations. In this sense Guo claims in his 1923 "Postscript": "*Shi jing* has been buried by the traditional commentaries. The decaying nature of the traditional commentary is not worthy of our fascination, and does not even deserve our criticism."[31] In place of poetic education, he offers lyrical spontaneity, which is emblematic of the institutionalization of a new literary language, rhetoric, and ideology in May Fourth China.

This valorization of lyrical intuition also contains Guo's response to the problem of poetic translatability. Whether poetry is translatable (or how to translate poetry) has long been hotly debated in translation theory. Guo's resistance to literal translation is in fact most sufficiently expressed in his definition of modernizing translation. In his preface to *Cockleburs*, he announces his translation method: "My method of interpretation is not purely that of word-by-word literal translation. Freely I translate, and I don't believe that poetic translation should be limited to literal translation."[32] He uses Tagore's self-translation from Bengali into English as an example.[33] In his essay "The Issue of Modernizing Translation of Ancient Works," Guo not only prepares a long list of modern English translations of *Beowulf* to argue for modernizing translation, he also resorts again to the liberties Edward Fitzgerald took in his translation of *Rubáiyát of Omar Khayyám*.[34]

As I indicated in chapter 1, Guo's proposal for the translator's subversive freedom should not be understood only within the frame of "literalness versus fluency."[35] What lies behind his resistance to literal translation is once again his monism of poetry. When dealing with the issue of translatability in "The Issue of Modernizing Translation of Ancient Works," Guo insists that the approach of literal translation is what makes translation impossible: "It is, after all, impossible to do poetic

30. Yu Pingbo, "Qizhiliaoheng shi du shi zha ji: Zhounan Juan'er," 10.
31. Guo, "*Juan'er ji* zi ba," in *GQJ/W*, 5:208.
32. Guo, "*Juan'er ji* xu," 4.
33. Ibid.
34. Guo, "Gu shu jinyi wenti," 8.
35. For a discussion of the theory of literalness versus fluency in modern China, see Chan, ed., *Twentieth-Century Chinese Translation Theory*, especially 15–28, 179–80.

translation in a word-by-word, sentence-by-sentence fashion as if decoding a telegram."[36] In other words, if the translator seeks the purely linguistic equivalence, then, to use Jakobson's language, "poetry is by definition untranslatable." In poetic translation, "only creative transposition is possible."[37] Likewise, for Guo, poetry is actually translatable insofar as the translation is "the translator's re-presentation [*fuxian* 復現] of the feeling that he or she experiences in the original."[38] The form and wording become far less important than the resonance of the poetic feeling.

More important, Guo brings this translational relationship into the relationship between the modern and the ancient. For a rediscovery of China's national origins of lyricism, he also demands the lyrical immediacy:

> Our nation was originally a very free, very beautiful one. Unfortunately, shackled by the traditional codes and ethics [*li jiao* 禮教] for thousands of years, our nation has virtually become a mummy of a dead elephant. Shame! What a shame! Our most ancient, beautiful popular literature, [*Shi jing*], has long become a fossil. I aim to breathe life into this fossil, and I aim to revitalize this dead elephant mummy—this is the ultimate intention of my translating these tens of poems.[39]

Modern Chinese intellectuals have routinely traced China's "lyrical tradition" or "lyricism" to *Shi jing*: "The glory of Chinese literature lies . . . in lyric poetry. *Shi jing*, a book that has long been renowned, is its origin."[40] Such a recognition certainly involves a modern "reinvention of tradition."[41] Yet in the recent revival of interest in "lyrical modernity," Guo's translation of the national lyrical origin goes largely unmentioned. Based on the life of poetic creativity, the ancient is the ever-new, and tradition is not the preservation of transhistorical origins but their burial. The modern then must be the revitalization of origins. This is not merely

36. Guo, "Gu shu jinyi wenti," 8.
37. Jakobson, "On Linguistic Aspects of Translation," 131.
38. Guo, "Gu shu jinyi wenti," 8.
39. Guo, "*Juan'er ji* xu," 5.
40. Chen Shih-hsiang, "Lun Zhongguo shuqing chuantong," 46.
41. Huang Jinshu, "Shuqing chuantong yu xiandaixing," 688.

a vision similar to many other May Fourth efforts to find "indigenous alternatives" to traditional Chinese culture and seek "radical inspirations" from China's past.[42] It is comparable to the conception of the origin (*Ursprung*) in modern German culture, according to which an *Ursprung* signifies "a primal leap into being which at once reveals and determines the unfolding structure, the central dynamic of form in an organic or spiritual phenomenon."[43] Only through a creative and antitraditional rewriting can an ancient origin be truly reactivated as an unfolding structure. Guo states: "Our current task of urgency is to experience the true beauty directly [*zhijie* 直接] in ancient poetry, and refuse to continue to debate with the pedantic Confucians."[44]

As a result, his revitalization/translation is not only intertwined with the invention of lyricism as a literary ideology but also gives rise to a new lyrical subjectivity of historical imagination. Amid a number of critical reviews, Hong Weifa 洪爲法, a Creationist, wrote a positive review of *Cocklebursr*. He contended that Guo's efforts embodied "a revolutionary spirit," overthrowing the "despicable spirit" of the traditional interpretation and positivistic philology.[45] This revolutionary spirit alone was a great "accomplishment of *Cockleburs*."[46] The new "path for our interpretation of *Shi jing*" meant nothing but the emphasis on the interpreter's own poetic subjectivity.[47] In fact, Hong noted that many of Guo's interpretations were not satisfactory, but based on this revolutionary spirit one could overthrow Guo's modernizing translation just as he had overthrown traditional commentary. Hong pushed Guo's logic to the extreme by rephrasing Guo's statement: "All traditional commentaries, and also Guo Moruo's interpretations, are just for references."[48]

This "revolutionary" attitude shows to us an important dimension of the May Fourth reevaluation of ancient traditions. On the surface, Guo's modernizing translation seems to have followed the general trend of liberating classics from traditional exegetical frames. Yet it is worth

42. Schneider, *Ku Chieh-Kang and China's New History*, 2.
43. Steiner, "Introduction," 16.
44. Guo, "*Juan'er ji* zi ba," in *GQJ/W*, 5:208.
45. Hong Weifa, "Du *Juan'er ji*," 349.
46. Ibid., 350.
47. Ibid., 352.
48. Ibid., 353.

mentioning that around the time of the publication of *Cockleburs*, Guo and other Creationists voiced their discontent with the "reorganization of the national heritage" (*zhengli guo gu* 整理國故) advocated by Hu Shi, the standard-bearer of the May Fourth enlightenment. Guo shared much in common with Hu Shi and his associates in terms of their opposition to traditional ideologies. But for Guo and Hong, the "national heritage" scholarship treated ancient history only as dead material and fell short of the "creation of new values."[49] Cao's criticism opposed "objective investigation" (*kaoju* 考據) to Guo's "intuition."[50] While for Guo's opponents the interpretation of the ancient meant a cognitive comprehension, for Guo it involved a poetic "experience," an experience of the affinity of the present with antiquity. In opposition to positivistic "objective" historicism, Guo's modernizing translation represents a historical consciousness that paradoxically entails a dehistoricization to "revitalize" the ancient.

This perspective draws close to Pound's radical approach to poetic interpretation: "All ages are contemporaneous."[51] Guo and his fellow Creationists would also agree with Pound's proposal of a "literary scholarship" that "give[s] praise to beauty before referring to an almanack."[52] In line with the Poundian-Confucian ideal of interpretation as "making it new," Guo justifies his modernizing translation with a joking fantasy: "If Confucius were still alive, he would say 'it is Moruo who illuminates me!' "[53] In other words, Confucius the editor of *Shi jing* would identify himself with the lyrical modernity Guo proposes, since the latter grasps the ancient poetic spirit much more originally than the classical commentaries. Guo's first attempt of modernizing translation thus marks a moment of the penetration of lyrical imagination into the historical consciousness.

49. Guo, "Zhengli guo gu de pingjia," 3.
50. Cao Juren, "Du Juan'er," 19.
51. Pound, *The Spirit of Romance*, xiii.
52. Ibid., xiv.
53. Guo, "*Juan'er ji* xu," 2.

Exegetical Translation and Marxist Historiography

Poet and scholar Wen Yiduo once commented, with a sense of frustration, on the hermeneutic condition of *Shi jing* scholarship:

> The Han scholars were too utilitarian, using the three hundred poems as political textbooks; the Song scholars were a bit better, but never gave up the neo-Confucian philosophy—exuding a scholastic smell; the Qing scholars were more objective, but their philology was not poetry; the moderns have a bagful of scientific methods, looking sharp. Unfortunately, history—be it materialist or non-materialist—is still far from poetry. It is simply a book of folk songs, and why does no one seriously treat it as literature and art?![54]

Echoing Guo's early view, Wen's emphasis on the poetic nature of the book was itself a modern reconstruction of *Shi jing*, based on the logic of aesthetic autonomy. While denouncing the ancient exegesis, Wen resisted his contemporaries' application of modern social-scientific methods to the interpretation of *Shi jing*. "By choosing not to read the classic as a chronicle of Chou," as Haun Saussy remarks, "modern readers make it . . . into the anthology of unrelated poems that, for centuries, it had not been."[55] Modern-minded historians soon found a new value of this ancient book, using it as evidence of the social development in early China. When criticizing modern scholars for being obsessed with scientific methodology, Wen surely had Guo in his mind. A modernizing translator, Guo later became a pioneering scholar in applying the materialist conception of history to the interpretation of *Shi jing*. Here I trace the peculiar persistence of modernizing translation in his historical scholarship. For Wen, historiography was far from poetry; for Guo, the two were adjoined.

When embarking on his adventure into Marxist studies of ancient Chinese society, Guo considered *Shi jing* a "reliable ancient book."[56] "The

54. Wen Yiduo, "Kuang zhai chi du," 356.
55. Saussy, *The Problem of a Chinese Aesthetic*, 23.
56. Guo, *Zhongguo gudai shehui yanjiu*, in *GQJ/L*, 1:90.

Social Revolution and Its Reflection in Thought during the Epoch of the *Book of Songs* and *Book of Documents*" ("Shi Shu shidai de shehui biange yu qi zai sixiang shang zhi fanying" 《詩》《書》時代的社會變革與其在思想上之反映; "Shi Shu" hereafter) was originally composed in late 1928 and was included (with revisions) in Guo's *Studies*. No longer focusing exclusively on the "Airs of the States," he turned to the Odes (*ya* 雅, or Elegantiae) and the Hymns (*song* 頌), the parts of *Shi jing* in which one can find more textual clues to ancient production relations, political organization, and religious activity. The long essay interweaves vernacular translations—almost seamlessly—into the prose of his Marxist argumentation. When he uses the method of vernacular translation, the subjective literary intervention is not replaced by historiographical objectivity but contributes to the making of a politicized polemical style.

Let us look at some moments in which the historian's paraphrases of certain poems merge into modernizing translation in "Shi Shu." Discussing "The Seventh Month" ("Qi yue" 七月), a long poem about agricultural life, he uses a vernacular paraphrase to lament that ancient peasants' life is not idyllic but is full of suffering due to the yearlong forced labor and exploitation by the state. Dealing with a controversial couplet— 女子伤悲，殆及公子同归 ("A girl's heart is sick and sad / Till with her lord she can go home")[57]—he does not miss the opportunity to provide a combination of his translation and commentary:

> [After all these labors] girls seem to have another duty, that is, they would unavoidably be sexually abused, under the shining sun of the springtime, when the lords are driven by the spring fever of libido. This is nothing rare or surprising, and according to the studies of modern scholars, the patriarchs of many tribes have the "Jus primae noctis" over women. . . .
>
> This is the life of peasants, as represented in "The Seventh Month," day in, day out, four seasons, year after year. Aren't they slaves?![58]

Guo's paraphrasing translation makes this poem a powerful evidence for his argument of the existence of slavery in ancient China. This conclusion also amounts to a political protestation. He then jumps from Chi-

57. Cheng and Jiang, *Shi jing zhuxi*, 409; Waley, trans., *The Book of Songs*, 120.
58. Guo, *Zhongguo gudai shehui yanjiu*, in *GQJ/L*, 1:114.

na's slavery society directly to the CCP-led peasants' movements in his own revolutionary times: "Chinese peasants have been cheated by sages, heroes, poetic thieves, and literary hooligans, for thousands of years, but currently they are no longer as tamed."[59]

In contrast to the ancient peasants' miserable life, he interprets "Thick Star-Thistle" ("Chu ci" 楚茨; from Minor Odes) as a poem about the decadent lifestyle of the slave-owning nobilities. This poem describes the sacrifice-offering rites, and yet he translates in prose the last stanza about a postritual feast as the sexual orgy of the ruling class:

> The prayers were finished, and gods were drunk, so they were sent off with drums and bells; the remaining time was for the enjoyment of "lords and ladies," "uncles and brothers." The females were especially hurried, as if they couldn't wait, and after clearing away the dishes in a rush, they started to enjoy the feast with "uncles and brothers." They went off to the bedroom behind, and music followed there too. They were drunk and sated, and one more thing was not appropriate to be said explicitly, so they had to say "so lovely, so timely, all are happy to the uttermost." As a result, there would be "sons and grandsons, a never-ending line of offspring."[60]

This prose translation combines, as it were, a Freudian move and a Marxian motif in one stroke. The wish for a long line of offspring becomes an expression of the gratification of sexual desire; the monopoly of sexual pleasure, in turn, is portrayed as a significant aspect of class domination.

In Guo's analysis of "The Large Field ("Fu tian" 甫田), another Minor Ode about ancient agricultural labor, the line between prose translation and commentary is further blurred. Citing the effusive words the lord speaks to his laborers, he sometimes puts his vernacular translations in parentheses following the original lines; at other times, puts the original lines in parentheses following his vernacular translations. The poem ends with the lord's blessings intended for his hard-working laborers: "Long life to you, age unending!"[61] After citing this couplet, Guo injects his vernacular translation/commentary: "Long live the peasants, long live

59. Ibid.
60. Ibid., 115. Also see Waley, trans., *The Book of Songs*, 195–96.
61. Waley, trans., *The Book of Songs*, 200.

the workers! The longer is your life, the better—as long as you are hard-working and available for my exploitation—so long live! Long live! Long, long live! Huhhhh!"

This hyperbolic translation aims to unveil the unconscious internal monologue of the exploiting class underneath their seemingly well-intended praise of their slaves. Guo transforms his epistemological use of poetic-historical evidence into an occasion of political satire. The target of this satirical rendition is not only the ancient ruling class but also the GMD regime. According to Guo's footnote, when he was writing this historical essay, he noticed that the GMD "reactionaries" were setting up their own peasants' organizations and workers' unions.[62] Clearly, Guo's historiographical use of *Shi jing* furnishes a different mode of vernacular translation, in which interpretative paraphrase, Marxist analysis, and political criticism become inseparably entwined.

His 1944 essay "Nongshishi" marks a refraining from political over-interpretation of *Shi jing*. He composed this essay as an integral part of his wartime project of systematically revising his earlier views on ancient Chinese society.[63] As we saw in chapter 4, the young Guo once viewed the *jingtian* system as China's own primitive communism. Then in the late 1920s he argued that the *jingtian* system was merely a Confucian ideal of land distribution and never existed in the Zhou society. More than fifteen years later, he changed his position again in the "Nongshishi" essay and asserted that the *jingtian* system did exist in ancient China. Yet he believed that it functioned as a form of land ownership for state slavery rather than as a communal ownership, and therefore he maintained his general conclusion that the Zhou society was a slavery society.[64] Guo's change of position on the significant issue of *jingtian* system issue was anchored in yet another act of modernizing translation. What has escaped from the previous scholarly attention is the fact that in "Nongshishi" Guo systematically translates the ten poems that he defines as the Zhou georgics from *Shi jing*. In the middle of this essay, as his argument shifts from the analysis of the poems to the analysis of the Zhou society,

62. See *GQJ/L*, 1:117.

63. Guo, "Nongshishi," in *GQJ/L*, 1:405.

64. For Guo's self-criticism and his reexamination of the *jingtian* issue, see "Nongshishi," in *GQJ/L*, 1:426–29. For a more detailed discussion of Guo's change of position on the "*jintian* system" issue, see my essay, "Enlightenment as a 'Romantic Science?' "

he summarizes: "So far I examined all the georgic poems from the Zhou era, and moreover, I translated all of them."[65]

Compared with *Cockleburs*, Guo's renderings of these ten poems are more faithful to the content of the originals; some of them are prose translations. The poems are already discussed in the 1928 essay "Shi Shu," but in "Nongshishi" the translations are complete and separated from his historical analysis. He admits that he must overcome his earlier "emotional" (be it in a lyrical or political sense) interpretation of ancient poetry.[66] This time around, he aims for a more reliable and objective exegesis of the poems, so he can use them as evidence for his analysis of the Zhou society. For example, the satirical interpretation of the lord's prayers disappears for good. Whereas Guo's 1928 commentary of "The Large Field" mocks the ruling class's hypocrisy in wishing the best for the slaves, his 1944 translation refrains from any direct political labeling. Instead, the new rendering emphasizes the labor scene as an evidence of the massive use of slaves.[67]

One has to ask whether these translations are necessary for this scholarly essay on the Zhou society. These translations can be seen as standalone texts inserted into Guo's historical analysis. They seem to be a series of literary-hermeneutic monuments slowing the argumentative flow toward his conclusion. Why did he need to have them in the first place? It needs to be noted that the use of vernacular translation became more and more common in the historiographical writings since the May Fourth Movement but was intended primarily for popularization. For instance, in a series of lectures composed in the 1920s and 1930s, Gu Jiegang directly used his vernacular translations as substitutes for the original ancient texts and materials he cited.[68] Another example is *A Brief Account of the Complete History of China* (*Zhongguo tongshi jianbian* 中國通史簡編), written by another leftist historian, Fan Wenlan 范文瀾 (1893–1969). In this 1940s book, almost all quotations of ancient texts appear in the form of their vernacular translations. For Gu and Fan, two historians of different ideological orientations, the vernacularized versions of

65. Guo, "Nongshishi," in *GQJ/L*, 1:425.
66. Ibid., 405.
67. Ibid., 414–15.
68. See Gu Jiegang, *Chunqiu shi jiangyi* and *Guo shi jianghua*.

historical references serve to produce a national history accessible to "broad readership."[69]

Guo's translations, to be sure, are also intended to fulfill the need for popularization. But in addition to this general function, a rhetorical "surplus value" of this practice comes into relief. Guo's analysis of the ten georgics proceeds in the following manner: his philological commentary is a preparation for an accurate modern translation, and after the translations are achieved, these poems can be adduced for his argument about the Zhou society. His essay thus unfolds and makes visible the whole exegetical process of vernacular translation as a literary component of Marxist historical research (whereas in Gu's and Fan's works the traces of this process are erased).

In 1911, French sociologist and Sinologist Marcel Granet published *Fêtes et chansons anciennes de la Chine*. Relying on *Shi jing* as the "authentic documents" in an attempt to "understand some aspects of the religious antiquity of China," this seminal study offered line-by-line French translations of more than sixty-seven poems from the Confucian anthology and marked a significant beginning of modern reinvention of the poetic-historical "authenticity" of *Shi jing*.[70] Fourteen years before the publication of Waley's English translation, and more than three decades before Pound's *Classic Anthology Defined by Confucius*, the young Guo's *Cockleburs* provided China's own version of modernization/translation of *Shi jing*. One may find some similarities between Guo's early task as translator and Pound's. As L. S. Dembo observes, "Ezra Pound's conception of the ideal translator was no different from his conception of the ideal poet."[71] Translation is transcultural and even transhistorical: "In regard to translation, the poet is inspired by direct empathy with the mind of the original author . . . who voices the Kultur of his own epoch and therefore speaks to all epochs."[72] Pound's idea of translation as a transmission of one epoch to another is reminiscent of Guo's ideal of translatability. Whereas Pound aims to "emerge as a Confucian poet," *Cockleburs*

69. Fan Wenlan, *Zhongguo tongshi jianbian*, ii.
70. Granet, *Fêtes et chansons anciennes de la Chine*, 1, 27.
71. Dembo, *The Confucian Odes of Ezra Pound*, 1–2.
72. Ibid., 2.

aims to renew the Confucian poems and prioritizes the creative unfolding of the present.[73]

This literary mode of modernizing translation merges into Guo's Marxist historiography. Rather than being superseded by a pursuit of historical objectivity, it constitutes a kind of exegetical translation within a scientific-revolutionary conception of history. On a scholarly level, the fragments, passages, and mini-texts of modernizing translation in his sociohistorical discussions of *Shi jing* bear resemblance to the practice of translation in Granet's scholarship; on a literary level, they even remind us of Pound's exegetical translation of troubadour poets in *The Spirit of Romance*.[74] Similar to Guo's deciphering of pictographs, such intralingual translations suggest a hermeneutic circle: the poems are translated so as to become comprehensible in a modern/scientific historical framework, and in turn, such translations are used as evidence to reinforce a Marxist conception. Guo's impulse for modernizing translation evolves into an analytical method, a cultural-political intervention, and above all a literary-rhetorical surplus intrinsic to the revolutionary knowledge production.

Qu Yuan in People's China and Guo's Theory of Translation

Let us move to the year of 1953. Almost four years into its building of a People's Republic, the CCP reunited mainland China, recovered the national economy, and forced the United States to accept a cease-fire in the Korean peninsula. It was also supposed to be the 2,330th anniversary of the death of Qu Yuan. Guo led a Chinese delegation to the World Peace Congress, a Soviet-sponsored international organization with a mission of preventing the next world war. The Congress decided on a commemoration of "Four Giants of World Culture," in which Qu Yuan ranked with Copernicus, Rabelais, and José Martí. Guo must have

73. A. Fang, "Introduction," xiii.
74. See Pound, *The Spirit of Romance*; especially Sieburth, "Introduction," xi.

campaigned hard for the inclusion of a Chinese literary icon in this cosmopolitan mix.

Taking note of a "greater Chinese fervor in this supra-national celebration," Levenson sees the 1953 glorification of Qu Yuan as a "residual traditionalism" in China's revolutionary cosmopolitanism.[75] In his panoramic view of the 1953 commemoration of Qu Yuan, Schneider mentions in passing the contribution of vernacular renditions to the popularization of the Qu Yuan lore but offers no further discussion of Guo's *Modernizing Translations of Qu Yuan's Poetic Works*. As Zikpi has pointed out, "in his capacities as poet, literary scholar, Marxist historian, dramatist, and politician, Guo Moruo's work displays a lifelong dedication to Qu Yuan."[76] In chapter 5, I examined the importance of Guo's 1940s interpretation to the articulation of people's democracy. In what follows I show how his 1953 rendition of Qu Yuan's poetry furnished an occasion for Guo's theorization of literary translation. Moreover, this act of modernizing translation served as a bridge leading his pre-1949 historical imagination into the post-1949 cultural politics.

Modernizing Translations of Qu Yuan's Poetic Works includes Guo's renditions of twenty-five poems whose authorship he attributed to Qu Yuan, such as "On Encountering Trouble," *Nine Songs*, "Heavenly Questions" ("Tian wen" 天問), and even "Summons of the Soul" ("Zhao hun" 招魂), whose authorship had been more frequently attributed to Song Yu. The translation of "On Encountering Trouble" was drafted in 1935 and revised in 1942 and 1953; all others were newly accomplished.[77] On one hand, he returns to the mode of poetic translation in this project, underscoring, as he did in the case of *Cockleburs*, the literary nature of the original and the translated text. On the other hand, similar to what he did in "Nongshishi," he aims to convey objectively and faithfully the thought and content in Qu Yuan's poems. His modernizing translation is in this sense intended for a synthesis of scholarly faithfulness and poetic creativity. Such a task of the poet-translator-scholar is best summarized in his

75. Levenson, *Confucian China and Its Modern Fate*, 1:135.

76. Zikpi, "Revolution and Continuity in Guo Moruo's Representations of Qu Yuan," 178.

77. In the late 1940s, Guo translated several pieces by Qu Yuan, but textually these renditions are unrelated to the 1950s ones.

new definition of modernizing translation as a "versed exegesis" (*yunyu zhushu* 韻語註疏).[78]

The language Guo created for this versed exegesis draws close to the poetic language in his rendering of *Faust II*, showing a similar effort of combining the colloquial fluency with diverse metric effects. In some cases, his translation achieves a modernized prosody.

> Original text from "On Encountering Trouble":
> 紛吾既有此内美兮，又重之以脩能。扈江離與辟芷兮，紉秋蘭以為佩。[79]
>
> (Having from birth this inward beauty, / I added to it fair outward adornment: / I dressed in selinea and shady angelica, / And twined autumn orchids to make a garland.)[80]
>
> Guo's translation:
> 我的内部既有了這樣的美質，
> 我的外部又加以美好的裝扮。
> 我把蘼蕪和白芷都折取了來，
> 和秋蘭扭結著做成了個花環。[81]
>
> [As my interiority has such beauty, / My exteriority is enhanced with fine adornment. / I collected selinea and angelica, / And twined them with orchids to make a garland.]

In other cases, Guo's rendering suggests an imitation of folk-song colloquialism:

> Original text from *Nine Songs*:
> 吉日兮辰良，穆將愉兮上皇。[82]
>
> (On a lucky day with an auspicious name / Reverently we come to delight the Lord on High.)[83]

78. Guo, trans., *Qu Yuan fu jinyi*, in *GQJ/W*, 5:329.
79. Qu Yuan et al., *Chu ci ji zhu*, 3.
80. Qu Yuan et al., *The Songs of the South*, 68.
81. Guo, trans., *Qu Yuan fu jinyi*, in *GQJ/W*, 5:308. Ding Xiaohan, a reviewer of Guo's work on Qu Yuan, suggested that the translation of these lines is inaccurate. See Ding Xiaohan, "Ping Guo Moruo zhu Qu Yuan," in *GHY*, 9:411.
82. Qu Yuan et al., *Chu ci ji zhu*, 29.
83. Qu Yuan et al., *The Songs of the South*, 102.

Guo's translation:
日子好，天上出太陽，
高高興興，來敬東皇。[84]

[A good day, the sun rising in the sky, / Happily, we come to worship the Lord of East.]

Whether the rustic simplicity of this couplet echoes the indigenous shamanism in *Nine Songs* is an open question.

Translating "The Goddess of the Xiang" ("Xiang jun" 湘君) and "The Lady of the Xiang" ("Xiang furen" 湘夫人), two other famous pieces from *Nine Songs*, Guo resorts to a quasi-dramatic format. In his renditions, both the Goddess of Xiang and the Lady of Xiang end their monologues with the same couplet:

良辰美景不再來，
彷徨，彷徨，姑且散淡心腸。[85]

[The good and beautiful hour will not come again. / Wandering, wandering, I only wish to alleviate the feelings in my heart.]

The choice of words, rhyme, and syntax seems to fall into the typical language in the love scenes of traditional popular operas. In his "Interpretative Notes" ("Ti jie" 題解) on *Nine Songs*, he defends his translation of these two pieces as love poems by stating that "the ancient rituals in celebration of deities in fact provided opportunities for young men and women to develop their erotic love."[86] This obviously refers to the perspective of sexuality in Guo's study of the primitive religious rituals. Moreover, his theatrical translations draw implicitly on Wen's interpretation of such songs as the "ancient drama of singing and dancing" inserted into a religious ritual.[87]

A reviewer of Guo's work on Qu Yuan once pointed out that "few scholars . . . would like to do the work of translating ancient texts, which

84. Guo, trans., *Qu Yuan fu jinyi*, in *GQJ/W*, 5:257.
85. Ibid., 261, 263.
86. Ibid., 273.
87. See Wen Yiduo, "Shenme shi Jiuge" and "Jiuge gu ge wu ju xuanjie."

is very easy to invite criticism."[88] It is an almost impossible mission to produce a versed exegesis that is simultaneously philologically objective and aesthetically effective. Guo uses his interpretative notes to lament the difficulties facing modernization/translation: "Poetic translation is very difficult, and even more so for the translation of ancient poetry." Since the interpretation of ancient poetry sometimes cannot reach a finite conclusion, he proposes "a bolder approach to translation" as long as "the translation is based on certain evidence, and is reasonable and sensible in terms of logic and mood." After all, "translating poetry is a creative process." He confesses that his translation of *Nine Songs* "contains a lot of creative interpretations."[89]

Similarly, in his notes on his translation of "Heavenly Questions," Guo justifies a creative-interpretative approach: "The original is very hard to comprehend in the first place, and precisely because of this incomprehensibility, it demands a vernacular translation. In order to facilitate the readers that feel alien to the original, I decided to pay little heed to the experts' disagreements my version may invite, and went for a bold interpretation."[90] Dealing with Chinese mythology, "Heavenly Questions" includes a number of passages so obscure that the most prominent commentators find their meanings unfathomable. Zhu Xi, for example, has to use the term "unknown" (*wei xiang* 未詳) time and again when annotating this poem.[91] But Guo produces a fully elucidated rendition of the long poem—in versed form. The philological difficulties render necessary the method of creative translation.

Proposing creative interpretation as an essential complement to faithfulness, Guo offers his general theory of literary translation in his notes on *Nine Pieces* (*Jiu zhang* 九章). He asserts that his translations are "faithful" (*zhongshi* 忠實) based on his word-by-word scrutiny of the originals. But he admits the existence of subjective interpretations: "Translating the ancient language into the modern one, the language of Qu Yuan into *my own language*, [my work] of course cannot be as accurate as a photocopy."[92]

88. Tian Hua, "Du Guo Moruo Qu Yuan yanjiu guanjian," in *GHY*, 9:438.
89. Guo, trans., *Qu Yuan fu jinyi*, in *GQJ/W*, 5:273.
90. Ibid., 303.
91. See, for example, Qu Yuan et al., *Chu ci ji zhu*, 57.
92. Guo, trans., *Qu Yuan fu jinyi*, in *GQJ/W*, 5:369; emphasis added.

From an emphasis on fidelity, he arrives at the pursuit of artistic representation:

> Since this is translation rather than commentary, you have to make sure your translation is a piece of art. The translation has to be "trustworthy" [*xin* 信], but also "comprehensible" [*da* 達] and finally "elegant" [*ya* 雅]. The original is poetry, and then your translation has to be poetry. In order to do so, we have to allow for the translator's partial freedom. Sometimes he simply cannot do word-by-word hard translation [*ying yi* 硬譯]. He has the right to appropriate the original meaning and mold it into a new discourse [*xin ci* 新辭].[93]

The three principles of *xin*, *da*, and *ya* derive from the renowned late Qing translator Yan Fu 嚴復 (1854–1921)'s discourse on translation, which inaugurated "twentieth-century translation theory in China" and was "repeatedly debated by scholars throughout the last century."[94] "Hard translation" is a phrase originally coined by Lu Xun, in an effort to defend his rigid and rigorous translations of Marxist theories.[95] Resisting word-by-word translation and reconciling hermeneutic fidelity and artistic creativity, Guo's apology projects a double translatability of the content and the aesthetic style of the original. The emphasis of this ideology of literary translation falls again on "my own language" and the "new discourse." It grows out of his earlier argument for the translatability of ancient poetry and his whole career as a modern Chinese translator. His transmission of the Shelleyan "winds," his grasp of Goethe's *Faust* as a history of Zeitgeist, and his modernizing translations—all privilege a poetic-political interpretative subjectivity that remolds original texts, forms, and epochs.

93. Ibid.

94. Chan, ed., *Twentieth-Century Chinese Translation Theory*, 67. For Yan Fu's original statement, see Yan Fu, "Preface to *Tianyanlun* (1901)," 69. For an interpretation of Yan Fu's three principles of translation, see Wong, *Chong shi xin da ya*, 87–120.

95. See Lu Xun, "'Hard Translation' and the 'Class Character of Literature.'" For an account of the debates concerning "hard translation," see Wong, *Fanyi yu wenxue zhijian*, 299–333. Also see my essay, "The Promethean Translator and Cannibalistic Pains."

In other words, a modern translator, equipped with aesthetic sensibility and revolutionary consciousness, can and must seize the operative power of the present while "appropriating" the ancient. Zikpi observes that Guo's translation of Qu Yuan's poetry represents a "shift of emphasis from allegory to imagination."[96] She indicates in particular that Guo "reinterprets the social content of ['On Encountering Trouble'] in terms of modern revolutionary politics."[97] Empowering the translator with creative imagination, the 1953 modern renditions of Qu Yuan's work are permeated by Guo's continued effort to turn the ancient cultural hero into a modern revolutionary icon. He characterizes Qu Yuan as a poet in deep "love for his fatherland and people (*renmin*)."[98]

This agenda of popularization/glorification should be examined against a larger background of the cultural changes in the young People's Republic. In 1953, Guo's evaluation of Qu Yuan placed the emphasis unmistakably on a theme of patriotic populism as it was summarized in the discourse of people/*renmin*. The conception of the people/*renmin* had dominated 1940s revolutionary politics, in which Guo offered a historical imagination or articulation of *min* and *renmin*. The founding of the People's Republic in 1949 attested to the triumph of CCP's principle of people's democracy, which envisioned the alliance of all the revolutionary and patriotic social classes. In this young republic, the discourse of people/*renmin* was omnipresent, symbolizing the highest political legitimacy. In his 1953 preface, Guo pays microscopic attention to the figurations of *min*—which he has interpreted as the ancient lower classes of people/*renmin* on multiple occasions, as we have seen—in Qu Yuan's poems and refers to the following two couplets of Qu Yuan's sympathy for the people with his own vernacular renditions:

> Original text from "On Encountering Trouble":
> 長太息以掩涕兮，哀民生之多艱。
>
> (Having a long sigh, I brush away my tears, / Sad that *man's* life should be so beset with hardship.)

96. Zikpi, "Revolution and Continuity in Guo Moruo's Representations of Qu Yuan," 194.

97. Ibid., 190.

98. Guo, trans., *Qu Yuan fu jinyi*, in *GQJ/W*, 5:253.

Guo's translation:
我哀憐著人民的生涯多麼艱苦，
我長太息地禁不住要灑些眼淚。

[I lament how miserable the people's life is, / And I sigh and can't help dropping my tears.]

Original text from "The Outpouring of Sad Thoughts" ("Chou si" 抽思):
願搖起而橫奔兮，覽民尤以自鎮。

(I would like to rise up and fly to him unbidden, / But seeing how *others* have fared, I restrain myself.)[99]

Guo's translation:
想率性離開故鄉跑向國外，
看到人民的災難又鎮定了下來。[100]

[I want to leave my homeland and flee abroad, / But when I see the people's sufferings I calm down again.]

In both cases, Guo translates, emphatically, the ancient character *min* 民 as *renmin* 人民, the people. According to Zhu Xi's commentary, *min* refers to the subjects of the sovereign.[101] As Zikpi suggests, "the creation of solidarity is perhaps the most important intention of Guo's work on Qu Yuan."[102] Guo's modernizing use of *renmin* connects Qu Yuan's poetry to a new vision of the driving force of historical progress. The same citations of these passages appear in Guo's 1950 essay titled "Qu Yuan, the People's Poet" ("Renmin shiren Qu Yuan" 人民詩人屈原), with the same vernacular renditions. There, Guo claims that Qu Yuan "qualifies for the title of 'the people's poet.'"[103]

This was, however, not the first time that Qu Yuan had received such a title. In the 1940s, Wen Yiduo already enshrined Qu Yuan as "the poet of the people." His essay "The Poet of the People: Qu Yuan" ("Renmin de shiren—Qu Yuan" 人民的詩人— 屈原), obviously in conversation with

99. Qu Yuan et al., *The Songs of the South*, 70, 167; emphasis added.

100. For originals and Guo's translations, see *GQJ/W*, 5:253.

101. Commenting on the second couplet, Zhu Xi mentions the king's mistreatment of his subjects. See Qu Yuan et al., *Chu ci ji zhu*, 8, 85.

102. Zikpi, "Revolution and Continuity in Guo Moruo's Representations of Qu Yuan," 192.

103. Guo, "Renmin shiren Qu Yuan," in *GQJ/W*, 17:235.

Guo's study of the poet, situated Qu Yuan in the revolutionary trend of ancient China's liberation from slavery in the Warring States era. While in the 1940s Guo depicted Qu Yuan's life as a tragic entrapment of the progressive intelligentsia, Wen's Qu Yuan was a heroic herald of the "storming age" of "the people's revolution."[104] The similarity and difference between these interpretations prompt Schneider to characterize Guo's Qu Yuan as "Prometheus Bound" (an intellectual "chained to history") and Wen's Qu Yuan as "Prometheus Unbound" (a self-liberated slave representing a genuine *fanshen* or "turning-around").[105] Wen's more apocalyptic view was based on his radical analysis of Qu Yuan's class identity. Whereas most historians believed that Qu Yuan belonged to the class of nobility (for example, Marxist historian Hou Wailu would never agree with the title of "the people's poet"), Wen argued that "although Qu Yuan was from the same clan as the Chu royal family," he later became a "court performer" abused and oppressed by the ruling class, and therefore "belonged among the masses of the people [*renmin*]."[106]

The question about "individual creativity and class association" was at the center of the post-1949 literature on Qu Yuan, as intellectuals in New China were confronting the task of evaluating historical individuals as national heroes and as targets of revolutionary criticism.[107] In the 1940s, Guo largely left aside the issue of class and called the Chu poet a "southern Confucian." One should bear in mind that in Guo's 1940s writings, the Confucian school represented the revolutionary Zeitgeist of the Warring States era and was in fact a coded self-reference of modern Chinese progressive intelligentsia.[108] But in his 1950s writings, the association of Qu Yuan with Confucianism uncannily disappeared, indicating a silent change in his view of Confucian humanism in response to the new cultural politics in People's China. In his 1950 essay, Guo explicitly cautioned against Wen's classification of Qu Yuan as a member of the underclass and leader of the people's revolution.[109] Instead Guo held that even though Qu Yuan loved and sympathized with the people, as a noble

104. Wen Yiduo, "Renmin de shiren—Qu Yuan," 260–61.
105. Schneider, *A Madman of Ch'u*, 120, 124.
106. Wen Yiduo, "Renmin de shiren—Qu Yuan," 259–60.
107. Schneider, *A Madman of Ch'u*, 166.
108. Guo, "Qu Yuan yanjiu," 104.
109. Guo, "Renmin shiren Qu Yuan," in *GQJ/W*, 17:230.

he was unable to "awaken the people and organize the people."[110] But his 1953 essay, "The Great Patriotic Poet, Qu Yuan" ("Weida de aiguo shiren—Qu Yuan" 偉大的愛國詩人—— 屈原), implied another change in judgment: "Although Qu Yuan belonged to the same clan as the Chu royal family, he was simply a Chu plebeian citizen."[111] This statement came closer to Wen's view. In the preface to his modernizing translation of Qu Yuan, Guo provided a balanced conclusion: "Despite his noble origins, he had profound sympathies for the people."[112]

As Schneider summarizes, the post-1949 literature on Qu Yuan "conveyed the ambivalence of China's intellectual community about their relationship to the masses, about their place as creative individuals in a collectivist society."[113] It would not be too much to say that this ambivalence is indicative of a larger contradiction between the legacies of May Fourth individualism and the new demands of socialist transformations. Guo's "people-centrism," invented in the 1940s and tested in the 1950s, was once an imaginary solution to this contradiction. In Guo's historical vision of the people, the creative individuality (such as Qu Yuan and eventually Guo himself) could function as the mouthpiece of the masses. From Guo's ideal of translation as the lyre of the "cosmic winds" to his redefinition of the "people's poet," we have seen time and again this ideological mechanism of translatability between the creative individuality and the revolutionary Zeitgeist. Although the issue of class seems unsolvable, Guo indicates that the title of "the people's poet" is not only about class association. Qu Yuan's populism can be detected not only in the content of his poetry but also in its poetic form: "Qu Yuan's poetic forms were primarily developed from the folk-song forms, and his language was the people's language at that time."[114] It thus goes back to Guo's pursuit of a popular, colloquial, or even folk-song style in his vernacular modernizing translation. However, as the theme of class struggle came to saturate the Maoist historical thinking, the question about who deserved the title of "the people's poet" would continue to be open.

110. Ibid., 232.
111. Guo, "Weida de aiguo shiren," in *GQJ/W*, 17:165.
112. Guo, trans., *Qu Yuan fu jinyi*, in *GQJ/W*, 5:253.
113. Schneider, *A Madman of Ch'u*, 159.
114. Guo, trans., *Qu Yuan fu jinyi*, in *GQJ/W*, 5:254.

Du Fu, Maoist Scholarship, and Translation as Class Analysis

The approach of modernizing translation eventually found its way into the controversial uses and abuses of ancient literary traditions under Maoism. In the years preceding the "Great Proletarian Cultural Revolution," Qu Yuan was not the only one enshrined as a "poet of the people." Another ancient poet receiving that honor in socialist China was Du Fu, the Tang poet who had also been glorified in premodern China as the sage of poetry. A poet living through the catastrophic years of the An Lushan Rebellion (755–763), Du Fu focused his poetry on personal experience and witness of the human sufferings, and thus he produced a "poetic history" (*shi shi* 詩史) of the fall of the Tang dynasty from its golden times into tumult.[115] His loyalty to the court, to the nation, and to its people earned him the high reputation as a Confucian role model. In socialist China, literary historians ranked Du Fu and Li Bai as peaks of the high Tang poetry.

Guo's last major scholarly work focused on Du Fu. In late 1971, now a septuagenarian and a revolutionary culture veteran, he published *Li Bai and Du Fu*. The appearance of this book, first, was an important cultural event during Mao's Cultural Revolution—a continued revolution within China's socialist revolution. Since much of the socialist system of cultural and knowledge production was damaged or interrupted in the late 1960s, *Li Bai and Du Fu* was a rare monument of intellectual activity during the Cultural Revolution. The peculiar position of this scholarly project implies a question central to the Maoist agenda: how to appraise ancient literature in the age of cultural revolution?

Second, the polemical content of Guo's book conceals the tensions within his own post-1949 literary-historical scholarship in particular and the whole socialist historiography in general. Divided into two long parts—"A Study of Li Bai" and "A Study of Du Fu"—Guo's book reflects a preference of Li Bai the romantic over Du Fu the realist. While Guo's

115. "Tu Fu is the greatest Chinese poet. . . . The peculiar nature of Tu Fu's greatness lies beyond the limited scope of literary history." Thus Stephen Owen starts his reading of Du Fu's lifework. Owen, *The Great Age of Chinese Poetry*, 183.

identification with Li Bai's colorful life and his criticism of this Tang poet's political weakness may contain an autobiographical dimension of self-reflection or self-criticism, his analysis of Du Fu has a much stronger polemical drive and remains more controversial to this date.[116] Guo's choice of Du Fu as a target of criticism, on one hand, reaffirms the logic of reversing the verdict in the revolutionary rewriting of national antiquity. As he indicated in a letter, any criticism of Du Fu had become a "taboo" in traditional commentaries because of Du Fu's fame as a Confucian "sage of poetry": "Du Fu should be positively evaluated, about which I don't have objection; what I object to is the way in which he was treated as a 'sage', a sacrosanct 'taboo.' "[117] Guo's diagnosis of Du Fu's "feudal class consciousness" is yet another example of leftist historiographical efforts to demystify traditional ideological narratives, "restore the truth," or "reverse what has been reversed."[118] However, similar to the case of Guo's post-Liberation historical plays, such a reversal of the verdict, despite its rebellious energies, actually followed the latest Maoist political line.

Thus, in the discourse of Maoism, the revolutionary destructive potentials and the omniscient authoritative guidance were interconnected and mutually conditioned. Within such a party-state of the continued revolution, the whole enterprise of historical knowledge was then both subversive and subordinate. Guo's politicization of ancient literature in his account of Du Fu (as well as in many other post-Liberation writings) should be approached within this larger cultural contradiction. I propose to see Guo's embrace of Maoist cultural revolution as a problematic or ironic fulfillment of his earlier Shelleyan vision: the interpretative subjectivity became a lyre or harp of the political wind in Maoist China. While Guo's scholarship distanced itself from ultraleftism, his discursive performance of subversion and self-subversion was at least partially tuned with and empowered by the momentum of the Cultural Revolution.

116. See Liu Maolin, "Xiang mu chun feng yang liu si—zai lun Guo Moruo de 'Li Bai yu Du Fu' "; Wang Jinhou, "Lue lun dui 'Li Bai yu Du Fu' de piping."

117. Cited in Wang Jinhou, "Lue lun dui 'Li Bai yu Du Fu' de piping," in *GHY*, 9:581.

118. Mao Zedong, "Kanle *Bishang Liangshan* hou xie gei Yang Shaoxuan Qi Yanming er tongzhi de xin," 3.

Third and more specifically, Guo's study of Du Fu amounts to a miniature "cultural revolution" within the Chinese Revolution, exposing on a micro level the tensions intrinsic to the knowledge production in socialist China. Guo's target of criticism is not limited to Du Fu's ancient halo as a sage but also includes the title of "people's poet" given to Du Fu in the socialist period. Guo lays bare his polemical intentions on the opening pages of his "Study of Du Fu":

> Du Fu sided fully with the ruling class, the landlord class. This class consciousness and outlook is the defining spine of Du Fu's thought, manifested throughout the majority of his poetry and prose. . . . The literati-gentries of ancient feudal times praised this consciousness, which is not surprising at all. What is surprising is that a number of scholars, around the time of the Liberation [in 1949], accepted this old approach, assuming an uncritical attitude towards Du Fu and praising him effusively—with a new rhetoric. Scholars of previous times called Du Fu "a sage of poetry," and contemporary scholars call him a "poet of the people." When [Du Fu] was called a "sage," the people did not have a right to ask why; when he is called a "poet of the people," I'm afraid that the people today need to ask why.[119]

Finding the poet's humanistic touch appealing, a number of socialist scholars praised Du Fu's work and personality from a progressive and populist perspective (which was similarly assumed in the post-1949 evaluation of Qu Yuan). Such a reading can be traced to Feng Zhi's book *A Biography of Du Fu* (*Du Fu zhuan* 杜甫傳, 1952). Feng Zhi, whose work I touched on in chapter 3, wrote this biography immediately after the founding of the People's Republic to position Du Fu's legacy in a new light: "Nowadays, the people have won the sovereign power. . . . Nothing will prevent [Du Fu's poems] from shining their radiance."[120] His book focuses thematically on the contradiction of Du Fu's lifework: on one hand, Du Fu's identification with the ruling class; on the other, his experience of the people's atrocities beyond his own class identity. "How did [Du Fu] transcend his own class limitations and experience the sufferings of the exploited, oppressed people, and in doing so contribute to

119. Guo, *Li Bai yu Du Fu*, 124–25.
120. Feng Zhi, *Du Fu zhuan*, 1.

the gigantic development of Tang poetry? In this process, he went through countless transformations and contradictions. This biography attempts to narrate all those transformations and contradictions in his life."[121]

Here one can discern a logic similar to that of Guo's argument for Qu Yuan. Feng's book describes how Du Fu became closer to the people during the second half of his life because of the social turmoil, and how his poetry functioned as a mirror of that "complicated and changeful age."[122] Feng's account of Du Fu's witness of the people's suffering is also reminiscent of what the Chinese intelligentsia experienced in the 1930s and 1940s. Just as Feng's study of *Faust II* can be read as a self-analysis of the May Fourth intellectuals in the 1940s, so his biography of Du Fu conceals a symbolic self-justification of the nonpartisan intellectuals' role in a progressive-populist politics represented now by the "people's regime" in the early 1950s.

Xiao Difei 蕭滌非 (1907–91), another interpreter of Du Fu's oeuvre in New China, expressed an equally profound acceptance of this people-centered historical consciousness, and his comprehensive work *A Study of Du Fu* (*Du Fu yanjiu* 杜甫研究), divided into two parts and published respectively in 1956 and 1957, offered an even more sympathetic reading. Applying "Mao Zedong's thought of literature and art" and Marxist aesthetic theory in a more self-conscious way, Xiao praised the "popular character" (*renmin xing* 人民性) of Du Fu's work and pinpointed the "vast scope," "profundity," and "sincerity" of Du Fu's attachment to the people. Once again, Xiao's definition of Du Fu's thought as the "love for the fatherland and the people" reminds us of the discourse Guo once used to glorify Qu Yuan.[123] It is also noteworthy that after Guo's death, Xiao struck a blow to Guo's *Li Bai and Du Fu*, asserting again that Du Fu surely deserves the title of the "poet of the people."[124]

It is worth mentioning in passing that in 1962 socialist China's literary community celebrated the 1,250th anniversary of Du Fu's birth. Feng gave a keynote address at the conference in commemoration of Du Fu in Beijing and published two historical short stories based on the poet's life.

121. Ibid.
122. Ibid., 140.
123. Xiao Difei, *Du Fu yanjiu, shang juan*, 60.
124. Xiao Difei, "Guanyu Li Bai yu Du Fu," in *GHY*, 9:540.

Together with other literary accounts, Feng's 1962 depictions of Du Fu could be read as a veiled and indirect protestation against the "people's sufferings" during the "Three Years of Difficulties" that had resulted from Maoist economic voluntarism.[125] Guo, in contrast, published a series of commentary notes on the Qing poet Yuan Mei's poetics in 1962. He complained that although his commentary only contained minor criticism of Du Fu, he received questions of disagreement from his readers. He then defended himself by arguing that it is "an exaggeration to repeat the title [of the 'sage']," but he did not yet mention the issue of the "poet of the people."[126] Guo's discontent with the socialist high evaluation of Du Fu in the 1960s may have been a trigger for his writing of *Li Bai and Du fu*.[127]

In his 1971 study, Guo singled out Feng and Xiao for criticism, and his tone was sometimes quite politicized or dramatized. For example, he writes: "Can it be that easy to 'transcend one's class'?"[128] This sentence questions Feng's approach without naming him. On another occasion, Guo indicates that Feng's "defense of Du Fu" is "ridiculous."[129] Although sometimes Guo can at least cite Feng in a positive sense, he makes harsh political judgments on Xiao's scholarship: "This is a typical revival of the feudalist consciousness."[130]

Published during the Cultural Revolution, *Li Bai and Du Fu* opens with two quotations from Mao on the pages preceding the title-author page. One quote is from the famous "On New Democracy": "A splendid old culture was created during the long period of Chinese feudal society. . . . It is imperative to separate the fine old culture of the people which had a more or less democratic and revolutionary character from all the decadence of the old feudal ruling class."[131] This directive for the revolutionary transformation of antiquity is the original definition of the perspective of people/*renmin*. Guo, Feng, and Xiao in fact shared the same political paradigm of historical thinking, that is, the Maoist discourse of

125. See two appendixes in Feng Zhi, *Du Fu zhuan*, 141–94.

126. Guo, *Suiyuan shi hua zhaji*, in *GQJ/W*, 16:399.

127. For a contextualization of Guo's scholarly intentions in the long reception history of Li Bai and Du Fu, see Xie Baocheng, *Long hu dou yu ma niu feng*, 331–69.

128. Guo, *Li Bai yu Du Fu*, 141.

129. Ibid., 188.

130. Ibid., 225.

131. Ibid., inside cover. Also see Mao Zedong, "On New Democracy," 381.

progressive populism. The works of all three of them belonged to a new socialist scholarship. Feng and Xiao consciously mobilized this perspective in their favorable positioning of Du Fu on the side of the people's culture, but Guo's 1971 recategorization of Du Fu into the camp of decadence exposed the political tension within the socialist reevaluation of the ancient culture. The hegemonic discourse of people-centrism now led to its own self-reversal and became a destructive continued revolution against an existing scholarship of its own.

Last but not least, it turns out that modernizing translation is tied up with this intellectual-political performance of subversion. To accomplish a class analysis of Du Fu, Guo once again resorts to the method of modernizing translation. He notes that six narrative poems have received particular attention from socialist "new experts," and have been considered as "most powerful in the populist tendencies" among Du Fu's works.[132] These poems are "Sanbie" 三别—"Parting of the New Weds," "Parting of the Senior Couple," and "Parting of the Homeless"—and "Sanli" 三吏—"The Xinan Official," "The Shihao Official," and "The Tongguan Official." Together they document the poet's witness of the human atrocities under the military disasters and contain criticism of the unbearable burdens the dynasty put on its subjects. Guo singles out these canonized works and decides to "translate them word-by-word and sentence-by-sentence into the vernacular, so as to add more precision to my interpretation."[133]

Guo's renditions of these six poems are generally as literal as he promises; yet they still show the impulse for rhymed translation (Du Fu's originals assume the *yuefu* 樂府 ancient style, which gives the author a certain degree of freedom for rhymes and meters). For instance, on one occasion he sacrifices literalness for the sake of the rhyme, translating *letu* 樂土 (a word meaning a happy land, traceable to *Shi jing*) into *tao huayuan* 桃花源 (the Peach Blossom Spring, the name of the utopia in ancient poet Tao Yuanming's literary work).[134] In fact, Guo's analysis of these classics is not entirely far from what Feng and Xiao have to say about them. Just as Feng and Xiao has to note Du Fu's political limitations, Guo

132. Guo, *Li Bai yu Du Fu*, 125.

133. Ibid.

134. Ibid., 128.

has to recognize Du Fu's realistic depiction of the human tragedies. In translating these poems, Guo concedes to Feng and Xiao that the six poems "leave us a [document of] the miserable conditions of the people in the war-inflicted regions, which is indeed very valuable."[135] The defining difference, however, is an ideological sleight of hand, or a shift of political optics: by putting the originals side by side with the translations, Guo places the accent on the side of the feudalist weaknesses of Du Fu's poetry: "When we conduct a class analysis, the limitation of [Du Fu's] poetry can no longer be disguised." He argues that the poet's sympathy for the people is "cheap."[136] He translates these poems in such a way that the words seem to be the miserable individuals' monologues, and as a result the poet is a "speechless detached observer."[137] According to Guo, "Du Fu assumes a standing of the landlord class." Because of this "class consciousness," in these six poems the poet "identifies himself with the officials," and the "people" are portrayed as "tame as lambs and purged of any bit of rebellious sentiments."[138]

After pointing out that "the popular character of 'Sanli' and 'Sanbie' is exaggerated," Guo uses this form of "parallel translation"—to "avoid any errors of my understanding"[139]—for two more poems by Du Fu, both written during the latter's exile in Chengdu. "My Thatched Roof Is Ruined by the Autumn Wind" ("Maowu wei qiufeng suo po ge" 茅屋爲秋風所破歌) is a renowned poem that many commentators refer to as an example of the progressive-populist vision because Du Fu not only laments his own miserable condition of living but envisions "a great roof for the poorest gentlemen of all this world."[140] Guo's vernacular rendition, however, pays excessive attention to the matter of class. By turning to a literal translation, Guo indicates that Du Fu condemns the village children as "bandits" when they take away his thatches, whereas this condemnation is usually taken as a show of the poet's humorous self-mocking. More symptomatic is that Guo insists on keeping the word *han shi* 寒士 intact and untranslated in his vernacular version. Although

135. Ibid., 125.
136. Ibid., 132.
137. Ibid., 133
138. Ibid., 136, 135.
139. Ibid., 136.
140. Du Fu, "My thatched roof is ruined by the autumn wind," 802.

this Chinese word is commonly understood as referring to "the poor gentlemen," Guo argues that it refers to a very specific social class of the literati-gentry eligible for more social wealth and standing.[141] In other words, "the great roof" in Du Fu's imagination is not for all the lower social classes. Consequently, Guo contends that this poem actually discloses Du Fu's lack of compassion for the people/*renmin*—a reading that deconstructs the humanistic image of Du Fu and forms an ironic contrast to Guo's high praise of Qu Yuan.

The next poem Guo translates is "Being Treated with Wine by Old Farmer Tian and Hearing Him Praise Yan Wu the Mayor" ("Zao Tian fu ni yin mei Yan zhongcheng" 遭田父泥飲美嚴中丞). This poem, narrating Du Fu's wine drinking at his neighbor's place, can be considered to indicate how close the poet became to the lower-class people. But Guo's rendition presents Du Fu as someone who distances himself from the rustic manners of the host farmer. Guo even categorizes this farmer as belonging among the "rich peasantry" or kulaks—a category of Leninist-Maoist class analysis—and claims that the poet's intention in writing this poem was to praise Yan Wu, a high-ranking politician who aided Du Fu.[142] The sensitivity to class consciousness in his renditions of these two Chengdu poems reminds us of Mao's own characterization of Du Fu's work as "political poetry."[143]

In other words, modernizing translation figures prominently in the most central and contentious part of Guo's study of "Du Fu's class consciousness." Similar to the situation we encountered in our discussion of "Nongshishi," to carry out his deconstructive reading it is not necessary in the first place to vernacularize Du Fu's poems (especially considering that his poetic language is far more intelligible to modern readers than the pre-Qin language in *Shi jing* and Qu Yuan's poetry). Feng and Xiao, for example, do not use the method of vernacular translation and have little difficulty in making their arguments accessible. Yet Guo sees the process of vernacular translation as essential for the "correctness" of a new understanding of Du Fu. The shift of focus from "popular character" onto "class consciousness," however, was a discursive performance of Maoist

141. Guo, *Li Bai yu Du Fu*, 138.
142. Ibid., 140.
143. Mao Zedong, *Jian guo yilai Mao Zedong wengao*, 7:166.

subversion, whose "correctness" was virtually a rhetorical effect. It was the literary practice of modernizing translation that provided the power of political persuasion.[144] One can conclude that as a lyrical, intellectual, and political device in line with the revolutionary project of language, modernizing translation was fixed in Guo's interpretation of antiquity.

In this chapter, we are once again confronted with the centrality of translation in the cultural logic of the Chinese Revolution. The revolutionary rewriting of antiquity determined a mode of translation that was intralingual, interpretative, poetic, and polemical. So far I have pinpointed a series of moments of the inventive practice of modernizing translation of ancient poetry from the May Fourth age to the final years of Maoism. They constitute a site where poetry, ancient history, and revolutionary politics become inextricably inseparable. First, Guo's early renditions of *Shi jing* contributed to the invention of a national lyricism, according to which the modern lyrical subjectivity would illuminate the ancient origin. Second, Guo heralded the practice of vernacular translation as a literary-rhetoric component of national heritage scholarship. Third, the practice of modernizing translation is refunctionalized into the Marxist hermeneutics of progressive populism. Eventually the politicization of literary historiography exhausted the potential of such a modernization/translation.

At the core of all these modes of modernizing translation, I argue, is their synchronization of the ancient originals into a now-time dramatized by the creative potentials and destructive energies of revolutionary cultural politics. With an overemphasis on the "present" or *jin*, this literary and political synchronization not only means a linguistic modernization but also brings about a "displacement of the angle of vision," within which the past is revalued, reappraised, and reinvented.[145] The past needs to be translated to beat the same literary-political pulse with the present. Put differently, the historical interpretation involves a constant process of literary, epistemological, and political translation. Throughout this book I

144. A similar case can be found in Zhao Jibin 趙紀彬's 1974 study of Confucius, in which vernacular translations of all the cited ancient documents served the purpose of popularizing an anti-Confucian argument. Yet Zhao's transcoding of ancient Sage's words into a monologue of class consciousness did not need to address the issue of poetic effect. See Zhao Jibin, *Guanyu Kong Qiu sha Shaozheng Mou wenti*.

145. Benjamin, *The Arcades Project*, 459.

have argued that Guo's case offers a perspective from which to see the dialectical interactions between translation, historical time, and the Chinese Revolution. Modernizing translation, in this sense, is an occasion where translation and historical imagination merge into a cultural logic of revolution as reinterpretation.

CONCLUSION, OR, SOME FINAL VARIATIONS

On August 5, 1973, Mao Zedong, an ailing eighty-year-old revolutionary leader, recited a new poem to his wife Jiang Qing 江青 (1914–91), letting her transcribe it. The poem was addressed to Guo Moruo, an eighty-one-year-old man who continued to function as the symbol of the intelligentsia's identification with the Maoist party after surviving the craze of the early days of the Cultural Revolution. Titled "To Guo the Senior After Reading 'On Feudal System,' Written in *qilü* Style" ("Qilü, du *Fengjian lun* cheng Guo lao" 七律·讀《封建論》呈郭老), Mao's poem reads:

> My friend, please stop criticizing Qin Shi Huang;
> His actions of burning books and burying the Confucians should be reevaluated.
> The founding emperor is long gone, but the achievements of Qin remain,
> And notwithstanding its high renown, the learning of Confucius is in fact worthless chaff.
> All later generations followed the political-legal system of Qin,
> And your book *Ten Critiques* is not a good treatise.
> Please carefully reread the Tang thinker [Liu Zongyuan]'s "On Feudal System,"
> And don't retreat from Liu to the King Wen of Zhou.[1]

1. Mao Zedong, "Qilü, du *Fengjian lun* cheng Guo lao," 361.

I started this book with a snapshot reference to this peculiar poetic dialogue. To end my study, I delve into this coda of not only Guo's sinuous career but also China's revolutionary century. According to Alain Badiou's periodization, the Cultural Revolution was a decisive implosion of the party-state, and its ebbing signaled the closure of a global revolutionary sequence. In the fading twilight of Maoist politics, why did the controversy of Confucius versus Qin Shi Huang figure so prominently? Why did Guo's book *Ten Critiques* suddenly—and anachronistically—become so important? And why did the revolutionary helmsman want to express his critique in an ancient poetic form?

Conversing with Chairman Mao in Ancient Style

In the early 1970s, China was living the aftermath of the destructiveness and inventiveness of radical Maoism from 1966 to 1968, a "political episode of the highest importance."[2] The rebellious overflows destabilized the party-state system that was the achievement of China's New Democratic Revolution and socialist transition. But they failed to translate into any "strategic and reproducible propositions."[3] Since the defection and death of Lin Biao 林彪 (1907–71), the Maoist regime was marked by the antagonism between the ultra-left group, represented by the Shanghai faction or Gang of Four, and the revolutionary veterans, who attempted to restore the order.[4] A senile cultural leader, a protégé of Zhou Enlai, and a literary friend of Mao's, Guo became active again, resuming some diplomatic responsibilities (as China's international stage was rapidly expanding due to the thawing of the Sino-US relationship in 1972) and orchestrating the restoration of the scholarly activities that had been largely disrupted in the late 1960s.

The period of 1972–76, as an extended ending of the whole sequence of China's revolutionary movements, was not without spasms and actu-

2. Badiou, "The Cultural Revolution: The Last Revolution?," 488.

3. Ibid.

4. For a historical account of the second half of the Cultural Revolution, see MacFarquhar and Schoenhals, *Mao's Last Revolution*, chapters 19–23.

ally saw an ambivalent "process of rethinking the Cultural Revolution."[5] The year of 1973 witnessed yet another Maoist stirring. Recovering from the blow struck by the Lin Biao Incident, Mao eventually decided on one of his last targets of critique: it was neither bourgeoisie nor revisionists, but an ancient Chinese sage, Confucius. In particular, Mao's denunciation of the Confucian school (*ru jia* 儒家) was accompanied by a renewed interest in the tradition of Legalism (*fa jia* 法家), an ancient Chinese school of political philosophy that helped the kingdom of Qin put an end to the Warring States era and unified China in 221 BCE. The campaign of "criticizing Lin Biao and Confucius" (*pi Lin pi Kong* 批林批孔) soon turned into an agenda of "appraising Legalism and criticizing Confucianism" (*ping fa pi ru* 評法批儒), which is sometimes considered an attempt to make the "second Cultural Revolution."[6] Seen from the poem, Mao's sympathies clearly went to Qin Shi Huang. For Mao, the negative verdict on Qin Shi Huang had to be reversed. The emperor's brutal rule of law, unification of thought, and standardization of political institutions laid the true foundation of a progressive social transformation in premodern China, whereas the Confucian value of benevolence was nothing more than the ideological "chaff" of that historical process. Here, national antiquity reemerged as a battleground of symbolic anachronism within the Chinese Revolution.

Guo wrote in early 1974 a response poem, also in *qilü* style, titled "Spring Thunders" ("Chun lei" 春雷). The regulated verse shows an unconditional acceptance of Mao's new verdict:

> Shaking the earth, the spring thunders herald the message of revitalization;
> All the oceanic dragons, competing with each other, disgorge their pearls.
> You affirm the legacy of Qin Shi Huang that has benefited hundreds of generations;
> You put Confucius the second son on trial for his inexpiable guilt.
> The grave error of my book *Ten Critiques* is now as clear as fire,
> And the high view of Liu Zongyuan's treatise as shining as cinnabar.
> I would like to join the march of the workers and peasants,
> Cleansing my own dirt and painting a new vision.[7]

5. Weigelin-Schwiedrzik, "The Campaign to Criticize Lin Biao and Confucius," 163.
6. Ibid.," 174.
7. Cited in Feng Xigang, *Guo Moruo de wannian suiyue*, 323. This poem was not published during Guo's lifetime.

Soon after this self-criticism, Guo was hospitalized for fever and pneumonia, his lyrical conversation with Mao cut short. Amid the "spring thunders" of 1974, his political fate was again at nadir. But in this difficult moment, he received in the hospital a visit from Mao's messenger. Mao sent this messenger for Guo's 1962 book *Notes on* Suiyuan Discourses on Poetry (*Suiyuan shi hua zhaji* 《隨園詩話》札記), a collection of comments on traditional poetics. The revolutionary philosopher-king's request of Guo's more recent work—a highly symbolic act that was characteristic of the obscure style of China's political life during Mao's final years—implied that Mao continued to see Guo worthy as his literary comrade and thereby immediately saved him from any further political persecution.

The last poetic-political conversation between Guo and Mao is saturated with a sense of anachronism. First, one is made to ponder why Mao eventually returned to the debate of Confucius versus Qin Shi Huang. The most obvious anachronism lies in the fact that after decades of revolutionary social transformation, he still picked Confucius as his final enemy, although "Confucius Inc." had already been exposed to iconoclastic attacks during the May Fourth Movement. Since the ultra-leftist practice had failed to institutionalize itself into a new social order, the later Mao was discontented with the centrifugal tendencies of the revolutionary veterans who had "never progressed beyond the stage of the bourgeois democratic revolution."[8] As a result, his political thinking resonated with the Qin system of centralism, as he was rereading Liu Zongyuan 柳宗元's "On the Feudal System" ("Fengjian lun" 封建論). Confucian conservatism idealized the feudal system designed by the founding fathers of the Zhou dynasty, whereas Liu's renowned essay criticized the separatist tendencies under the feudal system and supported the efforts for centralization from the perspective of the objective historical "propensity" (*shi* 勢).[9] As Stuart Schram puts it, "the Cultural Revolution, which had opened with manifestos in favor of the Paris Commune model of mass democracy, closed with paeans of praise to the most implacable of centralizing despots, the first Ch'in emperor."[10] Mao decided

8. Mao Zedong, "Mao zhuxi zhongyao zhishi," 487.
9. See Liu Zongyuan, "Fengjian lun."
10. Schram, "Mao Tse-Tung's Thought from 1949–1976," 484.

to "avert a reversal of verdicts on the Cultural Revolution" by linking revolutionary politics with the Qin legacies and defending it against Confucian criticisms.[11] Schram observes that a major impulse of Mao's thought after 1949 "was to enrich Marxism with ideas and values drawn from the national past."[12] Weigelin-Schwiedrzik also suggests that in the final years of the Cultural Revolution, "the traditional method of analogy was integrated into Marxist historiography."[13] The long Chinese Revolution, drawing to an anticlimactic (or tragic-farcical?) end, was bound with the untimely return of the ancient.

The second dimension of this anachronistic situation is that to sentence Confucianism to death one more time, Mao chose, as a negative example, a book from the period of the New Democratic Revolution, Guo's *Ten Critiques*. As I demonstrated in chapter 5, *Ten Critiques*, written and published in the mid-1940s, argued that Confucian humanism represented the "revolutionary current" of "the people's interests" and "people's demands" during pre-Qin China's "social revolution," whereas the triumph of Qin Shi Huang meant a brief "restoration of slavery."[14] Based on this redemption of Confucianism, Guo's historical perspective of "people-centrism" formed an active intervention into the articulation of "the people," a central figure of the New Democratic Revolution that was to be enshrined in the very title of New China—the People's Republic.

However, Mao's "continued revolution" in the 1960s and 1970s was meant to be an attempt to go beyond the New Democratic Revolution. Perhaps this tendency of self-negation and self-supersession (traceable to the Creation Society's radical vision of *Aufhebung/aofuhebian*) can at least partly explain why in the mid-1970s Guo's earlier praise of Confucianism received attention from Mao, who anxiously noted that some "old comrades" did not understand "the socialist revolution," that is, the continued Cultural Revolution.[15] Guo seemed to be one of those "old comrades," as his leftist historical scholarship represented the legacies of

11. MacFarquhar and Schoenhals, *Mao's Last Revolution*, 413.

12. Schram, "Mao Tse-Tung's Thought from 1949–1976," 396.

13. Weigelin-Schwiedrzik, "The Campaign to Criticize Lin Biao and Confucius," 157.

14. Guo, *Shi pipan shu*, 61, 74, 404.

15. Mao Zedong, "Mao zhuxi zhongyao zhishi," 487.

people's democracy or the "bourgeois democratic revolution." The ultraleftist Gang of Four saw Mao's criticism of Guo's 1940s scholarship as an opportunity to resist the normalization of the party-state. Enduring several long sessions of questioning at his Beijing residence, Guo dismissed all accusations and insisted that his denigrations on Qin Shi Huang had been intended as innuendo, a disguised denunciation of Jiang Jieshi's rule in the 1940s.[16] In this whole "historiography of innuendo" from the 1940s to the 1970s, the changing valence of ancient history, to be sure, shows the danger of historical discourses at the service of political struggle. Nevertheless, it presents the Chinese Revolution as a permanent metahistorical crisis. On a deeper level, the reappearance of *Ten Critiques* pointed to a profound temporal standstill within the Chinese Revolution: a confusion between national antiquity and revolutionary modernity was inscribed in a tension between the New Democratic Revolution and the continued revolution.

The third dimension of anachronism involved in this Mao–Guo conversation is the easiest to be overshadowed by the intellectual subject matter, yet in my view, the most significant: their revolutionary reevaluation of Confucianism was conducted in an ancient poetic form, the *qilü* style. This style, which requires eight seven-syllable lines with sophisticated tonal and rhyming rules, represents a zenith of the refinement in classical Chinese prosody. The persistence of such traditional formality in a dialogue of two revolutionary figures is symptomatic—especially considering that Guo's literary career was initiated with his contribution to the vernacular New Poetry.

The lure of ancient-style poetry, as it turned out, was no less irresistible for many May Fourth intellectuals than was the lure of the modern. Recent scholarship has drawn attention to the persistence of the ancient-style poetic writing among the revolutionary writers from the late Qing period all the way to the socialist era, questioning the orthodox May Fourth binary division of the ancient and modern and the paradigm of linear progression from one to the other.[17] For example, Haosheng Yang's study argues that "modern Chinese writers' persistent engagement with

16. See Yu Liqun, "Hua beitong wei liliang," 512.

17. See, for example, Kiyama Hideo, *Ren ge ren ku da qi qian*; Wu, *Modern Archaics*; and Yang, *A Modernity Set to a Pre-Modern Tune.*

the aesthetic and rhetoric of the traditional genre was central to their critical response to the present."[18] Even in the heyday of the Literary Revolution, Guo entertained himself with the composition of ancient-style poetry. This fact is not surprising; as can be recalled from chapter 1, for Guo the form and language were secondary to the universal spirit of poetry. We have also seen how Guo recycled many elements of ancient-style poetry in his translations.

The War of Resistance Against Japanese Aggression witnessed a further politicization of this lingering of traditional forms. Guo's return to China from his exile in 1937, for example, was announced by his poem composed in *qilü* style: "Again a time comes when I have to throw away my pen and ask for a military assignment; / Parting my wife and abandoning my children, I must cut off the lotus root silk binding my heart."[19] Based on the dramatic tension between the national calling and his transnational familial obligations, this patriotic poem immediately won the hearts of the reading public. In the wartime capital Chongqing, the writing of ancient-style poetry created a "community of rhyme" that contributed to the establishment of a united front of anti-GMD activists, progressive intellectuals, and the reading public.[20] Notably, Guo's memory of the democratic movements in Chongqing was entangled with a poetic friendship among the prodemocracy activists. He remembered his composition of a *qilü* poem on the occasion of a welcome back party held for Zhou Enlai: "The torch bearer has returned from the northern land."[21] It was also in Chongqing that Mao's ancient-style poetry became known to the public during the postwar CCP-GMD negotiations. The publication of "Snow, to the Tune of *Qin Yuan Chun*" ("Qin yuan chun: xue" 沁園春：雪) was a literary/political event and virtually drew the "community of rhyme" to the CCP's side.

Guo's literary exchanges with Mao started with a poem in response to "Snow," and intensified in the socialist period.[22] In the 1960s, their poetic conversations attested to the Maoist shift of focus to a continued revolution (see fig. 9). Despite China's self-induced economic difficulties

18. Yang, *A Modernity Set to a Pre-Modern Tune*, 1.
19. Guo, "Gui guo za yin," in *GQJ/W*, 2:44.
20. Liu Kui, *Shiren gemingjia*, 109.
21. Guo, "Minzhu yundong zhong er san shi," in *GQJ/W*, 20:187.
22. See Ji Guoping, *Mao Zedong yu Guo Moruo.*

FIGURE 9 Guo Moruo and Mao Zedong, 1964. Courtesy of Guo Pingying.

in the late 1950s and early 1960s, Guo remained faithful to Maoist heroism and wrote in *qilü* style "On Seeing 'The Monkey King's Three Combats with the White-Boned Demon'" ("Kan Sun Wukong san da Baigu Jing" 看孫悟空三打白骨精, 1961). In that poem, Guo implicitly compared Mao's fighting spirit with the power of the legendary Monkey King, using the pun of *da sheng mao* 大聖毛, which means at the same time "the Monkey King's [magic] hair" and "the Great Sage Mao."[23] Mao used his response poem to clarify why he reemphasized the need of political struggle: "A thunderstorm burst over the earth / And a demon rose from a heap of white bones. . . . / Today, a miasmal mist once more rising, / We hail Su Wukong, the Great Sage."[24]

Another example is Guo's "Written on the New Year Day of 1963, to the Tune of *Man Jiang Hong*" ("Man jiang hong, yijiuliusan nian yuandan shuhuai" 滿江紅，一九六三年元旦書懷). The poem was a celebration

23. Guo, "Kan Sun Wukong san da Baigu Jing," in *GQJ/W*, 4:326.

24. Mao Zedong, "Reply to Comrade Kuo Mo-jo—a *lu shih*," 41 (translation modified).

of the strong comeback that Mao's China had made. Rather than paying due respect to the Thermidorian bureaucrats, he sang the hymn to the visionary leader fighting against Soviet revisionism. The escalation of the China-Soviet split and the isolation of Red China added to his dramatization of the heroic defiance of Mao and his people: "When the seas are in turmoil / Heroes are on their mettle."[25] As Yang's reading indicates, "the more hostile the environment, the stronger his hero-worship grew."[26] In Guo's figurative language, Mao Zedong Thought is the true gold, temporary difficulties are melting ice mountains, four volumes of Mao's *Selected Works* are the columns that support the collapsing sky, and the criticism from the Soviet Union is nothing but the barking of a dog. When the East receives the dawning light of 1963, "the red flag of revolution is unfurling, / The universe is glowing red."[27] The rhetoric of a reddened universe reminds us of the young Guo's pantheistic vision of an active universe, as discussed in earlier chapters. As early as 1920, Guo sang a "wild song of the cosmic revolution."[28] In his celebration of erotic drive, he also stated that in springtime "the whole universe is a most immense pornographic work."[29] The imagination of an all-pervading cosmic renewal, frequently appearing in Guo's poems after 1949, eventually merged into an endorsement of Mao's philosophy of permanent struggle, a philosophy that was in its own way as cosmological as dialectical.

Only one week after the publication of this poem, Mao wrote his response in the same style of *man jiang hong*. The poem famously declares: "Ten thousand years are too long, / Seize the day, seize the hour!" The chairman concluded the response poem with a sublime global landscape:

> The Four Seas are rising, clouds and waters raging,
> The Five Continents are rocking, wind and thunder roaring.
> Our force is irresistible,
> Away with all pests![30]

25. Guo, "Man jiang hong, yijiuliusan nian yuandan shuhuai," in *GQJ/W*, 4:119.
26. Yang, *A Modernity Set to a Pre-Modern Tune*, 177.
27. Guo, "Man jiang hong, yijiuliusan nian yuandan shuhuai," in *GQJ/W*, 4:120.
28. Guo, "Yuzhou geming de kuang ge," 29.
29. Guo, "Kaermeiluo guniang," in *GQJ/W*, 9:215.
30. Mao Zedong, "Reply to Comrade Kuo Mo-jo, to the Tune of *Man Jiang Hong*," 46–47 (translation modified).

Commenting on Mao's romantic aesthetic of the sublime, Ban Wang notes that most of Mao's poems "address the grand themes of revolution, history, and the destiny of the Chinese nation and people."[31] What I want to further emphasize is the peculiar significance that the ancient poetic formality held in the 1960s and 1970s. Creating an anachronistic relationship with the radicalization of Maoist cultural politics, the old style as an active cultural memory provided a symbolic value and communicative affect to the revolutionary discourse. As a founding poet of China's vernacular modern poetry, Guo ended up modernizing the traditional literati-scholar's function of commemoration and commentary and contributed to the making of an "esoteric form of communication."[32] Revolutionary modernity was in cohabitation with an old poetic tradition. In chapter 6, I focused on Guo's modernizing translation of ancient poetry, a translation of the ancient poetic language into a vernacularized/revolutionized aesthetics and knowledge. In Guo–Mao poetic exchanges, we are confronted with a reversed translation, a translation of revolutionary content into traditional form, of contemporary exigencies into ancient codes.

Through the allegorical facades of ancient forms and references, the twilight of the Chinese revolutionary century can be seen as an extreme experience of historicity marked with an anachronistic translation of the ancient. Regarding the Maoist criticism of Confucianism, Weigelin-Schwiedrzik suggests that Maoism introduced the traditional view of "reversibility" into the modern outlook of linear evolution, and as a result "deviates from the basic Marxist belief in the irreversibility."[33] But the experience of historical repetition and translation is actually central to the Marxist revolutionary consciousness in general. Commenting on the imitation of the ancient in bourgeois modernity, Marx once famously described the repetition of the tragic as the farcical, and emphasized the inevitability of the "translation" of the new into an ancient language or form. Only in this light can the content and form of the Guo–Mao poetic exchanges be fully understood. The Zeitgeist that Guo—and Mao—had

31. Ban Wang, *The Sublime Figure of History*, 108.
32. Weigelin-Schwiedrzik, "The Campaign to Criticize Lin Biao and Confucius," 171.
33. Ibid., 159.

been eager and confident to grasp was exhausted by a tragic-farcical "translation" of the ancient. The irruption and vanishing of the political subjectivity at the end of China's revolutionary century was thus overdetermined by a confusion or coexistence of multiple historical lineages. In his final "supreme instructions," delivered from late 1975 through early 1976, Mao once again stressed the need to move beyond the "bourgeois democratic revolution"; interestingly, his argument for more revolutions extending into the next "one thousand years" was wrapped up with a reading list on ancient Chinese thought: "In addition, one may want to look into the pro-Confucius, anti-Legalist component of the senior Guo's *Ten Critiques*."[34] Thus reads one of the philosopher-king's final directives on revolution.

"Marx Enters the Temple of Confucius"

The jostling of historical-allegorical frames in the Mao–Guo dialogue also leads me to conclude with a summary of the ambivalent role of Confucianism in Guo's lifework. His modernization of Confucius/Confucianism is emblematic of a central theme of this book, that is, the cultural-political translation between antiquity and revolution, between national history and Western modernity. Let us flash back to 1925, during which Guo wrote a short piece scandalously titled "Marx Enters the Temple of Confucius" ("Makesi jin wen miao" 馬克斯進文廟).

It is a literary piece that defies easy categorization. As a short story, it lacks plot development and reads more like a philosophical dialogue or a polemical satire. Here is what happens in this work of fantasy: Marx pays a visit to the temple of Confucius, strangely located in modern Shanghai, while Confucius is eating the annual sacrificial offerings with his disciples. Confucius welcomes Marx: "To have friends coming in from far quarters, not a delight? Mr. Marx, do you have anything to teach me?" Marx then asks Confucius a widely debated question: "Is there any possibility that my ism will be fulfilled in a China that is permeated by your

34. Mao Zedong, "Mao zhuxi zhongyao zhishi," 487–88, 490.

thought?"[35] Marx indicates that for him, communism means a world where everyone can fully and freely develop his or her potential at the service of all of humanity.[36] Proposing his age-old idea of great universality or *datong*, Confucius sees no difference between his own social ideal and Marx's communism. Marx, in his turn, cautions against such a synthesis, maintaining that while Confucius's idea represents utopian socialism, Marxism offers scientific understanding of productive forces and social relations. Confucius then elaborates on his own economic thoughts, arguing that he discovered the rules of political economy as early as 2,000 years ago. Marx is convinced that in front of him stands a Chinese comrade of communism, but he continues to ask: "Then why do some people believe that my thought is in discordance with yours and cannot be implemented in China?"[37] Confucius replies with a sigh, indicating that actually the Chinese have only paid lip service to his ideas. As soon as he expresses admiration for Confucius, Marx decides to bid his goodbye; as he explains, he starts to miss his wife, Jenny. Confucius makes fun of Marx's attachment to monogamous marriage. Referring to his own ideas of solidarity and fraternity, Confucius jokingly says: "Your wife can be my wife." Marx is surprised, if not frightened. "Your thought is more dangerous than mine."[38] These are his final words to Confucius.

This piece testifies to Guo's apprenticeship in Marxist social theory; in particular, it bears an unmistakable influence of the Japanese Marxist Kawakami Hajime's focus on the productive forces and the accumulation of capital.[39] Although some of Guo's peers reproached him for overemphasizing Confucius's socialist ideal and overlooking the incommensurability between Confucianism and Marxism, one may even see the piece as an early attempt to Sinicize Marxism.[40] I want to draw particular attention to the imaginative structure underneath this unlikely translatability between Confucianism and Marxism. I propose to define Guo's historical fantasy as a rhetorical performance of transcultural anachronism. It is fascinating to note that Guo did not forget to mention the

35. Guo, "Makesi jin wen miao," in *GQJ/W*, 10:162.
36. Ibid., 164.
37. Ibid., 168.
38. Ibid., 169.
39. Ibid., 165. Also see Kawakami Hajime, *Shehui zuzhi yu shehui geming.*
40. See, for example, Tao Qiqing, "Makesi daodi buneng jin Wen Miao."

necessary existence of interpreters in this conjectured conversation between Marx and Confucius.[41] While poking fun at the arrogance and insufficiency of the early Chinese translators of Marxist thought, in fact the narrator of this piece is the true "interpreter" behind this ahistorical encounter.[42] In concluding this book, I would go as far as to argue that Guo's cultural-political practice as a whole embodied the function of that "interpreter," that is, an interpretative mechanism intrinsic to the Chinese Revolution, imaginatively communicating between the national and the foreign and provocatively coalescing different historical temporalities.

A lot of ink has been spilled about the attitudes of modern Chinese intellectuals toward Confucianism.[43] On one hand, Guo's praise of Confucianism seems to form a contrast to the antitraditional trend; on the other hand, it should not be confused with the traditionalist or neo-Confucian defense of Confucius. Levenson refers to Guo's critique of "both traditionalists and westerners" in a discussion of communist China's "iconoclast-nativist synthesis."[44] Xiaoming Chen's study situates Guo's mingling of Confucianism and communism in the May Fourth search for a "solution to the issue of Chinese tradition versus Western modernity."[45] He argues: "Guo's continuity with Confucianism tells us that the May Fourth intellectual movement was not . . . anti-traditional."[46] Chen's questioning of the rigid division between modernity and tradition also resonates with Levenson's argument about Chinese communism as a combination of Chinese-ness and revolutionary cosmopolitanism. Going one step further, my book has been an examination of this transcultural anachronism that energizes a new historical imagination and brings together Marx, Confucius, and Chinese modernity.

41. Guo, "Makesi jin wen miao," in *GQJ/W*, 10:162.

42. Ibid., 165.

43. For an account of May Fourth anti-Confucianism, see Chou, *The May Fourth Movement*, 300–314. For the continuity between late imperial Confucianism and the Chinese Revolution, see Mizoguchi Yuzo, *Zhongguo shixiang shi*, 164–70.

44. Levenson, *Confucian China and Its Modern Fate*, 1:141.

45. Xiaoming Chen, *From the May Fourth Movement to Communist Revolution*, 110.

46. Ibid., 4.

Guo's modernizing reportrayal of Confucius can be traced all the way back to the beginning of his literary career. Amid the May Fourth iconoclastic current, he never shied away from his worship of the personality of Confucius and the social-political ideal of Confucianism. As I mentioned in chapter 3, the young Guo ranked Confucius with Goethe. In his cosmopolitan perspective, Confucius is a political thinker of *datong*, a "philosopher of pantheism," a musician, an educator of citizenship, a preserver of vernacular poetry.[47] In a 1923 essay "On the Traditional Spirit of Chinese Culture" (originally written in Japanese and published in Chinese), the young Guo was generous with his effusive words for Confucius. "We worship Confucius." He stated: "As for those who say that we are *anachronistic*, we have to let them say so, but we still worship Confucius—in a way entirely incompatible to the psychological condition of blindly taking pleasures in the antiques. What we see in Confucius is a genius combining Kant and Goethe, a harmoniously developed personality, a giant of ever-new life. He developed his own individuality to the extreme."[48] Based on this eulogy, Guo defined the spirit of Chinese tradition: "Under the vision of pantheism, to purify oneself and enrich oneself to the utmost, and aspiring for the godlike greatness and benevolence, to strive for the unity of the human compatriots around the globe and the fulfillment of the world republic."[49]

Perhaps no other modern evaluations of Confucius can be more utopian and visionary. Differing from the May Fourth positivistic and enlightenment approaches, Guo's preference of original Confucianism is a crucial yet neglected proof of the transcultural "hermeneutic radicalism" that pervaded the force-field of the May Fourth New Culture in particular and the discursive regime of China's long revolution in general.[50] To extrapolate what I suggested in chapter 4, for Guo, the valorization of modern enlightenment was inseparable from a romantic reimagination of history. Mixing Kant and Goethe, anarchism and pantheism, romantic nostalgia and modern individualism, the reinterpretation of the Con-

47. See Guo, Tian, and Zong, *San ye ji*, 12–15.

48. Guo, "Zhongguo wenhua zhi chuantong jingshen," in *GQJ/L*, 3:259, emphasis added.

49. Ibid., 262.

50. Zhang Xudong, "Wu si yu zhongguo xiandaixing wenhua de jijin quanshi xue," 12.

fucian *datong* myth in Guo's pre-Marxist work prioritized a subjectivity of cultural-political imagination.

In his early years Guo did not refrain from the tendency for anachronism, but after being baptized in Marxist historicism, he came to see anachronism as an intellectual fallacy. In his historical studies in the 1920s and 1930s, he distanced himself from the *datong* myth, as he came to doubt the historical existence of the well-field system in ancient China. Nevertheless, as I have shown in chapter 5, Confucianism appeared as an ancient spirit of "people's liberation" in his rewriting of pre-Qin history during the 1940s. Hence Marx indeed enters the temple of Confucius in a historiographical sense. In this genealogy of revolutionization of Confucianism, tradition and modernity do not form a simple lineage of continuity or rupture; rather, it is the cultural-political vibration of the present that constantly reinvents the ancient and transcodes the foreign. The figure of Confucius is more of a catalyst, metaphor, and fulcrum for Guo's evolving vision of communism, social revolution, and the people's liberation. On this note, I want to bring his translation of *Faust* and his argument for revolutionary Confucianism into parallel. The interpretation of the Faustian tragedy as an evolution of the modern Zeitgeist, on one hand, and the progressive appraisal of Confucius's role in pre-Qin China, on the other, formed the same discourse of people-centrism as an intervention within the leftist articulation of "people's democracy." It has been the task of this book to interrogate these dialectical interactions of translation, historical imagination, and revolution.

"Revolutionary Romanticism" and the Problem of Reversibility/Translatability

The reimagination of Confucianism as a critique of the present leads us back to Michael Löwy's thesis on the affinity between the communist revolutionary outlook and romanticism. My discussion of Guo's translingual-anachronistic interventions then needs to have a final confrontation with the problem of revolutionary romanticism. No critical accounts of Guo's lifework can afford avoiding the term "revolutionary romanticism" (*geming langmanzhuyi* 革命浪漫主義). Just as preexisting

Chinese studies on Guo have long been bound up with various conceptions of revolutionary romanticism, scholars in the English-speaking world generalize his journey as a transition from "romanticism to Marxism-Leninism" and see him as a typical "left romantic."[51] It is always tempting to explain away Guo's work by recognizing it as a rendezvous of revolution and romanticism, but it does not say much unless one further problematizes the label of "revolutionary romanticism" and trace its genealogy. I deem it necessary to conclude this study with a theoretical reflection on revolutionary romanticism as an aesthetic tendency, as a spiritual structure, and ultimately as a malaise of the historical imagination in twentieth-century China that has loomed in the background of all my preceding discussions.

With the birth of the leftist literary movement, the phrase "revolutionary romanticism" came into wide circulation in China. The advent of revolutionary literature at the end of the 1920s was accompanied by a critical reevaluation of romanticism. During the "revolutionary literature debates," romanticism was denounced as an internal malaise of the Chinese left. This was clearly shown in Qu Qiubai's critique of "the revolutionary romantic" (*geming de luomandike* 革命的羅曼諦克) in his 1932 essay of the same title. In this review of Creationist Yang Hansheng's fictional works, Qu reproached a tendency of "Schillerism" for mystifying the reality and using personalities as mouthpieces of revolutionary ideas: "Such romanticism is an obstacle to the emergence of new literature."[52] As may be recalled from chapter 5, Marx criticized the Schillerian style, which imposes an abstractly or subjectively imagined "spirit of the times" on historical details. In Qu's Marxist jargon, "Schillerism" became the code name for a dubious revolutionary romanticism.

If Qu's analysis saw romanticism as a petit-bourgeois ethos, then Zhou Yang's perspective redeemed romanticism as a method of literary imagination. In contrast to Qu, he suggested that revolutionary romanticism be a necessary complement to realism. Romanticism was no longer considered petit-bourgeois idealism but an aesthetic "trend" or an "element." Clarifying the difference of his use of this phrase from Qu's,

51. See Roy, *Kuo Mo-jo*, 134–61; Lee, *The Romantic Generation of Modern Chinese Writers*, 283–86.

52. Qu Qiubai, "Geming de luomandike," 459.

Zhou indicates that "revolutionary romanticism [*geming de langmanzhuyi* 革命的浪漫主義] is an element intrinsic to socialist realism."[53] In his praise of the colorful allegories in the Russian literary master Maxim Gorky's romanticism, it becomes clear that what he meant by romanticism was a literary method, mode, or style associated with subjective imagination and fantasy. Qu banished romanticism as subjectivism from revolutionary literature, but Zhou reserved a place of revolutionary fantasy for romanticism.

Zhou's idea of revolutionary romanticism was apparently a Chinese variation of the Soviet discourse of "positive romanticism" as a visionary view of history. This perspective predetermined a critical language in the canonization of Guo's early pantheistic work in China's leftist cultural tradition.[54] Furthermore, it is along this line that Mao, more than two decades later, schematized his idea of the "antithetical synthesis of revolutionary realism and revolutionary romanticism" against the backdrop of the feverish Great Leap Forward.[55] It is evident that this promotion of revolutionary romanticism was a literary correlative of Maoist voluntarism in historical practice in the age of socialist revolution.

Guo, a veteran of May Fourth romanticism who kept silent about romanticism and paid lip service to realism from the 1930s onward, expressed his feeling of liberation on receiving Mao's latest instruction in 1958: "Comrade Mao Zedong's poetry . . . has restored the reputation of romanticism. As a result, I can admit frankly that I am a romantic. I had no such courage in the past thirty years."[56] By the "past thirty years," he obviously referred to the period during which revolutionary literature was dominated by the discourse of realism. This announcement comes from his 1958 essay "Romanticism and Realism" ("Langmanzhuyi he

53. Zhou Yang, "Guanyu shehuizhuyi de xianshizhuyi yu geming de langmanzhuyi," 113.

54. See, again, Zhou Yang, "Guo Moruo he ta de Nüshen," in *GZL*, 669–75.

55. Mao proposed the "antithetical synthesis of realism and romanticism" in a speech in Chengdu in 1958. The speech was not published, but Zhou Yang disseminated this proposal as the "combination of revolutionary realism and revolutionary romanticism." See Zhou Yang, "Xin minge kaituo le shige de xin daolu," 462. Also see Hong Zicheng, *Zhongguo dangdai wenxue shi*, 178–81. For a detailed study of Maoist literary policies and the rise of revolutionary romanticism, see Fokkema, *Literary Doctrine in China and Soviet Influence*, chapter 6.

56. Guo, "Langmanzhuyi he xianshizhuyi," in *GQJ/W*, 17:10.

xianshizhuyi" 浪漫主義和現實主義), one of the first elaborations on Mao's ideal of the realism-romanticism combination.

"Romanticism and Realism" opens with Guo's argument that realism and romanticism are often undistinguishable from each other in literary creations. According to Guo, Qu Yuan, Marx, and Lu Xun are all realists and romanticists at one and the same time. What follows is then Guo's effusive celebration of Mao the poet as the "supreme exemplar" of "the combination of revolutionary realism and revolutionary romanticism."[57] All this later became the cliché in the industry of socialist literary criticism. Rather than consigning this piece to the trash bin of history, I suggest that we pay more attention to the ways Guo revalorized romanticism at that historical moment. First, it should be immediately noticed that in Guo both realism and romanticism, as two aesthetic concepts, are stripped of any historical content or reference. Instead, they are generalized or even psychologized into two aspects of creative ethos: realism means being rational and objective, romanticism being subjective and idealist. Second, with these two generalized dispositions of creativity, he argues that the attainment of the combination of realism and romanticism has nothing to do with styles, techniques, or methods of artistic creation, but only concerns the transformation of one's political consciousness. Third and last, as his idea of romanticism now hinges on an intensive interfusion between subjectivity and history, Guo's essay takes another turn and evolves into a narrative account of his own participation in the Great Leap Forward Movement in a county in Zhangjiakou, northwest to Beijing. His observation concludes with a characterization of his epoch: "The current age of the Great Leap Forward should be recognized as a revolutionary-romantic epoch, and also a revolutionary-realist epoch. The reality advances much ahead of artists and writers."[58] So romanticism and realism now become the characteristics of a revolutionary age, reminiscent of Guo's formula of the Zeitgeist. Let us look at the romantic nature of the age depicted by Guo:

> How intimate is the human-to-human relation nowadays! . . . A new social relation pervades and expands in a very lively way, making everyone

57. Ibid., 9.
58. Ibid., 14.

> feel enthusiastic. Grasses, trees, birds and animals; mountains, rocks, mines; I suspect that they all have sensed this atmosphere of the new age. Look: with the [East] wind, pigs are growing, fruits are growing, crops are growing, and steel is growing, as if they were also making effort to accomplish the General Guideline, and in doing so, they were achieving an intimate solidarity with each other.[59]

This is where a theoretical essay on romanticism reveals itself to be a revolutionary-romantic work in its own right. Whereas in Zhou Yang's theory romanticism should only be a complementary element within realism, in Guo's account there is no contradiction between subjective fantasy and history. Rather, a surreal pantheism of political subjectivity is supposed to lie at the heart of the configuration of the real.[60] Inviting us to experience the fantastic as the real, the rhetoric of this "revolutionary-romantic epoch" interestingly bears a striking resemblance to the early Guo's pantheistic idea of the ancient *datong* communism.

According to the Soviet tradition of Marxist aesthetic theory, "Marx's and Engels' analysis of West European romanticism" distinguished two faces of the post–French Revolution development: "Considering romanticism a reflection of the age beginning after the Great French Revolution, of all its inherent social contradictions, [Marx and Engels] distinguished between revolutionary romanticism, which rejected capitalism and was striving towards the future, and romantic criticism of capitalism from the point of view of the past."[61] Clearly, this orthodox definition highlights "revolutionary romanticism" as a historical imagination that is closely related to utopian traditions. A more recent theorization of revolutionary romanticism by Michael Löwy and Robert Sayre reformulates this perspective of historical imagination, as I mentioned in chapter 4. Despite the diverse and sometimes self-contradictory manifestations of romanticism in different contexts and periods (romanticism, for example, is "simultaneously [or alternately] revolutionary and counterrevolutionary"), Löwy and Sayre redefine romanticism as a critique of

59. Ibid., 14–15.

60. For a discussion of similar subject articulations and ensuing lyricism in Maoist China, see Cai Xiang, *Revolution and Its Narratives*, 154.

61. Krylov, "Preface," 33.

capitalistic modernity that mobilizes the imagination of an idealized past and sometimes involves a vision of utopian redemption.[62] They argue that Marxism has an ambivalent attitude of "attraction/repulsion with respect to Romanticism."[63] The striving toward the future is inseparable from the critical revival of a lost past: "The Marxist conception of socialism is intimately connected with this radical critique of modern civilization. It implies a qualitative change, a new social culture, a new way of life, a different type of civilization that would reestablish the role of the 'human and natural qualities' of life."[64]

Although the case of Chinese romanticism is missing in Löwy and Sayre's account, Guo's utopian phantasmagoria of the socialist leap forward evidently produced yet another romantic-scientific perspective: the social transformation based on scientific Marxism prepares the conditions for a re-enchantment—rather than disenchantment—of human relations that defies realist representation. His early pantheism transformed into a socialist animism: every natural and social object actively sensed the "atmosphere of the new age." As Guo's utopian fantasy had once been a remystification of prehistorical *datong*, in the late 1950s it was posited as a "primal leap" into socialist actuality.[65] He also contributed to the campaign for revolutionary romanticism by hailing the Maoist "new folk songs" as "today's *Airs of the States* and tomorrow's *Songs of the South*."[66] The futuristic experience of the immediate leap into socialism demanded the ancient exemplars.

Leo Lee has discerned a romantic outlook among some modern Chinese writers of the 1920s: "What is emphasized in this outlook is impulse, not result; motive, not objective; creative will, not retrospective analysis; feeling and sensitivity, not reason and ritualization."[67] This outlook, one may say, partially merged into Maoist utopianism, which led to

62. Löwy and Sayre, *Romanticism Against the Tide of Modernity*, 1.

63. Ibid., 88.

64. Ibid., 98.

65. Here, I link the Maoist-romantic conception of the Great Leap Forward with the meaning of *Ursprung*/origin, that is, a primal leap into being.

66. Guo, "Wei jintian de xin guofeng, mingtian de xin chuci huanhu," in *GQJ/W*, 17:156.

67. Lee, *The Romantic Generation of Modern Chinese Writers*, 295.

"one of the great utopian episodes in world history."[68] According to Maurice Meisner's account of the Great Leap Forward vision of the future, the "idyllic and almost pastoral vision of communism [in Marxism] was entirely in harmony with the Maoist expectation of the time that 'new men' of 'all-round' abilities would soon produce a [new] society."[69] Guo's discourse had little to do with the idealization of "ascetic values" in Maoism, but it obviously reinforced a revolutionary-romantic historical imagination within Maoism.[70]

But during the Cultural Revolution, this supporter of Mao's revolutionary romanticism secretly picked up the practice of literary translation. In 1969, Guo translated fifty short modern English poems from a selection of English poetry he had received as a gift from a Japanese friend. His translations were handwritten as marginalia on the pages of the book and were discovered posthumously and published as late as 1981. Guo may have done his translations simply as a pastime. But the resumption of poetic translation as a private hobby came at a personally and politically acute moment. The translations were accomplished either right before or after the Ninth National Congress of the CCP, in which Mao declared the victory of the Cultural Revolution and Guo was promoted to the Central Committee. The use of a vernacular language and colorful rhetoric in Guo's artistic "wrestling"[71] with those English, Scottish, and Irish poets, as many have noted, formed a stark contrast to the three hyperbolic poems he wrote about the same time in a traditional tune of *man jiang hong* in commemoration of the Ninth National Congress. It is also interesting to note that, like his private translation drafts, these ancient-style poems, although being political-propagandist in nature, were not intended for publication. So on one hand, he hailed the "continued revolution under the dictatorship of the proletariat" and expressed an identification with Maoist politics ("China will be red for thousands of generations to come, / And the proletariat will be young forever, never getting old"; "The Congress of solidarity is as timely as the rain, and there is the hope

68. Meisner, *Marxism, Maoism, and Utopianism*, xii.

69. Ibid., 192.

70. See ibid., chapter 4. Also see Hong Zicheng, *Zhongguo dangdai wenxue shi*, chapter 13.

71. Cheng Fangwu, "Xu," i.

for opening up a new universe"), fulfilling the role of a gramophone.[72] On the other hand, he privately wrote down his rendition of Wordsworth's "Daffodils."

Moreover, according to the comments Guo handwrote about some of those poems, he distanced himself from the acclaimed romantics such as Wordsworth, criticizing the latter for the "cheap pedagogic words"—a criticism that ironically seems to be equally suitable to his own revolutionary lyrics.[73] Rather, the poem he seemed to love most among those translations was Irish poet Charles Wolfe's "The Burial of Sir John Moore at Corunna," which Guo found "concrete," "unmannered," and "moving":

> But we steadfastly gazed on the face that was dead,
> And we bitterly thought of the morrow.
>
> 我們堅定地凝視著死者的面，
> 只沉痛地在想到明天。[74]
>
> [We steadfastly gazed on the face of the dead / And bitterly we thought of nothing but tomorrow.]

No contrast is sharper than this bitter thought of tomorrow with the same translator-poet's political hope of a red universe. One may link the mourning mood to the tragic loss of Guo's two sons during the Cultural Revolution. As a worshiper of the starry sky of pantheistic life and the reddened universe of revolution, he now admired Russell Green's "Meditations" on "the stars": "I could not bow before infinity, / The silent grandeur could not conquer me." Guo's comment is worthy of notice: "I have had similar feelings, but impure."[75] The ambiguous relationship of such translations with his other later works in Maoist China points to the complexity of the social existence of this senior revolutionary literati-scholar. The reversal or reversibility between a moment of translation as melancholy self-reflection on one hand and an internalized function of political commemoration on the other also forces one to ask: was Guo's revolutionary romanticism, torn between party propaganda and

72. Cited in Feng Xigang, *Guo Moruo de wannian suiyue*, 202, 203.
73. Guo, trans., *Ying shi yi gao*, 35.
74. Ibid., 135, 132, 133.
75. Ibid., 114, 115.

individual authenticity, exempt of aesthetic-political seriousness and substance?

The revolutionary-romantic imagination seems therefore vulnerable to a criticism based on Carl Schmitt's famous theory of "political romanticism." With a penetrating diagnosis of the German romantics, Schmitt discovers an "occasionalist structure of romanticism:" "By means of a simple reversal, the [romantic] subject has become the creator of the world. It designates as the world only what served it as the occasion of an experience."[76] This occasionalism leads to an unduly liberal subjectivity that is directed to "a kind of lyrical paraphrase of experience." Although agitated and excited, this subjectivity exists "without making its own decision and assuming its responsibility and risk;"[77] "where political activity begins, political romanticism ends."[78] In other words, political romanticism ironically means an aestheticization/depoliticization of subjectivity: "political romanticism is apolitical."[79]

On the surface, Guo's case seems to fall into Schmitt's categorization of "subjective occasionalism," given the multiple reversals of his positions and the large number of the occasional works he composed. Some of Guo's works may well be read as a surrender to the ever-changing political winds. In his later work, this ironic actualization of the Shelleyan model of the lyre spiraled into an aesthetic scandal, which seems to confirm Schmitt's criticism: "[The] superiority [of political romanticism] over present, which is taken in a purely occasional fashion, undergoes an extremely ironical reversal: Everything that is romantic is at the disposal of other energies that are unromantic, and the sublime elevation above definition and decision is transformed into a subservient attendance upon alien power and alien decision."[80]

On closer inspection, however, Schmitt's emphasis on the political romantic's "incapacity to hold fast to an important political idea" is not applicable to the Chinese case.[81] Whereas the representatives of German romanticism Schmitt studies seldom took part in revolutionary activism

76. Schmitt, *Political Romanticism*, 97.
77. Ibid., 159.
78. Ibid., 160.
79. Oakes, "Translator's Introduction," xxxi.
80. Schmitt, *Political Romanticism*, 162.
81. The quote is from Schmitt, *Political Romanticism*, 51.

(but sometimes ensnared themselves in conservative politics), Guo's lifework was punctuated by a series of political decisions and interventions at critical moments of the long Chinese Revolution. Guo's aesthetical-political ethos of self-conscious submission, displaying a paradox of activeness/passiveness, was not opportunism but meant a subjectivity of metamorphosis (*tuibian*, in Guo's and Feng Zhi's terms) and a fidelity to party politics. Nor was the romantic productivity of his cultural practice only a "concomitant emotive response to political events."[82] One only needs to recall his returns to translating *Faust* in 1927–28 and 1947, respectively. In both cases, his "retreats" from direct political activity embodied decisive interventions into the ambiguous conjunctures of revolutionary standstill. Then in his "subservience" to the Maoist power, the poetic occasion shows an ambivalent structure of simultaneous politicization and lyricization (depoliticization) at the center of China's revolutionary century. A partisan fidelity led to his ancient-style poetic translation of Maoist discourse, whose propagandist lyricism ironically became alienated from political actuality, whereas his final melancholy practice of translation as an occasional retreat from the party-state may have contained an untimely return of the truly political potential of lyric poetry.

Such a dialectic of occasionalism and decisionism is what I have tried to capture in the relationship between Guo's career and the making of a revolutionary culture. Its central mechanism can be characterized as a translation, transcoding, or transformation of a series of historical conjunctures into a now-time pregnant with the unstable, mutable momentum of political intervention and occasional lyricization. This book has focused on the interpenetration of translation and historical imagination in Guo's lifework in response to the changeful field of political possibilities. At the core of the cultural legacy of China's revolutionary century, there is a deep mode of translation as historical imagination, as can be seen in Guo's translation of *Faust*; there is also a poetics of history as translation, revealed in subversive rewritings of national antiquity. In this sense, the significance of Guo's case as a Chinese prototype of revolution-

82. Ibid., 58.

ary romanticism consists in the experience, imagination, or production of "the now of translatability."[83]

To summarize this revolutionary-romantic mode, I turn again to the Chinese character *fan*, which links together the domains of translation, hermeneutic reversal, revolutionary subversion, and self-transformation. "Here everything can be substituted for everything else."[84] Thus Carl Schmitt complains of the occasional character of romanticized objects, just as Antoine Berman discovers in the same early German romantics the "method of reversal" and the "principle of the translatability of everything into everything."[85] For Schmitt, this kind of translatability/reversibility shows the "untruthfulness" of "romantic productivity."[86] Insofar as Guo's case is concerned, however, the cultural logic of translatability/reversibility shows both the productivity and destructiveness of *fan*, and must be recognized as an unstable occasion or a permanent crisis of the political actuality and truthfulness of the Revolution—a crisis within which subjectivity figures and simultaneously vanishes, is intensified and simultaneously instrumentalized.

My study has tried to demonstrate how the logic of translatability/reversibility took form historically and rhetorically as an inner symptom and structure of the Chinese Revolution. I started this book with a periodization of the Chinese Revolution as multiple temporalities compressed into a short century. Now I conclude by contending that this revolutionary century gave rise to and hinged on a problematic translatability and reversibility of the Zeitgeist. I challenged the one-dimensional views of China's revolutionary culture as destructive romanticism or derailed propaganda. I showed how the lyrical sovereignty functioned as "history's lyre" between creative writing and translation. I traced the translingual imprints of the experience of revolutionary crises. I unearthed in Guo's translation of *Faust* some key moments of linguistic-poetic inventions and cultural-political interventions. I argued that the rewritings of ancient history produced new contestations or imaginations about the leftist

83. This phrase is based on Walter Benjamin's idea of "the now of recognizability" underlying the "actuality of genuine historiography." See Benjamin, "Paralipomena to 'On the Concept of History,'" 405.

84. Schmitt, *Political Romanticism*, 158.

85. Berman, *The Experience of the Foreign*, 77, 82.

86. Schmitt, *Political Romanticism*, 158, 159.

agenda. I also demonstrated how a reinterpretation of classical poetry exhausted the energies of literary-political reversal. I hope this book offers some new methodologies and perspectives that do at least partial justice to its challenging subject matter and help demarcate the dialectics and impasses of translation, historical imagination, and revolution. I am conscious that my approach is not innocent but derives from a desire for new cultural translation/transcoding. Most important, the issue of translatability/reversibility calls for more contemporary debates on the complexity of a bygone revolutionary century.

Bibliography

Writings by Guo Moruo

"Bili shan tou zhanwang" 筆立山頭展望 [Panorama from Fudetate Yama]. In *N*, 97–98.

"*Cai Wenji* xu" 《蔡文姬》序 [Preface to *Cai Wenji*]. In *GQJ/W*, vol. 8, 3–12.

"Can chun" 殘春 [Lingering spring]. In *GQJ/W*, vol. 9, 20–35.

"Chen an" 晨安 [Good morning]. In *N*, 93–96.

"Chi fandong wenyi" 斥反動文藝 [A refutation of reactionary literature and art]. In *GQJ/W*, vol. 16, 288–96.

Chuangzao shinian 創造十年 [The ten years of the Creation Society]. In *GQJ/W*, vol. 12.

Chuangzao shinian xubian 創造十年續編 [The ten years of the Creation Society: a sequel]. In *GQJ/W*, vol. 12.

"Chuangzao zhe" 創造者 [The creator]. *Chuangzao jikan* 創造季刊 [Creation quarterly] 1, no. 1 (1922): 1–4.

"Chun zhi taidong" 春之胎動 [Fetal stirrings of spring]. In *N*, 212–14.

"Cong dianxing shuo qi" 從典型說起 [To begin with type]. In *GQJ/W*, vol. 16, 195–200.

"Da Sun Mingchuan jun" 答孫銘傳君 [A reply to Mr. Sun Mingchuan]. *Chuangzao ri huikan* 創造日匯刊 [Creation daily: a compilation, 1923]: 205–10.

"De le anxi" 得了安息 [Resting in peace]. In *GQJ/W*, vol. 1, 372–73.

"*Deyizhi yishixingtai* xu" 《德意志意識形態》 序 [Preface to the *German Ideology*]. In Karl Marx and Friedrich Engels, *Deyizhi yishixingtai* 德意志意識形態 [The German ideology], translated by Guo Moruo, i. Shanghai: Qunyi-Haiyan-Yunhai, 1947.

"Di er bu yi hou ji" 第二部譯後記 [Translator's postscript to Part II]. In Goethe, *Fushide di er bu*, translated by Guo Moruo, 384–88.

"Diqiu, wo de muqin" 地球，我的母親 [O Earth, my mother]. In *N*, 116–19.

Fanzheng qianhou 反正前後 [Around the time of the 1911 revolution]. In *GQJ/W*, vol. 11.

"Feng huang niepan" 鳳凰涅槃 [The nirvana of the Feng and Huang]. In *N*, 43–79.

Five Historical Plays. Translated by Peng Fumin, Bonnie McDougall, Yang Xianyi, and Gladys Yang. Beijing: Foreign Languages Press, 1984.

"Fushide jian lun" 浮士德簡論 [A concise interpretation of *Faust*]. In Goethe, *Fushide* 浮士德 [Faust], translated by Guo Moruo, 3–14. Beijing: Renmin wenxue, 1978.
"Geming yu wenxue" 革命與文學 [Revolution and literature]. In *GQJ/W*, vol. 16, 32–43.
"Gu hong—zhi Cheng Fangwu de yifeng xin" 孤鴻—— 致成仿吾的一封信 [A letter from abroad: a letter to Cheng Fangwu]. In *GQJ/W*, vol. 16, 6–21.
"Gu shu jinyi wenti" 古書今譯問題 [The issue of modernizing translation of ancient works]. *Chuangzuo zhoubao* 創造週報 [Creation weekly], no. 37 (1924): 7–11.
"Guan ju de fanyi" 《關雎》的翻譯 [A translation of "The Ospreys Cry"]. In *GQJ/W*, vol. 1, 360–61.
"Gudai shehui yanjiu da ke nan" 古代社會研究答客難 [On the study of ancient society: a reply]. In *GQJ/L*, vol. 3, 416–20.
"Gui guo za yin" 歸國雜吟 [Random lines on coming back to homeland]. In *GQJ/W*, vol. 2, 44–48.
"Guilai" 歸來 [Homecoming]. In *GQJ/W*, vol. 1, 369–71.
Guo Moruo quan ji, kaogu bian 郭沫若全集•考古編 [Complete works, volumes of archeological works]. 10 vols. Beijing: Kexue chubanshe, 1982 (abbreviated *GQJ/K*).
Guo Moruo quan ji, lishi bian 郭沫若全集•歷史編 [Complete works, volumes of historical works]. 8 vols. Beijing: Renmin chubanshe, 1982 (abbreviated *GQJ/L*).
Guo Moruo quan ji, wenxue bian 郭沫若全集•文學編 [Complete works, volumes of literary works]. 20 vols. Beijing: Renmin wenxue, 1982 (abbreviated *GQJ/W*).
"Guo Moruo shizuo tan" 郭沫若詩作談 [An interview with Guo Moruo on poetry]. In *GZL*, edited by Wang Xunzhao et al., 212–20.
Guo Moruo shuxin ji 郭沫若書信集 [A collection of Guo Moruo's letters]. Edited by Huang Dunhao 黄敦浩. Beijing: Zhongguo shehui kexue, 1992.
"Guo Moruo tongzhi da qingnian wen" 郭沫若同志答青年問 [Comrade Guo Moruo answers youths' questions]. In *GZL*, edited by Wang Xunzhao et al., 342–47.
"Guo Moruo tongzhi jiu 'Li Bai yu Du Fu' yi shu gei Hu Zengwei tongzhi de fu xin" 郭沫若同志就《李白與杜甫》一書給胡曾偉同志的複信 [Comrade Guo Moruo's letter to Comrade Hu Zengwei concerning *Li Bai and Du Fu*]. Cited in *GHY*, edited by Yang Shengkuan and Cai Zhen, vol. 9, 581.
Guo Moruo yi wen ji 郭沫若佚文集 [Uncollected works of Guo Moruo]. Edited by Wang Jinhou 王錦厚 et al. Chengdu: Sichuan daxue chubanshe, 1988.
"Guzhu jun zhi er zi" 孤竹君之二子 [Two princes of Guzhu]. *Chuangzao jikan* 1, no. 4 (1923): 1–25.
"Hei mao" 黑貓 [A black cat]. In *GQJ/W*, vol. 11, 277–316.
"Houji" 後記 [Postscript]. In Goethe, *Fushide*, translated by Guo Moruo, 1–5 (the postscript is independently numbered). Shanghai: Xiandai shuju, 1930.
"Huifu" 恢復 [Convalescence]. In *GQJ/W*, vol. 1, 355–57.
"Jiao hou ji zhi er" 校後記之二 [The second postscript after revision]. In *GQJ/W*, vol. 7, 129.
"Jinqian de moli" 金錢的魔力 [The magic power of money]. In *GQJ/W*, vol. 1, 406–8.
"*Juan'er ji* xu" 卷耳集序 [Preface to *Cockleburs*]. In *Juan'er ji*, translated by Guo Moruo, 1–6 (separate pagination). Shanghai: Taidong, 1923.
"*Juan'er ji* zi ba" 卷耳集自跋 [Author's postscript to *Cockleburs*]. In *GQJ/W*, vol. 5, 208.

"Kaermeiluo guniang" 喀爾美蘿姑娘 [Donna Carmela]. In *GQJ/W*, vol. 9, 205–38.
"Kan Sun Wukong san da Baigu Jing" 看孫悟空三打白骨精 [On seeing "The Monkey King's Three Combats with the White-Boned Demon"]. In *GQJ/W*, vol. 4, 326.
"Kexue de chuntian" 科學的春天 [Springtime of science]. *Renmin ribao* 人民日報 [People's daily], April 1, 1978.
"Kua zhe donghai" 跨著東海 [Across the East China Sea]. In *GQJ/W*, vol. 3, 305–41.
"Langmanzhuyi he xianshizhuyi" 浪漫主義和現實主義 [Romanticism and realism]. In *GQJ/W*, vol. 17, 3–18.
Li Bai yu Du Fu 李白與杜甫 [Li Bai and Du Fu]. Beijing: Renmin wenxue, 1972.
"Li Hu zhiqian" 離滬之前 [Before departing from Shanghai]. In *GQJ/W*, vol. 13, 272–304.
"Li zai diqiu bianshang fanghao" 立在地球邊上放號 [Shouting on the rim of the globe]. In *N*, 101.
Lishi renwu 歷史人物 [Historical characters]. Beijing: Renmin wenxue, 1979.
"Liushengji de huiyin" 留聲機的回聲 [The replying echo of the gramophone]. *Wenhua pipan* 文化批判 [Cultural critique], no. 3 (1928): 1–12.
"Lixing yu shouxing zhi zhan" 理性與獸性之戰 [The war between reason and bestiality]. In *GQJ/W*, vol. 18, 153–55.
"Lun shi san zha" 論詩三札 [Three letters on poetry]. In *GQJ/W*, vol. 15, 334–42.
"Lun shi tongxin" 論詩通信 [On poetry—a letter]. In *GZL*, edited by Wang Xunzhao et al., 111–14.
"Makesi jin wen miao" 馬克斯進文廟 [Marx enters the temple of Confucius]. In *GQJ/W*, vol. 10, 161–70.
"Man jiang hong, yijiuliusan nian yuandan shuhuai" 滿江紅，一九六三年元旦書懷 [Written on the New Year Day of 1963, to the tune of *Man jiang hong*]. In *GQJ/W*, vol. 4, 119–20.
"Minzhu yundong zhong de er san shi" 民主運動中的二三事 [Two or three things about the democratic movements]. In *GQJ/W*, vol. 20, 182–93.
Nanjing yinxiang 南京印象 [Impressions about Nanjing]. In *GQJ/W*, vol. 14.
Nüshen: juqu shige ji 女神：劇曲詩歌集 [The goddesses: a book of poetry and poetic drama]. Shanghai: Taidong, 1921 (Abbreviated *N*).
Nüshen huijiaoben 女神匯校本 [A critical edition of *The Goddesses*]. Edited by Sang Fengkang 桑逢康. Changsha: Hunan renmin, 1983.
"Nüshen zhi zaisheng" 女神之再生 [The rebirth of the goddesses]. In *N*, 1–17.
"Piaoliu sanbuqu" 漂流三部曲 [The trilogy of wandering]. In *GQJ/W*, vol. 9, 241–81.
"Pipan Yimenhu yiben ji qita" 批判 "意門湖" 譯本及其他 [Comments on the translation of *Immensee* and other matters]. *Chuangzao jikan* 1, no. 2 (1922): 23–36 (of the Criticism section).
"Qing kan jinri zhi Jiang Jieshi" 請看今日之蔣介石 [Look at today's Jiang Jieshi]. In *GQJ/W*, vol. 13, 127–52.
Qu Yuan. Translated by Yang Xianyi and Gladys Yang. In *Five Historical Plays*. Beijing: Foreign Languages Press, 1984.
"Qu Yuan yanjiu" 屈原研究 [A study of Qu Yuan]. In *Lishi renwu*, 7–106. Beijing: Renmin wenxue, 1979.
"Qu Yuan yu Liya Wang" 《屈原》與《釐雅王》 [*Qu Yuan* and *King Lear*]. In *GQJ/W*, vol. 6, 408–9.

"Ren hu, ren hu, hun xi guilai" 人乎，人乎，魂兮歸來 [Human, human, your soul come back]. In *GQJ/W*, vol. 19, 411–12.

"Renmin shiren Qu Yuan" 人民詩人屈原 [Qu Yuan, the poet of the people]. In *GQJ/W*, vol. 17, 230–38.

"Ri chu" 日出 [Sunrise]. In *N*, 91–92.

San ye ji 三葉集 [Kleeblatt]. Coauthored with Tian Shouchang 田壽昌 and Zong Baihua 宗白華. Shanghai: Yadong, 1920.

Selected Poems from The Goddesses. Translated by John Lester and A. C. Barnes. Beijing: Foreign Languages Press, 1958 (abbreviated *SPG*).

"Shaonian shidai xu" 《少年時代》序 [Preface to *The Epoch of My Early Years*, the first volume of *Autobiography*]. In *GQJ/W*, vol. 11, 3–4.

"Shaonian Weite zhi fannao xuyin" 少年維特之煩惱序引 [Translator's introduction to *The Sorrows of Young Werther*]. *Chuangzao jikan* 1, no. 1 (1922): 1–9 (independent pagination).

"Shi chen zai" 釋臣宰 [Interpreting *chen* and *zai*]. In *GQJ/K*, vol. 1, 65–78.

"Shi de xuanyan" 诗的宣言 [A manifesto of poetry]. In *GQJ/W*, vol. 1, 374–75.

Shi pipan shu 十批判書 [Ten critiques]. Beijing: Renmin chubanshe, 1954.

Shi ti 豕蹄 [Pig's trotters]. In *GQJ/W*, vol. 10.

"Shi zu bi" 釋祖妣 [Interpreting *zu* and *bi*]. In *GQJ/K*, vol. 1, 19–64.

"Shu huai" 述懷 [Expressing my feeling]. In *GQJ/W*, vol. 1, 358–59.

"Si de youhuo" 死的誘惑 [The lure of death]. In *N*, 190–91.

Suiyuan shi hua zhaji 隨園詩話札記 [Notes on *Suiyuan Discourses on Poetry*]. In *GQJ/W*, vol. 16.

"Taiyang lizhan" 太陽禮讚 [Hymn to the sun]. In *N*, 143–44.

"Ti Cao Cao fan'an" 替曹操翻案 [A reversal of the verdict on Cao Cao]. In *GQJ/L*, vol. 3, 457–76.

"Tian di xuan huang" 天地玄黄 [The sickness of the heaven and the earth]. In *GQJ/W*, vol. 20, 5–6.

"Tian gou" 天狗 [The heaven hound]. In *N*, 81–82.

"Tuoli Jiang Jieshi yihou" 脱離蔣介石以後 [After escaping from Jiang Jieshi]. In *GQJ/W*, vol. 13, 153–208.

"Venus." In *N*, 181.

"Wang Yangming lizan" 王陽明禮讚 [In praise of Wang Yangming]. In *GQJ/L*, vol. 3, 288–301.

"Wei jintian de xin guofeng, mingtian de xin chuci huanhu" 爲今天的新 "國風" 、明天的新 "楚辭" 歡呼 [Hail today's *Airs of the States* and tomorrow's *Songs of Chu*]. In *GQJ/W*, vol. 17, 155–56.

"Weida de aiguo shiren—Qu Yuan" 偉大的愛國詩人—— 屈原 [The great patriotic poet Qu Yuan]. In *GQJ/W*, vol. 17, 165–75.

"Wenxue geming zhi huigu" 文學革命之回顧 [A retrospective of the literary revolution]. In *Chuangzao she ziliao*, edited by Rao Hongjing et al., 551–53. Beijing: Zhishi chanquan, 2010.

Wo de tongnian 我的童年 [My childhood]. In *GQJ/W*, vol. 11.

"Wo de xuesheng shidai" 我的學生時代 [My days as a student]. In *GQJ/W*, vol. 12, 5–19.

"Wo de zuoshi de jingguo" 我的作詩的經過 [My experience of writing poetry]. In *GZL*, edited by Wang Xunzhao et al., 224–31.
"Wo duiyu 'Juan'er' yi shi de jieshi" 我對於卷耳一詩的解釋 [My interpretation of "The Cocklebur"]. In *Juan'er taolun ji*, edited by Cao Juren, 20–25. Shanghai: Liangxi tushuguan, 1925.
"Wo shi Zhongguo ren" 我是中國人 [I am a Chinese]. In *GQJ/W*, vol. 13, 342–74.
"Wo xiangqi le Chen She Wu Guang" 我想起了陳涉吳廣 [I think of Chen She and Wu Guang]. In *GQJ/W*, vol. 1, 378–81.
"Wo zenme xie Tang di zhi hua" 我怎麼寫《棠棣之花》 [How I wrote *Twin Flowers*]. In *GQJ/W*, vol. 6, 272–79.
"Wo zenyang xie wu mu shi ju Qu Yuan" 我怎樣寫五幕史劇《屈原》 [How I wrote *Qu Yuan*]. In *GQJ/W*, vol. 6, 397–404.
"Woguo sixiang shi shang zhi Pengpai cheng" 我國思想史上之澎湃城 [A Pompeii in the intellectual history of our nation]. In *Guo Moruo yi wen ji*, edited by Wang Jinhou et al., 67–81. Chengdu: Sichuan daxue chubanshe, 1988.
"Women de huayuan" 我們的花園 [Our own garden]. *Chuangzao jikan* 2, no. 1 (1923): n.p.
"Wuxia de huiyi" 巫峽的回憶 [The memory of the Wuxia Gorge]. In *GQJ/W*, vol. 1, 397–98.
"Xian gei xianshi de pantao" 獻給現實的蟠桃 [The peaches offered to reality]. In *GZL*, edited by Wang Xunzhao et al., 286–87.
"Xiao xu" 小序 [A short preface]. *Chuangzao jikan* 1, no. 4 (1923): 19–20 (Shelley section).
"Xie zai Sange panni de nüxing houmian" 寫在《三個叛逆的女性》後面 [Proscript to *The Three Rebellious Women*]. In *GQJ/W*, vol. 6, 134–49.
"Xiesidieli" 歇斯迭里 [Hysteria]. In *GQJ/W*, vol. 1, 362–63.
"Xin hua song" 新华颂 [A hymn of New China]. In *GQJ/W*, vol. 3, 3–4.
"Xin wenyi de shiming" 新文藝的使命 [The mission of new literature and art], in *GQJ/W*, vol. 19, 379.
"Xing kong" 星空 [The starry sky]. *Chuangzao jikan* 1, no. 2 (1922): 139–41.
"Xiyi de canmeng" 蜥蜴的殘夢 [A lizard's residual dream]. In *GQW/L*, vol. 3, 71–78.
"Xu shi" 序詩 [Introductory poem]. In *N*, i–ii.
"Xu wo de shi" 序我的詩 [Introduction to my poetry]. In *GQJ/W*, vol. 19, 404–10.
"Xue zhao" 雪朝 [Morning snow]. In *N*, 120–21.
"Xuexi Mao zhuxi" 學習毛主席 [Learn from Chairman Mao]. In *GQJ/W*, vol. 17, 278–81.
"*Yan tie lun duben* xu" 《鹽鐵論讀本》序 [Introduction to *A Reader of the Discourse on Salt and Iron*]. In *GQJ/L*, vol. 8, 471–78.
"Ye" 夜 [Night]. In *N*, 177–78.
"Ye bu shili songlin" 夜步十里松林 [Pacing through Jurimatsubara at night]. In *N*, 141.
"Yi hou" 譯後 [Translator's postscript]. In Goethe, *Fushide*, translated by Guo Moruo, 1–6 (independent pagination). Shanghai: Xiandai shuju, 1930.
"Yi wan le 'Hualunsitan' zhihou" 譯完了《華倫斯坦》之後 [After translating *Wallenstein*, 1936]. In Schiller, *Hualunsitan*, translated by Guo Moruo, 471–76. Beijing: Renmin wenxue, 1955.

Yingjie xin Zhongguo: Guo lao zai Xianggang zhandou shiqi de yiwen 迎接新中國：郭老在香港戰鬥時期的佚文 [Welcoming the New China: uncollected writings of Guo the senior during his fighting days in Hong Kong]. Edited by Shanghai tushuguan 上海圖書館 (Shanghai Library) and Fudan daxue zhongwen xi 復旦大學中文系 (the Chinese Department of Fudan University). Shanghai: Fudan xuebao, 1979.

"Yingjie yi jiu qi qi nian" 迎接一九七七年 [Welcome the year of 1977]. In *GQJ/W*, vol. 5, 148.

"Yingxiong shu" 英雄樹 [The hero tree]. In *GQJ/W*, vol. 16, 44–50.

"Yinyi zhong tuxing wenzi zhi yi jie" 殷彝中圖象文字之一解 [Pictographs in the Shang bronze inscriptions: an interpretation]. In *GQJ/K*, vol. 4, 11–20.

"Yizhe bianyan" 譯者弁言 [Translator's introduction]. In Karl Marx and Friedrich Engels, *Deyizhi yishixingtai*, translated by Guo Moruo, 1–7. Shanghai: Qunyi-Haiyan-Yunhai, 1947.

"You Hu fu shuodao beiju jingshen" 由《虎符》說到悲劇精神 [From *The Tiger Tally* to the tragic spirit]. In *GQJ/W*, vol. 17, 249–51.

"You Zhoudai nongshishi lun dao Zhoudai shehui" 由周代農事詩論到周代社會 [Understanding the Zhou society by reading the Zhou georgics]. In *GQJ/L*, vol. 1, 405–33.

"Yuzhou geming de kuang ge" 宇宙革命的狂歌. In *Guo Moruo yi wen ji*, edited by Wang Jinhou et al., 28–29. Chengdu: Sichuan daxue chubanshe, 1988.

"Zhanqu" 戰取 [To seize]. In *GQJ/W*, vol. 1, 409.

"Zhengli guo gu de pingjia" 整理國故的評價 [An evaluation of the reorganization of the national heritage]. *Chuangzao zhou bao* 創造週報 [Creation weekly], no. 36 (1924): 1–3.

Zhongguo gudai shehui yanjiu 中國古代社會研究 [Studies of ancient Chinese society]. In *GQJ/L*, vol. 1.

"Zhongguo wenhua zhi chuantong jingshen" 中國文化之傳統精神 [The traditional spirit of Chinese culture]. In *GQJ/L*, vol. 3, 255–63.

"Zhu Tang di zhi hua de yanchu" 祝《棠棣之花》的演出 [In celebration of the staging of *Twin Flowers*]. In *GQJ/W*, vol. 6, 283.

Translations by Guo Moruo

Deguo shi xuan 德國詩選 [A selection of German poems]. Co-translated with Cheng Fangwu. Shanghai: Chuangzao she chubanbu, 1928.

Juan'er ji 卷耳集 [Cockleburs]. Shanghai: Taidong, 1923.

Moruo yi shi ji 沫若譯詩集 [A collection of poems translated by Moruo]. Beijing: Renmin wenxue, 1956.

Ying shi yi gao 英詩譯稿 [Translation drafts of English poetry]. Shanghai: Shanghai yiwen, 1981.

Goethe, Johann Wolfgang von. "*Faust* chaoyi" Faust 抄譯 [A translation excerpt from *Faust*]. *Shi shi xin bao: xue deng* 時事新報：學燈 [The China times: the lamp of learning], Oct. 10, 1919.

———. "Fengguang mingmei de difang" 風光明媚的地方 [Charming landscape]. *Shishi xinbao: xue deng*, March 20, 1920.

———. *Fushide* 浮士德 [Faust]. Shanghai: Xiandai shuju, 1930.

———. *Fushide di er bu* 浮士德：第二部 [Faust II]. Beijing: Renmin wenxue, 1978.

———. *Shaonian Weite zhi fannao* 少年維特之煩惱 [The sorrows of young Werther]. Beijing: Renmin wenxue, 1956.

Kawakami Hajime 河上 肇. *Shehui zuzhi yu shehui geming* 社會組織與社會革命 [Social organization and social revolution]. Shanghai: Shangwu, 1950.

Khayyám, Omar. *Lubai ji* 魯拜集 [The rubáiyát]. Shanghai: Chuangzao she, 1930.

Marx, Karl. *Yishu zuopin zhi zhenshixing* 藝術作品之眞實性 [The reality of artwork, a portion of *The Holy Family*]. Tokyo: Zhiwen she, 1936.

———. *Zhengzhi jingjixue pipan* 政治經濟學批判 [A critique of political economy]. Shanghai: Shenzhou guoguang she, 1939.

Marx, Karl, and Friedrich Engels. *Deyizhi yishixingtai* 德意志意識形態 [The German ideology]. Shanghai: Qunyi-Haiyan-Yunhai, 1947.

Qu Yuan 屈原. *Qu Yuan fu jinyi* 屈原賦今譯 [Modernizing translations of Qu Yuan's poetic works]. In *GQJ/W*, vol. 5.

Schiller, Friedrich. *Hualunsitan* 華倫斯坦 [Wallenstein]. Beijing: Renmin wenxue, 1955.

Shelley, Percy Bysshe. "Huanle de jingling" 歡樂的精靈 [Song]. *Chunagzao jikan* 1, no. 4: 23–26 (Shelley section).

———. "Xifeng song" 西風頌 [Ode to the west wind]. *Chunagzao jikan* 1, no. 4: 20–23.

———. "Xuelai de shi" 雪萊的詩 [Shelley's poems]. *Chuangzao jikan* 1, no. 4 (1923): 19–39.

———. "Zhao buxing ci" 招 "不幸" 辭 [Invocation to misery]. *Chuangzao jikan* 1, no. 4 (1923): 28–31.

———. "Zhuanxi" 轉徙 [Mutability]. *Chuangzao jikan* 1, no. 4 (1923): 31–33.

Other Primary Sources

"Aofuhebian" 奧伏赫變 [Aufheben]. *Wenhua pipan*, no. 1 (1928): 100.

Beijing daxue 北京大學, Beijing shifan daxue 北京師範大學, and Beijing shifan xueyuan 北京師範學院, eds. *Wenxue yundong shiliao xuan* 文學運動史料選 [Selected materials of literary movements]. 5 vols. Shanghai: Shanghai jiaoyu, 1979.

Benjamin, Walter. *The Arcades Project*. Translated by Howard Eiland and Levin McLaughlin. Cambridge, MA: Belknap Press of Harvard University Press, 1999.

———. "On the Concept of History." Translated by Harry Zohn. In *Selected Writings*, vol. 4 (1938–1940), edited by Howard Eiland and Michael W. Jennings, 389–400. Cambridge, MA: Belknap Press of Harvard University Press, 2003.

———. "Paralipomena to 'On the Concept of History.'" In *Selected Writings*, vol. 4 (1938–1940), edited by Howard Eiland and Michael W. Jennings, 401–11. Cambridge, MA: Belknap Press of Harvard University Press, 2003.

Bloch, Ernst. *Heritage of Our Times*. Translated by Neville Plaice and Stephen Plaice. Berkeley: University of California Press, 1990.

Cai Shangsi 蔡尚思, ed. *Zhongguo xiandai sixiang shi ziliao jianbian* 中國現代思想史資料簡編 [A concise collection of materials of modern Chinese intellectual history]. 5 vols. Hangzhou: Zhejiang renmin, 1983.

Cao Juren 曹聚仁. "Du Juan'er" 讀卷耳 [Reading "The Cocklebur"]. In *Juan'er taolun ji*, edited by Cao Juren, 13–20. Shanghai: Liangxi tushuguan, 1925.

———, ed. *Juan'er taolun ji* 卷耳討論集 [A collection of discussions on "The Cocklebur"]. Shanghai: Liangxi tushuguan, 1925.

Chan, Tak-hung Leo, ed. *Twentieth-Century Chinese Translation Theory: Modes, Issues and Debates*. Amsterdam: J. Benjamins, 2004.

Chen Mengjia 陳夢家. *Yinxu buci zongshu* 殷墟卜辭綜述 [A general study of Shang oracle inscriptions]. Beijing: Zhonghua shuju, 1988.

Cheng Fangwu 成仿吾. "Cong wenxue geming dao geming wenxue" 從文學革命到革命文學 [From literary revolution to revolutionary literature]. In *Geming wenxue lunzheng ziliao xuan bian*, edited by Zhongguo shehui kexue yuan, 130–37. Beijing: Renmin wenxue, 1981.

———. "Quanmian de pipan zhi biyao" 全面的批判之必要 [The need of a total critique]. *Chuangzao yuekan* 創造月刊 [Creation monthly] 1, no. 10 (1928): 1–8.

———. "Xin wenxue de shiming" 新文學的使命 [The mission of new literature]. *Chuangzao zhoubao*, no. 2 (1923): 1–7.

———. "Xu" 序 [Preface]. In Guo, trans., *Ying shi yi gao*, I–II. Shanghai: Shanghai yiwen, 1981.

———. "Zhuci" 祝辭 [Congratulatory words]. *Wenhua pipan*, no. 1 (1928): 1–2.

Cheng Junying 陳俊英 and Jiang Jianyuan 蔣見元. *Shi jing zhu xi* 詩經注析 [The annotated *Book of Songs*]. Beijing: Zhonghua shuju, 1991.

Chuangzao she 創造社 [Creation Society], ed. *Chuangzao jikan* 創造季刊 [Creation quarterly]. 1922–1924.

———, ed. *Chuangzao ri huikan* 創造日匯刊 [Creation daily: a compilation]. 1923.

———, ed. *Chuangzao yuekan* 創造月刊 [Creation monthly]. 1926–1929.

———, ed. *Chuangzao zhoubao* 創造週報 [Creation weekly]. 1923–1924.

———, ed. *Hongshui* 洪水 [Deluge]. 1924, 1925–1927.

———, ed. *Wenhua pipan* 文化批判 [Cultural critique]. 1928.

Coleridge, Samuel Taylor. "Effusion XXXV [The Eolian Harp]." In *Coleridge's Poetry and* Prose, edited by Nicholas Halmi, Paul Magnuson, and Raimonda Modiano, 17–20. New York: Norton, 2002.

Dai Jitao 戴季陶. "Zhonghua min guo li zhi zhi jiben guannian" 中華民國禮制之基本觀念 [Basic concepts of the institutionalization of the ritual of the Republic of China]. In *Zhongguo xiandai shixiang shi ziliao jianbian*, edited by Cai Shangsi, vol. 4, 950–51. Hangzhou: Zhejiang renmin, 1983.

Deng Xiaoping 鄧小平. "Zai Guo Moruo tongzhi zhuidao hui shang de daoci" 在郭沫若同志追悼會上的悼詞 [The speech at the memorial service of Comrade Guo Moruo]. In *Daonian Guo lao* 悼念郭老 [Remembering Guo the senior], edited by Xinhua yuebao ziliao shi 新華月報資料室, i–vi. Beijing: Sanlian, 1979.

Di'er lishi dang'an guan 第二歷史檔案館 [The second historical archive], ed. *Minguo shiliao dang'an huibian, 5 ji, 3 bian* 民國史料檔案彙編, 5 輯, 3 編 [Collected archival materials of the Republican era, series 5, vol. 3]. Nanjing: Jiangsu guji, 1994.

Du Fu 杜甫. "My Thatched Roof Is Ruined by the Autumn Wind." Translated by Stephen Owen. In *Classical Chinese Literature: An Anthology of Translations, Volume I: From Antiquity to the Tang Dynasty*, edited by John Minford and Joseph S. M. Lau,

802. New York: Columbia University Press and the Chinese University of Hong Kong, 2000.

Du Guoxiang 杜國庠. "Lue lun li yue qi yuan ji zhongguo li xue de fazhan (jielu)" 略論禮樂起源及中國禮學得發展(節錄) [A brief discussion of the origins of ritual and music and the development of Chinese discourse of ritual, an excerpt]. In *Zhongguo xiandai shixiang shi ziliao jianbian*, edited by Cai Shangsi, vol. 4, 952–57. Hangzhou: Zhejiang renmin, 1983.

Engels, Friedrich. *Anti-Dühring*. New York: International Publishers, 1970.

———. "Engels to Ferdinand Lassalle." In Karl Marx and Friedrich Engels, *On Literature and Art*, 101–7. Moscow: Progress, 1976.

———. "German Socialism in Verse and Prose." In *Marx/Engels Collected Works*, vol. 6, 235–73. New York: International Publishers, 1977.

———. *Ludwig Feuerbach and the End of German Classical Philosophy*. In *Marx/Engels Selected Works in One Volume*. New York: International Publishers, 1980.

———. *The Origin of the Family, Private Property and the State*. New York: International Publishers, 1972.

———. *Socialism: Utopian and Scientific*. In *Marx/Engels Selected Works in One Volume*. New York: International Publishers, 1980.

Fan Wenlan 范文瀾. *Zhongguo tongshi jianbian* 中國通史簡編 [A brief account of the complete history of China]. Shanghai: Xinzhi, 1947.

Feng Naichao 馮乃超. "Yishu yu shehui shenghuo" 藝術與社會生活 [Art and social life]. *Wenhua pipan*, no. 1 (1928): 3–13.

Feng Zhi 馮至. "Cong Fushide li de renzaoren luelun Gede de ziran zhexue" 從《浮士德》里的人造人略論歌德的自然哲學 [Goethe's philosophy of nature seen from the character of Homunculus]. In *Feng Zhi quan ji* 馮至全集 [Complete works of Feng Zhi], vol. 8, 46–59. Shijiazhuang: Hebei jiaoyu, 1999.

———. *Du Fu zhuan* 杜甫傳 [A biography of Du Fu]. Beijing: Renmin wenxue, 1980.

———. "Fushide li de mo" 浮士德里的魔 [On the devil in *Faust*]. In *Feng Zhi quan ji* 馮至全集 [Complete works of Feng Zhi], vol. 8, 25–45. Shijiazhuang: Hebei jiaoyu, 1999.

———. "Gede yu ren de jiaoyu" 歌德与人的教育 [Goethe and the education of man]. In *Feng Zhi quan ji* 馮至全集 [Complete works of Feng Zhi], vol. 8, 81–86. Shijiazhuang: Hebei jiaoyu, 1999.

Gao Jun 高軍, ed. *Zhongguo shehui xingzhi wenti lunzhan* 中國社會性質問題論戰 [The debates on the controversy of the characteristics of Chinese society]. Beijing: Renmin, 1982.

Goethe, Johann Wolfgang von. *Early Verse Drama and Prose Plays*. Edited by Cyrus Hamlin et al. New York: Suhrhamp, 1988.

———. *Faust*. A Norton Critical Edition (2nd ed.). Translated by Walter Arndt, edited by Cyrus Hamlin. New York: Norton, 2001.

———. *Faust: Texte*. Frankfurt: Deutscher Klassiker, 2005.

———. *Fausuto* ファウスト [Faust]. Translated (into Japanese) by Mori Ōgai 森 鷗外. In *Ogai zenshu* 鷗外全集 [Complete works of Ogai], vol. 12. Tokyo: Iwanami Shoten, 1972.

———. *The First Part of Goethe's Faust*. Translated by John Auster. London: Routledge, 1887.

———. *The Sorrows of Young Werther*. Translated by E. Mayer and L. Bogan. New York: Vintage, 1990.

Gramsci, Antonio. *Prison Notebooks*. Translated by Joseph A. Buttigieg and Antonio Callari. New York: Columbia University Press, 1992.

Granet, Marcel. *Fêtes et chansons anciennes de la Chine*. Paris: L'Université Paris, 1929.

Gu Jiegang 顧頡剛. *Chunqiu shi jiangyi* 春秋史講義 [Lecture notes on the history of the Springs and Autumns era]. In *Gu Jiegang quan ji* 顧頡剛全集 [Complete works of Gu Jiegang], vol. 4. Beijing: Zhonghua shuju, 2010.

———. *Guo shi jianghua* [Lectures on national history]. In *Gu Jiegang quan ji* 顧頡剛全集, vol. 13. Beijing: Zhonghua shuju, 2010.

———. "Shang shu Pangeng zhong pian jinyi" [A modern translation of "Pangeng," second part, from the *Book of Documents*]. In *Gu Jiegang quan ji* 顧頡剛全集, vol. 9, 1–7. Beijing: Zhonghua shuju, 2010.

Hazlitt, William. *The Spirit of the Age, or, Contemporary Portraits*. London: Henry Colburn, 1825.

He Ganzhi 何干之. *Zhongguo shehui xingzhi wenti lunzheng* 中國社會性質問題論爭 [The debate on the characteristics of Chinese society]. Shanghai: Shenghuo shudian, 1937.

Hegel, Georg Wilhelm Friedrich. *Early Theological Writings*. Translated by T. M. Knox. Chicago: University of Chicago Press, 1948.

———. *Phenomenology of Spirit*. Translated by A. V. Miller. Oxford: Oxford University Press, 1977.

Hölderlin, Friedrich. "Der Rhein." In *Hymns and Fragments*, translated by Richard Sieburth, 68–81. Princeton, NJ: Princeton University Press, 1984.

Hong Weifa 洪為法. "Du *Juan'er ji*" 讀《卷耳集》 [Reading *Cockleburs*]. *Chuangzao ri huikan* (1923), 347–53.

Hong Zicheng 洪子誠, ed. *Zhongguo dangdai wenxue shi shiliao xuan* 中國當代文學史史料選 [Selected historical materials on post-1949 Chinese literature]. Wuhan: Changjiang wenyi, 2002.

Hou Wailu 侯外廬. "Lun Qu Yuan sixiang" 論屈原思想 [On Qu Yuan's thought]. In *Hou Wailu shixue lunwen xuan ji* 侯外廬史學論文選集 [Selected historical essays of Hou Wailu], vol. 1, 340–62. Beijing: Renmin chubanshe, 1987.

Hou Wailu 侯外廬, Zhao Jibin 趙紀彬, and Du Guoxiang 杜國庠. *Zhongguo sixiang tongshi, di yi juan* 中國思想通史 [A history of Chinese thought, volume 1]. Beijing: Renmin chubanshe, 1957.

Hu Qiuyuan 胡秋原. "Makesizhuyi suojian de Gede" 馬克斯主義所見的歌德 [Goethe in the Marxist light]. *Dushu zazhi* 讀書雜誌 [Reading magazine] 2, no. 4 (1932): 1–46 (independent pagination).

Huang Renying 黄人影, ed. *Guo Moruo lun* 郭沫若論 [Critical essays on Guo Moruo]. Shanghai: Guanghua, 1931.

Ito Toramaru 伊藤 虎丸, ed. *Sōzōsha shiryō* 創造社資料 [Archives of the Creation Society]. 10 vols. Tokyo: Ajia shuppan, 1979.

Jakobson, Roman. "On Linguistic Aspects of Translation." In *The Translation Studies Reader*, edited by Lawrence Venuti, 3rd ed., 126–31. London: Routledge, 2012.

Jiang Qing 江青. "Tan jing ju gaige" 談京劇改革 [On the reform of the Beijing opera]. In *Zhongguo dangdai wenxue shi shiliao xuan*, edited by Hong Zicheng, 514–17. Wuhan: Changjiang wenyi, 2002.

Li Chuli 李初梨. "Zenyang de jianshe geming wenxue" 怎樣地建設革命文學 [How to build revolutionary literature]. *Wenhua pipan*, no. 2 (1928): 3–20.

Lin Lin 林林. "Zhe shi dang laba de jingshen" 這就是黨喇叭的精神 [This is the spirit of being the party's trumpet, 1979]. In *GZL*, edited by Wang Xunzhao et al., 429–40.

Liu Zongyuan 柳宗元. "Fengjian lun" 封建論 [On the feudal system]. In *Liu Hedong ji* 柳宗元集 [A collection of Liu Zongyuan's works], 43–48. Shanghai: Shanghai renmin chubanshe, 1974.

Lu Xun. "Befuddled Woolliness." In *Selected Works*, translated by Yang Hsien-yi and Gladys Yang, vol. 3, 15–22. Beijing: Foreign Language Press, 1964.

———. "A Glance at Shanghai Literature." In *Selected Works*, translated by Yang Hsien-yi and Gladys Yang, vol. 3, 127–41. Beijing: Foreign Language Press, 1964.

———. " 'Hard Translation' and the 'Class Character of Literature.' " In *Selected Works*, translated by Yang Hsien-yi and Gladys Yang, vol. 3, 75–96. Beijing: Foreign Language Press, 1964.

———. "Preface to *Old Stories Retold*." In *The Real Story of Ah-Q and Other Tales of China: The Complete Fiction of Lu Xun*, translated by Julia Lovell, 295–97. New York: Penguin Books, 2009.

———. "Xiao zagan" 小雜感 [Little miscellaneous thoughts]. In *Lu Xun quanji* 魯迅全集 [Complete works of Lu Xun], vol. 3, 554–58. Beijing: Renmin wenxue, 2005.

———. "Zuiyan zhong de menglong" 醉眼中的朦朧 [Befuddled woolliness]. In *Lu Xun quanji* 魯迅全集 [Complete works of Lu Xun], vol. 5, 61–72. Beijing: Renmin wenxue, 2005.

Lukács, György. "Blum Theses 1928–1929." In *Tactics and Ethics 1919–1929*, translated by Michael McColgan, 227–53. London: Verso, 2014.

———. *The Destruction of Reason*. Translated by Peter Palmer. London: Merlin, 1980.

———. *Goethe and His Age*. Translated by Robert Anchor. London: Merlin, 1968.

———. *The Historical Novel*. Translated by Hannah and Stanley Mitchell. Lincoln: University of Nebraska Press, 1983.

———. "Die Sickingendebatte zwischen Marx-Engels und Lassalle." In *Karl Marx und Friedrich Engels als Literaturhistoriker*, 5–62. Berlin: Aufbau, 1948.

———. *Soul and Form*. Translated by Anna Bostock. New York: Columbia University Press, 2010.

Mao Dun 茅盾. "Du 'Ni Huanzhi' " 讀《倪煥之》[Reading *Ni Huanzhi*]. In *Geming wenxue lunzheng ziliao xuanbian*, edited by Zhongguo shehui kexue yuan, 847–67. Beijing: Renmin wenxue, 1981.

———. *Mao Dun quanji* 茅盾全集 [Complete works]. Vol. 1. Beijing: Renmin wenxue, 1984.

Mao Zedong 毛澤東. "Carry the Revolution through to the End." In *Selected Works of Mao Tse-tung*, vol. 4, 299–308. Beijing: Foreign Languages, 1965.

———. *Jian guo hou Mao Zedong wengao* 建國后毛澤東文稿 [Mao Zedong's writings after the founding of the People's Republic]. Vols. 7 and 13. Beijing: Zhongyang wenxian, 1992.

———. "Kanle *Bishang Liangshan* hou xie gei Yang Shaoxuan Qi Yanming er tongzhi de xin" 看了《逼上梁山》后寫給楊紹萱齊燕銘二同志的信 [A letter to comrades Yang Shaoxuan and Qi Yanming after seeing *Forced to go to Liangshan*]. In *Wenxue yundong shiliao xuan*, edited by Beijing daxue et al., vol. 5, 3. Shanghai: Shanghai jiaoyu, 1979.

———. "Mao Zedong tongzhi gei Guo Moruo tongzhi de xin" 毛澤東同志給郭沫若同志的信 [Comrade Mao Zedong's letter to comrade Guo Moruo]. In *Wenxue yundong shiliao xuan*, edited by Beijing daxue et al., vol. 5, 140. Shanghai: Shanghai jiaoyu, 1979.

———. *Mao Zedong xuan ji* 毛澤東選集 [Selected works]. Beijing: Renmin, 1969.

———. "Mao zhuxi zhongyao zhishi" 毛主席重要指示 [Chairman Mao's important instructions, 1975–1976]. In *Jian guo hou Mao Zedong wengao*, vol. 13, 486–93. Beijing: Zhongyang wenxian, 1992.

———. "On New Democracy" (1940). In *Selected Works of Mao Tse-tung*, vol. 2, 339–84. Beijing: Foreign Languages, 1965.

———. "On the People's Democratic Dictatorship" (1949). In *Selected Works of Mao Tse-tung*, vol. 4, 411–24. Beijing: Foreign Languages, 1965.

———. "Peitaiho—to the Tune of Lang Tao Sha." In *Poems*, 30. Beijing: Foreign Languages, 1976.

———. "Qilü, du *Fengjian lun* cheng Guo lao" 七律·讀《封建論》呈郭老 [To Guo the senior after reading "On Feudal System"—written in *qi lü* style]. In *Jian guo hou Mao Zedong wengao*, vol. 13, 361–62.

———. "Ren de zhengque sixiang shi cong nali lai de" 人的正確思想是從哪裡來的 [Where do correct ideas come from, 1963]. In *Mao Zedong zhuzuo xuan du, yi zhong ben* 毛澤東著作選讀，乙種本 [Selected readings from Mao Zedong's works, the second volume], 192–94. Beijing: Zhongguo qingnian, 1965.

———. "Reply to Comrade Kuo Mo-jo—a *lu shih*." In *Poems*, 41. Beijing: Foreign Languages, 1976.

———. "Reply to Comrade Kuo Mo-jo, to the Tune of *Man Jiang Hong*." In *Poems*, 46–47. Beijing: Foreign Languages, 1976.

———. "Talks at Yenan Forum on Literature and Art." In *Selected Works*, vol. 3, 69–98. Beijing: Foreign Languages, 1965.

———. "Zhi Lu Dingyi" 致陸定一 [To Lu Dingyi]. In *Mao Zedong shuxin xuan ji* 毛澤東書信選集 [Selected letters of Mao Zedong], 598. Beijing: Renmin, 1983.

Marx, Karl. *The Communist Manifesto*. New York: Norton, 1988.

———. *The Eighteenth Brumaire of Louis Bonaparte*. In *Marx/Engels Selected Works in One Volume*. New York: International Publishers, 1980.

———. "Der leitende Artikel in Nr. 179 der 'Kölnischen Zeitung.'" In *Marx/Engels Werke*, Band 1, 86–104. Berlin: Dietz, 1981.

———. "Marx to Ferdinand Lassalle." In Karl Marx and Friedrich Engels, *On Literature and Art*, 98–101. Moscow: Progress, 1976.

———. "Preface to *A Contribution to the Critique of Political Economy*." In *Marx/Engels Selected Works in One Volume*, 181–85. New York: International Publishers, 1980.

———. "Towards a Critique of Hegel's *Philosophy of Right*: Introduction." In *Karl Marx: Selected Writings*, 2nd ed., edited by David McLellan, 71–82. Oxford: Oxford University Press, 2000.

———. "The Victory of Counter-Revolution in Vienna." In *Marx/Engels Collected Works*, vol. 7, 503–6. New York: International Publishers, 1977.

Morgan, Lewis H. *Ancient Society*. Chicago: Charles H. Kerr, 1877.

Peng Kang. "Chudiao Lu Xun de chudiao" 除掉魯迅的" 除掉" [Annihilate Lu Xun's "Annihilate"]. *Wenhua pipan*, no. 4 (1928): 57–64.

Pound, Ezra, trans. *Confucius: The Unwobbling Pivogt, the Great Digest, the Analects*. New York: New Directions, 1951.

———. "Guido's Relations." In *The Translation Studies Reader*, edited by Lawrence Venuti, 3rd ed., 84–91. London: Routledge, 2012.

———, trans. *Shih-ching, the Classic Anthology Defined by Confucius*. Cambridge, MA: Harvard University Press, 1982.

———. *The Spirit of Romance*. New York: New Directions, 2005.

Qian Xingcun 錢興邨. "Guo Moruo jiqi chuangzuo" 郭沫若及其創作 [Guo Moruo and his creative work]. In *Guo Moruo lun*, edited by Huang Renying, 17–54. Shanghai: Guanghua, 1931.

Qu Qiubai 瞿秋白. "Geming de luomandike" 革命的羅曼諦克 [The revolutionary romantic]. In *Qu Qiubai wenji, wenxuebian* 瞿秋白文集，文學編 [Works of Qu Qiubai, volumes in literature], vol. 1, 456–60. Beijing: Renmin wenxue, 1985.

———. "Lu Xun zagan xuan ji xuyan" 《魯迅雜感選集》序言 [Preface to *A Selection of Lu Xun's Essays*]. In *Qu Qiubai wenji, wenxuebian*, vol. 3, 95–123. Beijing: Renmin wenxue, 1985.

Qu Yuan 屈原 et al. *Chu ci ji zhu* 楚辭集註 [The Chu songs with collected commentaries]. Edited and annotated by Zhu Xi 朱熹. Shanghai: Shanghai guji, 1979.

———. *The Songs of the South: An Ancient Chinese Anthology of Poems by Qu Yuan and Other Poets*. Translated by David Hawkes. London: Penguin Books, 2011.

Rao Hongjing 饒鴻競, Chen Songsheng 陳頌聲, Li Weijiang 李偉江, Wu Hongcong 吳宏聰, Zhang Zhengwu 張正吾, Dong Xiuzhi 董修志, and Wang Peijuan 王珮娟, eds. *Chuangzao she ziliao* 創造社資料 [Archival materials of the Creation Society]. Beijing: Zhishi chanquan, 2010.

Rousseau, Jean-Jacques. *The Discourses and Other Early Political Writings*. Edited and translated by Victor Gourevitch. Cambridge: Cambridge University Press, 1997.

———. *The Social Contract and Other Later Political Writings*. Edited and translated by Victor Gourevitch. Cambridge: Cambridge University Press, 1997.

Ruan Yuan 阮元, ed. *Shi san jing zhu shu* 十三經註疏 [Collected commentaries on the thirteen classics]. Shanghai: Shanghai guji, 1997.

Schleiermacher, Friedrich. "On the Different Methods of Translating." Translated by Susan Bernofsky. In *The Translation Studies Reader*, edited by Lawrence Venuti, 3rd ed., 43–63. London: Routledge, 2012.

Schmitt, Carl. *Political Romanticism*. Translated by Guy Oakes. Cambridge, MA: MIT Press, 1986.

Shakespeare, William. *King Lear*. New Haven, CT: Yale University Press, 2007.

Shanghai shifan daxue zhongwen xi 上海師範大學中文系, ed. *Guo Moruo zhuan ji* 郭沫若專集 [Special collections on Guo]. 2 vols. Shanghai: Shanghai shifan daxue, 1980.

Shelley, Percy Bysshe. *Shelley's Poetry and Prose*, 2nd ed. Edited by Donald H. Reiman and Neil Fraistat. New York: Norton, 2002.

Shen Congwen 沈從文. "Lun Guo Moruo" 論郭沫若 [On Guo Moruo]. In *Guo Moruo lun*, edited by Huang Renying, 5–16. Shanghai: Guanghua, 1931.

Tao Qiqing 陶其情. "Makesi daodi buneng jin Wen Miao" 馬克斯到底不能進文廟 [After all Marx cannot enter the Temple of Confucius]. *Hongshui*, no. 14 (1926): 71–81.

Waley, Arthur, trans. *The Book of Songs*. Edited by Joseph R. Allen. New York: Grove Press, 1996.

Wang Guowei 王國維. "Yin Zhou zhidu lun" 殷商制度論 [On the Yin-Zhou institutional change]. In *Wang Guowei xiansheng quan ji* 王國維先生全集 [Complete works of Wang Guowei], 449–78. Taipei: Datong shuju, 1976.

Wang Xunzhao 王訓昭, Lu Zhengyan 盧正言, Shao Hua 邵華, Xiao Binru 蕭斌如, and Lin Minghua 林明華, eds. *Guo Moruo yanjiu ziliao* 郭沫若研究資料 [Selected materials on Guo Moruo]. Beijing: Zhichi chanquan, 2010 (abbreviated *GZL*).

Wen Yiduo 聞一多. "Jiuge gu ge wu ju xuanjie" 九歌古歌舞劇懸解 [An interpretation of *Nine Songs*]. In *Shenhua yu shi* 神話與詩 [Mythology and poetry], 305–34. Beijing: Guji chubanshe, 1956.

———. "Kuang zhai chi du" 匡齋尺牘 [Notes from Kuang Studio]. In *Shenhua yu shi*, 339–67. Beijing: Guji chubanshe, 1956.

———. "Nüshen zhi shidai jingshen" 《女神》之時代精神 [The Zeitgeist in *The Goddesses*]. *Chuangzao zhoubao*, no. 4 (1923): 3–8.

———. "Renmin de shiren—Qu Yuan" 人民的詩人—— 屈原 [The poet of the people: Qu Yuan]. In *Shenhua yu shi*, 259–62. Beijing: Guji chubanshe, 1956.

———. "Shenme shi Jiuge" 什麼是九歌 [What is *Nine Songs*?]. In *Shenhua yu shi*, 263–78. Beijing: Guji chubanshe, 1956.

Whitman, Walt. "Song of the Open Road." In *Poetry and Prose*, 297–307. New York: Library of America, 1996.

Xia Yan 夏衍. "Lishi yu fengyu" 歷史與諷喻 [History and allegory]. In *Liang ge kou hao lunzheng ziliao xuanbian* 兩個口號論爭資料選編 [Selected materials of the "Two Slogans" debate], edited by Zhongguo shehui kexue yuan 中國社會科學院, vol. 1, 248–52. Beijing: Renmin wenxue, 1982.

Xiang Peiliang 向培良. "Suowei lishi ju" 所謂歷史劇 [So-called historical drama]. In *GZL*, edited by Wang Xunzhao et al., 722–27.

Xie Kang 謝康. "Du le Nüshen zhihou" 讀了《女神》之後 [After reading *Goddesses*]. *Chuangzao jikan* 1, no. 2 (1922): 16–22 (criticism section).

Xu Chi 徐遲. "Guo Moruo, Qu Yuan he Cai Wenji" 郭沫若、屈原和蔡文姬 [Guo Moruo, Qu Yuan and Cai Wenji]. In *Guo Moruo zhuan ji*, vol. 2, 319–28.

———. "Xu Chi xiansheng laixin" 徐遲先生來信 [Mr. Xu Chi's letter]. In *GQJ/W*, vol. 6, 412–15.

Yan Fu 嚴復. "Preface to *Tianyanlun*." Translated by C. Y. Hsu. In *Twentieth-Century Chinese Translation Theory: Modes, Issues and Debates*, edited by Tak-hung Leo Chan, 69–71. Amsterdam: J. Benjamins, 2004.

Yu Dafu 郁達夫. "Riji wenxue" 日記文學 [Diary literature]. In *Yu Dafu wen ji* 郁達夫文集 [Works of Yu Dafu], vol. 5, 261–67. Guangzhou: Huacheng, 1983.

———. "Wu liu nian lai chuangzuo shenghuo de huigu" 五六年來創作生活的回顧 [A retrospective of my creative writings in last five or six years]. In *Yu Dafu wen ji*, vol. 7, 176–81. Guangzhou: Huacheng, 1983.

Yu Liqun 于立群. "Hua beitong wei liliang" 化悲痛爲力量 [To transform mourning into strength]. In *Daonian Guo lao* 悼念郭老 [Remembering Guo the senior], edited by Xinhua yuebao ziliao shi 新華月報資料室, 511–18. Beijing: Sanlian, 1979

Yu Pingbo 俞平伯. "Qizhiliaoheng shi du shi zha ji: Zhounan Juan'er" 葺芷繚衡室讀詩雜記：周南卷耳 [Notes on reading the *Book of Songs* in Qizhiliaoheng studio: "The Cocklebur" from the south of Zhou]. In *Juan'er taolun ji*, edited by Cao Juren, 5–12. Shanghai: Liangxi tushuguan, 1925.

Zeng Jianrong 曾健戎, ed. *Guo Moruo zai Chongqing* 郭沫若在重慶 [Guo Moruo in Chongqing, a collection of historical materials]. Xining: Qinghai renmin, 1982.

Zhang Ying 章罌. "Cong Tang di zhi hua tandao ping lishi ju" 從《棠棣之花》談到評歷史劇 [From *Twin Flowers* to criticism of the historical drama]. In *GZL*, edited by Wang Xunzhao et al., 769–73.

Zhao Jibin 趙紀彬. *Guanyu Kong Qiu sha Shaozheng Mao wenti* 關於孔丘殺少正卯問題 [On the issue of Confucius' killing of Shaozheng Mao]. Beijing: Renmin, 1974.

Zhongguo shehui kexue yuan 中國社會科學院, ed. *Geming wenxue lunzheng ziliao xuanbian* 革命文學論爭資料選編 [Archives of the revolutionary literature debate]. Beijing: Renmin wenxue, 1981.

———, ed. *Liang ge kou hao lunzheng ziliao xuanbian* "兩個口號" 論爭資料選編 [Selected materials of the "Two Slogans" debate]. Beijing: Renmin wenxue, 1982.

Zhou Enlai 周恩來. "Wo yao shuo de hua" 我要說的話 [What I want to say]. In *GZL*, edited by Wang Xunzhao et al., 368–72.

Zhou Xuepu 周學普. "Yizhe xu" 譯者序. In Goethe, *Fushide* [Faust], translated by Zhou Xuepu, 1–37. Shanghai: Shangwu, 1936.

Zhou Yang 周揚. "Beitong de huainian" 悲痛的懷念 [Saddening remembrances]. In *Daonian Guo lao* 悼念郭老 [Remembering Guo the senior], edited by Xinhua yuebao ziliao shi 新華月報資料室, 4–10. Beijing: Sanlian, 1979.

———. "Guanyu shehuizhuyi de xianshizhuyi yu geming de langmanzhuyi" 關於社會主義的現實主義與革命的浪漫主義 [On socialist realism and revolutionary romanticism]. In *Zhou Yang wenji* 周揚文集 [Works of Zhou Yang], vol. 1, 101–14. Beijing: Renmin wenxue, 1984.

———. "Guo Moruo he ta de Nüshen" 郭沫若和他的《女神》 [Guo Moruo and his *Goddesses*]. In *GZL*, edited by Wang Xunzhao et al., 669–75.

———. "Xin minge kaituo le shige de xin daolu" 新民歌開拓了詩歌的新道路 [New folk songs have broken a new path for poetry]. In *Zhongguo dangdai wenxue shi, shiliao xuan*, edited by Hong Zicheng, 459–64. Wuhan: Changjiang wenyi, 2002.

Zhou Zuoren 周作人. "Gu shi jinyi Apologia" 古詩今譯 Apologia [Apologia for modern translation of ancient poetry]. In *Zhou Zuoren sanwen quan ji* 周作人散文全集 [Collected essays of Zhou Zuoren], edited by Zhong Shuhe 鐘叔河, vol. 2, 12–13. Guilin: Guangxi Shifan, 2009.

Zhu Xi 朱熹. *Shi ji zhuan* 詩集傳 [Commentary on the *Book of Songs*]. Beijing: Zhonghua shuju, 1958.

Zong Baihua 宗白華. "Gede zhi rensheng qishi" 歌德對人生的啓示 [Goethe as an illumination of life]. In *Yi jing* 藝境 [Aesthetic realm], 36–56. Beijing: Beijing daxue chubanshe, 1987.

Secondary Sources

Abrams, M. H. *The Mirror and the Lamp: Romantic Theory and the Critical Tradition.* London: Oxford University Press, 1952.

———. *Natural Supernaturalism: Tradition and Revolution in Romantic Literature.* New York: Norton, 1973.

Agamben, Giorgio. "What Is a People." In *Means Without Ends*, translated by Vincenzo Binetti and Cesare Casarino, 29–36. Minneapolis: University of Minnesota Press, 2000.

Ai Yang 艾揚. "Shi lun Guo Moruo qianqi sixiang fazhan" 試論郭沫若前期思想發展 [On the early Guo's intellectual development, 1958]. In *GZL*, edited by Wang Xunzhao et al., 489–509.

Althusser, Louis, and Etienne Balibar. *Reading Capital.* Translated by Ben Brewster. London: Verso, 2009.

Anderson, Kevin. *Marxism at the Margins: On Nationalism, Ethnicity and Non-Western Societies.* Chicago: University of Chicago Press, 2010.

Badiou, Alain. "The Cultural Revolution: The Last Revolution?" Translated by Bruno Bosteels. *Positions: East Asia Cultures Critique*, vol. 13, no. 3 (Winter 2005): 481–513.

———. *Le Siècle.* Paris: Seuil, 2005.

Bartels, Nora. "Goethes *Faust* bei Mori Rintarō und Guo Moruo. Vorstudien zum Verständnis ihrer Übersetzungen." *Japonica Humboldtiana* 15 (2012): 77–150.

Berman, Antoine. *The Experience of the Foreign: Culture and Translation in Romantic Germany.* Translated by S. Heyvaert. Albany: State University of New York Press, 1992.

Bloom, Harold. "The Art of Reading Poetry." In *Best Poems of the English Language*, selected by Harold Bloom, 1–29. New York: Harper Collins, 2004.

———. *Shelley's Mythmaking.* Ithaca, NY: Cornell University Press, 1969.

Boar, Bruce Gordon. "Images of Women in the Dramas of Guo Moruo: The Case of *Empress Wu*." In *Drama in the People's Republic of China*, edited by Constance Tung and Colin Mackerras, 54–92. Albany: State University of New York Press, 1987.

Brown, Jane K. *Goethe's* Faust*: The German Tragedy.* Ithaca, NY: Cornell University Press, 1986.

Büttgen, Philippe. "Aufheben." Translated by Steven Rendall. In *Dictionary of Untranslatables*, edited by Barbara Cassin, translated and edited by Emily Apter, Jacques Lezra, and Michael Wood, 71–76. Princeton, NJ: Princeton University Press, 2013.

Button, Peter. *Configurations of the Real in Chinese Literary and Aesthetic Modernity.* Leiden: Brill, 2009.

Cai Xiang 蔡翔. *Revolution and Its Narratives: China's Socialist Literary and Cultural Imaginaries, 1949–1966.* Edited and translated by Rebecca E. Karl and Xueping Zhong. Durham, NC: Duke University Press, 2016.

Cai Zhen 蔡震. *Guo Moruo shengping wenxian shiliao kaobian* 郭沫若生平文獻史料考辨 [A critical examination of historical materials about Guo's life]. Beijing: Shehui kexue wenxue chubanshe, 2014.

———. "Guo Moruo yan jiu san yi" 郭沫若研究三論 [Three discourses on Guo Moruo studies]. In *GHY*, edited by Yang Shengkuan and Cai Zhen, vol. 13, 408–16.

Cao Jian 曹劍, ed. *Gongzheng pingjia Guo Moruo* 公正評價郭沫若 [On justly valuating Guo Moruo]. Beijing: Zhongyang dangxiao, 1999.

Chandler, James K. *England in 1819: The Politics of Literary Culture and the Case of Romantic Historicism*. Chicago: University of Chicago Press, 1998.

Chang, Kwang-chih. *The Archaeology of Ancient China*, 4th ed. New Haven, CT: Yale University Press, 1986.

Chen Shih-hsiang 陳世驤. "Lun zhongguo shuqing chuantong" 論中國抒情傳統 [On Chinese lyrical tradition]. In *Shuqing zhi xiandaixing: Shuqing chuantong lunshu yu zhongguo wenxue yanjiu* 抒情之現代性：抒情傳統論述與中國文學研究 [The modernity of lyricism: essays on Chinese lyrical tradition], edited by Chen Guoqiu 陳國球 and David Der-wei Wang, 45–51. Beijing: Sanlian, 2014.

Chen, Xiaomei. *Acting the Right Part: Political Theater and Popular Drama in Contemporary China*. Honolulu: University of Hawai'i Press, 2002.

Chen, Xiaoming. *From the May Fourth Movement to Communist Revolution: Guo Moruo and the Chinese Path to Communism*. Albany: State University of New York Press, 2007.

Chen Yongzhi 陳永志. *Guo Moruo sixiang zhengti guan* 郭沫若思想整體觀 [A holistic perspective on Guo Moruo's thought]. Shanghai: Shanghai wenyi, 1992.

Cheng Kai 程凱. *Geming de zhangli: Da Geming qianhou xin wenxue zhishifenzi de lishi chujing yu sixiang tanqiu* 革命的張力：大革命前後新文學知識份子的歷史處境與思想探索 [Tensions of the revolution: revolutionizing the May Fourth intellectuals]. Beijing: Beijing daxue chubanshe, 2014.

Chou, Ts'e-tsung. *The May Fourth Movement: Intellectual Revolution in Modern China*. Cambridge, MA: Harvard University Press, 1960.

Cohen, Paul A. *Speaking to History: The Story of King Goujian in Twentieth-Century China*. Berkeley: University of California Press, 2009.

Comay, Rebecca. *Mourning Sickness: Hegel and the French Revolution*. Stanford, CA: Stanford University Press, 2011.

Culler, Jonathan D. "Apostrophe." In *The Pursuit of Signs: Semiotics, Literature, Deconstruction*, 135–54. Ithaca, NY: Cornell University Press, 1981.

Deleuze, Gilles. *Expressionism in Philosophy: Spinoza*. Trans. Martin Joughin. New York: Zone Books, 1990.

De Man, Paul. "Autobiography as De-facement." In *The Rhetoric of Romanticism*, 67–82. New York: Columbia University Press, 1984.

———. "Thematic Criticism and the Theme of Faust." In *Critical Writings, 1953–1978*, edited by Lindsay Waters, 76–89. Minneapolis: University of Minnesota Press, 1989.

Dembo, L. S. *The Confucian Odes of Ezra Pound: A Critical Appraisal*. Berkeley: University of California Press, 1963.

Denton, Kirk A. "General Introduction." In *Modern Chinese Literary Thought: Writings on Literature, 1893–1945*, edited by Kirk Denton, 1–61. Stanford, CA: Stanford University Press, 1996.

———. *The Problematic of Self in Modern Chinese Literature: Hu Feng and Lu Ling.* Stanford, CA: Stanford University Press, 1998.

Ding Dong 丁東, ed. *Fansi Guo Moruo* 反思郭沫若 [Reflecting on Guo Moruo]. Beijing: Zuojia chubanshe, 1998.

Ding Xiaohan 丁霄漢. "Ping Guo Moruo zhu Qu Yuan" 評郭沫若著《屈原》 [On Guo Moruo's *Qu Yuan*]. In *GHY*, edited by Yang Shengkuan and Cai Zhen, vol. 9, 402–14.

Dirlik, Arif. *Revolution and History: The Origins of Marxist Historiography in China, 1919–1937*. Berkeley: University of California Press, 1978.

Dong Bingyue 董炳月. *"Guomin zuojia" de lichang: Zhong Ri xiandai wenxue guanxi yanjiu* 國民作家" 的立場：中日現代文學關係研究 [The standpoint of the "national writer:" studies in the relationship between modern Chinese and Japanese literatures]. Beijing: Sanlian, 2006.

Duara, Prasenjit. *Rescuing History from the Nation: Questioning Narratives of Modern China*. Chicago: University of Chicago Press, 1995.

Dye, Ellis. "Figurations of the Feminine in Goethe's *Faust*." In *A Companion to Goethe's* Faust*: Parts I and II*, edited by Paul Bishop, 95–121. Rochester, NY: Camden House, 2001.

Eastman, Lloyd. *The Abortive Revolution: China under Nationalist Rule, 1927–1937.* Cambridge, MA: Harvard University Press, 1990.

Fairbank, John King. *The Great Chinese Revolution, 1800–1985*. New York: Harper & Row, 1987.

Fang, Achilles. "From Imagims to Whitmanism in Recent Chinese Poetry: A Search for Poetics That Failed." In *Indiana University Conference on Oriental-Western Literary Relations*, edited by Horst Frenz and George Lincoln Anderson, 177–92. Chapel Hill: University of North Carolina Press, 1955.

———. "Introduction." In *Shih-ching: The Classic Anthology defined by Confucius*, translated by Ezra Pound, ix–xvi. Cambridge, MA: Harvard University Press, 1982.

Fang Shiming 方詩銘 and Liu Xiuming 劉修明. "Minzhu yundong yu renmin benwei sixiang" 民主運動與人民本位思想 [The democratic movement and the thought of people-centrism]. In *GHY*, edited by Yang Shengkuan and Cai Zhen, vol. 9, 230–59.

Farrelly, Daniel J. *Goethe in East Germany, 1949–1989: Toward a History of Goethe Reception in the GDR*. Rochester, NY: Camden House, 1998.

Feng Xigang 馮錫剛. *Guo Moruo de wannian suiyue* 郭沫若的晚年歲月 [Guo Moruo's last years]. Beijing: Zhongyang wenxian, 2004.

———. *Wenge qian de Guo Moruo* 文革前的郭沫若 [Guo Moruo before the Cultural Revolution]. Beijing: Zhongyang wenxue, 2005.

Fokkema, D. W. *Literary Doctrine in China and Soviet Influence, 1956–1960*. The Hague: Mouton, 1965.

Gálik, Marián. *The Genesis of Modern Chinese Literary Criticism: 1917–1930*. London: Curzon Press, 1980.

———. "Gothic Chamber in Goethe's *Faust* and a Tiny Room in Hakozaki: Some Comments on Guo Moruo's Translation from October 10, 1919." In *Conference Pro-*

ceedings of the 2010 IGMA Annual Meeting. Jinan: Shandong Normal University, 2010.

Gamsa, Mark. *The Chinese Translation of Russian Literature: Three Studies.* Leiden: Brill, 2008.

———. *The Reading of Russian Literature in China: A Moral Example and Manual of Practice.* New York: Palgrave, 2010.

Gong Jimin 龔濟民 and Fang Rennian 方仁念. *Guo Moruo nianpu* 郭沫若年譜 [Guo Moruo: a chronology]. Tianjin: Tianjin renmin, 1992.

———. *Guo Moruo zhuan* 郭沫若傳 [A biography of Guo Moruo]. Beijing: Shiyue wenyi, 1988.

Hamlin, Cyrus. "The Composition of Faust." In Goethe, *Faust*, 505–13. New York: Norton, 2001.

———. "Interpretative Notes." In Goethe, *Faust*, 345–491. New York: Norton, 2001.

———. "Tracking the Eternal-Feminine in Goethe's *Faust II*." In *Interpreting Goethe's* Faust *Today*, edited by Jane Brown, Meredith Lee, and Thomas Saine, 142–55. Rochester, NY: Camden House, 1994.

Harootunian, Harry D. *Marx After Marx: History and Time in the Expansion of Capitalism.* New York: Columbia University Press, 2015.

———. *Overcome by Modernity: History, Culture, and Community in Interwar Japan.* Princeton, NJ: Princeton University Press, 2000.

He Guimei 賀桂梅. *Zhuanzhe de shidai: 40–50 niandai zuojia yanjiu* 轉折的時代：40 至 50 年代作家研究 [An epoch of turning: studies on Chinese writers in the 1940s–50s]. Jinan: Shangdong jiaoyu chubanshe, 2003.

Hill, Michael. *Lin Shu, Inc.: Translation and the Making of Modern Chinese Culture.* New York: Oxford University Press, 2013.

Hinton, William H. *Fanshen: A Documentary of Revolution in a Chinese Village.* New York: Monthly Review, 1966.

Hobsbawm, Eric J. *The Age of Extremes: A History of the World, 1914–1991.* New York: Pantheon Books, 1994.

Hockx, Michel. "Literary Association (*Wenxue yanjiu hui*)." In *Literary Societies of Republican China*, edited by Michel Hockx and Kirk A. Denton, 79–102. Lanham, MD: Lexington Books, 2008.

Hong Zicheng 洪子誠. *1956: baihua shidai* 1956：百花時代 [1956: The age of the hundred flowers]. Jinan: Shangdong jiaoyu, 1998.

———. *Zhongguo dangdai wenxueshi* 中國當代文學史 [A history of Contemporary Chinese literature]. Beijing: Beijing daxue, 1999.

Hsia, C. T. *A History of Modern Chinese Fiction*, 3rd ed. Bloomington: Indiana University Press, 1999.

Hsia, Tsi-an. *The Gate of Darkness: Studies on the Leftist Literary Movement in China.* Seattle: University of Washington Press, 1968.

Hu Ying. *Tales of Translation: Composing the New Woman in China, 1899–1918.* Stanford, CA: Stanford University Press, 2000.

Huang Houxing 黃侯興. *Guo Moruo: "Qingchun xing" de shiren* 郭沫若：“青春型”的詩人 [Guo Moruo: a young style]. Jinan: Shandong renmin, 1994.

Huang Jinshu 黃錦樹. "Shuqing chuantong yu xiandaixing: chuantong zhi faming, huo chuangzaoxing de zhuanhua" 抒情傳統與現代性：傳統之發明，或創造性的轉化 [Lyrical tradition and modernity: the invention of tradition or the creative transformation]. In *Shuqing zhi xiandaixing: Shuqing chuantong lunshu yu zhongguo wenxue yanjiu* 抒情之現代性：抒情傳統論述與中國文學研究 [The modernity of lyricism: essays on Chinese lyrical tradition], edited by Chen Guoqiu and David Der-wei Wang, 677–717. Beijing: Sanlian, 2014.

Huang Xiaowu 黃曉武. *Makesizhuyi yu zhutixing: Kangzhan shiqi Hu Feng de zhuguan lun yanjiu* 馬克思主義與主體性：抗戰時期胡風的主觀論研究 [Marxism and subjectivity: a study of Hu Feng's discourse of the subjective during the War of Resistance]. Beijing: Zhongyang bianyi chubanshe, 2012.

Huters, Theodore. *Bringing the World Home: Appropriating the West in Late Qing and Early Republican China*. Honolulu: University of Hawai'i Press, 2005.

Isaacs, Harold. *The Tragedy of the Chinese Revolution*. London: Secker & Warburg, 1938.

Ito Toramaru 伊藤虎丸. *Lu Xun, Chuangzao she yu ribenwenxue* 魯迅、創造社與日本文學 [Lu Xun, the Creation Society, and Japanese literature]. Translated by Sun Meng 孫猛, Xu Jiang 徐江, and Li Dongmu 李冬木. Beijing: Beijing daxue, 2005.

Jameson, Fredric. "Cultural Revolution." In *Valences of the Dialectic*, 267–278. London: Verso, 2009.

———. *The Hegel Variations: On the* Phenomenology of Spirit. London: Verso, 2010.

———. "Introduction." In György Lukács, *The Historical Novel*, 1–8. Lincoln: University of Nebraska Press, 1983.

———. *The Political Unconscious: Narrative as a Socially Symbolic Act*. Ithaca, NY: Cornell University Press, 1982.

Jaspers, Karl. *The Way to Wisdom: An Introduction to Philosophy*. New Haven, CT: Yale University Press, 2003.

Ji Guoping 季國平. *Mao Zedong yu Guo Moruo* 毛澤東與郭沫若 [Mao Zedong and Guo Moruo]. Beijing: Beijing chubanshe, 1998.

Jiang Tao 姜濤. *Gongyu li de ta: 1920 niadai zhongguo de wenxue yu qingnian* 公寓里的塔： 1920 年代中國的文學與青年 [A tower in the apartment: Chinese literature and youth in the 1920s]. Beijing: Beijing daxue chubanshe, 2015.

———. *"Xinshi ji" yu zhongguo xinshi de fasheng* "新詩集" 與中國新詩的發生 ["New Poetry books" and the emergence of Chinese New Poetry]. Beijing: Beijing daxue chubanshe, 2005.

Jiang Zheng 姜錚. *Ren de jie fang yu yi shu de jie fang: Guo Moruo yu Gede* 人的解放與藝術的解放：郭沫若與歌德 [The liberation of man and the liberation of art: Guo Moruo and Goethe]. Changchun: Shidai wenyi, 1991.

Jin Dakai 金達凱. *Guo Moruo zong lun: sanshi zhi bashi niandai Zhonggong wenhua huodong de suoying* 郭沫若總論：三十至八十年代中國文化活動的縮影 [A full commentary on Guo Moruo: a miniature of the CCP regime's cultural activities from the 1930s to 80s]. Taipei: Shangwu, 1988.

Jin Qiu. "Between Power and Knowledge: Defining Moments in Guo Moruo's Career." *Modern China Studies*, vol. 17, no. 2 (2010): 127–68.

Jones, Andrew F. *Developmental Fairy Tales: Evolutionary Thinking and Modern Chinese Culture*. Cambridge, MA: Harvard University Press, 2011.

Judge, Joan. *The Precious Raft of History: The Past, the West, and the Woman Question in China*. Stanford, CA: Stanford University Press, 2008.

Karl, Rebecca E. *Staging the World: Chinese Nationalism at the Turn of the Twentieth Century*. Durham, NC: Duke University Press, 2002.

Kaske, Elisabeth. *The Politics of Language in Chinese Education, 1895–1919*. Boston: Brill, 2008.

Kawai Kozo 川合 康三. *Zhongguo de zizhuan wenxue* 中國的自傳文學 [Chinese autobiographical literature]. Translated by Cai Yi 蔡毅. Beijing: Zhongyang bianyi, 1999.

Keaveney, Christopher T. *The Subversive Self in Modern Chinese Literature the Creation Society's Reinvention of the Japanese Shishōsetsu*. New York: Palgrave Macmillan, 2004.

Kiyama Hideo 木山 英雄. *Ren ge ren ku da qi qian: Mao Zedong shidai de jiuti shi* 人歌人哭大旗前：毛澤東時代的舊體詩 [People are singing, and people are crying, in front of the great flag: old-style poetry in the era of Mao Zedong]. Translated by Zhao Jinghua 趙京華. Beijing: Sanlian, 2016.

Koselleck, Reinhart. *Futures Past: On the Semantics of Historical Time*. Translated by Keith Tribe. Cambridge, MA: MIT Press, 1985.

Krylov, B. "Preface." In Marx and Engels, *On Literature and Art*, 15–37. Moscow: Progress, 1976.

Kubin, Wolfgang. "'Invincible for Aye!': Melancholy and Wrath, or Toward the Utopia of Purges." *Chinese Literature Today*, no. 4 (2014): 76–81.

Kwok, D. W. Y. *Scientism in Chinese Thought, 1900–1950*. New Haven, CT: Yale University Press, 1965.

Laclau, Ernesto, and Chantal Mouffe. *Hegemony and Socialist Strategy: Towards a Radical Democratic Politics*. London: Verso, 2014.

Larson, Wendy. *From Ah Q to Lei Feng: Freud and Revolutionary Spirit in Twentieth Century China*. Stanford, CA: Stanford University Press, 2009.

———. *Literary Authority and the Modern Chinese Writer: Ambivalence and Autobiography*. Durham, NC: Duke University Press, 1991.

Laughlin, Charles A. *Chinese Reportage: The Aesthetics of Historical Experience*. Durham, NC: Duke University Press, 2002.

Lee, Leo Ou-fan. "Literary Trends: The Quest for Modernity, 1895–1927." In *An Intellectual History of Modern China*, edited by Merle Goldman and Leo Lee, 142–95. New York: Cambridge University Press, 2002.

———. "Literary Trends: The Road to Revolution, 1927–1949." In *An Intellectual History of Modern China*, edited by Merle Goldman and Leo Lee, 196–266. New York: Cambridge University Press, 2002.

———. *The Romantic Generation of Modern Chinese Writers*. Cambridge, MA: Harvard University Press, 1973.

———. "In Search of Modernity: Some Reflections on a New Mode of Consciousness in Twentieth-Century Chinese History and Literature." In *Ideas across Cultures: Essays on Chinese Thought in Honor of Benjamin I. Schwartz*, edited by Paul Cohen and Merle Goldman, 109–36. Cambridge, MA: Harvard University Press, 1990.

Lefevere, André. *Translation, Rewriting, and the Manipulation of Literary Fame*. London: Routledge, 1992.

Levenson, Joseph R. *Confucian China and Its Modern Fate: A Trilogy*. Berkeley: University of California Press, 1968.

———. *Revolution and Cosmopolitanism: The Western Stage and the Chinese Stages.* Berkeley: University of California Press, 1971.

Li Chun 李春. *Wenxue fanyi yu wenxue geming: Wusi zuojia de wenxue fanyi yanjiu* 文學翻譯與文學革命：五四作家的文學翻譯研究 [Literary translation and literary revolution: a study on literary translations of the May Fourth writers]. Ph.D. diss., Peking University, 2010.

Li Huoren 黎活仁. *Lukaqi dui zhongguo wenxue de yingxiang* 盧卡契對中國文學的影響 [The influence of Lukács on Chinese literature]. Taipei: Wenshizhe chubanshe, 1996.

Lin Ganquan 林甘泉 and Huang Lie 黃烈, eds. *Guo Moruo yu zhongguo shixue* 郭沫若與中國史學 [Guo Moruo and Chinese historiography]. Beijing: Zhongguo shehui kexue, 1992.

Liu, Jianmei. *Zhuangzi and Modern Chinese Literature*. New York: Oxford University Press, 2016.

Liu Kui 劉奎. *Shiren gemingjia: kangzhan shiqi de Guo Moruo* 詩人革命家：抗戰時期的郭沫若 [The poet as revolutionist: Guo Moruo in the years of the War Against Japanese Aggression]. Ph.D. diss., Peking University, 2015.

Liu, Lydia H. *Translingual Practice: Literature, National Culture, and Translated Modernity—China, 1900–1937*. Stanford, CA: Stanford University Press, 1995.

Liu Maolin 劉茂林. "Xiang mu chun feng yang liu si—zai lun Guo Moruo de 'Li Bai yu Du Fu'" 向暮春風楊柳絲—— 再論郭沫若的《李白與杜甫》 [The willow tree grows new branches in the late spring wind: re-reading Guo Moruo's *Li Bai and Du Fu*]. In *GHY*, edited by Yang Shengkuan and Cai Zhen, vol. 9, 602–16.

Löwith, Karl. *From Hegel to Nietzsche: The Revolution in Nineteenth-Century Thought.* Translated by David Green. Garden City, NY: Anchor Books, 1967.

Löwy, Michael. *Marxisme et romantisme révolutionnaire*. Paris: Le Syncomore, 1979.

Löwy, Michael, and Robert Sayre. *Romanticism against the Tide of Modernity.* Translated by Catherine Porter. Durham, NC: Duke University Press, 2001.

Lu, Yan. *Re-Understanding Japan: Chinese Perspectives, 1895–1945*. Honolulu: University of Hawai'i Press, 2004.

Luo, Liang. *The Avant-Garde and the Popular in Modern China: Tian Han and the Intersection of Performance and Politics*. Ann Arbor: University of Michigan Press, 2014.

MacFarquhar, Roderick, and Michael Schoenhals. *Mao's Last Revolution*. Cambridge, MA: Belknap Press of Harvard University Press, 2006.

McFarland, Thomas. *Coleridge and the Pantheist Tradition*. Oxford: Clarendon, 1969.

Meisner, Maurice J. *Marxism, Maoism, and Utopianism: Eight Essays*. Madison: University of Wisconsin Press, 1982.

Mi, Jiayan. *Self-Fashioning and Reflexive Modernity in Modern Chinese Poetry, 1919–1949*. Lewiston: Ed. Mellen Press, 2004.

Miao Yue 繆鉞. "Du Guo Moruo zhu Qu Yuan yanjiu" 讀郭沫若著《屈原研究》 [On Guo Moruo's *Study of Qu Yuan*]. In *GHY*, edited by Yang Shengkuan and Cai Zhen, vol. 9, 426–32.

Minford, John, and Joseph S. M. Lau, eds. *Classical Chinese Literature: An Anthology of Translations, Volume I: From Antiquity to the Tang Dynasty*. New York: Columbia University Press and the Chinese University of Hong Kong, 2000.

Mizoguchi Yuzo 溝口 雄三. *Zhongguo sixiang shi: Song dai zhi jindai* 中國思想史：宋代至近代 [Intellectual history of China, Song Dynasty to modern times]. Translated by Gong Ying 龔穎 et al. Beijing: Sanlian, 2014.

Moretti, Franco. *Modern Epic: The World-System from Goethe to García Márquez*. Translated by Quintin Hoare. London: Verso, 1996.

Ng, Janet. *The Experience of Modernity: Chinese Autobiography of the Early Twentieth Century*. Ann Arbor: University of Michigan Press, 2003.

Nida, Eugene. "Principles of Correspondence." In *The Translation Studies Reader*, edited by Lawrence Venuti, 3rd ed., 141–55. London: Routledge, 2012.

Oakes, Guy. "Translator's Introduction." In Carl Schmitt, *Political Romanticism*, ix–xxxv. Cambridge, MA: MIT Press, 1986.

Osborne, Peter. *The Politics of Time: Modernity and Avant-Garde*. London: Verso, 1995.

Owen, Stephen. *The Great Age of Chinese Poetry: The High T'ang*. New Haven, CT: Yale University Press, 1981.

Průšek, Jaroslav. *The Lyrical and the Epic: Studies of Modern Chinese Literature*. Edited by Leo Ou-fan Lee. Bloomington: Indiana University Press, 1980.

Qi Xuemin 戚學民. "Zai lun Shi pipan shu de zhuanzhu dongji yu lunxue zongzhi" 再論《十批判書》的撰著動機與論學宗旨 [Reexamining the motivation and intention behind the writing and argument of *Ten Critiques*]. In *GHY*, edited by Yang Shengkuan and Cai Zhen, vol. 9, 363–96.

Qian, Kun. *Imperial-Time-Order: Literature, Intellectual History, and China's Road to Empire*. Leiden: Brill, 2016.

Qian Liqun 錢理群. *1948: Tian di yuan huang* 1948：天地玄黄 [1948: The sickness of the heaven and the earth]. Jinan: Shandong jiaoyu, 2001.

Qin Chuan 秦川. *Wenhua juren Guo Moruo* 文化巨人郭沫若 [Guo Moruo, a cultural giant]. Beijing: Zhongguo qingnian, 1992.

Roy, David Tod. *Kuo Mo-jo: The Early Years*. Cambridge, MA: Harvard University Press, 1971.

Sartre, Jean-Paul. *Critique de la raison dialectique*, tome 1. Paris: Gallimard, 1960.

Saussy, Haun. *The Problem of a Chinese Aesthetic*. Stanford, CA: Stanford University Press, 1993.

Schlaffer, Heinz. *Faust zweiter Teil: die Allegorie des 19. Jahrhunderts*. Stuttgart: J. B. Metzler, 1998.

Schneider, Laurence A. *Ku Chieh-Kang and China's New History: Nationalism and the Quest for Alternative Traditions*. Berkeley: University of California Press, 1971.

———. *A Madman of Ch'u: The Chinese Myth of Loyalty and Dissent*. Berkeley: University of California Press, 1980.

Schram, Stuart. "Mao Tse-Tung's Thought from 1949–1976." In *An Intellectual History of Modern China*, edited by Merle Goldman and Leo Lee, 395–498. New York: Cambridge University Press, 2002.

Shen Zhihua 沈志華. *Zhonghua renmin gongheguo shi, di san juan: sikao yu xuanze* 中華人民共和國史・第三卷：思考與選擇 [A history of the People's Republic of China, volume

3: the reflection and decision]. Hong Kong: Chinese University of Hong Kong Press, 2008.

Shi Jian 史劍. *Guo Moruo pipan* 郭沫若批判 [A critique of Guo Moruo]. Hong Kong: Yazhou chubanshe, 1954.

Shih, Shu-mei. *The Lure of the Modern: Writing Modernism in Semicolonial China, 1917–1937*. Berkeley: University of California Press, 2001.

Sieburth, Richard. "Introduction." In Pound, *The Spirit of Romance*, vii–xii.

Song Yaozong 宋耀宗. "Dui Guo Moruo qianqi sixiang fazhan de yixie lijie" 對郭沫若前期思想發展的一些理解 [Some reflections on the early Guo's intellectual development]. In *GZL*, edited by Wang Xunzhao et al., 510–24.

Spivak, Gayatri Chakravorty. "The Politics of Translation." In *The Translation Studies Reader*, edited by Lawrence Venuti, 3rd ed., 312–30. London: Routledge, 2012.

Steiner, Goerge. *After Babel: Aspects of Language and Translation*, 3rd ed. Oxford: Oxford University Press, 1998.

———. "Introduction." In Walter Benjamin, *The Origin of German Tragic Drama*, 7–24. London: Verso, 2003.

Su Chi 素癡. "Ping Guo Moruo Zhongguo gudai shehui yanjiu" 評郭沫若《中國古代社會研究》 [A review of Guo Moruo's *Studies of Ancient Chinese Society*]. In *GHY*, edited by Yang Shengkuan and Cai Zhen, vol. 9, 10–17.

Sun, Lung-Kee. "Chinese Intellectuals' Notion of 'Epoch' (Shidai) in the Post–May Fourth Era." *Chinese Studies in History* 20, no. 2 (Winter 1986–87): 44–74.

Tan Qixiang 譚其驤. "Lun Cao Cao" 論曹操 [On Cao Cao]. In *GHY*, edited by Yang Shengkuan and Cai Zhen, vol. 9, 445–57.

Tang, Xiaobing. *Global Space and the Nationalist Discourse of Modernity: The Historical Thinking of Liang Qichao*. Stanford, CA: Stanford University Press, 1996.

Tang, Xiaobing, with Michel Hockx. "The Creation Society." In *Literary Societies of Republican China*, edited by Michel Hockx and Kirk A. Denton, 103–36. Lanham, MD: Lexington Books, 2008.

Terray, Emmanuel. *Marxism and "Primitive" Society*. Translated by M. Klopper. New York: Monthly Review, 1972.

Tian Hua 天華. "Du Guo Moruo zhu Qu Yuan yanjiu guanjian" 讀郭沫若屈原研究管見 [My thoughts on Guo Moruo's *Study of Qu Yuan*]. In *GHY*, edited by Yang Shengkuan and Cai Zhen, vol. 9, 433–38.

Tsu, Jing. *Failure, Nationalism, and Literature: The Making of Modern Chinese Identity, 1895–1937*. Stanford, CA: Stanford University Press, 2005.

———. *Sound and Script in Chinese Diaspora*. Cambridge, MA: Harvard University Press, 2010.

Tung, Constance, and Colin Mackerras, eds. *Drama in the People's Republic of China*. Albany: State University of New York Press, 1987.

Unger, Jonathan, ed. *Using the Past to Serve the Present: Historiography and Politics in Contemporary China*. Armonk, NY: M.E. Sharpe, 1993.

Venuti, Lawrence. *The Translator's Invisibility: A History of Translation*. New York: Routledge, 1995.

Vuilenmier, Victor. "Guo Moruo ershi niandai baihua shixuan li de Gede yi shi" 郭沫若二十年代白話詩選里的歌德譯詩 [Guo Moruo's translations of Goethe's poems in *Vernacular Poetry* in the 1920s]. Unpublished conference article.

Wagner, Rudolf G. *The Contemporary Chinese Historical Drama: Four Studies*. Berkeley: University of California Press, 1990.

Wang, Ban. *The Sublime Figure of History: Aesthetics and Politics in Twentieth-Century China*. Stanford, CA: Stanford University Press, 1997.

Wang, David Der-wei. *The Lyrical in Epic Time: Modern Chinese Intellectuals and Artists through the 1949 Crisis*. New York: Columbia University Press, 2015.

Wang Feng 王風. *Shi yun tuiyi yu wenzhang xingti: Zhongguo jindai wenxue lun ji* 世運推移與文章興替：中國近代文學論集 [Shifts of history and literature: essays on late Qing and early Republican literature]. Beijing: Beijing daxue chubanshe, 2015.

Wang Furen 王富仁. "Shenmei zhuiqiu de maoluan yu shicuo" 審美追求的瞀亂與失措 [The malaise and deficiency of an aesthetic pursuit]. In *Guo Moruo pingshuo jiushi nian* 郭沫若評說九十年 [Nine decades of critical receptions of Guo Moruo], edited by Li Yi 李怡 and Cai Zhen 蔡震, 153–58. Beijing: Wenhua yishu, 2010.

Wang Hui 汪暉. "Depoliticized Politics, From East to West." *New Left Review*, no. 41 (2006): 29–45.

———. *The Politics of Imagining Asia*. Edited and translated by Theodore Huters. Cambridge, MA: Harvard University Press, 2011.

———. *Wenhua yu zhengzhi de bianzou: yi zhan yu zhongguo de sixiang zhan* 文化與政治的變奏：一戰與中國的思想戰 [The variations of culture and politics: World War I and China's intellectual war]. Shanghai: Shanghai renmin, 2014.

———. *Xiandai zhongguo sixiang de xingqi* 現代中國思想的興起 [Rise of modern Chinese thought]. Beijing: Sanlian, 2004.

Wang Jian 汪籛. "Wu Zetian" 武則天. In *Wang Jian Sui Tang shi lun gao* 汪籛隋唐史論稿 [Wang Jian's essays on Sui and Tang history], 118–31. Beijing: Zhongguo shehui kexue, 1981.

Wang Jinhou 王錦厚. "Lue lun dui *Li Bai yu Du Fu* de piping" 略論對《李白與杜甫》的批評 [On the criticisms of *Li Bai and Du Fu*]. In *GHY*, edited by Yang Shengkuan and Cai Zhen, vol. 9, 579–93.

Wang, Pu. "Enlightenment as a 'Romantic Science?' Cultural Politics and Guo Moruo's Rewriting of Ancient Chinese History." In *Rethinking Enlightenment in Global and Historical Contexts*, edited by Nakajima Takahiro and Xudong Zhang, 45–68. Tokyo: University of Tokyo UTCP Booklet Series, 2011.

———. "The Promethean Translator and Cannibalistic Pains: Lu Xun's 'Hard Translation' as a Political Allegory." *Translation Studies* 6, no. 3 (2013): 324–38.

Wang, Q. Edward. *Inventing China through History: The May Fourth Approach to Historiography*. Albany: State University of New York Press, 2000.

Wang, Xiaojue. *Modernity with a Cold War Face: Reimagining the Nation in Chinese Literature across the 1949 Divide*. Cambridge, MA: Harvard University Asia Center, 2013.

Wang Yao 王瑤. "Guo Moruo de langmanzhuyi lishiju chuangzuo lilun" 郭沫若的浪漫主義歷史劇創作理論 [The romantic theory of historical drama in Guo Moruo]. In *GHY*, edited by Yang Shengkuan and Cai Zhen, vol. 7, 105–22.

Wasserman, Earl R. *Shelley: A Critical Reading*. Baltimore: Johns Hopkins University Press, 1971.

Wei Jian 魏建. "Guo Moruo lishiju yanjiu shuping" 郭沫若歷史劇研究述評 [A review of scholarship on Guo's historical drama]. *Guo Moruo yanjiu* 郭沫若研究 [Journal of Guo Moruo studies], no. 5 (1988): 213–33.

Weigelin-Schwiedrzik, Susanne. "The Campaign to Criticize Lin Biao and Confucius and the Problem of 'Restoration' in Chinese Marxist Historiography." In *Challenge of Linear Time: Nationhood and the Politics of History in East Asia*, edited by Viren Murthy and Axel Schneider, 155–77. Leiden: Brill, 2013.

Wellbery, David E. *The Specular Moment: Goethe's Early Lyric and the Beginnings of Romanticism*. Stanford, CA: Stanford University Press, 1996.

Wen Fu 文甫. "Ping Guo Moruo Zhongguo gudai shehui yanjiu" 評郭沫若《中國古代社會研究》 [A review of Guo Moruo's *Studies of Ancient Chinese Society*]. In *GHY*, edited by Yang Shengkuan and Cai Zhen, vol. 9, 3–9.

White, Hayden. *Metahistory: The Historical Imagination in Nineteenth-Century Europe*. Baltimore: Johns Hopkins University Press, 1973.

Williams, Raymond. *Keywords: A Vocabulary of Culture and Society*. New York: Oxford University Press, 1983.

Wong, Lawrence Wang-Chi. *Chong shi xin da ya* 重釋信達雅 [Reinterpreting trustworthiness, comprehensibility and elegance]. Beijing: Qinghua daxue chubanshe, 2007.

———. *Fanyi yu jindai zhongguo* 翻譯與近代中國 [Translation and modern China]. Shanghai: Fudan daxue chubanshe, 2014.

———. *Fanyi yu wenxue zhijian* 翻譯與文學之間 [Between translation and literature]. Nanjing: Nanjing daxue chubanshe, 2011.

———. *Politics and Literature in Shanghai: The Chinese League of Left-Wing Writers, 1930–1936*. Manchester: Manchester University Press, 1991.

Wu, Shengqing. *Modern Archaics: Continuity and Innovation in the Chinese Lyric Tradition, 1900–1937*. Cambridge, MA: Harvard University Asia Center, 2014.

Xiao Difei 蕭滌非. *Du Fu yanjiu, shang juan* 杜甫研究，上卷 [A study of Du Fu, part 1]. Jinan: Shandong renmin, 1956.

———. "Guanyu Li Bai yu Du Fu" 關於《李白與杜甫》[On *Li Bai and Du Fu*]. In *GHY*, edited by Yang Shengkuan and Cai zhen, vol. 9, 539–60.

Xiaomin 小民. "Juan'er ji de zanci" 《卷耳集》的讚詞 [A praise of *Cockleburs*]. In *Juan'er taolun ji*, edited by Cao Juren, 12–13. Shanghai: Liangxi tushuguan, 1925.

Xie Baocheng 謝保成. *Long hu dou yu ma niu feng: lun zhongguo xiandai shixue yu shijia* 龍虎鬥與馬牛風：論中國現代史學和史家 [The dragon-tiger fight and the horse-cow mating: on modern Chinese historical scholarship and historians]. Beijing: Sanlian, 2012.

Yang, Haosheng. *A Modernity Set to a Pre-Modern Tune: Classical-Style Poetry of Modern Chinese Writers*. Leiden: Brill, 2016.

Yang Shengkuan 楊勝寬 and Cai Zhen 蔡震, eds. *Guo Moruo yanjiu wenxian huiyao* 郭沫若研究文獻匯要 [A compilation of Guo Moruo studies]. 14 vols. Shanghai: Shanghai shudian, 2012 (abbreviated *GHY*).

Yang Wuneng 楊武能. *Gede yu zhongguo* 歌德與中國 [Goethe and China]. Beijing: Sanlian, 1991.

Ye Jun 葉雋. "Die Veränderung der Faustrezeption als Spiegel der Entwicklung des nationalen Aufbaus im modernen China (1920–1940er Jahre)." In *Orient und Okzident–Zur Faustrezeption in nicht-christlichen Kulturen*, edited by Jochen Golz and Adrian Hsia, 233–48. Koeln: Boehlau, 2008.

Yeh, Michelle. *Modern Chinese Poetry: Theory and Practice since 1917*. New Haven, CT: Yale University Press, 1991.

Yin, Zhiguang. *Politics of Art: The Creation Society and the Practice of Theoretical Struggle in Revolutionary China*. Leiden: Brill, 2014.

Zeng Liping 曾立平. “Ping lishi ju chuangzuo zhong de fan lishizhuyi qingxiang (jiexuan)” 評歷史劇創作中的反歷史主義傾向（節錄） [On the anti-historicist tendency in the creation of the historical drama, an excerpt]. In *GHY*, edited by Yang Shengkuan and Cai Zhen, vol. 7, 197–209.

Zhang Xudong 張旭東. “Wu si yu zhongguo xiandaixing wenhua de jijin quanshi xue” 五四與中國現代性文化的激進詮釋學 [The May Fourth and the radical hermeneutic of China’s cultural modernity]. In *Wenhua zhengzhi yu zhongguo daolu* 文化政治與中國道路 [Cultural politics and the Chinese way], 3–13. Shanghai: Shanghai renmin, 2015.

Zikpi, Monica E. M. “Revolution and Continuity in Guo Moruo’s Representations of Qu Yuan.” *Chinese Literature: Essays, Articles, Reviews* (2014): 175–200.

Zou Jianjun 鄒建軍. “Geming fengbao de yuyan shi—du ‘Zhanqu’ ” 革命風暴的預言詩——讀《戰取》 [A prophetic poem of the revolutionary storm: reading “To Seize”]. In *Guo Moruo ming shi jianshang cidian* 郭沫若名詩鑑賞辭典 [A dictionary of Guo Moruo’s renowned poems along with interpretations], edited by Zang Kejia 臧克家, 236–37. Beijing: Zhongguo heping chubanshe, 1993.

Index

Page numbers for figures are in italics.

D

E

T

U

V

W